Merriam-Webster's Vocabulary Builder

Merriam-Webster's Vocabulary Builder

Mary Wood Cornog

MERRIAM-WEBSTER, INCORPORATED
Springfield, Massachusetts

A GENUINE MERRIAM-WEBSTER

The name *Webster* alone is no guarantee of excellence. It is used by a number of publishers and may serve mainly to mislead an unwary buyer.

Merriam-Webster™ is the name you should look for when you consider the purchase of dictionaries or other fine reference books. It carries the reputation of a company that has been publishing since 1831 and is your assurance of quality and authority.

Introduction

Merriam-Webster's Vocabulary Builder is designed to achieve two goals: to add a large number of words to your permanent working vocabulary, and to teach the most useful of the classical word-building roots to help you continue expanding your vocabulary in the future.

In order to achieve these goals, *Merriam-Webster's Vocabulary Builder* employs an original approach that takes into account how people learn and remember. Many vocabulary builders simply present their words in alphabetical order, many provide little or no discussion of the words and how to use them, and a few even fail to show the kinds of sentences in which the words usually appear. But memorizing a series of random and unrelated things, especially for more than a few hours, can be difficult and time-consuming. The fact is that we tend to remember words easily and naturally when they appear in some meaningful text, when they have been shown to be useful and therefore worth remembering, and when they have been properly explained to us. Knowing precisely how to use a word is just as important as knowing what it means, and this book provides that needed additional information.

Greek and Latin have been the sources of most of the words in the English language. (The third principal source is the family of Germanic languages.) Almost all of these words were added to the language long after the fall of the Roman Empire, and they continue to be added to this day. New words are constantly being invented, and most of them, especially those in the sciences, are still making use of Greek and Latin roots. Many words contain more than one root, as you'll see in the following pages, and some mix Greek and Latin (and even Germanic) roots.

The roots in this book are only a fraction of those that exist, but they include the roots that have produced the largest number of common English words. These roots (sometimes called *stems*) all formed part of Greek and Latin words. Some are shown in more than one form (for example, FLECT/FLEX), which means that they changed form in the original language, just as *buy* and *bought* are forms of the same English word. A knowledge of Greek and Latin roots will help you to remember the meanings of the words in this book, but it will also enable you to guess at the meanings of new words that you run into elsewhere. Remember what a root means and you will have at least a fighting chance of understanding a word in which it appears.

Each of the 200 roots in this book is followed by four words based on the root. Each group of eight words (two roots) is followed by two quizzes. Every fifth group is a special eight-word section which may contain words based on classical mythology or history, words borrowed directly from Greek or Latin, or other special categories of terms. Each set of 40 words makes up a unit. Thus, the 25 units in the book discuss in detail a total of 1,000 words. In addition, the brief paragraphs discussing each word include in *italics* many words closely related to the main words, in order to at least suggest how those related words may be used as well. Mastering a single word—for example, *phenomenon*—can thus increase your vocabulary by several words—for example, *phenomenal, phenomenally,* and the plural form *phenomena*.

The words presented here are not all on the same level of difficulty—some are quite simple and some are truly challenging—but the great majority are words that could be encountered on the Scholastic Aptitude Test (SAT) and similar standardized tests. Most of them are in the vocabularies of well-educated Americans, including professionals such as scientists, lawyers, professors, doctors, and editors. Even those words you feel familiar with may only have a place in your *recognition* vocabulary—that is, the words that you recognize when you see or hear them but that you are not sure enough about to use in your own speech and writing.

Each main word is followed by its most common pronunciation. A few of the pronunciation symbols may be unfamiliar to you, but they can be learned very easily by referring to the pronunciation key on page xi.

The definition comes next. We have tried to provide only the most common senses or meanings of the word, in simple and straightforward language, and no more than two definitions of any word are given. A more complete range of definitions can be found in a college dictionary such as *Merriam-Webster's Collegiate Dictionary, Tenth Edition.*

An example sentence marked with a bullet (●) follows the definition. This sentence by itself can indicate a great deal about the word, including the kind of sentence in which it often appears. It can also serve as a memory aid, since when you meet the word in the future you may recall the example sentence more easily than the definition.

An explanatory paragraph rounds out your introduction to each word. The paragraph may do a number of things: It may tell you what else you need to know in order to use the word intelligently and correctly, since the example sentence can't do this all by itself. It may tell you more about the word's roots and its history. It may discuss additional meanings. It will often give you additional example sentences that demonstrate various ways to use the word and to expect to see it used. It may demonstrate the use of closely related words. The paragraph may even offer an informative or entertaining glimpse into a subject not strictly related to the word. The intention is to make you as comfortable as possible with each word in turn and to enable you to start using it immediately, without fear of embarrassment.

The quizzes immediately following each eight-word group, along with the review quizzes at the end of each unit, will test your memory. Many of these quizzes are similar to those used on standardized tests such as the SAT. Some of them ask you to identify *synonyms*, words with the same or very similar meaning, or *antonyms*, words with the opposite meaning. Perhaps more difficult are the *analogies*, which ask that you choose the word that will make the relationship between the last two words the same as the relationship between the first two. Thus, you may be asked to complete the analogy "calculate : count :: expend : _____" (which can be read as "*Calculate* is to *count* as *expend* is to _____") by choosing one of four words: *stretch, speculate, pay,* and *explode.* Since *calculate* and *count* are nearly synonyms, you will choose a near synonym for *expend,* so the correct answer is *pay.*

Studies have shown that the only way a new word will remain alive in your vocabulary is if it is regularly reinforced through use and through reading. Learn the word here and look and listen for it elsewhere—you'll probably find yourself running into it frequently, just as when you have bought a new car you soon realize how many other people own the same model.

Carry this book in your shoulder bag or leave it on your night table. Whenever you find yourself with a few minutes to spare, open it to the beginning of a brief root group. (There's no real need to read the units in any particular order, since each unit is entirely self-contained. However, studying the book straight through from the beginning will ensure that you make maximum use of it.) Pick a single word or a four-word group or an eight-word section; study it, test yourself, and then try making up new sentences for each word. Be sure to pronounce every new word aloud at least once, along with its definition.

Start using the words immediately. As soon as you feel confident with a word, start trying to work it into your writing wherever appropriate—your papers and reports, your diary and your poetry. An old saying goes, "Use it three times and it's yours." That may be, but don't stop at three. Make the words part of your *working* vocabulary, the words that you can not only recognize when you see or hear them but that you can comfortably call on whenever you need them. Astonish your friends, amaze your relatives, astound *yourself* (while trying not to be too much of a showoff), and have fun.

Acknowledgments: This book has benefited from the contributions of numerous members of the Merriam-Webster staff. Michael G. Belanger, John M. Morse, Brett P. Palmer, Stephen J. Perrault, and Mark A. Stevens edited the manuscript. Brian M. Sietsema and Eileen M. Haraty entered the pronunciations. James G. Lowe prepared the answer key. Florence A. Fowler undertook the immense task of preparing the manuscript for typesetting. The text was proofread by Susan L. Brady, Rebecca R. Bryer, Paul F. Cappellano, Jennifer N. Cislo, Jill J. Cooney, Jennifer S. Goss, Donna L. Rickerby, Michael D. Roundy, Katherine C. Sietsema, Amy West, and Karen L. Wilkinson, under the direction of Maria A. Sansalone and Madeline L. Novak.

Pronunciation Symbols

ə .... abut, collect, suppose

'ə, ˌə . humdrum

ər .... operation, further

a .... map, patch

ā .... day, fate

ä .... bother, cot, father

à .... a sound between \a\ and \ä\, as in an Eastern New England pronunciation of aunt, ask

aù ... now, out

b .... baby, rib

ch .... chin, catch

d .... did, adder

e .... set, red

ē .... beat, easy

f .... fifty, cuff

g .... go, big

h .... hat, ahead

hw .... whale

i .... tip, banish

ī .... site, buy

j .... job, edge

k .... kin, cook

l .... lily, cool

m .... murmur, dim

n .... nine, own

ⁿ .... indicates that a preceding vowel is pronounced through both nose and mouth, as in French bon \bōⁿ\

ŋ .... sing, singer, finger, ink

ō .... bone, hollow

ȯ .... saw

ȯi .... toy

p .... pepper, lip

r .... rarity

s .... source, less

sh ... shy, mission

t .... tie, attack

th .... thin, ether

th .... then, either

ü .... boot, few \'fyü\

ù .... put, pure \'pyùr\

v .... vivid, give

w .... we, away

y .... yard, cue \'kyü\

z .... zone, raise

zh ... vision, pleasure

\ .... slant line used in pairs to mark the beginning and end of a transcription: \'pen\

' .... mark at the beginning of a syllable that has primary (strongest) stress: \'shəf-əl-ˌbȯrd\

ˌ .... mark at the beginning of a syllable that has secondary (next-strongest) stress: \'shəf-əl-ˌbȯrd\

- .... mark of a syllable division in pronunciations

Merriam-Webster's Vocabulary Builder

Unit 1

BELL comes from the Latin word meaning "war." *Bellona* was the little-known Roman goddess of war; her husband, Mars, was the god of war.

---

antebellum \‚an-ti-'be-ləm\ Existing before a war, especially before the American Civil War (1861–65).

● When World War I was over, the French nobility found it impossible to return to their extravagant antebellum way of life.

Often the word *antebellum* summons up images of ease, elegance, and entertainment on a grand scale that disappeared in the postwar years. That way of life in the American South depended on a social structure that collapsed after the war. The years after the Civil War—and many other wars—were colored for some people by nostalgia and bitterness (Margaret Mitchell's *Gone with the Wind* shows this through the eyes of the Southern gentry), and for others by relief and anticipation.

bellicose \'be-li-‚kōs\ Warlike, aggressive, quarrelsome.

● The country often elected the more bellicose party after a period of tension along the border, hoping that military action would result.

The international relations of a nation with a bellicose foreign policy tend to be stormy and difficult, since such a nation looks for opportunities to fight rather than to negotiate. Combative by nature, it is happiest when quarreling or, better yet, actively engaged in battle.

belligerence \bə-'li-jə-rəns\ Aggressiveness, combativeness.

• The belligerence in Turner's voice told them that the warning was a serious threat.

The belligerence of Marlon Brando's performance as the violent Stanley Kowalski in *A Streetcar Named Desire* electrified the country. *Belligerent* speeches by leaders of the Soviet Union and the United States throughout the Cold War kept the world on edge for years. Iraq's shocking belligerence toward Kuwait and its own Kurdish people resulted in hundreds of thousands of deaths.

rebellion \ri-'bel-yən\ Open defiance and opposition, sometimes armed, to a person or thing in authority.

• The substitute teacher attempted to end the student rebellion by insisting on absolute quiet.

These days, some degree of rebellion against parents and other authority figures is viewed as a normal part of growing up, as long as it is not destructive and does not go on too long. Rebellion, armed or otherwise, has often served to alert those in power to the discontent of those they control. The American War of Independence was first viewed by the British as a minor rebellion that would soon run its course.

PAC/PEAS is related to the Latin words for "agree" and "peace." The *Pacific Ocean*—that is, the "Peaceful Ocean"—was named by Magellan because it seemed so calm after the storms near Cape Horn. (He obviously never witnessed a Pacific hurricane.)

---

pacify \'pa-sə-,fī\ (1) To soothe anger or agitation. (2) To subdue by armed action.

• It took the police hours to pacify the angry demonstrators.

Unhappy babies are often given a rubber device for sucking called a *pacifier* to make them stop crying. In the same way, someone stirred up by anger or some other strong emotion can usually be pacified by resolving or removing its causes. In a usage that became popular during the Vietnam War, *pacification* of an area meant using armed force to neutralize the enemy there and to quiet the local people who may have been supporting them.

pacifist \\'pa-sə-fist\\ A person opposed to war or violence, especially someone who refuses to bear arms or to fight, on moral or religious grounds.

• Always a strong pacifist, in later life he took to promoting actively the cause of peace and nonviolence.

Pacifists have not always met with sympathy or understanding. Refusing to fight ever for any reason, or even just in a particular situation when the reasons for fighting seem clear to many others, calls for strong faith in one's own moral or religious convictions, since it has often resulted in persecution by those who disagree. The Quakers and the Jehovah's Witnesses are *pacifist* religious groups; Henry D. Thoreau and Martin Luther King are probably the most famous American pacifists.

pact \\'pakt\\ An agreement between two or more people or groups; a treaty or formal agreement between nations to deal with a problem or to resolve a dispute.

• The girls made a pact never to reveal what had happened on that terrifying night in the abandoned house.

Since a pact often ends a period of unfriendly relations, the word has "peace" at its root. *Pact* is generally used in the field of international relations, where we often speak of an "arms pact" or a "fishing-rights pact." But it may also be used for a solemn agreement or promise between two people.

appease \\ə-'pēz\\ To make peaceful and quiet; to calm, satisfy.

• The Aztecs offered mass human sacrifices—of 80,000 prisoners on one occasion!—in order to appease their gods.

When the European nations agreed to let Adolf Hitler take over part of Czechoslovakia in 1938, in a vain attempt to prevent a larger war, their opponents shouted that they were practicing a foolish *appeasement* that was doomed to fail. (They were right—within months Hitler had violated the *pact*.) A child's anger may be appeased with a little effort; an angry god or goddess may demand something extreme. We may speak of hunger being appeased by food. Appeasing usually involves giving something, whereas *pacifying* can refer to anything from stroking a baby to using armed force to stop an uprising.

Quizzes

A. Match the word on the left to the correct definition on the right:

1. antebellum
2. appease
3. rebellion
4. pacify
5. pacifist
6. belligerence
7. pact
8. bellicose

a. quarrelsome
b. solemn agreement
c. to make peaceful
d. before the war
e. aggressiveness
f. opposition to authority
g. to calm by satisfying
h. one who opposes war

B. Fill in each blank with the correct letter:

a. antebellum
b. pacifist
c. pact
d. appease

e. rebellion
f. bellicose
g. pacify
h. belligerence

1. The native _____ began at midnight, when a gang of youths massacred the Newton family and set the house afire.
2. The grand _____ mansion has hardly been altered since it was built in 1841.
3. The Senate Republicans, outraged by their treatment, were in a _____ mood.
4. To _____ the younger managers, the company will double their bonuses this year.
5. The cease-fire _____ that had been reached with such effort was shattered by the news of the slaughter.
6. Their relations during the divorce proceedings had been mostly friendly, so his _____ in the judge's chambers surprised her.
7. The world watched in amazement as the gentle _____ Gandhi won India its independence with almost no bloodshed.
8. Her soft lullabies could always _____ the unhappy infant.

HOSP/HOST comes from the Latin word *hospes* and its stem *hospit-* meaning both "host" and "guest." Many words based on it came to English through French, which often dropped the *-pi-*, leaving *host-*. *Hospitality* is what a good *host* or *hostess* offers to a guest. A *hospital* was once a house for religious pilgrims and other travelers, or a home for the aged.

hostage \'häs-tij\ A person given or held to ensure that an agreement, demand, or treaty is kept or fulfilled.

• The kidnappers released their hostage unharmed once all their demands were met.

Opponents in war sometimes exchange hostages to ensure that a truce or treaty remains unbroken. Hostages may also be taken by kidnappers or terrorists or rebels to use in bargaining for money or concessions. It may seem strange that the word *hostage* is connected with *host* and in fact with *guest* as well, since hostages are now unwilling guests, at the mercy of their *hostile* hosts.

hospice \'häs-pəs\ A place or program to help care for the terminally ill.

• Uncle Harold was moved to the hospice only after my aunt had almost collapsed with exhaustion while caring for him.

In the Middle Ages, hospices run by monks and nuns gave shelter and food to travelers and the poor. Now, hospices are institutions that take care of people who are too ill to be at home but whose lives cannot be saved by hospital care—often those with incurable cancer or AIDS, for example. More and more Americans are relying on "home hospice care"—care by visiting nurses and volunteers for terminally ill patients who have decided to live their last months at home.

hostel \'häs-təl\ An inexpensive, supervised place for young travelers to stay overnight.

• Generations of American college students have traveled through Europe cheaply by staying at hostels instead of hotels.

Throughout Europe and in some other parts of the world, a network of youth hostels provides cheap, safe (although not always quiet) overnight shelter for younger bicyclists, hikers, and canoeists. The United States has over 200 youth hostels, many of them in New England. Worldwide, there are more than 5,000.

inhospitable \,in-hä-'spi-tə-bəl\ (1) Not welcoming or generous; unfriendly. (2) Providing no shelter or food (such as a desert).

• Shot down by government agents, the smuggler struggled for survival on the rocky, inhospitable island.

An inhospitable host fails to make his guests comfortable, in order to show them they are unwelcome. An inhospitable territory, such as Death Valley or Antarctica, may be barren and harsh in its climate. In a similar way, a country may be called inhospitable to democracy, just as a company may be called inhospitable to new ideas.

AM/IM comes from the Latin word *amare,* "to love." *Amiable* means "friendly or good-natured," and *amigo* is Spanish for "friend."

---

amicable \'a-mi-kə-bəl\ Friendly, peaceful.

• Their relations with their in-laws were generally amicable, despite some bickering during the holidays.

Amicable often describes relations between two groups or especially two nations—for example, the United States and Canada, which are proud of sharing the longest unguarded border in the world. When *amicable* describes personal relations, it tends to indicate a rather formal friendliness.

enamored \i-'na-mərd\ Charmed or fascinated; inflamed with love.

• Rebecca quickly became enamored of the town's rustic surroundings, its slow pace, and its eccentric characters.

Computer hackers are always enamored of their new programs and games. Millions of readers have found themselves enamored with Jane Austen's novels. And Romeo and Juliet were utterly enamored of each other. (Note that both *of* and *with* are commonly used after *enamored.*)

inimical \i-'ni-mi-kəl\ Hostile, unfriendly, or harmful.

• This latest report, like so many earlier ones, found that too great a concern with test scores was inimical to a broad education.

The *in-* with which *inimical* begins negates the meaning of the root. This word rarely describes a person; instead, it is generally used to describe forces, concepts, or situations. For example, high inflation may be called inimical to economic growth; tolerance of racist comments in an office may be seen as inimical to minorities; and rapid population growth may be inimical to a country's standard of living.

paramour \\'par-ə-,mur\\ A lover, often secret, not allowed by law or custom.

• He was her paramour for many years before she finally divorced her husband.

Paramour includes the prefix *par -*, "by or through." This implies a relationship based solely on love, often physical love, rather than on a social custom or ceremony. Today it usually refers to the lover of a married man or woman.

Quizzes

A. Choose the odd word:

1. hostel   a. shelter b. hotel c. prison d. dormitory
2. inimical   a. unfriendly b. sympathetic c. antagonistic
        d. harmful
3. hospice   a. nursing b. travel c. hospital d. illness
4. amicable   a. difficult b. friendly c. pleasant
        d. peaceful
5. enamored   a. strengthened b. charmed c. fond
        d. fascinated
6. inhospitable   a. inimical b. barren c. unfriendly
        d. inviting
7. paramour   a. lover b. husband c. mistress
        d. significant other
8. hostage   a. exchange b. guarantee c. pledge d. hotel

B. Complete the analogy:

1. charming : enchanting :: inimical : _____
        a. sublime b. harmful c. direct d. cautious

2. lush : barren :: inhospitable : _____
   a. deserted b. sunny c. rocky d. welcoming
3. house : mortgage :: hostage : _____
   a. treaty b. gunman c. terrorist d. prisoner
4. gentle : tender :: enamored : _____
   a. lively b. charmed c. cozy d. enraged
5. picnic : dinner :: hostel : _____
   a. restaurant b. supper c. bar d. inn
6. frozen : boiling :: amicable : _____
   a. calm b. comfortable c. shy d. unfriendly
7. auditorium : arena :: hospice : _____
   a. spa b. nursing home c. club d. motel
8. friend : companion :: paramour : _____
   a. lover b. theater c. mother d. wife

CRIM comes from the Latin for "fault or crime" or "accusation," and produces such English words as *crime* and *criminal*.

criminology \ˌkri-mə-'nä-lə-jē\ The study of crime, criminals, law enforcement, and punishment.

• His growing interest in criminology led him to become a probation officer.

Criminology includes the study of all aspects of crime and law enforcement—criminal psychology, the social setting of crime, prohibition and prevention, investigation and detection, apprehension and punishment. Thus, many of the people involved—legislators, social workers, probation officers, judges, etc.—could possibly be considered *criminologists,* though the word usually refers to scholars and researchers only.

decriminalize \dē-'kri-mə-nə-ˌlīz\ To remove or reduce the criminal status of.

• An angry debate over decriminalizing doctor-assisted suicide raged all day at the statehouse.

Decriminalization of various "victimless crimes"—crimes that do not directly harm others, such as private gambling and drug-taking—has been recommended by conservatives as well as liberals, who claim that it would ease the burden on the legal system and decrease the amount of money flowing to criminals. Decriminalization is sometimes distinguished from legalization, since it may still call for a small fine like a traffic ticket, or it may apply only to use or possession, leaving the actual sale of goods or services illegal.

incriminate \in-'kri-mə-ˌnāt\ To show evidence of involvement in a crime or a fault.

• The muddy tracks leading to and from the cookie jar were enough to incriminate them.

We often hear of *incriminating* evidence, the kind that strongly links a suspect to a crime. Verbal testimony may incriminate by placing the suspect at the scene of the crime or describe behavior that involves him or her in it. We can also say that a virus has been incriminated as the cause of a type of cancer, and that television has been incriminated in the decline in study skills among young people.

recrimination \rē-ˌkri-mə-'nā-shən\ An accusation in retaliation for an accusation made against oneself; the making of such an accusation.

• Their failure to find help led to endless and pointless recriminations over the responsibility for the accident.

Defending oneself from a verbal attack by means of a counterattack is almost as natural as physical self-defense. So a disaster often brings recriminations among those connected with it, and divorces and battles over child custody usually involve recriminations between husband and wife.

PROB/PROV comes from the Latin words for "prove or proof" and "honesty or integrity." To *prove* a statement is to "make it honest," and *probate* court is where the genuineness of the wills of deceased people must be *proved*.

---

approbation \ˌa-prə-'bā-shən\ A formal or official act of approving; praise, usually given with pleasure or enthusiasm.

● The senate signaled its approbation of the new plan by voting for it unanimously.

Approbation indicates both formal recognition of an accomplishment and happy acceptance of it. An official commendation for bravery is an example of approbation. Getting reelected to office usually indicates public approbation. The social approbation that comes from being a star quarterback in high school makes all the pain worthwhile.

disprove \dis-'prüv\ To show that something is not what it has been claimed to be; refute.

● A week before the election he was still struggling to disprove his opponent's lies about his connections to organized crime.

Disprove, which includes the negative prefix *dis-,* is clearly the opposite of *prove.* One may have to disprove something for which the evidence has already been accepted, so the *disprover* often encounters violent objections to the new evidence that weakens the old. Galileo was forced to deny the new findings with which he and Copernicus had disproved the old conception of the earth's being at the center of the planetary system.

probity \'prō-bə-tē\ Absolute honesty and uprightness.

● Her unquestioned probity helped win her the respect of her fellow judges.

Probity is a quality the American public generally hopes for in its elected officials but doesn't always get. Bankers, for example, have traditionally been careful to project an air of probity; the savings-and-loan scandal of the 1980s has made it even more necessary. An aura of probity surrounds such public figures as Walter Cronkite and Bill Moyers, men to whom many Americans would entrust their children and their finances.

reprobate \'re-prə-ˌbāt\ A person of thoroughly bad character.

● Finally, on the verge of physical and financial ruin, the reprobate dropped his lowlife friends, joined AA, and begged his wife to come back.

Reprobate (which includes the prefix *re-*, "back or backward") is often said in a tone of joshing affection. The related verb is *reprove* or "scold," since the reprobate deserves a constant scolding. Shakespeare's great character Falstaff—a lazy, lying, boastful, sponging drunkard—is the model of an old reprobate.

Quizzes

A. Indicate whether the following pairs of words have the same or different meanings:

1. decriminalize / tolerate   same ___ / different ___
2. probity / fraud   same ___ / different ___
3. criminology / murder   same ___ / different ___
4. incriminate / acquit   same ___ / different ___
5. disprove / distinguish   same ___ / different ___
6. recrimination / approbation   same ___ / different ___
7. reprobate / scoundrel   same ___ / different ___
8. approbation / criticism   same ___ / different ___

B. Match the definition on the left to the correct word on the right:

1. utter honesty   a. approbation
2. approval   b. reprobate
3. rascal   c. recrimination
4. demonstrate as false   d. criminology
5. study of illegal behavior   e. probity
6. accuse   f. disprove
7. reduce penalty for   g. decriminalize
8. counterattack   h. incriminate

GRAV comes from the Latin word meaning "heavy, weighty, serious." Thus, a *grave* matter is serious and important.

gravid \'gra-vəd\ Pregnant or enlarged with something.

● The gravid sow moved heavily from trough to tree, where she settled into the shaded dust and lay unmoving for the rest of the afternoon.

Gravid implies weight and bulk, but actually describes a pregnant female even at an early stage of her pregnancy. It has the related senses of inflation that results from any cause and that will lead to a change of some kind. Thus, a writer may be gravid with ideas as she sits down to write; a speaker may make a gravid pause before announcing his remarkable findings; and a cloud may be gravid with rain.

gravitas \'gra-və-ˌtäs\ Great or very dignified seriousness.

• The head of the committee never failed to carry herself with the gravitas she felt was appropriate to her office.

This word comes to us straight from Latin. Among the Romans, gravitas was thought to be essential to the character and functions of any adult (male) in authority. Even the head of a household or a low-level official would strive for this important quality. We use *gravitas* today to identify the same solemn dignity in men and women.

gravitate \'gra-və-ˌtāt\ To move or be drawn toward something, especially by natural tendency or as if by an invisible force.

• During hot weather, the town's social life gravitated toward the lake.

To gravitate implies a natural, perhaps irresistible, response to a force that works like *gravity,* drawing things steadily to it as if by their own weight. Thus, moths gravitate to a flame, children gravitate to an ice-cream truck, gawkers gravitate to an accident, and everyone at a party gravitates to the bar.

gravity \'gra-və-tē\ Weighty importance, seriousness, or dignity.

• Laughing and splashing each other, they failed to realize the gravity of their situation until the canoe was within twenty feet of the falls.

Although closely related to *gravitas, gravity* can apply to situations and problems as well as to people. Gravity in the physical sense is, of course, what gives us weight and holds us on the earth. But weight can also mean seriousness. Thus, gravity in the nonphysical sense can mean seriousness in a person's manner but also the seriousness or danger in a situation.

LEV comes from the Latin adjective *levis,* meaning "light," and the verb *levare,* meaning "to raise or lighten." *Levitation* is the magician's trick in which a body seems to rise into the air by itself. And a *lever* is a bar used to lift something by means of *leverage*.

alleviate \ə-'lē-vē-ˌāt\ To lighten, lessen, or relieve, especially physical or mental suffering.

• Cold compresses alleviated the pain of the physical injury, but only time could alleviate the effect of the insult.

Physical pain or emotional anguish, or a water shortage or traffic congestion, can all be alleviated by providing the appropriate remedy. However, some pain or anguish or shortage or congestion will remain: to alleviate is not to cure.

elevate \'e-lə-ˌvāt\ (1) To lift up or raise. (2) To raise in rank or status.

• Last year's juniors have been elevated to the privileged status of seniors.

An *elevator* lifts things up. You may elevate a sprained ankle to reduce the swelling. When a Boy Scout reaches the rank of Eagle Scout, his rank is as *elevated* as it can get. *Elevated* language is language that, as in many poems and speeches, sounds formal or intellectual or in some way "higher" than common speech.

leavening \'le-və-niŋ\ Something that lightens and raises; something that modifies, eases, or animates.

• The speech was on a dull subject—"Microeconomic Theory in the 1970s"—but its leavening of humor made the time pass quickly.

The word *leavening,* when used in the kitchen, usually refers to yeast or baking powder. (*Unleavened* bread is often hard and dense; when it is used in religious ceremonies, it may be intended as a reminder of past hardship.) Young children may provide the leavening at a family reunion, and a cheerful receptionist may be the leavening in an otherwise dull office.

levity \'le-və-tē\ Frivolity, lack of appropriate seriousness.

• The Puritan elders tried to ban levity of all sorts from the community's meetings.

Levity originally was thought to be a physical force exactly like gravity but pulling in the opposite direction. Even as late as the last century, scientists were arguing about its existence. But today *levity* refers to lightness in manner. This was once regarded as almost sinful, so the word has an old-fashioned ring to it and is usually used in a half-serious tone of disapproval.

Quizzes

A. Fill in each blank with the correct letter:

a.	gravid	e.	alleviate
b.	gravitate	f.	leavening
c.	gravitas	g.	levity
d.	gravity	h.	elevate

1. As the _____ of the situation slowly became apparent, the crowd's mood changed from anxiety to hysteria.
2. With no _____, the muffins came out dense, chewy, and inedible.
3. At their father's funeral they showed the same solemn _____ at which they had often laughed during his lifetime.
4. Uncomfortable with their mean jokes, he tried to _____ the tone of the conversation.
5. Attracted magically by the music, all animals and natural objects would _____ toward the sound of Orpheus's lyre.
6. The lightning hung in the air for a _____ moment before the explosion of thunder.
7. The neighboring nations organized an airlift of supplies to _____ the suffering caused by the drought.
8. The board meeting ended in an unusual mood of _____ when a man in a gorilla suit burst in.

B. Match the word on the left to the correct definition on the right:

1. levity   a. solemn dignity
2. gravitas   b. relieve
3. gravid   c. lift, raise

4.	alleviate	d.	something that lightens
5.	elevate	e.	move toward as if drawn
6.	gravity	f.	lack of seriousness
7.	leavening	g.	pregnant
8.	gravitate	h.	seriousness

Words from Mythology and History

cicerone \ˌsi-sə-'rō-nē\ A guide, especially one who takes tourists to museums, monuments, or architectural sites and explains what is being seen.

● While in Paris, they placed themselves in the care of a highly recommended cicerone to ensure that they saw and learned what was most noteworthy.

Cicerones (or *ciceroni*) take their name from the Roman statesman and orator Cicero, who was renowned for his long-windedness as well as for his elegant style, though they rarely match his scholarship or eloquence.

hector \'hek-tər\ To bully; to intimidate or harass by bluster or personal pressure.

● He would swagger around the apartment entrance with his friends and hector the terrified inhabitants going in and out.

In the *Iliad,* Hector was the leader of the Trojan forces, and the very model of nobility and honor. In the war against the Greeks he killed several great warriors before being slain by Achilles. His name began to take on its current meaning only after it was adopted by a crowd of bullying young rowdies in late-17th-century London.

hedonism \'hē-də-ˌni-zəm\ An attitude or way of life based on the idea that pleasure or happiness should be the chief goal.

● In her new spirit of hedonism she went for a massage, picked up champagne and chocolate truffles, and made a date with an old boyfriend for that evening.

Derived from the Greek word for ''pleasure,'' hedonism over the ages has provided the basis for several philosophies. The ancient Epicureans and the more modern Utilitarians both taught and pursued *hedonistic* principles. Hedonism is often said to be more typical of those living in southern and tropical climates than of northerners, but it varies greatly from person to person everywhere.

nestor \'nes-,tȯr\ A senior figure or leader in one's field.

● After dinner the guest of honor, a nestor among journalists, shared some of his wisdom with the other guests.

Nestor was another character from the *Iliad,* the eldest of the Greek leaders at Troy. He was noted for his wisdom and his talkativeness, both of which increased as he aged. These days a nestor need not go on at such length; he may share his knowledge or give advice with few words.

spartan \'spär-tən\ Marked by simplicity and often strict self-discipline or self-denial.

● His spartan life bore no relation to the lush language of his poetry.

In ancient times, the Greek city of Sparta had a reputation for enforcing a highly disciplined, severe way of life among its citizens so as to keep them ready for war at any time. The city required physical training for men and women and maintained a common dining hall and communal child care, but provided few physical comforts. The term *spartan* today may sometimes suggest communal life (for example, in the army) but always signifies strictness and frugality.

stentorian \sten-'tȯr-ē-ən\ Extremely loud, often with especially deep richness of sound.

● Even without a microphone, his stentorian voice broadcast the message of peace to the farthest reaches of the auditorium.

Stentor, like Hector, was a warrior in the *Iliad,* but on the Greek side. His unusually powerful voice made him the natural choice for delivering announcements and proclamations to the assembled Greek army. One who speaks in a stentorian voice thus can be heard clearly at a considerable distance.

stoic \'stō-ik\ Seemingly indifferent to pleasure or pain.

• She bore the pain of her broken leg with stoic patience.

The *Stoics* were members of a philosophical movement that first appeared in ancient Greece and lasted through the Roman era. They taught that humans should seek to free themselves from joy, grief, and passions of all kinds in order to attain wisdom. They have given their name to a personal attitude that some cultures and individuals still proudly cultivate.

sybaritic \ˌsi-bə-'ri-tik\ Marked by a luxurious or sensual way of life.

• Eventually their sybaritic excesses consumed all their savings and forced them to lead a more restrained life.

The ancient city of Sybaris, founded by the Greeks in Italy, was famous for the wealth and hedonistic self-indulgence of its citizens, whose love of extravagance and sensuality made *sybaritic* a term for such leanings in any era.

Quiz

Choose the closest definition:

1. hedonism   a. preference for males b. habit of gift-giving c. tendency to conceal feelings d. love of pleasure
2. hector   a. encourage b. harass c. deceive d. swear
3. cicerone   a. guide b. cartoon character c. orator d. lawyer
4. spartan   a. cheap b. militaristic c. severe d. luxurious
5. nestor   a. journalist b. long-winded elder c. domestic hen d. judge
6. stoic   a. pleasure-seeking b. bullying c. repressed d. unaffected by pain
7. sybaritic   a. pleasure-seeking b. free of luxury c. sisterly d. ice-cold
8. stentorian   a. obnoxious b. muffled c. loud d. dictated

Review Quizzes

A. Fill in each blank with the correct letter:

a.	belligerence	h.	inhospitable
b.	stentorian	i.	incriminate
c.	appease	j.	gravitate
d.	sybaritic	k.	hector
e.	gravid	l.	enamored
f.	alleviate	m.	stoic
g.	inimical	n.	pacify

1. Councillor Hawkins had a folksy drawl, but his simplest statements were ＿＿ with meaning.
2. The mood at the resort was ＿＿, and the drinking and dancing continued long into the night.
3. To rattle the other team, they usually ＿＿ them constantly.
4. The judge was known for issuing all his rulings in a ＿＿ voice.
5. With its thin soil and long winters, the area is ＿＿ to farming.
6. Thoroughly ＿＿ of the splendid Victorian house, they began to plan their move.
7. She attempted to ＿＿ his anxiety by convincing him he wasn't to blame.
8. Whenever she entered a bar alone, the lonely men would always ＿＿ toward her.
9. Their refusal to cease work on nuclear weapons was seen as an ＿＿ act by the neighboring countries.
10. There was nowhere for miles where he could ＿＿ his intense nicotine craving.
11. Unable to calm the growing crowd, he finally ordered the police to ＿＿ the area by force.
12. Whenever her boyfriend saw anyone looking at her, his ＿＿ was alarming.
13. He bore all his financial losses with the same ＿＿ calm.
14. Who would have guessed that it would take the killer's own daughter to ＿＿ him.

B. Choose the closest definition:

1. hedonism   a. fear of heights b. hatred of crowds
      c. liking for children d. love of pleasure
2. levity   a. lightness b. policy c. leverage d. literacy
3. gravity   a. disturbance b. danger c. engraving
      d. seriousness
4. reprobate   a. researcher b. commissioner
      c. scoundrel d. reformer
5. bellicose   a. fun-loving b. warlike c. impatient d. jolly
6. decriminalize   a. discriminate b. legalize c. legislate
      d. decree
7. antebellum   a. preventive b. unlikely c. impossible
      d. prewar
8. hostage   a. prisoner b. hostess c. criminal d. hotel
9. pact   a. bundle b. form c. agreement d. presentation
10. amicable   a. technical b. sensitive c. friendly d. scenic
11. criminology   a. crime history b. crime book c. crime
      study d. crime story
12. approbation   a. approval b. resolution c. reputation
      d. substitution

**C. Match the definition on the left to the correct word
    on the right:**

1.	secret lover	a.	elevate
2.	show as false	b.	gravitas
3.	accusation	c.	disprove
4.	integrity	d.	probity
5.	shelter	e.	recrimination
6.	nursing service	f.	paramour
7.	peace lover	g.	hospice
8.	raise	h.	hostel
9.	dignity	i.	rebellion
10.	revolt	j.	pacifist

Unit 2

AG comes from the Latin word for "do, go, lead, drive." An *agenda* is a list of things to be done. An *agent* is usually someone who does things on behalf of another, just as an *agency* is an office that does business for others.

agitate \'a-jə-,tāt\ (1) To move something with an irregular, rapid, violent action. (2) To stir up or excite.

• Philip found Louisa highly agitated at the news of her son's disappearance.

Agitate can mean to shake or stir something physically, but more often its meaning is emotional or political. *Agitation* for a cause—a new union, civil rights, a change of government—involves talking it up, passing out information, and holding meetings, though sometimes as secretly as possible. An *agitated* person or animal usually feels severely anxious and upset, not pleasantly excited.

litigate \'li-tə-,gāt\ To carry on a lawsuit by judicial process.

• If the company chooses to litigate, it may give the protesters the chance to make their points even more effectively in the courts and newspapers.

Litigation has become almost a way of life in America, where there are many more lawyers than in any other country on earth. In this increasingly *litigious* society, the courts have been overwhelmed with petty disputes. Television has responded to the trend by producing heroes like Judge Wapner of *People's Court*, a man who can show *litigants* the absurdity of their case while rendering a just verdict. (The Latin *litigare* includes the root *lit*, "lawsuit," and thus means basically "to drive a lawsuit.")

prodigal \'prä-də-gəl\ Recklessly or wastefully extravagant; spendthrift.

● Rodney had been the most prodigal with his expected inheritance and had the most to gain from a redistribution of the estate.

The Latin *prodigere* means "to squander"—that is, to "drive away" money and goods. In the biblical story of the prodigal son, the father welcomes home the spendthrift and now-penniless young man, despite his *prodigality*, just as the Church stands ready to welcome back the repenting sinner. *Prodigal* can apply to more than money. Farmers may make prodigal use of their soil, or may give their animals prodigal amounts of antibiotics. Rich countries are almost always prodigal with their resources. In a bloody and pointless war, lives are lost on a prodigal scale.

synagogue \'si-nə-ˌgȯg\ The center of worship and communal life of a Jewish congregation; temple.

● Though the neighborhood was now dangerous at night, the older members refused to move and abandon the beloved synagogue they had attended since the 1940s.

Synagogue begins with the prefix *syn-*, "together," so the word refers basically to "coming together." Synagogues have existed for more than 2,500 years. The oldest synagogue in America, dating from 1763, was built in Rhode Island, the most religiously tolerant of the original thirteen colonies.

VEN/VENT comes from *venire,* the Latin verb meaning "come." To *intervene* in a case or an argument is to "come between" the two opponents. An *avenue* is a street, or originally an access road by which to "come toward" something. Groups "come together" at a *convention.*

---

advent \'ad-ˌvent\ A coming or arrival; a coming into use.

● The advent of spring was always marked by the blue crocuses pushing up through the snow.

Advent includes the prefix *ad-,* "to or toward," and thus means basically a "coming toward." The Advent season in the Christian religion consists of the weeks leading up to Christmas, when the coming of Christ is anticipated. The advent of mass printing with Gutenberg's printing press in the mid-15th century had an enormous effect on European society and politics; the advent of the computer in the mid-20th century has promised to change ours even more profoundly.

provenance \'präv-nəns\ Origin or source.

• The wedding guests wondered about the provenance of this mysterious woman, about whom Seth had never breathed a word.

Provenance refers to any source or origin in general, but is used particularly to refer to the history of ownership of a piece of art, which may be necessary to prove that a work is authentic. The provenance of Rubens's paintings is varied; some have been in a single family or in a single museum for centuries, while some have been lost without a trace, leaving their provenance a mystery. Tracing the provenance of an idea or invention such as television may be a complicated task.

venturesome \'ven-chər-ˌsəm\ Inclined to seek out risk or danger; bold, daring, adventurous.

• Kate, with her bungee jumping, free-falling, and rock climbing, had always been the most venturesome of the four.

America, perhaps with a touch of arrogance, likes to think of itself as a land of venturesome people who push fearlessly forward in all ages and in all fields, and it clearly took a venturesome spirit to mount the successful flight to the moon that ended in July 1969. In past centuries, however, the most venturesome explorers were to be found in Greece, Italy, Spain, Portugal, and Britain—that is, the rich countries on the sea or ocean.

venue \'ven-ˌyü\ (1) The place where a trial is held. (2) The locale of an event.

• To Dr. Slaughter the important thing was to get a change of venue; hoping to conceal his past, he wanted a judge who knew him neither by sight nor by reputation.

The importance of venue in jury makeup and the subsequent outcome of a trial was vividly shown in the famous Rodney King case.

A suburban jury acquitted the men accused of beating King; after a change of venue, an urban jury convicted two of the men. The venues of championship boxing matches, on the other hand, are chosen with maximum profits in mind.

Quizzes

A. Choose the correct synonym:

1. synagogue   a. courthouse b. arena c. temple d. cinema
2. provenance   a. part of France b. origin c. Italian cheese d. invitation
3. prodigal   a. brilliant b. poor c. missing d. lavish
4. venturesome   a. daring b. western c. forthright d. timid
5. agitate   a. soothe b. vibrate c. consume d. shake up
6. advent   a. propaganda b. arrival c. commerce d. departure
7. litigate   a. select a jury b. judge c. argue in court d. negotiate
8. venue   a. jury b. place c. menu d. decision

B. Complete the analogy:

1. venturesome : timid :: _____ : _____
   a. stiff : flexible b. antique : artificial c. attractive : shapely d. bellicose : belligerent
2. litigate : argue :: _____ : _____
   a. border : enclose b. negotiate : discuss c. demonstrate : describe d. scold : praise
3. synagogue : worship :: _____ : _____
   a. theater : ticket b. church : mosque c. stadium : match d. hymn : song
4. provenance : destination :: _____ : _____
   a. travel : itinerary b. menu : meal c. recording : transcript d. birthplace : hometown
5. agitate : placate :: _____ : _____
   a. alternate : switch b. hesitate : rush c. blame : scold d. modify : alter

---

6. venue : locale :: ____ : ____
    a. arrival : departure b. country : nation c. court :
    jury d. prosecutor : judge
7. advent : departure :: ____ : ____
    a. Christmas : New Year's b. poverty : wealth
    c. rainfall : precipitation d. journey : expedition
8. prodigal : spendthrift :: ____ : ____
    a. stingy : miserly b. cautious : reckless c. artificial :
    natural d. opposite : similar

CAP/CEP/CIP comes from *capere,* the Latin verb meaning
"take, seize." *Capture,* which is what a *captor* does to a *captive,*
has the same meaning. *Captivate* once meant literally "capture,"
but now means only to capture mentally through charm or appeal.
In some other English words this root produces, its meaning is
harder to find.

---

reception \ri-'sep-shən\ (1) The act of receiving. (2) A social gathering where guests are formally welcomed.

• Although the reception of her plan was enthusiastic, it was
months before anything was done about it.

Reception is the noun form of *receive.* So at a formal reception
guests are received or welcomed or "taken in." If your idea for a
great practical joke gets a lukewarm reception, it has not been well-
received or *accepted.* Bad TV reception means the signal isn't
being received well. And when a new novel receives good reviews
we say it has met with a good critical reception.

incipient \in-'si-pē-ənt\ Starting to come into being or to become
evident.

• He felt the stirrings of incipient panic as he riffled through the
file and realized that the letter had been removed.

An incipient career as an actor in New York tends to involve a lot
of waiting on tables while waiting for auditions. Identifying a cancer at its incipient stage may allow its development to be slowed
or reversed. An environmental pessimist may speak of the incipient
extinction of whales or bald eagles.

perceptible \pər-'sep-tə-bəl\ Noticeable or able to be felt by the senses.

• Her change in attitude toward him was barely perceptible, and he couldn't be sure that he wasn't imagining it.

Perceptible includes the prefix *per-*, meaning "through," so the word refers to whatever can be taken in through the senses. A *perceptive* person picks up hints and shades of meaning that others can't *perceive*. Such people rely on their sharp *perceptions*, their observations of whatever kind. So very often what is perceptible to one person—a tiny sound, a slight change in the weather, a different tone of voice—will not be to another.

susceptible \sə-'sep-tə-bəl\ (1) Open to some influence; responsive. (2) Able to be submitted to an action or process.

• Impressed with her intelligence and self-confidence, he was highly susceptible to her influence.

With its prefix *sus-*, "up," *susceptible* refers to what "takes up" or absorbs like a sponge. When negotiating the settlement of World War II at Yalta with Churchill and Roosevelt, Stalin may have found the other two susceptible to his threats and bullying and thus managed to hold on to much of Eastern Europe. Students are usually susceptible to the teaching of a strong and imaginative professor. In a similar way, a sickly child will be susceptible to colds, and an unlucky adult will be susceptible to back problems.

FIN comes from the Latin word for "end" or "boundary." *Final* describes last things, and a *finale* or a *finish* is an ending. But its meaning is harder to trace in some of the other English words derived from it.

---

affinity \ə-'fi-nə-tē\ (1) Sympathy; attraction. (2) Relationship.

• He knew of Carl's affinity to both wine and violence, and intended to take advantage of them.

Affinity gives a sense of things touching along their boundaries and therefore being of interest to each other. Felix Mendelssohn showed an affinity for music at a very early age and composed several fully developed symphonies while still in his teens; Stevie Wonder revealed his own musical affinity long before he made his debut at the age of 10. A strong affinity for another person may deepen into love. A critic may notice affinities between the works of two writers. A naturalist may speak of the affinity between two bird species—that is, their close physical relation to each other.

definitive \di-'fi-nə-tiv\ (1) Authoritative and final. (2) Specifying perfectly or precisely.

• The team's brilliant research provided a definitive description of the virus and its strange mutation patterns.

Something definitive is complete and final. A definitive example is the perfect example. A definitive biography contains everything we'll ever need to know about someone. Ella Fitzgerald's 1950s recordings of American popular songs have even been called definitive, though no one has ever wanted them to be the last.

infinitesimal \ˌin-ˌfi-nə-'te-sə-məl\ Extremely or immeasurably small.

• Looking more closely at the research data, he now saw an odd pattern of changes so infinitesimal that they hadn't been noticed before.

Infinitesimal includes the negative prefix *in-*, "not"; the resulting word describes something endlessly small. When Antonie van Leeuwenhoek invented the microscope in the 17th century, he was able to see organisms that had been thought too *infinitesimally* small to exist. But today's electron microscope allows us to see infinitesimal aspects of matter even he could not have imagined.

finite \'fī-ˌnīt\ Having definite limits.

• Her ambitions were infinite, but her wealth was finite.

It came as a shock to America in the early 1970s to realize that world and national resources were finite rather than unlimited. The debate continues as to whether the universe is finite or *infinite* and, if it is finite, how to think about what lies beyond it. Religion has always concerned itself with the question of the finite (that is, human life on earth) versus the infinite (God, eternity, and infinity).

But *finite* is mostly used in scientific writing, often with the meaning "definitely measurable."

Quizzes

A. Fill in each blank with the correct letter:

a. affinity   e. finite
b. susceptible   f. incipient
c. definitive   g. infinitesimal
d. reception   h. perceptible

1. By the fall there had been a _____ change in the mood of the students.
2. An _____ speck of dust on the lens can keep a CD player from functioning.
3. They waited weeks to hear about the board's _____ of their proposal.
4. She feels an _____ to her imaginary friend that she has never felt to her parents.
5. Small children are often _____ to nightmares after hearing ghost stories in the dark.
6. When the power failed as the wind began to reach gale force, she sensed _____ disaster.
7. We have a _____ number of choices, in fact maybe only three or four.
8. This may be the best book on the subject so far, but I wouldn't call it _____.

B. Match the word on the left to the correct definition on the right:

1. affinity   a. noticeable
2. susceptible   b. ultimate
3. definitive   c. beginning
4. reception   d. easily influenced
5. finite   e. tiny
6. incipient   f. attraction
7. infinitesimal   g. receiving
8. perceptible   h. limited

JAC/JEC comes from *jacere,* the Latin verb meaning "throw" or "hurl." To *reject* something is to throw (or push) it back. To *eject* something is to throw (or drive) it out. To *object* is to throw something in the way of something else.

adjacent \ə-'jā-sənt\ (1) Near, neighboring. (2) Sharing a common boundary or border.

● The warehouse was adjacent to the junction of the two raging rivers, so the body could have been quickly disposed of.

Adjacent contains the prefix *ad-,* "near or toward," so what is adjacent lies near its neighbor. In the former Yugoslavia, the Serbs and Croats have seized adjacent land from the Bosnians. Anyone buying a house is naturally curious about who lives on the adjacent lots. In geometry we speak of adjacent sides and angles. Though in each of these cases *adjacent* means "touching," it may also mean simply "neighboring" or "nearby."

conjecture \kən-'jek-chər\ To guess.

● They could conjecture that he had met his end in the Andes at the hands of the guerrillas.

Formed with the prefix *con-, conjecture* means literally "to throw together"—that is, to produce a theory by putting together a number of facts. From his calculations, Columbus conjectured that he would reach Asia if he sailed westward. His later *conjecture* of a Northwest Passage from the Atlantic to the Pacific over the North American continent was eventually proved correct, but only after hundreds of years had passed.

dejected \di-'jek-təd\ Downcast, depressed.

● Despite the glorious weather, they walked home from the hospital dejected.

Dejected, which includes the prefix *de-,* meaning "down," literally means "thrown down" or "cast down." It usually refers to a temporary state of mind—for example, the mood of a losing football team or a *rejected* lover—rather than ongoing depression.

trajectory \trə-'jek-tə-rē\ The curved path that an object makes in space, or that a thrown object follows as it rises and falls to earth.

● Considering the likely range, trajectory, and accuracy of a bullet fired from a cheap handgun at 150 yards, the murder seemed incredible.

Formed with part of the prefix *trans-*, "across," *trajectory* means a "hurling across." By calculating the effect of gravitational and other forces, the trajectory of an object launched into space at a known speed can be computed precisely. Missiles stand a chance of hitting their target only if their trajectory has been plotted accurately. Though the word is most used in physics and engineering, we can also say, for example, that the trajectory of a whole life may be set in a person's youth, or that a historian has described the long trajectory of the French empire in a new book.

TRACT comes from *trahere*, the Latin verb meaning "drag or draw." Something *attractive* draws us toward it. A *tractor* drags other vehicles behind it, with the help of the *traction* of its wheels.

detract \di-'trakt\ To decrease the importance, value, or effectiveness of something.

● None of the gossip in the new biography detracts in the least from her greatness as a writer.

With the prefix *de-*, meaning "away," *detract* means "draw away from." A fact that doesn't match up with the rest of the prosecution's case detracts from it. Richard Nixon's involvement in the Watergate coverup was felt to detract so seriously from his ability to carry out his presidential duties that he had to resign, especially after his *detractors* had impeached him. (Don't confuse *detract* with *distract*, which means "take attention away from.")

protracted \prō-'trak-təd\ Drawn out, continued, or extended.

● No one was looking forward to a protracted struggle for custody of the baby.

Protracted usually applies to something drawn out in time. A protracted strike may cripple a company; a protracted rainy spell may rot the roots of vegetables. Before Jonas Salk and Albert Sabin discovered vaccines to prevent polio, the many victims of the disease had no choice but to suffer a protracted illness and its permanent aftereffects.

retraction \ri-'trak-shən\ A taking back or withdrawal; a denial of what one has previously said.

• The following week, the newspaper reluctantly printed a retraction of the errors in the article, but the damage had been done.

The prefix *re-* ("back") gives *retraction* the meaning of "drawing back." Someone who has been wrongly accused may demand a retraction from his accuser—though today it seems more likely that he'll just go ahead and sue. Thousands of citizens were forced to publicly *retract* their "wrong" ideas by the Soviet government in the 1930s and the Chinese government in the 1960s. Retractions tend to be rather formal and rarely private.

intractable \in-'trak-tə-bəl\ Not easily handled, led, taught, or controlled.

• The army's corruption was known to be the country's intractable problem, and all foreign aid ended up in the colonels' pockets.

Intractable simply means "untreatable," and even comes from the same root. It may describe both people and conditions. An intractable alcoholic goes back to the bottle immediately after "drying out." A cancer patient may suffer intractable pain that doctors are unable to treat. Homelessness is now regarded by many as an intractable problem—though it hardly existed twenty years ago.

Quizzes

A. Choose the odd word:

1. conjecture   a. suppose   b. conclude   c. guess   d. know
2. protracted   a. lengthened   b. continued   c. circular
       d. extended
3. dejected   a. excited   b. downcast   c. depressed   d. forlorn
4. retraction   a. withdrawal   b. regret   c. disavowal
       d. denial

---

5. trajectory a. curve b. path c. line d. target
6. detract a. decrease b. diminish c. defy d. minimize
7. adjacent a. near b. adjourned c. touching d. bordering
8. intractable a. impossible b. uncontrollable
    c. stubborn d. unteachable

B. Match each definition on the left to the correct word on the right:

1. denial   a. protracted
2. assume   b. adjacent
3. depressed   c. trajectory
4. difficult   d. retraction
5. take away   e. conjecture
6. drawn out   f. intractable
7. curved path   g. detract
8. nearby   h. dejected

DUC, from the Latin verb *ducere,* "to lead," shows up constantly in English. *Duke* means basically "leader." The Italian dictator Mussolini was known simply as "Il Duce." But such words as *produce* and *reduce* also contain the root, even though their meanings show it less clearly.

conducive \kən-'dü-siv\ Tending to promote, encourage, or assist; helpful.

• She found the atmosphere there conducive to study and even to creative thinking.

Something conducive "leads to" a desirable result. A cozy living room may be conducive to relaxed conversation, just as a boardroom may be conducive to more intense discussions. Particular tax policies are often conducive to savings and investment, whereas others are conducive to consumer spending. Notice that *conducive* is almost always followed by *to*.

deduction \dē-'dək-shən\ (1) Subtraction. (2) The reaching of a conclusion by reasoning.

• Foretelling the future by deduction based on a political or economic theory has proved to be extremely difficult.

A tax deduction is a subtraction from your gross income allowed by the government for certain expenses, which will result in your paying lower taxes. To *deduct* is simply to subtract. But *deduction* also means "reasoning," and particularly reasoning based on general principles to produce specific findings. Mathematical reasoning is almost always deduction, for instance, since it is based on general rules. But when Dr. Watson exclaims "Brilliant deduction, my dear Holmes!" he simply means "brilliant reasoning," since Sherlock Holmes's solutions are based on specific details he has noticed rather than on general principles.

induce \in-'düs\ (1) Persuade, influence. (2) Bring about.

• To induce him to make the call we had to promise we wouldn't do it again.

Inducing often refers to gentle persuasion—inducing a friend to go to a concert, or inducing a child to stop crying, for instance. But an *inducement* may occasionally be a bit menacing, such as the Godfather's "Make him an offer he can't refuse." *Induce* also sometimes means "produce"; thus, doctors must at times induce labor in a pregnant woman. *Induction* often means the opposite of *deduction*, and is in fact closer to what Sherlock Holmes was actually doing.

seduction \si-'dək-shən\ (1) Temptation to wrong, especially temptation to sexual intercourse. (2) Attraction or charm.

• The company began its campaign of seduction of the smaller firm by inviting its top management to a series of weekends at expensive resorts.

Seduction, with its prefix *se-*, "aside," means basically "led aside or astray." In Nathaniel Hawthorne's novel *The Scarlet Letter*, Hester Prynne has to wear a scarlet A, for "adulteress," for all to see after it is revealed that she has been *seduced* by the Reverend Dimmesdale. Seduction also takes less physical forms. Advertisements constantly try to seduce us (often using sex as a temptation) into buying products we hadn't even known existed.

SEC/SEQU comes from the Latin verb *sequi,* meaning "to follow." A *sequel* follows the original novel, film, or television show. The *second* follows the first. But a *non sequitur* is a conclusion that does "not follow" from what was said before.

consequential \ˌkän-sə-ˈkwen-shəl\ (1) Resulting. (2) Important.

• None of our discussions thus far has been very consequential; next week's meeting will be the important one.

Something that is consequential follows or comes along with something else. The "resulting" meaning of *consequential* is usually seen in legal writing. For example, "consequential losses" are losses that are claimed to have resulted from some improper behavior, about which the lawyer's client is suing. But normally *consequential* means "significant" or "important," and is especially used for events that will produce large *consequences* or results.

execute \ˈek-si-ˌkyüt\ (1) To carry out or perform. (2) To put to death legally or formally.

• He was aware that he hadn't been hired to think independently but rather simply to execute the governor's policies.

Execute joins *ex-*, "out," and *sec* to produce the meaning "follow through" or "carry out." An artist executes (or produces) a painting or sculpture only after having planned it first. A policy or regulation must have been prepared before it can be executed (or put into practice). And a person may be executed (or put to death) by the state only after a death sentence has been issued.

obsequious \äb-ˈsē-kwē-əs\ Excessively submissive, obedient, or flattering.

• Since he loves flattery, he surrounds himself with obsequious people, none of whom he ever really trusts.

A man may be obsequious toward his overbearing wife, or vice versa. Obsequious assistants are often called "yes-men" or "toadies" or even less complimentary things behind their backs. (Uriah Heep, in *David Copperfield,* is probably the most famous example in literature.) *Obsequiousness* has never been admired, but it has often been adopted as a good strategy.

sequential \si-'kwen-chəl\ (1) Arranged in order or in a series. (2) Following in a series.

• In writing the history of the revolution, he found it hard to put some of the events in sequential order.

Things in *sequence,* or regular order, are arranged *sequentially*. Most novels and films move sequentially, but some use techniques such as flashbacks that interrupt the movement forward in time. Sequential courses in college must be taken in the proper order, just as sequential tasks or steps must be done in order.

Quizzes

A. Match the definition on the left to the correct word on the right:

1.	flattering	a.	deduction
2.	persuade	b.	obsequious
3.	temptation	c.	induce
4.	subtraction	d.	execute
5.	helpful	e.	seduction
6.	ordered	f.	consequential
7.	produce	g.	conducive
8.	significant	h.	sequential

B. Fill in each blank with the correct letter:

a.	conducive	e.	consequential
b.	deduction	f.	execute
c.	induce	g.	obsequious
d.	seduction	h.	sequential

1. The detectives insisted on a detailed and _____ account of the evening's events.
2. She fended off all his clumsy attempts at _____.
3. Conditions on the noisy hallway were not at all _____ to sleep.
4. She was barely able to _____ the task in the time allotted.
5. He sometimes thought that missing that plane had been the most _____ event of his life.
6. They arrived at the correct conclusion by simple _____.

> 7. The assistant's _____ manner drove the other employees wild.
> 8. He had tried to _____ sleep by all his usual methods, with no success.

Words from Mythology

apollonian \ˌa-pə-'lō-nē-ən\ Harmonious, ordered, rational, calm.

● After years of Romantic emotionality, many artists began to adopt a more apollonian style, producing carefully detailed patterns and avoiding extremes of all kinds.

The god Apollo governed the sun, light, and music. Due partly to the work of Nietzsche and other German scholars, we now associate Apollo with the forces of calm rationality and may call anything that has these qualities *apollonian*. This is not the whole story, however. Apollo was also the god of prophecy, so he was not entirely a force of reason; he had a terrible temper and an appetite for young girls as well.

bacchanalian \ˌba-kə-'nāl-yən\ Frenzied, orgiastic.

● The bacchanalian partying on graduation night resulted in three wrecked cars, two lawsuits by unamused parents, and more new experiences than most of the participants could remember the next day.

The Roman god of drama, wine, and ecstasy, Bacchus was the focus of a widespread celebration, the *Bacchanalia,* at which there was wine in abundance and celebrants were expected to cut loose from normal restraints and give in to all sorts of wild desires. The festivities got so out of hand that in 186 B.C. the Roman authorities had them banned. Much the same bacchanalian spirit fills New Orleans' Mardi Gras carnival each year.

delphic \'del-fik\ Unclear, ambiguous, or confusing.

● All she could get from the old woman were a few delphic comments that left her more confused than ever about the missing documents.

Delphi in Greece was the site of a temple to Apollo at which there was an oracle, a woman through whom Apollo would speak, foretelling the future. The Greeks consulted the oracle frequently on matters both private and public. The prophecies were given in obscure poetry that had to be interpreted by priests, and even then was subject to disastrous misinterpretation. Modern-day descendants of the oracle include some political commentators, who continue to utter words of delphic complexity each week.

Dionysian \ˌdī-ə-ˈni-zhē-ən\ Frenzied, orgiastic.

● Only in the tropics did such festivals become truly Dionysian, he said, which was why he was booking his flight to Rio.

Dionysus was the Greek forerunner of Bacchus. He was the inventor of wine, the first intoxicant, which he gave to the human race. For that gift and for all the uninhibited behavior that it led to, Dionysus became immensely popular, and he appears in a great many myths. He is often shown with a wine goblet, his hair is full of vine leaves, and he is frequently attended by a band of goat-footed satyrs and wild female spirits called maenads. The Greek Dionysian worship began as solemn rituals but eventually became great celebrations with much drunken lewdness.

jovial \ˈjō-vē-əl\ Jolly, expansively good-natured.

● Their grandfather was as jovial as their grandmother was quiet and withdrawn.

Jove, or Jupiter, was the Romans' chief god. He was generally a cheerful, sociable, fatherly figure, although his anger could destroy offenders in a flash. Every department-store Santa Claus strives to attain this appearance of generous *joviality*.

mercurial \mər-ˈkyu̇r-ē-əl\ Having rapid and unpredictable changes of mood.

● His mother's always mercurial temper became even more unpredictable, to the point where the slightest thing would trigger a violent fit.

The god Mercury and the planet named for him were thought to govern eloquence and cleverness. As the gods' messenger, with his winged cap and sandals, he was the very symbol of speed. The planet Mercury was named for him because it is the fastest of the planets. His name was also given to the liquid silver metal that skitters out of one's hand so quickly it is almost impossible to hold. A mercurial person isn't necessarily physically quick, but changes moods with bewildering speed.

olympian \ō-'lim-pē-ən\ Lofty, superior, and detached.

• The mafia don's manner grew increasingly olympian as he aged, but the old-timers could still remember when he was a hotheaded young thug.

The Greek gods lived high atop Mount Olympus, which allowed them to watch what went on in the human realm below and intervene as they saw fit. But they tended not to worry much about the affairs of these weak and short-lived creatures, although they did insist on being properly worshiped by them. We American voters sometimes feel that Congress treats us in an olympian manner as it determines how our money will be spent.

venereal \və-'nir-ē-əl\ Having to do with sexual intercourse or diseases transmitted by it.

• In the 19th century syphilis especially was often fatal, and venereal diseases killed some of the greatest figures of the time.

Venus was the Roman goddess of love, the equivalent of the Greek Aphrodite. Since she governed all aspects of human sensuality and sexuality, she has given her name to the diseases acquired through sexual contact. Most of these venereal diseases have been around for centuries, but only in this century have doctors devised tests to identify them or medicines to cure them. Today the official term is *sexually transmitted disease,* or STD; but even this name turns out to be ambiguous, since some of these diseases can be contracted in other ways as well.

Quiz

Choose the correct synonym and the correct antonym:

1. Dionysian   a. frenzied b. angry c. calm d. fatal
2. apollonian   a. fruity b. irrational c. single
    d. harmonious

3. mercurial   a. stable b. changeable c. sociable
      d. depressed
4. jovial   a. youthful b. mean-spirited c. merry
      d. magical
5. olympian   a. involved b. lame c. detached d. everyday
6. venereal   a. sensual b. intellectual c. diseased
      d. arthritic
7. bacchanalian   a. restrained b. dynamic c. orgiastic
      d. forthright
8. delphic   a. clear b. dark c. stormy d. ambiguous

Review Quizzes

A. Choose the closest definition:

1. venue   a. prosecution b. justice c. location d. street
2. incipient   a. sensitive b. beginning c. visible d. final
3. affinity   a. eternity b. attraction c. intensity
      d. retraction
4. deduction   a. addition b. flirtation c. tax d. reasoning
5. execute   a. dismiss b. carry out c. disturb d. announce
6. sequential   a. important b. noticeable c. consecutive
      d. distant
7. obsequious   a. powerful b. official c. notorious
      d. obedient
8. agitate   a. excite b. amaze c. explain d. exclaim
9. prodigal   a. poor b. departed c. wasteful d. returning
10. synagogue   a. palace b. temple c. club d. society

B. Match the definition on the left to the correct word on the right:

1. guess   a. olympian
2. arrival   b. perceptible
3. lengthy   c. conjecture
4. godlike   d. venturesome
5. ordered   e. protracted
6. bold   f. advent
7. noticeable   g. susceptible

8. sensitive	h. dejected
9. significant	i. sequential
10. unhappy	j. consequential

C. Fill in each blank with the correct letter:

a. mercurial	f. litigate
b. obsequious	g. bacchanalian
c. intractable	h. detract
d. provenance	i. retraction
e. adjacent	j. trajectory

1. Before deciding to _____ the matter, they had tried to negotiate a solution out of court.
2. Nothing his enemies could say managed to _____ from his heroic public image.
3. The prison situation is _____, and likely to get worse.
4. The company issued a _____ the next day, apologizing to those who had been offended.
5. The new study of the painting's _____ proved it to be a genuine Monet.
6. Because they lived _____ to the paint factory, their garden suffered from the effects of pollution.
7. The disappointing _____ of his career often puzzled his friends.
8. The smilingly _____ sales clerk bustled off in search of more jackets.
9. By 2:00 a.m. the party was a scene of _____ frenzy.
10. Her only excuse for her behavior was her well-known _____ temper.

Unit 3

AMBI/AMPHI means "on both sides" or "around"; *ambi-* comes from Latin and *amphi-* from Greek. An *ambidextrous* person can use the right and the left hand equally well. An *amphibian*, such as a frog or salamander, is able to live and breathe both on land and in the water.

ambiguous \am-ˈbi-gyü-wəs\ (1) Doubtful or uncertain especially from being obscure or indistinct. (2) Unclear in meaning because of being understandable in more than one way.

• Successful politicians are good at giving ambiguous answers to questions on controversial issues.

Ambiguous comes from the Latin verb *ambigere*, "to be undecided," which in turn includes the verb *agere*, "to drive." Something that is ambiguous drives the observer in two directions. When we speak of eyes as being of an ambiguous color, we mean that we cannot decide which color they are—blue or green? The *ambiguity* of the smile of the Mona Lisa makes us wonder about what she's thinking about. An ambiguous order is one that can be taken in at least two ways. An order to "shut up!," on the other hand, may be very rude, but at least it's *unambiguous*.

ambient \ˈam-bē-ənt\ Existing or present on all sides.

• The ambient lighting in the restaurant was low, but there was a bright candle at each table.

A scientist might measure how long it takes a heated substance to cool to the ambient temperature, the temperature of the surrounding air. Ambient light is the light that fills an area or surrounds something that is being viewed, like a television screen or a painting. A restaurant with low ambient light and candles at each table is probably trying for a romantic *ambience,* or atmosphere.

ambivalent \am-'bi-və-lənt\ (1) Holding opposite feelings and attitudes at the same time toward someone or something. (2) Continually wavering between opposites or alternate courses of action.

● He was extremely ambivalent about the trip: he badly wanted to travel but hated to miss the summer activities at home.

Ambivalent is a fairly new word, less than a hundred years old, but it is ultimately related to the Latin verb *valere,* which means "to be strong." An ambivalent person is someone who has strong feelings on more than one side of a question or issue. We might feel *ambivalence* about accepting a high-paying job that requires us to work long hours, or about lending money to someone we like but don't know well. Anyone who has ever been on a diet and been offered something like a Tutti-Frutti Chocolate Banana Sundae El Supremo probably knows what it's like to feel ambivalent.

amphitheater \'am-fə-ˌthē-ə-tər\ (1) An oval or circular building with an open area ringed by rising tiers of seats, used in ancient Rome for contests and spectacles. (2) A large modern theater or stadium.

● The Romans held popular contests between gladiators or between gladiators and wild beasts in their amphitheaters.

The basic design of an amphitheater reflects the forms of entertainment for which it was originally built: gladiatorial contests and other spectacles. The most famous of the ancient amphitheaters was Rome's Flavian Amphitheater, now more commonly known as the Colosseum. Built between 70 and 82 A.D., this structure could hold nearly 50,000 people. The ruins of more than 75 amphitheaters have been found in the ancient lands that were once part of the Roman Empire.

EP/EPI comes from Greek and means variously "upon," "besides," "attached to," "over," "outer," or "after." An *epiphenomenon* is a phenomenon that occurs as a result of the original phenomenon. An *epicenter* is the portion of the earth's surface directly over the focus of an earthquake. The *epidermis* is the outer layer of the skin, overlying the inner layer or "dermis."

ephemeral \i-'fe-mə-rəl\ (1) Lasting a day only. (2) Lasting a very short time.

• The benefits from the strategy will only be ephemeral, but we'll be paying for it for years to come.

Something that is literally ephemeral is "over" in a day, *hēmera* being the Greek word for "day." Ephemeral plants such as day-lilies have blooms that last only a day. More often, though, *ephemeral* is not to be taken quite so literally. In the world of show business, for example, fame is apt to be breathtakingly ephemeral, a year in the limelight followed by total obscurity.

epiphyte \'e-pi-ˌfīt\ A plant that obtains its nutrients from the air and the rain and usually grows on another plant for support.

• The strangler fig begins life as an epiphyte on a tree branch, drops its tendrils to take root in the ground around the trunk, and slowly covers and strangles the tree to death.

Epiphytic plants are sometimes also known as "air plants" because they seemingly survive on thin air. They rely on their host plants merely for physical support, not nourishment. Tropical epiphytes include orchids, ferns, and members of the pineapple family. To a newcomer in the tropical rainforest, the sight of a great tree with large epiphytes hanging from every level can be eerie and astonishing. The less interesting epiphytes of the temperate zone include lichens, mosses, and algae.

epitaph \'e-pi-ˌtaf\ An inscription on a grave or tomb in memory of the one buried there.

• The great English architect Christopher Wren designed London's majestic St. Paul's Cathedral, the site of his tomb and epitaph: "Si monumentum requiris, circumspice" ("If you seek my monument, look around you").

Epitaph includes the root from the Greek word *taphos*, "tomb" or "funeral." Traditionally, *epitaph* refers to a tombstone inscription, but it can also refer to brief memorial statements that resemble such inscriptions. One of the most famous is Henry Lee's epitaph for George Washington: "First in war, first in peace, and first in the hearts of his countrymen."

epithet \'e-pi-,thet\ (1) A descriptive word or phrase occurring with or in place of the name of a person or thing. (2) An insulting or demeaning word or phrase.

● King Richard I was known by the epithet "Lionhearted."

Sometimes an epithet follows a given name, as in Erik the Red and Billy the Kid. Other times, the epithet precedes the personal name, as in Mahatma ("Great-souled") Gandhi. Still other times, the epithet is used in place of the actual name, as in the case of El Greco ("the Greek") and El Cid ("the Lord"). In its other commonly used sense, *epithet* refers to a name intended to insult or mock someone. When enemies are said to be "hurling epithets" at each other, it means they are exchanging angry insults.

Quizzes

A. Fill in each blank with the correct letter:

a.	ambiguous	e.	epithet
b.	epiphyte	f.	ambivalent
c.	ambient	g.	ephemeral
d.	epitaph	h.	amphitheater

1. An _____ seems to live on air and water alone.
2. When the _____ light is low, photographers use a flash.
3. She felt _____ about the invitation, and couldn't decide whether to accept or decline.
4. Is any _____ inscribed on Grant's Tomb?
5. Andrew Jackson's _____, describing his lean toughness, was "Old Hickory."
6. Lord Raglan's _____ order confused the commander of the Light Brigade and led to its disastrous charge.
7. Spring and all its blossoms are _____, here but a moment and then gone.
8. On New Year's Day, the _____ known as the Rose Bowl becomes the site of one of college football's great face-offs.

B. Match each word on the left with its correct definition on the right:

1. ambivalent   a. having more than one
2. epithet   meaning

3. amphitheater	b. surrounding
4. epiphyte	c. wavering
5. ambiguous	d. grave inscription
6. epitaph	e. stage surrounded with tiered seats
7. ambient	f. descriptive nickname
8. ephemeral	g. short-lived
	h. non-parasitic plant growing on another

HYPO/HYP as a prefix can mean variously "under," "beneath," "down," or "below normal." Many *hypo-* words are medical. A *hypodermic* needle injects medication under the skin. *Hypotension*, or low blood pressure, can be just as unhealthy as *hypertension*, and *hypoglycemia*, low blood sugar, just as unhealthy as diabetes.

---

hypochondriac \\ˌhī-pō-ˈkän-drē-ˌak\ A person unduly concerned with health and often suffering from delusions of physical disease.

● Hercule Poirot, the dapper hero of Agatha Christie's mysteries, is a notorious hypochondriac, always trying to protect himself from drafts.

One disease a hypochondriac really does suffer from is *hypochondria*, which is the mental depression that comes from worrying too much about health and is often accompanied by delusions of physical ailments. Somewhat surprisingly, *hypochondria* derives from *hypo-* and *chondros*, the Greek word for "cartilage." The cartilage in question is that of the sternum, or breastbone. From ancient times medical authorities had believed that certain internal organs or regions were the seat of various diseases, both physical and mental. The region beneath the centrally located breastbone was thought to be the seat of hypochondria.

hypocrisy \hi-ˈpä-krə-sē\ A pretending to be what one is not or to feel what one does not really feel.

● The protesters were objecting to the hypocrisy of doing business with a government whose racist policies were condemned by everyone.

Hypocrisy comes from a Greek word that means "the act of playing a part on a stage." A *hypocrite* is a person who says or does one thing while thinking or feeling something entirely different underneath. Most of us are good at detecting *hypocritical* behavior in others, but we don't always see it so easily in ourselves.

hypothermia \ˌhī-pō-'thər-mē-ə\ Subnormal temperature of the body.

• By the time rescuers were able to pull the skater from the pond's icy waters, hypothermia had reached a life-threatening stage.

Hypothermia may constitute a grave medical emergency. Typical causes include submersion in icy water and prolonged exposure to cold. Hypothermia begins to be a concern when body temperature dips below 95°F. Below 90°F, the point at which the normal reaction of shivering ceases, emergency treatment is called for.

hypothetical \ˌhī-pə-'the-tə-kəl\ (1) Involving an assumption made for the sake of argument or for further study or investigation. (2) Imagined for purposes of example.

• The presidential candidate refused to say what she would do if faced with a hypothetical military crisis.

Hypothetical and its parent word *hypothesis* come from *hypo-* and the Greek verb *tithenai,* "to put." To *hypothesize* is to suppose, or to put (something) under consideration. *Hypothetical* applies to something that is assumed to be true so that it can serve as the basis for a line of reasoning. Thus, the theory that the dinosaurs became extinct because of a giant meteor striking the earth involves the hypothesis that such a collision would have certain effects on the earth's climate.

THERM/THERMO comes from the Greek word meaning "warm." A *thermometer* measures the amount of warmth in a body, the air, or an oven; a *thermostat* makes sure the temperature stays at the same level. In a *thermodynamic* process, heat affects the behavior of atoms, particles, or molecules. *Thermoelectricity* is produced by the direct action of heat on certain combinations of metals.

---

thermal \'thər-məl\ (1) Of, relating to, or caused by heat. (2) Designed to insulate in order to retain body heat.

● The glider circled slowly, seeking a thermal updraft from a plowed field that would take it spiraling upward.

Before polypropylene and thermal weave, union suits—that is, long thermal underwear that covered the entire body—were sometimes donned in October and not taken off until April. Worn by sodbusters, cowboys, and townsfolk alike, they kept America warm during its formative years. They undoubtedly also kept America itchy and a little on the smelly side through the cold months. But then, bathing even once a week was considered the height of cleanliness until very recently.

thermocline \'thər-mə-ˌklīn\ The region in a body of water that divides the warmer, oxygen-rich surface layer from the colder, oxygen-poor deep water.

● The warm water above the thermocline is relatively shallow: for most of the world's oceans the top layer is only about 150 to 300 feet deep.

The -*cline* of *thermocline* comes from a Greek word meaning "to slope" and refers to the gradual series of temperature changes that occur in this kind of zone. In a freshwater lake there is very little mixing between the layers of warm and cold water during the summer. During the autumn, however, a major turnover occurs. The oxygen-rich surface water cools and sinks to the bottom, and the nutrient-rich water near the bottom is displaced to the top. The cycle is reversed the following spring.

thermocouple \'thər-mō-ˌkə-pəl\ A device for measuring temperature that makes use of the way different metals respond to heat.

● Thermocouples can be used to measure temperatures as high as 2300°C or as low as -270°C, far beyond the range of ordinary thermometers.

Thermocouples use wires made of two different metals, such as copper and iron. The wires are joined at both ends; one end is placed against the object whose temperature is being measured, while the other end is kept at a known, constant temperature. The thermocouple generates a voltage that depends on the difference in temperature between the two joined ends of the wires and can be measured to obtain the temperature of the object.

thermonuclear \thər-mō-'nü-klē-ər\ Of or relating to the changes in the nucleus of atoms with low atomic weight, such as hydrogen, that require a very high temperature to begin.

• During the 1950s and 1960s American families built thousands of home underground shelters to protect themselves from thermonuclear blasts.

The sun's light comes from a sustained thermonuclear reaction deep within it. On earth, such thermonuclear reactions have been used to develop the hydrogen bomb, a bomb based on a fusion reaction that must be triggered by a fission bomb that uses uranium or plutonium. "Little Boy" and "Fatman," the bombs dropped on Hiroshima and Nagasaki to end World War II, were fission bombs. The thermonuclear era began only in 1952, and has produced bombs hundreds of times more powerful.

Quizzes

A. Choose the closest definition:

1. hypothermia   a. excitability   b. subnormal temperature   c. external temperature   d. warmth
2. thermocline   a. area of warm water   b. area of cold water   c. area between warm and cold water   d. deep ocean water
3. hypocrisy   a. dislike   b. low energy   c. insincerity   d. nickname
4. thermal   a. keeping out   b. keeping warm   c. keeping safe   d. keeping cold
5. hypothetical   a. typical   b. substandard   c. sympathetic   d. assumed
6. hypochondriac   a. person with imaginary visions   b. person with heart congestion   c. person with imaginary ailments   d. person with imaginary relatives
7. thermocouple   a. temperature gauge   b. nuclear reaction trigger   c. ocean current gauge   d. altitude gauge

8. thermonuclear a. nuclear reaction requiring high heat b. chemical reaction requiring a vacuum c. biological reaction producing bright light d. nuclear reaction based on distance from the sun

B. Indicate whether the following pairs of words have the same or different meanings:

1. thermocouple / hot bodies   same ___ / different ___
2. hypochondriac / invalid   same ___ / different ___
3. thermal / insulating   same ___ / different ___
4. thermonuclear / destructive   same ___ / different ___
5. hypocrisy / truthfulness   same ___ / different ___
6. hypothetical / supposed   same ___ / different ___
7. thermocline / warm hillside   same ___ / different ___
8. hypothermia / low blood sugar   same ___ / different ___

POLY comes from *polys,* the Greek word for "many." *Polysyllabic* words, of which there are a few in this book, are words of many syllables. *Polygamy* is marriage in which one has many spouses, or at least more than the legal limit of one. A *polygraph* is an instrument for recording variations in many different bodily pulsations simultaneously to reveal whether someone is lying.

---

polychromatic \pä-lē-krō-'ma-tik\ Showing a variety or a change of colors; multicolored.

• *The Wizard of Oz* begins in black and white but suddenly becomes gloriously polychromatic once Dorothy and Toto land in Oz.

Male peacocks are almost miraculously polychromatic, with their feathers of gleaming blue, green, white, and brown. The polychromatic content of light becomes apparent when it passes through a prism like mist or a faceted piece of glass; the prism organizes it into its distinct wavelengths, each creating a band of color in the rainbow. *Polychromatic* takes its meaning straight from its roots: *poly-,* "many," and *chrom-,* "color."

polyglot \\'pä-lē-ˌglät\ (1) One who can speak or write several languages. (2) Having or using several languages.

● As trade between countries increases, there is more need for polyglots who can act as negotiators.

Polyglot contains the root *glot*, meaning "language." It is used both as a noun and as an adjective. An international airport is bound to be polyglot, with people from all over the world speaking their native languages. One of history's more intriguing polyglots was the Holy Roman Emperor Charles V. He claimed that he addressed his horse only in German, he conversed with women in Italian and with men in French, but he reserved Spanish for his talks with God.

polymer \\'pä-lə-mər\ A chemical compound formed by a reaction in which two or more molecules combine to form larger molecules with repeating structural units.

● Nylon, a polymer commercially introduced in 1938, can be spun and woven into fabrics or cast as tough, elastic blocks.

There are natural polymers, such as shellac and rubber, but synthetic polymers came into being in 1870 with Celluloid, which, although a synthetic compound, is made from natural cotton and camphor. After many decades of development, the *polymeric* compounds now include *polypropylene,* used in milk crates, luggage, and hinges; *polyurethane,* used in paints, adhesives, molded items, rubbers, and foams; and *polyvinyl chloride,* used to make pipes that won't rust.

polyphony \pə-'li-fə-nē\ Music consisting of two or more independent but harmonious melodies.

● At concerts she preferred Mahler and Beethoven, but when she was working she listened only to Renaissance polyphony.

Polyphony is usually avoided in American folk and popular music, which almost always employs a strong melody with a much less important accompaniment. But it is typical of Dixieland, bluegrass, and almost any kind of music where more than one musician improvises at once. *Polyphony* is used primarily for music of the Renaissance and Baroque eras from about 1400 to 1750; J. S. Bach is the most famous master of polyphony.

PRIM comes from *primus,* the Latin word for "first." Something that is *primary* is first in time, development, rank, or importance. A *primer* is a book of first instructions on a subject. A *primate* is a bishop or archbishop of the first rank—but also a monkey or ape. Something *primitive* is in its first stage of development. Something *primeval* had its origin in the first period of world or human history.

primal \'prī-məl\ (1) Original or primitive. (2) First in importance.

• She argued that to restore the economy, the primal necessity was to reform the health care system.

We might speak of the primal innocence of youth, or of the primal intensity of someone's devotion to a cause. Certain psychologists employ "primal scream" therapy, in which patients relive painful experiences from their past and express their frustration and anger through screaming and even violence.

primiparous \prī-'mi-pə-rəs\ (1) Bearing a first offspring. (2) Having borne only one previous offspring.

• The purpose of the study was to compare the average duration of labor for primiparous women with that of multiparous women.

Primiparous is used of animals as well as humans. It is typically used with *multiparous,* "having had one or more previous pregnancies." The terms are common in laboratory research, veterinary science, and human obstetrics. An individual who is a *primipara* may exhibit certain characteristics, or be subject to certain circumstances, that are peculiar to first pregnancies.

primogeniture \prī-mō-'je-nə-chùr\ An exclusive right of inheritance belonging to the eldest son of a single set of parents.

• Many of the world's monarchies descend by the principle of primogeniture.

Primogeniture arose in England following the Norman Conquest of 1066. The practice began as a means of ensuring that fiefs (that is, estates) would not be broken up among the sons of a vassal. Eventually the right of the eldest son to inherit all of his father's estate was written into law. Primogeniture was one of the English practices that Americans were eager to abolish once independence had been attained. Leading the campaign against it was Thomas Jefferson.

primordial \prī-'mȯr-dē-əl\ (1) First created or developed. (2) Existing in or from the very beginning.

• Many astronomers think the universe is continuing to evolve from a primordial cloud of gas.

Primordial can be traced back to the Latin word *primordium,* or "origin." It applies to something that is only the starting point in a course of development or progression. The substance out of which the earth was formed and all life on it evolved is commonly spoken of as "the primordial ooze." A primordial cell is the first formed and least specialized in a line of cells. A primordial landscape is one that bears no sign of human use.

Quizzes

A. Fill in each blank with the correct letter:

a. primiparous   e. polychromatic
b. polyglot   f. primordial
c. primogeniture   g. polymer
d. polyphony   h. primal

1. In the 1980s many women chose to remain _____, content with just one child.
2. Rubber is a natural _____ that remains the preferred material for many applications.
3. The asteroids in our solar system may be remnants of a _____ cloud of dust.
4. The Beatles occasionally experimented with _____, sometimes imitating the music of Bach.
5. Royal titles are still passed from one generation to the next on the basis of _____.
6. Having gone to school in four countries as a child, she was already a fluent _____.
7. They were charmed by the _____ innocence of the little village.
8. The house, once white, was now dazzlingly _____.

B. Indicate whether the following pairs of words have the same or different meanings:

1. polychromatic / overly dramatic   same ___ / different ___
2. primogeniture / first generation   same ___ / different ___
3. polymer / molecule with
    repeating units   same ___ / different ___
4. primiparous / firstborn   same ___ / different ___
5. polyglot / speaking many
    languages   same ___ / different ___
6. primal / most important   same ___ / different ___
7. polyphonic / many-colored   same ___ / different ___
8. primordial / primitive   same ___ / different ___

HOM/HOMO comes from *homos*, the Greek word for "same." In an English word it can mean "one and the same" or "similar" or "alike." A *homograph* is one of two or more words spelled alike but different in meaning or derivation or pronunciation. A *homosexual* is a person who exhibits sexual desire toward others of the same sex.

homonym \'hä-mə-ˌnim\ One of two or more words pronounced and/or spelled alike but different in meaning.

• The *pool* of "a pool of water" and the *pool* of "a game of pool" are homonyms.

Homonym is a troublesome word because it can refer to three distinct classes of words. Homonyms can be words that merely sound alike—such as *to*, *too*, and *two*—but are different in spelling and meaning. Homonyms can also be words that are spelled alike—such as *bow* (of a ship) and *bow* (and arrow)—but are different in pronunciation and meaning. Finally, homonyms can be words with identical spellings and pronunciations but different meanings—such as *quail* (the bird) and *quail* (to cringe). Some writers and speakers prefer to limit *homonym* to this last sense.

homogeneous \ˌhō-mə-'jē-nē-əs\ (1) Of the same or a similar kind. (2) Of uniform structure or composition throughout.

• Though she was raised in a small town, she liked living in the city because the population there wasn't so homogeneous.

A slab of rock is homogeneous if it consists of the same material throughout, like granite or marble. A neighborhood might be called homogeneous if all the people in it are similar, having pretty much the same background, education, and outlook. *Homogeneity* is fine in a rock, but some people find it a little boring in a neighborhood. Foods can be homogeneous too. Milk, for example, is *homogenized* so that its fatty part, the cream, is spread evenly throughout, giving the milk a consistent, homogeneous texture.

homologous \hō-'mä-lə-gəs\ Developing from the same or a similar part of a remote ancestor.

• Arms and wings are homologous structures that reveal our ancient relationship to the birds.

In his discussion of the panda's thumb, Stephen Jay Gould carefully explains how this thumb is not homologous to the human thumb. Although in function the two digits are similar, the panda's thumb developed from a bone in its wrist and is an addition to the five "fingers" of its paw. The panda's thumb is indispensable for stripping bamboo of its tasty leaves, the staple of the panda's diet; but it did not develop *homologously* with our thumb. The tiny stirrup and anvil bones of our inner ear, however, do seem to be homologous with the bones that allow a garter snake to swallow a frog whole.

homophone \'hä-mə-,fōn\ One of two or more words pronounced alike but different in meaning or derivation or spelling.

• The words *wood* and *would* are familiar homophones.

Since *phon-* means "sound," homophones basically sound the same. *Tide* and *tied, made* and *maid, horse* and *hoarse* are pronounced identically, but differ in meaning, derivation, and spelling. This occasionally leads to confusion. If Groucho Marx had said "I'm a little hoarse," we might well have expected him to give a little whinny. Puns depend on *homophonic* pairs for their effect; while many find that homophonic humor grates, others think it is just great.

DIS comes from Latin, where it means "apart." In English, its meanings have increased to include "do the opposite of" (as in *disestablish*), "deprive of" (as in *disfranchise*), "exclude or expel from" (*disbar*), "the opposite or absence of" (*disunion, disaffection*), "not" (*disagreeable*), and "completely" (*disannul*). The original meaning can still be seen in a word like *dissipate*, which means "to break up and scatter."

diffraction \di-'frak-shən\ (1) The bending or spreading of a beam of light especially when it passes through a narrow opening or is reflected from a ruled surface. (2) Similar changes in other waves, such as sound waves.

• Through the occurrence of diffraction, the thin bands of light passing through venetian blinds become a sea of soft light on the opposite wall.

Diffraction contains the root *fract-*, "broken" (*dis-* here has changed to *dif-*), so *diffracted* light is light that is broken up. Diffracted sound is also broken up. The diffraction of the sound waves bends them around the corner, so a conversation carried on in one room can be overheard in another.

dissension \di-'sen-shən\ Disagreement in opinion.

• There was so much dissension at the meeting that nothing got done, and everyone went home angry.

Dissension is a common feature of our political system. One party suggests a new law or policy, and then the other party often *dissents*, arguing that the new law or policy will have a terrible effect on the country, and proposing a different new law or policy of its own. This leads the first party to dissent in turn, and so on. Things usually get worked out in the end. Since *dissentious* behavior of this kind keeps everyone on their toes, most people feel that it's a good thing overall. But not everyone agrees.

disseminate \di-'se-mə-ˌnāt\ To spread widely as if by sowing seeds.

• Television and computer networks now make it possible to disseminate information throughout the world very quickly.

In *disseminate,* the prefix *dis-* keeps its original Latin sense "apart." This prefix was attached in Latin to the verb *seminare,* "to sow," which itself was derived from the noun *semen,* "seed." The image lying behind *disseminate* is that of a farmer sowing seeds over a wide area by throwing them with a sweep of the arm, the same image that has given us *broadcast* (which has the basic sense "to cast broadly"). It's appropriate, then, that one of the best ways to bring about the *dissemination* of news is by broadcasting it over television and radio.

dissipate \'di-sə-ˌpāt\ (1)To cause to spread out to the point of vanishing; disperse. (2) To spend wastefully or foolishly; squander.

● The moderator's good humor slowly dissipated the tension that had filled the meeting room.

Dissipate suggests a gradual disintegration or vanishing, as if by crumbling, scattering, or evaporation. A police force dissipates an unruly mob. The sun dissipates the morning mist. In its second sense, *dissipate* implies frittering away something until it is exhausted. A foolish lottery winner might dissipate his or her money in extravagant spending sprees, buying 18 Ferraris, say, or a lifetime supply of expensive imported underwear.

Quizzes

A. Choose the closest definition:

1. dissipate   a. drink slowly b. scatter c. make pale
     d. undo
2. homonym   a. word meaning the same as another
     b. word spelled and sounded the same as another
     c. one with same name as another d. one who loves
     another of the same sex
3. disseminate   a. spread widely b. plant in rows
     c. dissolve d. make longer
4. homogeneous   a. self-loving b. unusually brilliant
     c. having many parts d. consistent throughout
5. diffraction   a. breaking up of friendships b. breaking up
     of light waves c. breaking up of meetings d. breaking
     up of atoms

6. homologous   a. of different length b. of similar size
   c. of different stages d. of similar origin
7. dissension   a. confusion b. disagreement
   c. satisfaction d. curiosity
8. homophone   a. word that sounds like another b. word
   that means the same thing as another c. word that
   looks like another d. word relating to sexual desire

**B. Match the definition on the left to the correct word
on the right:**

1. word spelled like another   a. dissension
2. spend foolishly   b. homophone
3. having a consistent   c. diffraction
   texture   d. homonym
4. conflict   e. disseminate
5. evolutionarily related   f. homologous
6. spread over a wide area   g. dissipate
7. word sounding like   h. homogeneous
   another
8. breaking up of light or
   sound waves

Latin Borrowings

ad hoc \'ad-'häk\ Formed or used for a particular purpose or for immediate needs.

● The faculty formed an ad hoc committee to deal with the question of first-amendment rights on campus.

Ad hoc literally means "for this" in Latin, a meaning clearly reflected in its uses in English. An ad hoc investigating committee is authorized to look into a matter of limited scope and not to go on a fishing expedition for other wrongdoing. An ad hoc ruling by an athletic council is intended to settle a particular case, and is not meant to serve as a model for later rulings. Problems that come up in the course of a project often require immediate, ad hoc solutions.

ad hominem \\'ad-'hä-mə-nem\\ Marked by an attack on an opponent's character rather than by an answer to the arguments made or the issues raised.

● The presidential debates often consist of ad hominem attacks rather than serious discussion of important issues.

Ad hominem in Latin means "to the man." It comes from the field of rhetoric (that is, speaking and writing), where it was first used to describe arguments that appeal to the listener's emotions and not to the intellect. The easiest way to do this is to engage in personal attacks against one's opponent. When debaters cannot justify their own positions or prove their opponents wrong, they may resort to ad hominem charges. Ad hominem arguments require neither truth nor logic to be effective. Consequently, the popularity of such arguments has never waned.

alter ego \\'òl-tər-'ē-gō\\ (1) A trusted friend or personal representative. (2) The opposite side of a personality.

● The White House chief of staff is a political alter ego: he knows, or should know, who and what the President considers important.

In Latin, *alter ego* literally means "second I." An alter ego can be thought of as a person's clone or second self. A professional alter ego might be a trusted aide who knows exactly what the boss wants done. A personal alter ego might be a close friend who is almost like a twin. *Alter ego* can also refer to the second, hidden side of one's own self. In Robert Louis Stevenson's classic *The Strange Case of Doctor Jekyll and Mr. Hyde,* Dr. Jekyll is a good-hearted, honorable man. But after taking a potion, his alter ego, the loathsome and diabolical Mr. Hyde, takes control over his personality.

de facto \\dē-'fak-tō\\ Being such in practice or effect, although not formally recognized; actual.

● Although there was never a general declaration of war, the two countries were in a de facto state of war for almost a decade.

Literally meaning "from the fact," *de facto* in English is applied to whatever has the substance of something but not the formal name. A de facto government is one that operates with all of the power of a regular government, but without the official recognition. De facto segregation does not stem from any legislative order, but it is just as real and deep-rooted as segregation that has been authorized by law.

de jure \dē-'jùr-ē\ By right of law.

• With the completion of the adoption proceedings, the Millers became the de jure as well as the de facto parents of the child.

Literally meaning "by right" in Latin, *de jure* is typically used in sentences where it is set in opposition to *de facto*. It is used with reference to things that have the force of law or operate under a right recognized by law. A de jure president is one duly elected under a nation's laws. A de facto ruler, on the other hand, may be exercising power that has been acquired through illegal means.

ex post facto \,eks-,pōst-'fak-tō\ Done, made, or formulated after the fact.

• Most of Carl's so-called reasons are merely ex post facto excuses for impulsive behavior.

Ex post facto is Latin for "from a thing done afterward." Approval for a project that is given ex post facto—after the project already has been begun or completed—is mainly given to save face. An ex post facto law is one that criminalizes an action after it was committed, even though the action was not a crime at the time that it was committed.

modus operandi \'mō-dəs-,ä-pə-'ran-,dī\ A usual way of doing something.

• A criminal who commits repeated crimes can often be identified by his modus operandi.

Modus operandi is Latin for "method of operating." Although often associated with police work and a favorite word of mystery writers, *modus operandi* is used in other contexts as well. For example, a frequent gambler who likes to play the horses may have a particular modus operandi for picking winners. The modus operandi of a cutthroat retailer may be to undersell competitors, drive them out of business, and then raise prices afterwards.

modus vivendi \'mō-dəs-vi-'ven-dē\ (1) A practical compromise or arrangement that is acceptable to all concerned. (2) A way of life.

• During the budget crisis, the Democratic governor and the Republican legislature established a modus vivendi that let them put aside their differences and tackle the problem at hand.

Modus vivendi literally means "manner of living" in Latin, and it sometimes has that meaning in English as well. Usually, though, a modus vivendi is a working arrangement that disputing parties can live with, at least until a more permanent solution can be found. Typically, a modus vivendi is an arrangement that ignores differences and difficulties. Two people going through a bitter divorce may be able to arrive at a modus vivendi that allows them to at least maintain an appearance of civility and dignity.

Quiz

Choose the closest definition:

1. alter ego   a. church structure b. bad conscience
     c. intimate friend d. self-love
2. modus vivendi   a. pie with ice cream b. compromise
     c. stalemate d. immoral conduct
3. ad hoc   a. for this purpose b. permanent c. long-
     range d. for many reasons
4. ex post facto   a. in anticipation b. sooner or later
     c. coming after d. someday
5. ad hominem   a. based on personalities b. based on
     logic c. based on issues d. based on sexual preference
6. modus operandi   a. procedure b. way of moving
     c. crime d. arrest
7. de facto   a. in transit b. in effect c. in debt d. in theory
8. de jure   a. by might b. by claim c. by right d. by word

Review Quizzes

A. Complete the analogy:

1. monochromatic : dull :: polychromatic : _____
     a. neutral b. bland c. sharp d. vivid
2. peace : tranquility :: dissension : _____
     a. cooperation b. disagreement c. unity
     d. communication

3. brief : lengthy :: ex post facto : _____
   a. beforehand b. afterward c. during d. actually

4. local : here :: ambient : _____
   a. there b. somewhere c. nowhere d. everywhere

5. marriage : dowry :: primogeniture : _____
   a. favoritism b. flattery c. inheritance d. divorce

6. antonym : up / down :: homophone : _____
   a. pause / paws b. three / tree c. imagine / dream
   d. retreat / advance

7. seek : flee :: ad hominem : _____
   a. to the time b. to the issue c. to the end d. to the
   maximum

8. desirable : despised :: thermal : _____
   a. cool b. soft c. warm d. springy

B. Fill in each blank with the correct letter:

a.	ad hoc	i.	diffraction
b.	ambivalent	j.	modus vivendi
c.	modus operandi	k.	primiparous
d.	epithet	l.	alter ego
e.	thermonuclear	m.	polyglot
f.	de jure	n.	hypochondriac
g.	polymer	o.	amphitheater
h.	homogeneous		

1. A real _____, she could speak four languages and read
   three others.

2. The independent-minded teenager and her overprotective
   parents struggled to arrive at a _____ that both sides
   could accept.

3. The usual _____ for the songwriters was for one to write
   the lyrics first and then for the other to compose the
   music.

4. She is such a close friend that she seems like my _____.

5. The de facto segregation in the North closely resembled
   the _____ segregation of the South.

6. _____ explains why sound can be heard around a corner,
   even though no straight path between source and hearer
   exists.

7. Much thought has gone into the designing of _____ power plants that run on nuclear fusion.

8. The development of the first synthetic _____ for use as fabric revolutionized the garment industry.

9. "Gray-eyed" is the standard _____ used to describe the goddess Athena.

10. The _____ mothers were shown to have on average more complications during pregnancy.

11. Jessica was _____ about going to the party: it sounded exciting, but she wouldn't know any of the other guests.

12. In her middle age she became a thorough _____, always convinced she was suffering from some new disease.

13. You should blend all ingredients thoroughly to produce a _____ mixture.

14. An _____ committee should be named to come up with ideas for redecorating the waiting room.

15. The play was presented in the open-air _____ under the stars.

C. Indicate whether the following pairs have the same or different meanings:

1. de facto / actually   same __ / different __
2. hypothermia / heat prostration   same __ / different __
3. primordial / existing from the beginning   same __ / different __
4. thermocline / cold ocean depths   same __ / different __
5. polyphonic / religious   same __ / different __
6. primal / first   same __ / different __
7. ambiguous / unclear   same __ / different __
8. modus operandi / way of life   same __ / different __
9. homologous / blended   same __ / different __
10. disseminate / broadcast   same __ / different __
11. thermocouple / lovebirds   same __ / different __
12. epiphyte / parasite   same __ / different __
13. de jure / legally   same __ / different __
14. epitaph / grave inscription   same __ / different __
15. dissipate / dispel   same __ / different __

Unit 4

VOR, from the Latin verb *vorare*, means "to eat." The ending *-ivorous* shows up in words that refer to eaters of certain kinds of food. *Frugivorous* (for "fruit-eating"), *granivorous* (for "grain-eating"), and *graminivorous* (for "grass-eating") are somewhat common. Some *-ivorous* words such as *insectivorous* and *nectarivorous,* are easy to understand at a glance. Others can get pretty complex; insects that feed on the sap of plants, for instance, are *phytosuccivorous*.

carnivorous \kär-'ni-və-rəs\ Meat-eating or flesh-eating.

● The dragonfly lives up to its name by being a carnivorous terror that can pluck its prey out of midair at speeds up to 30 miles per hour.

Usually when we think of carnivorous beings we think of large animals such as lions, tigers, or cheetahs. However, many smaller animals, including some kinds of mice and the tiny creatures that make up coral reefs, are also *carnivores*. And there are even a few carnivorous plants, such as the Venus's-flytrap, the pitcher plant, and the sundew, all of which *devour* their insect prey after trapping them by ingenious means.

herbivorous \hər-'bi-və-rəs\ Plant-eating.

● In spite of their frightening appearance, marine iguanas are peaceable herbivorous animals that feed mostly on seaweed.

While many herbivorous animals (such as rabbits and cows) are noted for their passive ways, such behavior is not universal among *herbivores*. A rhinoceros is herbivorous but capable of inflicting serious damage if threatened. Among dinosaurs, the herbivorous

Diplodocus had a thick tail that could be used as a lethal weapon against attacking carnivorous enemies.

omnivorous \äm-'ni-və-rəs\ (1) Feeding on both animals and plants. (2) Intensely interested in everything.

• Good writers are often also omnivorous readers who enjoy equally fiction and nonfiction, prose and poetry, philosophy and science.

We tend to think of human beings as omnivorous, but in fact there are many kinds of plants that we simply cannot digest. Bears are truer *omnivores*. Their diet can include bulbs, berries, nuts, young plant shoots, insects, grubs, and dead animals, including fish, deer, and beaver. Humans do seem to possess an omnivorous curiosity. And it probably took that kind of curiosity—plus a good deal of courage—to be the first human to eat an oyster.

voracious \və-'rā-shəs\ (1) Having a huge appetite. (2) Very eager.

• One of the hardest parts of dieting is watching skinny people with voracious appetites consume large amounts of food without gaining weight.

Voracious can be applied to both people and their appetites. Teenagers are voracious eaters because they have voracious appetites. Some vacationers become voracious readers; others are voracious for other kinds of pleasure. *Voracious* often suggests an appetite in excess of what is good for us. We are sometimes told that we are a nation of voracious borrowers because of our voracious demand for consumer goods and voracious government spending, and none of this is good news.

CARN comes from the Latin *carn-*, the stem of *caro*, "flesh," and words including this root usually refer to flesh in some form. The word *carnivore*, for example, which we met in the preceding section, means "an eater of meat."

---

carnage \'kär-nij\ Great destruction of life (as in a battle); slaughter.

• People from around the world made appeals to parties on all sides of the conflict to stop the carnage of the war in Bosnia.

Carnage does not refer only to slaughter on the battlefield. As long as tens of thousands of people die each year in automobile accidents, it is appropriate to speak of carnage on the nation's highways. And in some contexts *carnage* can simply mean violence or its results. Those concerned about the effect of all of the violence we are exposed to each day point in particular to the carnage on television and in the movies.

carnal \'kär-nəl\ Having to do with bodily pleasures.

• The news stories about students going on Spring Break focused as usual on the carnal pleasures associated with the annual ritual.

Carnal is sometimes used to mean "having to do with the human body," but more often it refers solely to the pleasures and appetites of the body. Most religions stress the superiority of spiritual enlightenment over carnal pleasures. Very frequently, *carnal* simply means "sexual," especially when the sexual activity is mostly physical in nature. Novels about Hollywood often rely heavily on detailed descriptions of the carnal adventures of their main characters.

carnival \'kär-nə-vəl\ (1) A season of merrymaking just before Lent; an occasion for festivities and excess. (2) A traveling group that presents a variety of amusements.

• Whether in Argentina, Brazil, or Trinidad, carnival is one of the most exciting events of the year, involving parades, parties, and dressing up in costume.

Just before Lent many cities hold a time of merrymaking called a carnival. The roots that apparently make up *carnival* mean "flesh" and "remove," and a common result of carnival was the eating up of meat that wouldn't keep through the 40-day season of Lent, a time of fasting and self-discipline when meat was indeed removed from the table. In the Americas, carnival is most famous in Rio de Janeiro and New Orleans (whose version of carnival is called Mardi Gras), but carnival takes place in most parts of the world where Lent is observed.

incarnation \‚in-kär-'nā-shən\ (1) A particular physical form or version of something. (2) A person showing a trait to a marked degree.

● During the Gulf War, press reports depicted Saddam Hussein as the incarnation of evil.

Incarnation originally referred to gods and deities taking on fleshly form, but now it more commonly refers to anything in the physical world that clearly illustrates some principle. The crowded streets of Hong Kong are said to be the incarnation of business and commerce. Sometimes *incarnation* can simply mean "a version" or "a form or state." An old building, for instance, can pass through several incarnations—as first an inn, then a private home, and then a store—before being returned to its original purpose.

Quizzes

A. Indicate whether the following pairs have the same or different meanings:

1. carnage / slaughter   same ___ / different ___
2. omnivorous / grazing   same ___ / different ___
3. incarnation / burial   same ___ / different ___
4. voracious / extremely hungry   same ___ / different ___
5. carnal / spiritual   same ___ / different ___
6. herbivorous / vegetarian   same ___ / different ___
7. carnival / Lent   same ___ / different ___
8. carnivorous / meat-eating   same ___ / different ___

B. Fill in each blank with the correct letter:

a. incarnation   e. voracious
b. omnivorous   f. herbivorous
c. carnage   g. carnal
d. carnivorous   h. carnival

1. Sheep, cattle, and antelope are ___; unlike dogs and cats, they show no interest in meat.
2. The school tried to shield students from ___ temptations.
3. It took an hour and several full picnic baskets to satisfy the bear's ___ appetite.

4. My sister and I rode the Ferris wheel every night the _____ was in town.
5. From the variety of books on his shelves, we could tell he was an _____ reader.
6. Even the ambulance drivers were horrified by the _____ of the accident.
7. As a child she loved to watch them throw meat to the _____ ones, especially the lions and tigers.
8. In Greek mythology the _____ of Zeus could be in the form of a bull or a swan or golden rain as well as a human.

CRED comes from *credere,* the Latin verb meaning "to believe." If something is *credible* it is believable, and if it is *incredible* it is almost unbelievable. We have a good *credit* rating when institutions believe in our ability to repay a loan, and we carry *credentials* so that others will believe we are who we say we are.

---

credence \\'krē-dəns\\ Mental acceptance of something as true or real; belief.

• He scoffed and said that no one still gives any credence to the story of the Loch Ness monster.

Credence is close in meaning to *belief,* but there are differences. Unlike *belief, credence* is seldom used in connection with faith in a religion or philosophy. Instead *credence* is often used in reference to reports, rumors, and opinions. Claims that a political candidate can become the next President gain credence only after the candidate wins a few primaries. Stories about Elvis sightings persist, but they lack credence for most people.

creditable \\'kre-di-tə-bəl\\ Worthy of praise.

• Even though the young team did not win the tournament, they turned in a creditable performance in the playoffs.

A creditable performance is one that makes us believe in the worth or value of the performer. A creditable effort, a creditable first novel, or a creditable new restaurant are all worthy of praise. Don't let the similarity in spelling fool you: *creditable* does not mean the same thing as *credible*.

credulity \kri-'dü-lə-tē\ Readiness and willingness to believe on the basis of little evidence.

• Thrillers and action movies only succeed if they don't strain our credulity too much.

Credulity most often appears in the phrase "to strain credulity," but a particularly far-fetched story may also be said to stretch credulity or to put demands on or make claims on our credulity. Credulity is not always a bad thing. There is no limit to the credulity of Boston and Chicago baseball fans, for example, and that probably makes life bearable for them. The related adjective is *credulous*. F. Scott Fitzgerald once defined advertising as "making dubious promises to a credulous public"—that is, a naive or gullible public.

creed \'krēd\ (1) A statement of the basic beliefs of a religious faith. (2) A set of guiding principles or beliefs.

• She had made her money on Wall Street by following the simple creed: Buy low, sell high.

We get the word *creed* from the Latin *credo,* "I believe," which is the first word of many religious creeds, such as the Apostles' Creed and the Nicene Creed. *Creed* can refer both to the statement of beliefs of a religion and to the religion itself; hence our common phrase "regardless of race, creed, or color." It can also be applied to any guiding principles. Reducing the size of company workforces—making companies "lean and mean"—has become the central creed for many corporate executives.

FID comes from *fides,* the Latin word for faith. *Fidelity* is another word for "faithfulness." *Confidence* is having faith in someone or something. And an *infidel* is someone who lacks a particular kind of religious faith.

---

affidavit \a-fə-'dā-vət\ A sworn statement made in writing.

● Each member of the family had signed an affidavit stating that he or she believed the will to be valid.

In Latin *affidavit* means "he or she has sworn an oath," and affidavits are always sworn written documents. During the McCarthy era in the 1950s, many people were forced to make affidavits in which they swore that they were not members of the Communist party. Affidavits are usually made without an opposing lawyer being present. When police officers file an affidavit to get a search warrant, they don't inform anyone except the judge of their intent. In this respect, affidavits are different from depositions, which are made with attorneys for both parties present and able to ask questions.

diffident \\'di-fə-dənt\\ (1) Lacking confidence; timid. (2) Cautious or unassertive.

● The teacher tried to encourage even the most diffident students to make a try at public speaking.

Diffident means lacking faith in oneself. It often refers to a distrust in one's abilities or opinions that leads to hesitation in acting or speaking. For example, many patients feel diffident around their doctors and don't dare ask them many questions. A helpful friend tries to instill confidence in place of *diffidence*.

fiduciary \\fi-'dü-shē-,er-ē\\ (1) Having to do with a confidence or trust. (2) Held in trust for another.

● Managers of pension funds have a fiduciary responsibility to invest funds for the sole and exclusive benefit of those who will receive the pensions.

A fiduciary relationship is one in which one person places faith in another. Stockbrokers and real-estate agents have fiduciary duties to their clients, which means that they must act in the clients' best financial interests. Similarly, members of a company's board of directors have a fiduciary responsibility to protect the financial interests of shareholders. There are legal requirements for those with fiduciary responsibility, and they can be sued for breach of fiduciary duty if they fail in their responsibilities.

perfidy \\'pər-fə-dē\\ Faithlessness, disloyalty, or treachery.

● While working for the CIA he became a double agent for another country, and it seems he paid a high price for his perfidy.

The Latin phrase *per fidem decipere,* meaning "to betray the trust of," may have been the original source of *perfidus,* from which *perfidy* comes. The most famously *perfidious* figure in U.S. history is probably Benedict Arnold, the American army officer in the Revolutionary War who plotted with the British to surrender West Point to them—an act that made his name an epithet for traitor.

Quizzes

A. Fill in each blank with the correct letter:

a. perfidy   e. creed
b. creditable   f. affidavit
c. diffident   g. fiduciary
d. credulity   h. credence

1. She gave little ____ to his story about his deranged girlfriend and the kitchen knife.
2. This is a ____ piece of work, one of the best reports I've received this year.
3. For her own best friend to take up with her former husband was ____ that could never be forgiven.
4. He's so ____ that you'd never believe he gives talks in front of international organizations.
5. The family trust had been so badly mismanaged that it appeared there had been a violation of ____ responsibility.
6. Their longtime ____ had been one of respect for the environment and all animal life.
7. The ____ stated that no oral agreement had ever been made.
8. Her ____ is enormous; no story in the supermarket tabloids is too far-fetched for her.

B. Match the definition on the left to the correct word on the right:

1. bad faith   a. perfidy
2. timid   b. creditable
3. acceptance   c. diffident

4.	trust-based	d.	credulity
5.	sworn document	e.	creed
6.	well-done	f.	affidavit
7.	principles	g.	fiduciary
8.	trustfulness	h.	credence

CURR/CURS comes from *currere,* the Latin verb meaning "to run." Although the sense of speed may be lacking from words based on this root, the sense of movement remains. *Current,* for instance, refers to running water in a stream or river. And an *excursion* is a trip from one place to another.

concurrent \kən-'kər-ənt\ Happening or operating at the same time.

● The convicted killer was sentenced to serve three concurrent life terms in prison.

Things that are concurrent usually not only happen at the same time but also are similar to each other. So, for example, multitasking computers are capable of performing concurrent tasks. When we take more than one medication at a time, we run the risks involved with concurrent drug use. And most movie theaters today run several movies concurrently.

cursory \'kər-sə-rē\ Hastily and often carelessly done.

● Having spent the weekend going to parties, she was only able to give the chapter a cursory reading before class on Monday.

Unlike the other words in this section, *cursory* always implies speed but also stresses a lack of attention to detail. When citizens complain about a cursory police investigation of a crime, they are distressed by its lack of thoroughness, not its speed. Cursory observations are made quickly, but more importantly they are probably shallow or superficial.

discursive \dis-'kər-siv\ Passing from one topic to another.

● Some days he allowed himself to write long discursive essays in his diary instead of his usual simple reporting of the day's events.

The Latin verb *discurrere* meant "to run about," and from this word we get our word *discursive,* which often means rambling about over a wide range of topics. A discursive writing style is generally not encouraged by writing teachers. But some of the great writers of the 19th century, such as Charles Lamb and Thomas de Quincey, have shown that the discursive essay, especially when gracefully written and somewhat personal in tone, can be a pleasure to read.

precursor \'prē-ˌkər-sər\ One that goes before and indicates the coming of another.

• Scientists are trying to identify special geological activity that may be a precursor to an earthquake, which will help them predict the quake's size, time, and location.

A precursor is literally a "forerunner," but the two words function a little differently. A forerunner may simply come before another thing, but a precursor generally paves the way for something. The Office of Strategic Services in World War II was the precursor of today's Central Intelligence Agency. The blues music of the 1930s and 1940s was a precursor to the rock and roll of today. The war in Bosnia could be a precursor to more armed conflict in Eastern Europe and the former Soviet Union.

PED comes from the Latin *ped-,* the stem of *pes,* meaning "foot," which is related to the Greek *pod-* and *pous,* with the same meaning. From *ped-* we get *pedicure,* "care of the feet, toes, and toenails." From *pod-* we get *podiatrist,* "a foot doctor."

---

expedient \ik-'spē-dē-ənt\ Suitable for bringing about a desired result, often without regard for what is fair or right.

• Reporters suggested that it would be politically expedient to nominate a vice-presidential candidate from a state with a large number of electoral votes.

Expedient comes from the Latin verb *expedire,* meaning "to prepare" or "to be useful"—perhaps because the best way to prepare for something is to get your feet moving. *Expedient* can simply mean "desirable" or "advantageous." For instance, it is often more expedient to take the train to New York than to drive and try to find a parking place. However, *expedient* often indicates placing self-interest ahead of moral concerns. As a company faces more and more lawsuits over its defective products, for example, it may realize that the expedient solution is to declare bankruptcy.

expedite \'ek-spə-ˌdīt\ To speed up the process or progress of.

• The sales department was looking for ways to expedite the shipping and billing of incoming orders.

Expedite comes from the same Latin verb as *expedient,* but *expedite* usually indicates only speed or efficiency and doesn't involve moral issues at all. Many people concerned about health-care issues, for example, have campaigned to get the FDA to expedite its approval of new drugs. And new kinds of educational software are expected to expedite the learning process.

impediment \im-'pe-də-mənt\ Something that interferes with movement or progress.

• Her poorly developed verbal ability was the most serious impediment to her advancement.

Impediment comes from a Latin verb that meant ''to interfere with'' or ''to get in the way of progress''—perhaps by catching one's feet. In English, *impediment* still suggests an obstruction or obstacle along a path; for example, a lack of adequate roads and bridges is an impediment to economic development. Impediments usually get in the way of something we want. We speak of an impediment to communication, marriage, or progress, but something that slows the progress of aging, disease, or decay isn't usually called an impediment.

pedestrian \pə-'des-trē-ən\ Commonplace, ordinary, or unimaginative.

• While politicians endlessly discussed the great issues facing Russia, the Russians worried about such pedestrian concerns as finding enough food, shelter, and clothing.

A *pedestrian* is, of course, someone who travels on foot. But the sense of this word as defined above is actually its original meaning. To be pedestrian was to be drab or dull, as if plodding along on foot rather than speeding on horseback or by coach. *Pedestrian* is often used to describe a writing style that is colorless or lifeless, but it can also describe politicians, public tastes, and personal qualities and possessions. In comparison with the elaborate stage shows put on by today's rock artists, for instance, most of the stage antics of the rock stars of the 1960s seem pedestrian.

Quizzes

A. Fill in each blank with the correct letter:

a.	concurrent	e.	cursory
b.	expedite	f.	impediment
c.	precursor	g.	discursive
d.	pedestrian	h.	expedient

1. The warm days in March were a ____ to spring floods that were sure to come.
2. They hoped the new computer system would ____ the delivery of supplies.
3. After only a ____ look at the new car, he knew he had to have it.
4. The presence of her little sister was a definite ____ to her romantic plans for the evening.
5. She came to enjoy the ____ style of the older, rambling essays.
6. Putting the blame on others for her mistakes was the ____ solution, but it enraged her coworkers.
7. Convention-goers had to decide which of the ____ meetings to attend.
8. His sister's trips to Borneo made his vacations at the seashore seem ____.

B. Match the definition on the left to the correct word on the right:

1. simultaneous   a. impediment
2. obstacle   b. precursor
3. hasty   c. expedient
4. forerunner   d. discursive
5. convenient   e. pedestrian

6.	speed up	f.	expedite
7.	rambling	g.	cursory
8.	ordinary	h.	concurrent

FLECT/FLEX comes from *flectere*, the Latin verb meaning "to bend." Things that are *flexible* can be bent. When light is *reflected*, it is bent and bounces back to us.

---

deflect \di-'flekt\ To turn aside, especially from a straight or fixed course.

• The stealth technology used on some of our bombers and fighter planes works by deflecting radar energy.

The physical meaning of *deflect* is frequently used. Thus, residents along rivers will build levees to deflect flood waters away from their homes, and workers wear eye shields to deflect tiny particles flying out of machines. But the nonphysical meaning is also common. Politicians make highly publicized trips to deflect attention from scandals or a terrible economy. Celebrities make a show of giving to charity to deflect resentment over the amount of money they make. And we all have tried to change the subject to deflect questions we really didn't want to answer.

flexor \'flek-₁sȯr\ A muscle that bends a part of the body, such as an arm or a leg.

• Her fitness instructor told her she could improve her posture by strengthening her hip flexors.

Flexors are any muscles that act to bend a part of the body, from neck to baby toe and all the *flexible* parts in between. Each flexor is paired with an *extensor* that acts to straighten the part after it is bent. Though you'll encounter *flexor* in reading about health and fitness, it is mostly a technical term. For instance, the names for the flexors that move the little toe (it takes three) are *flexor digiti minimi brevis, flexor digitorum brevis,* and *flexor digitorum longus.*

genuflect \'jen-yů-₁flekt\ To kneel on one knee and then rise as an act of respect.

● Pilgrims in China not only genuflect before religious shrines but also may lay themselves flat on the ground and light incense as well.

Genuflection, which contains the root *genu-*, "knee," has long been a mark of respect and obedience. King Arthur's Knights of the Round Table genuflected not only when he knighted them but whenever they greeted him formally. This custom remains in countries today that are still ruled by royalty, and in some churches each worshiper is expected to genuflect whenever entering or leaving a pew on the central aisle. By genuflecting you show loyalty to a human or god and admit your duty to obey his or her orders.

inflection \in-'flek-shən\ A change in the pitch, tone, or loudness of the voice.

● She couldn't understand her grandfather's words, but she knew from his inflection that he was asking a question.

Changing the pitch, tone, or loudness of our words are ways we communicate meaning in speech, though not on the printed page. A rising inflection on the last syllable of a sentence generally indicates a question and a falling inflection indicates a statement, for example. Another way of *inflecting* words is by adding endings. We add *-s* to make nouns plural and *-ed* to put verbs in the past tense, and these changes are also referred to as inflections.

POST comes from a Latin word meaning "after" or "behind." A *postscript* is a note that comes after an otherwise completed letter, usually as an afterthought. *Postpartum* refers to the period following childbirth and all of its related events and complications. To *postdate* a check is to give it a date after the day when it was written.

---

posterior \pō-'stir-ē-ər\ Situated toward or on the back; rear.

● One of the goals of his fitness program was to reduce the dimensions of the posterior parts of his anatomy.

Posterior comes from the Latin word *posterus*, meaning "coming after." *Posterior* is often used as a technical term in biology and medicine to refer to the back side of things. It is the opposite of *anterior,* which refers to the front side. For example, as more people took up running as a sport, doctors began to see an increase in stress fractures along the posterior as well as the anterior surface of the lower leg bones. When used as a noun, *posterior* simply means ''buttocks.''

posthumous \'päs-chə-məs\ (1) Published after the death of the author. (2) Following or happening after one's death.

• Vincent Van Gogh's rise to posthumous fame as one of the world's great artists came despite the fact that he scarcely sold a single painting during his lifetime.

Posthumous fame is fame that comes a little late, since the meaning of *posthumous* in Latin is ''late born.'' In fact, its original meaning in English is ''born after the death of the father.'' Bill Clinton is the posthumous son of a father who died in an automobile accident. The word is now mostly used of artistic works that appear after the death of the artist. From the poetry of Emily Dickinson to the diary of Anne Frank, posthumous works have often become legendary.

postmodern \ˌpōst-'mä-dərn\ Having to do with a movement in art, architecture, or literature that is a reaction against modernism and that calls for the reintroduction of traditional elements and techniques as well as elements from popular culture.

• The postmodern AT&T building in New York, with its ''Chippendale'' top that makes it look a little like an antique dresser, aroused a storm of criticism.

Although *postmodern* literally translates as ''after modern'' and would therefore seem likely to mean ''ultramodern,'' it usually really means ''antimodern.'' In the 1970s architects began to be dissatisfied with the stark simplicity of most modern architecture and began to include in their designs traditional elements such as columns, arches, and keystones, and also startling color contrasts such as might have come from advertising and pop culture. Similar developments took place in literature, and there too the movement has been greeted with a mixture of approval, disapproval, and sometimes amusement.

postmortem \ˌpōst-'mȯr-təm\ (1) Occurring after death. (2) Following the event.

• In their postmortem discussion of the election, the reporters tried to explain how the polls and predictions could have been so completely wrong.

Post mortem is Latin for "after death." In English, *postmortem* refers to an examination, investigation, or process that takes place after death. Postmortem examinations of bodies are often needed to determine the time and cause of death; rigor mortis, the temporary stiffening of muscles after death, is one postmortem change that doctors look at to determine time of death. We have come to use *postmortem* to refer to any examination or discussion that takes place after an event.

Quizzes

A. Choose the closest definition:

1. posthumous   a. before the event   b. born prematurely
      c. occurring after death   d. early in development
2. flexor   a. radar detector   b. muscle   c. sunscreen   d. bone
3. posterior   a. on the front   b. on the back
      c. underneath   d. on top
4. deflect   a. fold over   b. kneel   c. turn aside   d. protect
5. postmodern   a. ultramodern   b. traditional
      c. contemporary   d. using past styles
6. inflection   a. style in art   b. change in pitch
      c. muscle   d. part to the rear
7. genuflect   a. kneel   b. flex a muscle   c. fold back
      d. change one's tone of voice
8. postmortem   a. after the event   b. before the event
      c. caused by the event   d. causing the event

B. Complete the analogy:

1. postscript : letter :: postmortem : _____
      a. examination   b. death   c. body   d. morgue
2. flexor : extensor :: bend : _____
      a. fold   b. twist   c. straighten   d. break
3. prenatal : before birth :: posthumous : _____
      a. after birth   b. before life   c. after death   d. famous
4. deflect : shield :: reflect : _____
      a. shield   b. laser   c. metal   d. mirror

---

5. inflection : tone of voice :: hue : _____
   a. cry b. color c. tone d. rainbow
6. genuflect : obedience :: wave : _____
   a. friendship b. respect c. awe d. power
7. inferior : better :: posterior : _____
   a. in front b. behind c. beside d. above
8. abstract : painting :: postmodern : _____
   a. tradition b. design c. style d. architecture

Words from Mythology

calypso \kə-'lip-sō\ A folk song or style of singing of West Indian origin that has a lively rhythm and words that are often made up by the singer.

• If you take a Caribbean vacation in December you end up listening to a lot of Christmas carols played to a calypso beat.

In Homer's *Odyssey,* the nymph Calypso detains Odysseus for seven years on his way home from the Trojan War. She uses all her wiles to hold him on her lush, hidden island, but he still longs for home. The calypso music of the West Indian islands has the same captivating, bewitching power as the nymph. The lyrics that are often improvised to the melodies, however, often make fun of local people and happenings. Calypso may not have been the original name for this music; it may instead have simply replaced a similar-sounding native Caribbean word.

odyssey \'ä-də-sē\ (1) A long, wandering journey full of trials and adventures. (2) A spiritual journey or quest.

• Their six-month camping trip around the country was an odyssey they would always remember.

Odysseus, the hero of Homer's *Odyssey,* spends 20 years traveling home from the Trojan War. He has astonishing adventures and learns a great deal about himself and the world; he even descends to the underworld to talk to the dead. Thus, an odyssey is any long, complicated journey, often a quest for a goal, and may be a spiritual or psychological journey as well as an actual voyage.

palladium \pə-'lā-dē-əm\ A precious, silver-white metal related to platinum that is used in electrical contacts and as an alloy with gold to form white gold.

● Most wedding rings today are simple bands of gold, platinum, or palladium.

Pallas Athena was one of the poetical names given to the Greek goddess Athena, although it is no longer clear what *Pallas* was supposed to mean. When an asteroid belt was discovered between Mars and Jupiter, most of the asteroids were named after figures in Greek mythology, and one of the first to be discovered was named Pallas, in 1803. In the same year, scientists first isolated the element palladium, and they named the new element in honor of the recently discovered asteroid.

Penelope \pə-'ne-lə-pē\ A modest domestic wife.

● Critics of Hillary Rodham Clinton would perhaps have preferred her to be a Penelope, quietly keeping house and staying out of politics.

In the *Odyssey,* Penelope waits 20 long years for her husband Odysseus to return from Troy. During that time, she must raise their son and fend off the attentions of numerous rough suitors. She preserves herself for a long time by saying that she cannot remarry until she has finished weaving a funeral shroud for her aging father-in-law; however, what she weaves each day she secretly unravels each night. A Penelope, thus, appears to be the perfect, patient, faithful wife, and she uses her clever intelligence to keep herself that way.

procrustean \prō-'krəs-tē-ən\ Ruthlessly disregarding individual differences or special circumstances.

● The school's procrustean approach to education seemed to assume that all children learned in the same way and at the same rate.

Procrustes was a bandit in the Greek tale of the hero Theseus. He ambushed travelers and, after robbing them, made them lie on an iron bed. He would make sure they fit this procrustean bed by cutting off the parts that hung off the ends or stretching those that were too short. Either way, they died. Something procrustean, therefore, takes no account of individual differences but cruelly and mercilessly makes everything the same.

protean \'prō-tē-ən\ (1) Displaying great versatility or variety. (2) Able to take on many different forms or natures.

• He was attempting to become the protean athlete, with contracts to play professional baseball, football, and basketball.

Proteus was the figure in the *Odyssey* who revealed to Menelaus how to get home to Sparta with the notorious Helen of Troy. Before he would give up the information, though, Menelaus had to capture him—no mean feat, since he had the ability to change into any natural shape he chose. The word *protean* came to describe this ability to change into many different shapes or to play many different roles in quick succession.

sibyl \'si-bəl\ A female prophet or fortune-teller.

• Her mother treated her as if she were the family sibyl, able to predict what fate was about to befall her sisters.

The sibyls were ancient prophetesses who lived in Babylonia, Greece, Italy, and Egypt. The most famous was the Sibyl of Cumae in Italy, a withered crone who lived in a cave. Her prophecies were collected into twelve books, three of which survived to be consulted by the Romans in times of national emergencies. Whether or not she was the first sibyl, her name or title became the term for all such prophets.

siren \'sī-rən\ A woman who tempts men with bewitching sweetness.

• Reporters treated her like a sex symbol, but she lacked the graceful presence and air of mystery of a real siren.

The sirens were a group of partly human female creatures in Greek mythology that lured sailors onto destructive rocks with their singing. Odysseus and his men encountered the sirens after leaving Troy. The only way to sail by them safely was to make oneself deaf to their enchanting song, so Odysseus packed the men's ears with wax. But he himself, ever curious, wanted to hear, so he had himself tied to the mast to keep from flinging himself into the water or steering his ship toward sure destruction. A siren today is almost always a woman, though she need not sing or cause shipwrecks. But a *siren song* may be any appeal that lures a person to act against his or her better judgment.

Quiz

Fill in each blank with the correct letter:

a. odyssey   e. sibyl
b. calypso   f. procrustean
c. Penelope   g. siren
d. palladium   h. protean

1. They danced and sang to the rhythm of the _____ music long into the night.
2. While he was away on maneuvers, his wife stayed loyally at home like a true _____.
3. He took a _____ attitude toward the needs of his employees, enforcing a single set of work rules for everyone.
4. On their four-month _____ they visited most of the major cities of Asia.
5. The wedding rings were white gold, a mixture of gold and _____.
6. She won her reputation as the office _____ after her third successful prediction of who would get married next.
7. Actors like Robin Williams seem _____ in their ability to assume different characters.
8. In her fatigued state, sleep's _____ song lured her from her duties.

Review Quizzes

A. Choose the closest definition:

1. carnival   a. festival   b. feast   c. funeral   d. frenzy
2. precursor   a. shadow   b. forerunner   c. follower   d. oath
3. diffident   a. angry   b. different   c. aggressive   d. shy
4. pedestrian   a. useless   b. footlike   c. unusual   d. boring
5. credence   a. creation   b. belief   c. doubt   d. destruction
6. creditable   a. believable   b. acceptable
     c. praiseworthy   d. incredible
7. expedite   a. speed up   b. bounce off   c. slow down
     d. absorb

8. impediment   a. help   b. obstacle   c. footpath
       d. obligation
9. voracious   a. vast   b. hungry   c. fierce
       d. unsatisfied
10. protean   a. meaty   b. powerful   c. changeable
       d. professional

B. Indicate whether the following pairs of words have the same or different meanings:

1. procrustean / merciful   same ___ / different ___
2. credulity / distrust   same ___ / different ___
3. concurrent / simultaneous   same ___ / different ___
4. flexor / straightener   same ___ / different ___
5. odyssey / journey   same ___ / different ___
6. deflect / absorb   same ___ / different ___
7. perfidy / betrayal   same ___ / different ___
8. posterior / front   same ___ / different ___
9. siren / temptress   same ___ / different ___
10. herbivorous / plant-eating   same ___ / different ___

C. Complete the analogy:

1. fiduciary : trustworthy :: carnivorous : _____
       a. vegetarian   b. meat-eating   c. greedy   d. hungry
2. cursory : brief :: carnal : _____
       a. musical   b. festive   c. deadly   d. sexual
3. genuflect : kneel :: affidavit : _____
       a. financial affairs   b. courtroom testimony   c. legal
       advice   d. sworn statement
4. sibyl : future :: creed : _____
       a. belief   b. music   c. attraction   d. qualification
5. carnage : death :: Penelope : _____
       a. wife   b. mother   c. daughter   d. siren
6. palladium : metal :: surgeon : _____
       a. farmer   b. veterinarian   c. doctor   d. lawyer
7. expedient : effective :: discursive : _____
       a. fast   b. slow-moving   c. wide-ranging   d. all-knowing
8. procrustean : inflexible :: inflection : _____
       a. way of life   b. tone of voice   c. financial affairs
       d. part of speech

Unit 5

MAL as a combining form means "bad." *Malpractice* is bad medical practice. A *malady* is a bad condition—a disease or illness—of the body or mind. *Malodorous* things smell bad. And a *malefactor* is someone guilty of bad deeds.

malevolent \mə-'le-və-lənt\ Having or showing intense ill will or hatred.

• Captain Ahab sees Moby Dick not simply as a whale but as a malevolent, evil foe.

Malevolence runs deep. Malevolent enemies have bitter and lasting feelings of ill will. Malevolent racism and bigotry can erupt in acts of violence against innocent people. Malevolence can also show itself in hurtful words, and sometimes it can be seen in something as small as an angry look or gesture.

malicious \mə-'li-shəs\ Desiring to cause pain, injury, or distress to another.

• The boys didn't take the apples with any malicious intent; they were just hungry and didn't know any better.

Malicious and *malevolent* are closely related. Both refer to ill will that shows itself in a desire to see someone else suffer. While *malevolent* suggests deep and lasting dislike, however, *malicious* usually means petty and spiteful. Malicious gossipers may be simply envious of their neighbor's good fortune. Vandals take malicious pleasure in destroying and defacing property.

malign \mə-'līn\ To make harsh and often false or misleading statements about.

● Captain Bligh of the *Bounty* may be one of the most unjustly maligned figures in British naval history.

Malign is related to words like *defame, slander*, and *libel*. It implies that the person or group being maligned is the victim of false or misleading statements, but not necessarily that the *maligner* is guilty of deliberate lying. Something that is frequently criticized is often said to be "much maligned," which suggests that the criticism is not entirely fair or deserved.

malnourished \\ˌmal-'nər-isht\\ Badly or poorly nourished.

● When they finally found the children in the locked cabin, they were pale and malnourished but unharmed.

Malnourished people can be found in all types of societies. Famine and poverty are only two of the common causes of *malnutrition*. In more affluent societies, it is often the result of poor eating habits. Any diet that fails to provide the nutrients needed for health and growth can lead to malnutrition, and some of the malnourished are actually fat.

CATA comes from the Greek *kata*, one of whose meanings was "down." A *catalogue* is a list of items put down on paper. A *catapult* is an ancient military weapon for hurling missiles down on one's enemies.

---

cataclysm \\'ka-tə-ˌkli-zəm\\ (1) A violent and massive change of the earth's surface. (2) A momentous event that results in great upheaval and often destruction.

● World War I was a great cataclysm in modern history, marking the end of the old European social and political order.

A cataclysm causes great and lasting changes. An earthquake or other natural disaster that changes the landscape is one kind of cataclysm. We might also speak of the *cataclysmic* changes brought about by a political revolution. Even a new discovery or invention can be seen as cataclysmic if it brings great changes in how people think or work.

catacomb \\'ka-tə-ˌkōm\\ An underground cemetery of connecting passageways with recesses for tombs.

• The early Christian catacombs of Rome provide a striking glimpse into the ancient past for modern-day visitors.

About forty Christian catacombs have been found near the roads that once led into Rome. After the decline of the Roman empire these cemeteries were forgotten, not to be rediscovered until 1578. *Catacomb* has come to refer to different kinds of underground chambers and passageways. The catacombs of Paris are abandoned stone quarries that were not used for burials until 1787.

catalyst \\'ka-tə-list\\ (1) A substance that speeds up a chemical reaction or lets it take place under different conditions. (2) Someone or something that brings about or speeds significant change or action.

• The assassination of Archduke Ferdinand in Sarajevo in 1914 acted as the catalyst for World War I.

Although the Great Depression was a difficult and tragic period in this country, it served as the catalyst for many important social reforms. The Social Security Act of 1935 helped provide security for retired workers; it in turn became the catalyst for a number of laws concerning disabled and unemployed workers, health insurance, on-the-job safety, and dependents of deceased workers. The Depression was also the catalyst of many public-works projects, which were designed to put the unemployed back to work.

catatonic \\ˌka-tə-'tä-nik\\ (1) Relating to or suffering from a form of schizophrenia. (2) Showing an unusual lack of movement, activity, or expression.

• The audience sat in a catatonic stupor while the speaker droned on about the importance of a good vocabulary.

Catatonia is a form of the terrible mental disease known as schizophrenia. A common symptom is extreme muscular rigidity, so that catatonic patients may be ''frozen'' for hours or even days in a single position. In general use, *catatonic* most often describes people who are not ill but who likewise seem incapable of moving or of changing expression.

Quizzes

A. Choose the closest definition:

1. malevolent   a. wishing evil b. wishing well c. blowing violently d. badly done
2. cataclysm   a. loud applause b. feline behavior c. natural disaster d. inspiration
3. malign   a. speak well of b. speak to c. speak ill of d. speak of repeatedly
4. catacomb   a. underground road b. underground cemetery c. underground spring d. underground treasure
5. malicious   a. vague b. explosive c. confusing d. mean
6. catatonic   a. refreshing b. slow c. motionless d. boring
7. malnourished   a. fed frequently b. fed poorly c. fed excessively d. fed occasionally
8. catalyst   a. literary agent b. insurance agent c. cleaning agent d. agent of change

B. Indicate whether the following pairs of words have the same or different meanings:

1. catacomb / catastrophe   same ___ / different ___
2. malnourished / overfed   same ___ / different ___
3. cataclysm / disaster   same ___ / different ___
4. malign / slander   same ___ / different ___
5. catatonic / paralyzed   same ___ / different ___
6. catalyst / cemetery   same ___ / different ___
7. malicious / nasty   same ___ / different ___
8. malevolent / pleasant   same ___ / different ___

PROT/PROTO comes from Greek and has the basic meaning "first in time" or "first formed." *Protozoa* are one-celled animals, such as amoebas and paramecia, that are among the most basic members of the biological kingdom. A *proton* is an elementary particle that, along with neutrons, can be found in all atomic nuclei. A *protoplanet* is a whirling mass that is believed to give rise to a planet.

protagonist \prō-'ta-gə-nist\ The main character in a literary work.

● Macbeth is the ruthlessly ambitious protagonist of Shakespeare's play, but it is his wife who pulls the strings.

Struggle, or conflict, is central to drama. The protagonist or hero of a play is involved in a struggle, either against someone or something else or even against his or her own emotions. So the hero is the "first struggler," which is the literal meaning of the Greek word *prōtagōnistēs*. A character who opposes the hero is the *antagonist*, from a Greek verb that means literally "to struggle against."

protocol \'prō-tə-,kȯl\ (1) An original copy or record of a document. (2) A code of diplomatic or military rules of behavior.

● The guests at the governor's dinner were introduced and seated according to the strict protocol governing such occasions.

Protocol comes from a Greek word that refers to the first sheet of a papyrus roll. As an English word, *protocol* originally meant "a first draft or record," after which it came to mean specifically the first draft of a diplomatic document, such as a treaty. The "diplomatic" connection led eventually to its current meaning of "rules of behavior." Someone wearing Bermuda shorts and sandals to a State dinner at the White House would not be acting "according to protocol." *Protocol* is also now used to refer to other kinds of rules, such as those for doing a scientific experiment or for handling computer data.

protoplasm \'prō-tō-,pla-zəm\ The substance that makes up the living parts of cells.

● Protoplasm is a mixture of organic and inorganic substances, such as protein and water, and is regarded as the physical basis of life.

The term *protoplasm* was first used with its present meaning in 1846 by Hugo von Mohl, a German professor of botany. After studying plant cells, he conceived the idea that the nucleus was surrounded by a jellylike material that formed the main substance of the cell Von Mohl is also remembered for being the first to propose that new cells are formed by cell division.

prototype \\'prō-tō-ˌtīp\\ (1) An original model on which something is patterned. (2) A first, full-scale, usually working version of a new type or design.

● There was great excitement when, after years of top-secret development, the prototype of the new Stealth bomber first took to the skies.

A prototype is someone or something that serves as a model or inspiration. A successful fund-raising campaign can serve as a prototype for future campaigns. The legendary Robin Hood, the *prototypical* kindhearted, honorable outlaw, has been the inspiration for countless other romantic heroes. For over a century Vincent Van Gogh has been the prototype of the brilliant, tortured artist who is unappreciated in his own time.

ANTE is Latin for "before" or "in front of." *Antediluvian,* a word describing something very old or outdated, literally means "before the flood"—that is, the flood described in the Bible. *Antebellum* literally means "before the war," usually the American Civil War. *Antenatal* care is given during the period before birth.

---

antechamber \\'an-ti-ˌchām-bər\\ An outer room that leads to another and is often used as a waiting room.

● The antechamber to the lawyer's office was both elegant and comfortable, designed to inspire trust and confidence.

Antechamber suggests a room somewhat more formal than an *anteroom.* One expects to find an antechamber outside the private chambers of a Supreme Court Justice or leading into the great hall of a medieval castle. In the private end of the castle the lord's or lady's bedchamber would have its own antechamber, which served as a dressing room and sitting room, but could also house bodyguards if the castle came under siege.

antedate \\'an-ti-ˌdāt\\ (1) To date something (such as a check) with a date earlier than that of actual writing. (2) To precede in time.

● Nantucket Island has hundreds of beautifully preserved houses that antedate the Civil War.

Antedate is used when talking about things that can be given dates. Dinosaurs antedated the first human beings by about 65 million years, though this stubborn fact has never stopped cartoonists and moviemakers from having the two species inhabit the same story line. The oral use of a word often antedates its appearance in print by a number of years.

ante meridiem \\ˌan-ti-mə-ˈri-dē-ˌem\\ Before noon.

• On great ancient sundials the shadow crossed the central line at noon, dramatically marking the shift from ante meridiem to post meridiem.

Ante meridiem is almost always abbreviated as *a.m.* The term is spelled out only in the most formal contexts, such as laws and statutes. There is controversy about the use of *a.m.* and its counterpart *p.m.,* for *post meridiem,* when referring to twelve o'clock. Some people have argued that *12:00 a.m.* means midnight and *12:00 p.m.* means noon; others have insisted the opposite. There has never been any general agreement. If you want to avoid confusion, use *noon* or *midnight,* either alone or preceded by *12:00.*

anterior \\an-ˈtir-ē-ər\\ (1) Located before or toward the front or head. (2) Coming before in time or development.

• She joined the first-class passengers in the plane's anterior section and was delighted to recognize the governor in the next seat.

Anterior tends to appear in either technical or learned contexts. Anatomy books refer to the anterior lobe of the brain, the anterior cerebral artery, the anterior facial vein, etc. When used to refer to an earlier position in time or order, *anterior* is a somewhat formal word. Supporters of states' rights point out that the states enjoyed certain rights anterior to their joining the union. Prenuptial agreements are generally designed to protect the assets that one or both parties acquired anterior to the marriage.

Quizzes

A. Fill in each blank with the correct letter:

a. antedate	e. prototype
b. protoplasm	f. ante meridiem
c. anterior	g. protocol
d. protagonist	h. antechamber

1. The _____ of *The Wizard of Oz* is a Kansas farm girl named Dorothy.
2. According to official _____, the Ambassador from England precedes the Canadian Consul.
3. A butterfly's antennae are located on the most _____ part of its body.
4. There under the microscope we saw the cell's _____ in all its amazing complexity.
5. She was tempted to _____ the letter to make it seem that she had not forgotten to write it but only to mail it.
6. The engineers have promised to have the _____ of the new sedan finished by March.
7. Please step into the judge's _____; she'll be with you in a few minutes.
8. In Rome there were six "hours" _____ (that is, "before midday"), but the hours were shorter in winter than in summer.

B. Match the definition on the left to the correct word on the right:

1. to date before   a. protocol
2. cell contents   b. antechamber
3. morning   c. protagonist
4. rules of behavior   d. ante meridiem
5. toward the front   e. protoplasm
6. model   f. antedate
7. waiting room   g. prototype
8. hero or heroine   h. anterior

ORTH/ORTHO comes from *orthos*, the Greek word for "straight," "right," or "true." *Orthotics* is a branch of therapy that straightens out the stance or posture of the body by providing artificial support for weak joints or muscles. *Orthograde* animals, such as human beings, walk with their bodies in a "straight" or vertical position.

orthodontics \ˌȯr-thə-'dän-tiks\ A branch of dentistry that deals with the treatment and correction of crooked teeth and other irregularities.

• As much as she dreaded braces, Jennifer decided the time had come to consult a specialist in orthodontics.

Orthodontics of some kind has been practiced since ancient times, but the elaborate techniques and appliances familiar to us today were introduced only in the 20th century. Training to become an *orthodontist* usually consists of a two-year course following dental school. According to a 1939 text on dentistry, "Speech defects, psychiatric disturbances, personality changes, . . . all are correctable through *orthodontic* measures." Many adolescents, having endured the embarrassment of rubber bands breaking and even of entangling their braces while kissing, might disagree.

orthodox \'ȯr-thə-ˌdäks\ (1) Holding established beliefs, especially in religion. (2) Conforming to established rules or traditions; conventional.

• The O'Briens remain orthodox Catholics, faithfully observing the time-honored rituals of their church.

An orthodox religious belief or interpretation is one handed down by the founders or leaders of a church. When capitalized, as in *Orthodox Judaism, Orthodox* refers to branches within larger religious organizations that claim to honor the religion's original or traditional beliefs. The steadfast holding of established beliefs that is seen in religious *orthodoxy* is apparent also in other kinds of orthodox behavior. Orthodox medical treatment, for example, follows the established practices of mainstream medicine.

orthopedics \ˌȯr-thə-'pē-diks\ The correction or prevention of deformities of the skeleton.

• The surgery to correct the child's spinal curvature was done by a leading specialist in orthopedics.

Just as an orthodontist corrects crookedness in the teeth, so does an *orthopedist* correct crookedness in the skeleton. The word *orthopedics* is formed in part from the Greek word for "child," and many *orthopedic* patients are in fact children. But adults also often have need for orthopedic therapy, as when suffering from a disease of the joints like arthritis or when recovering from a broken arm or leg.

orthography \or-'thä-grə-fē\ (1) The spelling of words according to standard usage. (2) The part of language study concerned with letters and spelling.

• George Washington and Thomas Jefferson—and at least one recent vice president—were deficient in the skill of orthography.

Even as recently as the 19th century, the orthography of the English language was still unsettled. Not until primers like "McGuffey's Readers" and dictionaries like Noah Webster's came along did uniform spelling become established. Before that, there was much *orthographic* variation, even among the more educated. Many people, of course, still have problems with spelling. They can take heart from the words of Mark Twain, who once remarked, "I don't give a damn for a man that can spell a word only one way."

RECT comes from the Latin word *rectus,* which means "straight" or "right." A *rectangle* is a four-sided figure whose parallel, straight sides meet at right angles. *Rectus,* short for Latin *rectus musculus,* may refer to any of several straight muscles, such as those of the abdomen. To *correct* something is to make it right.

rectitude \'rek-tə-,tüd\ (1) Moral integrity. (2) Correctness of procedure.

• The school superintendent wasn't popular, but no one could question her moral rectitude.

We associate straightness with honesty, so if we think someone is being misleading we might ask if they are being "straight" with us. A person whose rectitude is unquestionable is a person whose straightness, or honesty, is always apparent in his or her dealings with other people. Such a person might be called *rectitudinous,* although this uncommon adjective can also suggest an undesirable quality of self-righteousness.

rectify \'rek-tə-,fī\ (1) To set right; remedy. (2) To correct by removing errors; revise.

• You must try to rectify this unfortunate situation before anyone else gets hurt.

We rectify something by straightening it out or making it right. We might rectify an injustice by seeing to it that a wrongly accused person is cleared. An error in a financial record can be rectified by replacing an incorrect number with a correct one. If the error is in our tax return, the Internal Revenue Service will be happy to rectify it for us. We might then have to rectify the impression that we were trying to cheat on our taxes.

rectilinear \,rek-tə-'li-nē-ər\ (1) Moving in or forming a straight line. (2) Having many straight lines.

• After admiring Frank Lloyd Wright's highly rectilinear buildings for years, the public was astonished by the giant spiral of the Guggenheim Museum.

Rectilinear is a term used widely in physics. Rectilinear motion is motion in which the speed remains constant and the path is a straight line. Rectilinear rays, such as light rays, travel in a straight line. Rectilinear patterns or constructions are those in which straight lines are strikingly obvious. The trunks of trees in a forest form a strongly rectilinear pattern.

rector \'rek-tər\ (1) A clergyman in charge of a church or parish. (2) The head of a university or school.

• We asked the rector of our church to perform the marriage ceremony.

The fiery American preacher Jonathan Edwards began as rector of a church in Massachusetts. He was so convinced of his own ideas about *rectitude* and so harsh in condemning those who opposed him that he was eventually dismissed and turned out of the parish *rectory* where he lived. He spent his remaining years attempting to *rectify* the beliefs of Native Americans.

Quizzes

A. Choose the closest definition:

1. orthodox a. straight b. pier c. conventional
    d. waterfowl
2. rectify a. redo b. make right c. modify d. make longer
3. orthopedics a. foot surgery b. children's medicine
    c. medical dictionaries d. treatment of skeletal defects

4. rector　a. warden　b. headmaster　c. direction　d. effect
5. orthography　a. correct color　b. correct map　c. correct direction　d. correct spelling
6. rectitude　a. roughness　b. integrity　c. certainty d. sameness
7. orthodontics　a. dentistry for children　b. dentistry for gums　c. dentistry for crooked teeth　d. dentistry for everyone
8. rectilinear　a. moving in a straight line　b. moving in a curved line　c. moving at a 45° angle　d. moving in a circle

B. Indicate whether the following pairs have the same or different meanings:

1. orthodox / crucial　　　　　same ___ / different ___
2. rectitude / honesty　　　　　same ___ / different ___
3. orthopedics / broken bones　same ___ / different ___
4. rector / follower　　　　　　same ___ / different ___
5. orthography / architecture　same ___ / different ___
6. rectilinear / straight　　　　same ___ / different ___
7. orthodontics / fixing of crooked teeth　　　　　　　　　　same ___ / different ___
8. rectify / damage　　　　　　same ___ / different ___

EU comes from the Greek word for "well"; in English words it can also mean "good" or "true." A person delivering a *eulogy* is full of good words, or praise, for the honoree. *Euthanasia* is regarded as a way of providing a hopelessly sick or injured person a "good" or easy death.

---

eugenic \yů-'je-nik\ (1) Relating to or fitted for the production of good offspring. (2) Relating to the science of improving the desirable traits of a race or breed through controlled breeding.

• Eugenic techniques have been part of cattle breeding for many years.

The word *eugenic* (like the name *Eugene*) was formed from the prefix *eu-* in combination with *-genes*, which in Greek means "born." Breeders of horses, cattle, and other animals hope that by using scientific, eugenic methods they can have better results, producing horses that run faster, for example, or cattle that provide more meat. Through *eugenics,* Guernsey cows have become one of the world's highest producers of milk. Earlier in this century there was much discussion of human eugenics, an idea that was taken up enthusiastically by the Nazis, with terrible consequences.

euphemism \'yü-fə-ˌmi-zəm\ (1) The use of an agreeable or inoffensive word or expression for one that may offend or disgust. (2) An expression used in this way.

● The Victorians, uncomfortable with the physical side of human existence, had euphemisms for most bodily functions.

Euphemism is an ancient part of the English language. While particular expressions come into and go out of vogue, the need for euphemism remains constant. *Golly* and *gosh* started out as euphemisms for *God,* and *darn* is a familiar euphemism for *damn. Shoot, shucks,* and *sugar* are all *euphemistic* substitutes for a well-known vulgar word. The standard household bathroom fixture has given rise to a host of euphemistic substitutes, including *convenience, head, john, potty, privy,* and *water closet.*

euphoria \yù-'fòr-ē-ə\ A feeling of well-being or great elation.

● The whole city was swept up in the euphoria of a Super Bowl victory.

Euphoria describes a temporary, almost overpowering feeling of health or elation. In medical use, it normally refers to abnormal or inappropriate feelings, such as might be caused by a drug or by mental illness. But euphoria can also be natural and appropriate. When the home team wins the championship, or when we win enough money in the lottery to buy a fleet of yachts and several small Pacific islands, we have good reason to feel *euphoric.*

evangelism \i-'van-jə-ˌli-zəm\ (1) The enthusiastic preaching or proclamation of the Christian gospel. (2) Militant or crusading zeal.

● Their evangelism for the new program won many converts among those who had previously doubted its merits.

Evangelism comes from *euangelion,* the Greek word for "gospel" or "good news." The firm belief that they are bringing "good news" has traditionally filled Christian *evangelists* with fiery zeal. *Evangelism* can now refer to crusading zeal in behalf of any cause. The *evangelical* enthusiasm of some environmentalists has won over some segments of the general public while alienating others.

DYS comes from Greek, where it means "bad" or "difficult." As a prefix in English, it has the additional meanings "abnormal" and "impaired." *Dysphagia* is difficult or labored swallowing, and *dyspnea* is difficult or labored breathing. *Dysphasia,* which literally means "impaired speech," refers to a disorder in which the ability to use and understand language is seriously impaired as a result of injury to or disease of the brain.

dysfunctional \dis-'fəŋk-shə-nəl\ Operating or functioning in an impaired or abnormal way.

• His sisters constantly claimed that the family was dysfunctional, but he could never see it.

Neurologists speak of dysfunctional brain stems, and psychiatrists treat patients for dysfunctional sexual response. Political scientists wonder if the American two-party system has become dysfunctional, and sociologists point to the rising crime rate as evidence of a dysfunctional society. Nowadays *dysfunctional* more often describes families than anything else. In popular usage, any family with problems is likely to be characterized as dysfunctional.

dyslexia \dis-'lek-sē-ə\ A disturbance or interference with the ability to read or to use language.

• She managed to deal with her dyslexia through careful tutoring all throughout elementary school.

Dyslexia is a neurological disorder that usually affects people of average or superior intelligence. *Dyslexic* individuals have an impaired ability to recognize and process words and letters. Dyslexia usually shows itself in the tendency to read and write words and letters in reversed order. Sometimes similar reversals occur in the person's speech. Dyslexia has been shown to be treatable through lengthy instruction in proper reading techniques.

dyspeptic \dis-'pep-tik\ (1) Relating to or suffering from indigestion. (2) Having an irritable temperament; ill-humored.

• For decades the dyspeptic columnist served as the newspaper's—and the city's—resident grouch.

Dyspepsia comes from the Greek word for "bad digestion." Interestingly, the Greek verb *pessein* can mean either "to cook" or "to digest"; a lot of bad cooking has been responsible for a lot of dyspepsia. Dyspepsia can be caused by many diseases, but often dyspeptic individuals are the victims of their own habits and appetites. Worry, overeating, inadequate chewing, and excessive smoking and drinking can all bring on dyspepsia. Today we generally use *dyspeptic* to mean "irritable"—that is, in the kind of mood that could be produced by bad digestion.

dystrophy \'dis-trə-fē\ Any of several disorders involving nerves and muscles, especially a hereditary disease marked by a progressive wasting of muscles.

• In cases involving the most devastating type of muscular dystrophy, infections or respiratory failure can result in the victim's death before the age of 30.

Dystrophy in its original sense refers to a disorder brought about through faulty nutrition. (The *-trophy* element in *dystrophy* comes from the Greek word for "nutrition.") Today *dystrophy* most often refers to the progressive wasting away of the muscles that is known as *muscular dystrophy*. Actually, there are several types of muscular dystrophy, the most common of which is Duchenne's, which strikes males almost exclusively. Duchenne's muscular dystrophy occurs in about one out of 3,300 male births.

Quizzes

A. Fill in each blank with the correct letter:

a. euphemism	e. dyslexia
b. dystrophy	f. euphoria
c. evangelism	g. dysfunctional
d. dyspeptic	h. eugenic

1. There is many a _____ for the word *death*, and many more for the word *drunk*.

2. Some pop psychologists claim that every family is _____ and impaired in some way.

3. The organization campaigns against drunk driving with remarkable _____.

4. Because his _____ was discovered early, he was able to receive the special reading instruction he needed.

5. The end of the war was marked by widespread _____ and celebration.

6. Ebenezer Scrooge, in *A Christmas Carol,* is a thoroughly _____ character.

7. Though the dog is the product of generations of _____ breeding, she is high-strung and has terrible eyesight.

8. The symptoms of muscular _____ can be relieved through physical therapy, various supportive devices, or surgery.

B. Match the word on the left to the correct definition on the right:

1.	dystrophy	a.	impaired
2.	euphemism	b.	beset by indigestion
3.	dyslexia	c.	muscular deterioration
4.	eugenic	d.	crusading zeal
5.	dysfunctional	e.	polite term
6.	euphoria	f.	reading disorder
7.	dyspeptic	g.	promoting superior offspring
8.	evangelism	h.	great happiness

Latin Borrowings

a fortiori \ˌä-ˌfȯr-tē-'ȯr-ē\ All the more certainly.

● If drug users are going to be subject to mandatory sentences, then a fortiori drug dealers should be subject to them also.

A fortiori in Latin literally means ''from the stronger (argument).'' It is used when drawing a conclusion that is even more obvious or convincing than the one just drawn. Thus, if teaching English grammar to native speakers is difficult, then, a fortiori, teaching English grammar to nonnative speakers is even more challenging.

a posteriori \ˌä-ˌpōs-tir-ē-ˈȯr-ē\ Relating to or derived by reasoning from known or observed facts.

● The President had come to the a posteriori conclusion that the booming economy was entirely due to his economic policies.

A posteriori is a term from logic. It is Latin for "from the latter." *A posteriori* usually refers to reasoning that derives causes from effects. This kind of reasoning can sometimes lead to false conclusions. The rising of the sun following the crowing of a rooster, for example, does not mean that the rooster's crowing caused the sun to rise.

a priori \ˌä-prē-ˈȯr-ē\ Relating to or derived by reasoning from self-evident propositions.

● Her colleagues rejected Professor Winslow's a priori argument because it rested on assumptions they felt were not necessarily true.

A priori is Latin for "from the former"; it is traditionally contrasted with *a posteriori*. It is usually applied to lines of reasoning or arguments that proceed from the general to the particular or from causes to effects. Whereas a posteriori knowledge is knowledge based solely on experience or personal observation, a priori knowledge is knowledge derived through the power of reasoning. An a priori argument is based on reasoning from what is self-evident; it does not rely on observed facts for its proof.

bona fide \ˈbō-nə-ˌfīd\ (1) Made in good faith, without deceit. (2) Authentic or genuine.

● They made a bona fide and sincere offer to buy the property at its fair market value.

Bona fide means "in good faith" in Latin. When applied to business deals and the like, it stresses the absence of fraud or deception. A bona fide sale of securities is an entirely aboveboard transaction. When used of matters outside of the legal or business worlds, *bona fide* implies sincerity and earnestness. A bona fide promise is one that the promisor has every intention of keeping. A bona fide proposal of marriage is one made by a suitor who isn't kidding around.

carpe diem \ˈkär-pā-ˈdē-ˌem\ Enjoy the pleasures or opportunities of the moment without concern about the future.

• He was convinced he would die young, so he told himself "carpe diem" and lived an adventurous life.

Carpe diem comes from Latin, where it literally means "Pluck the day," though it is usually translated as "Seize the day." A free translation might be "Enjoy yourself while you have the chance." Some people make *carpe diem* a kind of slogan for their lives, feeling that life is too short to spend it worrying about the future, and that we should grab the opportunities life gives us because they may not come again.

caveat emptor \'ka-vē-ˌät-'emp-tər\ Let the buyer beware.

• The best rule to keep in mind when buying anything from a pushcart is: "Caveat emptor."

"Without a warranty, the buyer must take the risk" is the basic meaning of the phrase *caveat emptor*. In olden days when buying and selling was carried on in the local marketplace, the rule was a practical one. Buyer and seller knew each other and were on equal footing. The nature of modern commerce and technology placed the buyer at a disadvantage, however, so a stack of regulations have been written by federal, state, and local agencies to protect the consumer against dangerous, defective, and ineffective products, fraudulent practices, and the like.

corpus delicti \'kȯr-pəs-di-'lik-ˌtī\ (1) The substantial and basic fact or facts necessary to prove that a crime has been committed. (2) The material substance, such as the murdered body, on which a crime has been committed.

• The police believed they had solved the crime, but they couldn't prove their case without the corpus delicti.

Corpus delicti literally means "body of the crime" in Latin. In its original sense the "body" in question refers not to a corpse but to the body of essential facts that taken together prove that a crime has been committed. In popular, nontechnical usage, *corpus delicti* also refers to the actual physical object upon which a crime has been committed. In a case of arson, it would be a ruined building.

In a murder case, as every fan of whodunits knows, it would be the victim's body.

curriculum vitae \kə-'ri-kyù-ləm-'vē-,tī\ A short summary of one's career and qualifications, typically prepared by an applicant for an academic job; résumé.

• The job advertisement asked for an up-to-date curriculum vitae and three recommendations.

Curriculum vitae is a term usually used in academic circles where teaching positions are the issue. The phrase means "the course of one's life," and is often abbreviated *CV*. In other fields, *résumé* is more commonly used.

Quiz

Fill in each blank with the correct letter:

a. a priori
b. curriculum vitae
c. caveat emptor
d. a posteriori
e. carpe diem
f. a fortiori
g. corpus delicti
h. bona fide

1. To ensure that all reservations are _____, the cruise line requires a nonrefundable deposit.
2. If these two medium-sized cars won't hold all of us and our luggage, _____ those smaller cars won't even come close.
3. The philosopher published his own _____ proof of the existence of God.
4. When we're afraid to pursue our dreams, we sometimes have to tell ourselves, _____.
5. She sent out a _____ full of impressive educational and professional credentials.
6. All of the elements were available to establish the _____ of the defendant's crime.
7. This art critic takes the _____ position that if Pablo Picasso painted it, it's a masterpiece of modern art.
8. When you go out to buy a used car, the best advice, warranty or no warranty, is still _____.

Review Quizzes

A. Complete the analogy:

1. antagonist : villain :: protagonist : _____
   a. maiden b. wizard c. knight d. hero
2. radical : rebellious :: orthodox : _____
   a. routine b. conventional c. sane d. typical
3. fake : fraudulent :: bona fide : _____
   a. copied b. certain c. authentic d. desirable
4. slang : vulgar :: euphemism : _____
   a. habitual b. polite c. dirty d. dumb
5. identify : name :: rectify : _____
   a. make over b. make new c. make right d. make up
6. superior : inferior :: anterior : _____
   a. before b. beside c. above d. behind
7. warranty : guarantee :: caveat emptor : _____
   a. explanation b. warning c. endorsement d. contract
8. jovial : friendly :: dyspeptic : _____
   a. grumpy b. sleepy c. dopey d. happy
9. hot : cold :: catatonic : _____
   a. active b. petrified c. feline d. tired
10. benevolent : wicked :: malevolent : _____
    a. evil b. silly c. noisy d. kindly

B. Fill in each blank with the correct letter:

a. antechamber   i. curriculum vitae
b. a posteriori   j. catacomb
c. euphoria   k. dystrophy
d. malign   l. eugenic
e. a fortiori   m. malnourished
f. orthography   n. protoplasm
g. prototype   o. orthodontics
h. rector

1. Before car makers produce a new model, they always build and test a _____.
2. Please include a _____ so that we can evaluate your qualifications for this position.
3. They were shown into an elegant _____ where they awaited their audience with the king.

4. After graduation from dental school, Kyle took a postgraduate course in _____.
5. The philosopher's conclusion was based on _____ reasoning.
6. The jellylike substance in cells is called _____.
7. These abused and _____ children can't be expected to pay attention in class.
8. With some milder types of muscular _____, victims can function well into adulthood.
9. They felt such _____ that they almost wept with joy.
10. Since they earned high honors for achieving a 3.7 average, _____ we should do so for getting a 3.8.
11. Obsessed with _____, the teacher seemed to care not for what his students wrote, only for how it was spelled.
12. It is common for boxers to _____ each other in crude terms before a big match.
13. The _____ of their church gives excellent sermons full of sensible advice.
14. When they went to Rome, they made sure to visit at least one underground _____.
15. _____ experimentation has produced a new breed of sheep with thick, fast-growing wool.

C. Indicate whether the following pairs have the same or different meanings:

1. corpus delicti / basic evidence   same ___ / different ___
2. ante meridiem / after noon   same ___ / different ___
3. malicious / mean   same ___ / different ___
4. protocol / rules of behavior   same ___ / different ___
5. a priori / determined later   same ___ / different ___
6. dyslexia / speech patterns   same ___ / different ___
7. cataclysm / religious teachings   same ___ / different ___
8. antedate / occur before   same ___ / different ___
9. orthopedics / shoe repair   same ___ / different ___
10. rectilinear / curvy   same ___ / different ___
11. evangelism / crusading   same ___ / different ___
12. carpe diem / look ahead   same ___ / different ___
13. dysfunctional / damaged   same ___ / different ___
14. catalyst / distributor   same ___ / different ___
15. rectitude / stubbornness   same ___ / different ___

Unit 6

ROG comes from *rogare,* the Latin verb meaning "to ask." The ancient Romans also used this word to mean "to propose," thinking perhaps that when we propose an idea, we are actually asking someone to consider it. So *interrogate* means "to question systematically," and a *surrogate* (for example, a surrogate mother) is a substitute, someone who is proposed to stand in for another.

abrogate \'a-brə-ˌgāt\ (1) To abolish or annul. (2) To ignore or treat as if nonexistent.

• The proposed constitutional amendment would abrogate fundamental rights of citizens that had long been protected by the courts.

The Latin prefix *ab-* sometimes functions like the English prefix *un-,* so if the ancient Romans wanted to "un-propose" something—that is, propose that something no longer be done—the verb they used was *abrogare,* from which we get *abrogate*. Today, members of our Senate might consider abrogating a treaty if serious questions were raised about the way in which it was negotiated. Similarly, a manufacturer faced with large increases in the cost of materials may feel justified in abrogating contracts with its customers. And policies requiring doctors to give out information about their patients are said to abrogate the confidential patient-doctor relationship.

arrogate \'ar-ə-ˌgāt\ To claim or seize without justification.

• With this legislation, Governor Burns insisted, the federal government was trying to arrogate powers previously held by the states.

A project team will probably succeed best if individual members do not try to arrogate decision-making authority to themselves. And many of us are annoyed when television evangelists try to arrogate to themselves the right to decide what kind of faith is acceptable. (Because of their similarity, it is all too easy to confuse *arrogate* with *abrogate*—and with *arrogant,* for that matter. Study them carefully.)

derogatory \di-'rä-gǝ-,tȯr-ē\ Expressing a low or poor opinion of someone or something.

● The radio talk-show host tried to discredit the politician by making derogatory remarks about his appearance.

Derogatory also comes from the "propose" sense of *rogare.* When Romans wanted to propose that something be taken out of a law, the verb they used was *derogare,* and this word developed the general meaning of "take away from." A derogatory comment is one that takes away because it detracts from a person's reputation or lowers the person in the eyes of others. Derogatory remarks are a specialty of some comedians, though their meanness sometimes detracts from their humor.

prerogative \pri-'rä-gǝ-tiv\ A special or exclusive right, power, or privilege that sets one apart from others.

● It is the prerogative of governors and presidents to grant reprieves and pardons.

In some meetings in ancient Rome, the person asked to vote first on an issue was called the *praerogativus.* Voting first was considered a privilege, and so the Romans also had the word *praerogativa,* meaning "preference" or "privilege," from which we get our word *prerogative,* meaning a special right that one has because of one's office, rank, or character. So a company's president may have the prerogative to occupy the largest office with the best view. In a less official sense, a successful writer may claim the prerogative to invent new words. Speaking frankly is sometimes thought to be the prerogative of the senior citizen, but it is probably best exercised with caution.

QUIS is derived from the Latin verb *quaerere*, meaning "to seek or obtain." You can see it in our word *acquisitive*, which means "having a strong wish to possess things." The roots *quer*, *quir*, and *ques* are also derived from this word and give us words such as *inquiry*, "a search or request for information," and *question*, "something asked."

inquisition \ˌin-kwə-ˈzi-shən\ A questioning or examining that is often harsh or severe.

• The President's choice for the cabinet position turned down the appointment, fearing that the confirmation hearings would turn into an inquisition into her past.

While *inquiry* is a general term and can apply to almost any search for truth, *inquisition* suggests an ongoing search for hidden facts that is thorough and involves long and harsh questioning. Originally *inquisition* had about the same meaning as *inquiry*, but our current use is very much influenced by the Spanish Inquisition, an ongoing trial which began in the Middle Ages and was conducted by church-appointed *inquisitors* who sought out nonbelievers and Jews and sentenced thousands of them to torture and to burning at the stake. Because of this historical connection, the word today almost always means ruthless questioning conducted with complete disregard for human rights.

perquisite \ˈpər-kwə-zət\ (1) A privilege or profit that is provided in addition to one's base salary. (2) Something claimed as an exclusive possession or right.

• A new car, a big house, and yearly trips to Europe were among the perquisites that made the presidency of Wyndam College such an attractive position.

A perquisite, often referred to simply as a *perk*, is usually something of value to which the holder of a particular job or position is entitled. The President of the United States, for instance, enjoys the perquisites of the use of the White House, Camp David, and Air Force One. Perhaps because perquisites are usually available to only a small number of people, the word sometimes refers to non-job-related privileges that are claimed as exclusive rights. It often is very close in meaning to *prerogative* (see above).

acquisitive \ə-'kwi-zə-tiv\ Eager to acquire; greedy.

● With each year the couple became more madly acquisitive, buying jewelry, a huge yacht, and two country estates.

Many have observed that we live in an acquisitive society, a society devoted to getting and spending, unlike most tribal societies and some older nations. America often makes successfully acquisitive people into heroes; even Ebenezer Scrooge, that model of miserly greed and *acquisitiveness,* was once defended by the White House chief of staff. An acquisitive nation may seek to *acquire* other territories by force. But mental *acquisition* of specialized knowledge or skills—or new vocabulary!—doesn't deprive others of the same information.

requisition \,re-kwə-'zi-shən\ A demand or request (such as for supplies) made with proper authority.

● The teachers had grown impatient with having to submit a requisition for even routine classroom supplies.

Requisition is both a noun and a verb. We can speak of sending a requisition to the purchasing department, but we also refer to soldiers *requisitioning* food from civilians. The word has a bureaucratic flavor, but one of Hollywood's bittersweet love stories begins when Omar Sharif, playing a World War II freedom fighter, says to Ingrid Bergman, who is the owner of a stately old yellow Rolls Royce, "I've come to requisition your car."

Quizzes

A. Choose the word that does not belong:

1. derogatory   a. critical b. unflattering c. admiring
       d. scornful
2. inquisition   a. examination b. interrogation
       c. pardon d. inquiry
3. abrogate   a. neglect b. abolish c. steal d. ignore
4. perquisite   a. privilege b. bonus c. salary d. right
5. prerogative   a. right b. persuasion c. power
       d. privilege
6. acquisitive   a. grateful b. grasping c. grabby d. greedy

7. requisition   a. purchase order   b. receipt   c. request
    d. demand
8. arrogate   a. claim   b. seize   c. grab   d. release

B. Fill in each blank with the correct letter:

a. prerogative   e. arrogate
b. requisition   f. acquisitive
c. derogatory   g. abrogate
d. perquisite   h. inquisition

1. She decided to _____ her family obligations for one day
to go to the fair.
2. You couldn't even get a pencil unless you filled out
a _____.
3. Rodney made _____ remarks about Philip's intelligence
that insulted and angered him.
4. Jeannette discovered that a _____ to membership in
Frank's family was the privilege of participating in all
their quarrels.
5. The mayor tried to _____ to himself sole control of local
political activity.
6. The whole family was _____ by nature, and there were
bitter legal battles over the will.
7. His status as newcomer did carry the special _____ of
being able to ask a lot of questions.
8. Louisa feared an _____ into her background and previous
involvements.

PLE comes from a Latin word meaning "to fill." It can be seen
in the word *complete,* meaning "possessing all necessary parts."
The *ple* root has a Greek equivalent, *pleth,* seen in the word *pleth-
ora,* which means "multitude or abundance."

---

complement \'käm-plə-mənt\ (1) Something that fills up or
makes perfect; the amount needed to make something complete.
(2) A counterpart.

• In an inventive mind, imagination often serves as a necessary
complement to reason.

A complement fills out or balances something. Salt is the complement of pepper, and the right necktie is a perfect complement to a good suit. *Complement* can also mean "the full quantity, number, or amount." A ship's complement of officers and crew is the whole force necessary for full operation. (Do not confuse with *compliment*, which means an expression of respect or affection.)

deplete \di-'plēt\ To reduce in amount by using up.

• Years of farming on the same small plot of land had left the soil depleted of minerals.

The *de-* prefix often means "do the opposite of," so *deplete* means the opposite of "fill." It can mean merely a lessening in amount; thus, food supplies can be rapidly depleted by hungry teenagers in the house. However, *deplete* usually suggests a reduction that endangers the ability to function. Desertions can deplete an army; layoffs can deplete an office staff; and too much exercise without rest can deplete a body's strength.

implement \'im-plə-ˌment\ To take steps to fulfill or put into practice.

• Senators and cabinet members were called in to discuss how to implement the President's new foreign policy.

Implement is usually used in connection with bills that have been passed, proposals that have been accepted, or policies that have been adopted. When companies develop new corporate strategies, they will often hire a new management team to implement the strategy; and when strategies succeed, credit should go to those responsible for both the original idea and its *implementation*.

replete \ri-'plēt\ Fully or abundantly filled or supplied.

• The retired professor's autobiography was a fascinating book, replete with details and anecdotes about academic life in the 1930s.

Replete implies that something is filled to capacity. Most people enjoy autumn weekends in New England, replete with colorful foliage, the smell of wood smoke, and a little chill in the air. Supermarket tabloids are usually replete with more details of stars' lives than anyone has any use for. After a big meal of lobster and all the trimmings, we feel replete and drowsy; better wait till later for any more volleyball.

METR comes to us from Greek by way of Latin; in both languages it refers to "measure." A *thermometer* measures heat; a *perimeter* is the measure around something; and things that are *isometric* are equal in measure.

---

metric \'me-trik\ (1) Relating to or based on the metric system. (2) Relating to or arranged in meter.

• Many Americans are beginning to become accustomed to metric units such as the liter, milligram, and kilometer.

The metric system, used in most of the world to measure distance, weight, and volume, is built in part on a unit length called the *meter*, from which it takes its name. Other metric units are the kilogram (the basic unit of weight) and the liter (the basic unit of volume). *Metric* can also refer to the meter, or rhythm, in songs and poetry, although the word *metrical* is used more often for this meaning. So while the scientists' measurements are usually metric, the poets' are usually metrical.

odometer \ō-'dä-mə-tər\ An instrument used to measure distance traveled.

• Jennifer watched the odometer to see how far she would have to drive to her new job.

Odometer includes the root from the Greek word *hodos,* meaning "road" or "trip." The odometer is what unscrupulous car salesmen illegally tamper with when they want to reduce the mileage a car registers as having traveled. One of life's little pleasures is watching the odometer when all of the numbers change at the same time.

symmetrical \sə-'me-tri-kəl\ (1) Having or exhibiting balanced proportions or the beauty that results from such balance. (2) Corresponding in size, shape, or other qualities on opposite sides of a dividing line or plane or around a center.

• Noting the dents in both front fenders, Robert comforted himself that at least his car was now symmetrical.

A key element in the appeal of most formal gardens is their symmetrical design, and *symmetry* plays a large part in the timeless beauty of Greek temples. Of course, the opposite can also be true. Cindy Crawford was not the first person to discover that a certain lack of symmetry can add interest to the human face.

tachometer \ta-'kä-mə-tər\ A device used to measure speed of rotation.

• Even though one purpose of having a tachometer is to help drivers keep their engine speeds down, most of us occasionally try to see how high we can make the needle go.

A tachometer is literally a "speed-measurer," since the Greek root *tach-* means "speed." This is clear in the name of the *tachyon,* a particle of matter that travels faster than the speed of light. If it exists, it is so fast that it is impossible to see. *Tachycardia* is a medical condition in which the heart races uncontrollably. Since the speed that a tachometer measures is speed of rotation, the numbers it reports are usually revolutions per minute, or rpm's.

Quizzes

A. Match the word on the left to the correct definition on the right:

1.	symmetrical	a.	drain
2.	tachometer	b.	put to use
3.	metric	c.	counterpart
4.	replete	d.	balanced
5.	odometer	e.	distance measurer
6.	deplete	f.	speed measurer
7.	implement	g.	full
8.	complement	h.	relating to a measuring system

B. Choose the closest definition:

1. deplete   a. straighten out   b. draw down   c. fold
   d. abandon
2. replete   a. refold   b. repeat   c. abundantly provided
   d. fully clothed
3. odometer   a. intelligence measurer   b. heart-rate measurer   c. height measurer   d. distance measurer

4. tachometer   a. speed measurer b. sharpness measurer
    c. fatigue measurer d. size measurer
5. complement   a. praise b. number required
    c. abundance d. usual dress
6. metric   a. relating to poetic rhythm b. relating to ocean
    depth c. relating to books d. relating to particles of
    matter
7. implement   a. put to death b. put to pasture c. put into
    practice d. put to sleep
8. symmetrical   a. uncomplicated b. measured
    c. unattractive d. balanced

AUD, from the Latin verb *audire,* is the root that has to do with
hearing. What is *audible* is hearable, and an *audience* is a group
of people that listens, sometimes in an *auditorium.*

---

auditor \'ȯ-də-tər\ A person who formally examines and verifies
financial accounts.

• It seems impossible that so many banks could have gotten
themselves into so much trouble in the 1980s if their auditors had
been doing their jobs.

We don't normally associate auditors with listening—looking and
adding up numbers seems more their line of work. But auditors do
have to listen to people's explanations, and perhaps that is the historical link. Both Latin and some old forms of French had words
similar to our *auditor* which meant "hearer," "judge's assistant,"
and "one who examines accounts." So listening and judging have
been intertwined with looking at the books for hundreds of years.

auditory \'ȯ-də-ˌtȯr-ē\ (1) Perceived or experienced through hearing. (2) Of or relating to the sense or organs of hearing.

• With the new sophisticated sound systems that are now available,
going to a movie has become an auditory experience almost as
much as a visual one.

Auditory is close in meaning to *acoustic* and *acoustical* as they all
relate to the hearing of sounds. *Auditory,* however, usually refers
more to hearing than to sound. For instance, many dogs have great

auditory powers. The nerve that allows us to hear by connecting the inner ear to the brain is the auditory nerve. *Acoustic* and *acoustical* refer especially to instruments and to the conditions under which sound can be heard. So architects concern themselves with the acoustic (or acoustical) properties of an auditorium, and instrument makers with those of a clarinet or piano.

audition \ȯ-'di-shən\ A trial performance to evaluate a performer's skills.

• Auditions for Broadway shows attract so many hopeful unknown performers that they are referred to as "cattle calls."

Most stars are discovered at auditions, where a number of candidates read the same part and the director chooses. Lana Turner, on the other hand, skipped the audition process altogether; once she was discovered sipping a soda at Schwab's, her future was secure. *Audition* can also be a verb. After Miss Turner won her stardom, the prize was the opportunity to audition to be her leading man.

inaudible \i-'nȯ-də-bəl\ Not heard or capable of being heard.

• The coach spoke to the young gymnast in a low voice that was inaudible to the rest of the team.

Inaudible adds the negative prefix *in-* to the adjective *audible* and turns it into its opposite. Modern spy technology (if movies like *Three Days of the Condor* or *Patriot Games* are accurate) can turn inaudible conversations into audible ones with the use of high-powered directional microphones. So if you think you're being spied on, make sure there's a lot of other noise around you.

SON is the Latin root meaning "sound," as in our word *sonata*, meaning a kind of music usually played by one or two instruments, and *sonorous*, usually meaning full, loud, or rich in sound.

---

dissonant \'di-sə-nənt\ (1) Clashing or discordant, especially in music. (2) Incompatible or disagreeing.

• Critics of the health-care plan pointed to its two seemingly dissonant goals: cost containment, which would try to control spending, and universal coverage, which could increase spending.

Dissonant includes the negative prefix *dis-*. What is dissonant sounds or feels unresolved, unharmonic, and clashing. Twentieth-century composers such as Arnold Schoenberg and his students Alban Berg and Anton Webern developed the use of *dissonance* in music as a style in itself. To many, such visual and jarring sounds are still unbearable; most listeners prefer music based on traditional tonality.

resonance \'re-zə-nəns\ (1) A continuing or echoing of sound. (2) A richness and variety in the depth and quality of sound.

• Audiences for both *Star Wars* and CNN are drawn to the resonance in the voice of James Earl Jones.

Many of the finest musical instruments possess a high degree of resonance which, by producing additional vibrations and echoes of the original sound, enriches and amplifies it. Violins made by the masters Stradivari and Guarneri, for example, possess a quality of resonance that modern violinmakers have not been able to duplicate.

sonic \'sä-nik\ (1) Having to do with sound. (2) Having to do with the speed of sound in air (about 750 miles per hour).

• With a sonic depth finder, they determined the depth of the lake by bouncing a sound signal off the bottom.

In 1947 a plane burst the sound barrier and created a sonic boom for the first time. Now even commercial jetliners, including the Concorde, leave sonic booms in their wake as they exceed the speed of sound.

ultrasound \'əl-trə-,saund\ The use of sound vibrations above the limits of human hearing to produce images with which to diagnose internal bodily conditions.

• His doctor, who loved new technology, used CAT scans, MRI, and ultrasound to view his various organs.

The root *son-* came to be spelled *soun-* in medieval English, which led to *sound* and all the English words that now contain it. Ultrasound, or *ultrasonography,* works on the principle that sound is reflected at different speeds by tissues or substances of different densities. *Sonograms,* the pictures produced by ultrasound, can reveal heart defects, tumors, and gallstones, but are most often used to display fetuses during pregnancy in order to make sure they are healthy.

Quizzes

A. Indicate whether the following pairs of words have the same or different meanings:

1. dissonant / jarring   same ___ / different ___
2. inaudible / invisible   same ___ / different ___
3. resonance / richness   same ___ / different ___
4. audition / tryout   same ___ / different ___
5. ultrasound / harmony   same ___ / different ___
6. auditor / performer   same ___ / different ___
7. sonic / loud   same ___ / different ___
8. auditory / hearing   same ___ / different ___

B. Match the word on the left to the correct definition on the right:

1. inaudible   a. involving sound
2. auditory   b. impossible to hear
3. ultrasound   c. diagnostic technique
4. resonance   d. a critical hearing
5. auditor   e. relating to hearing
6. sonic   f. unharmonious
7. dissonant   g. financial examiner
8. audition   h. continuing or echoing sound

ERR, from the Latin verb *errare*, means "to wander" or "to stray." This root is easily seen in the word *error*, which means a wandering or straying from what is correct or true. We also use the word *erratum* to mean "a mistake" in a book or other printed material; its plural is *errata*, and the *errata* page is the book page that lists mistakes found too late to correct before publication.

---

aberrant \ə-'ber-ənt\ Straying or differing from the right, normal, or natural type.

● Richard's aberrant behavior began to make his colleagues fear that the stress of the project was getting to be too much for him.

Something that is aberrant has wandered away from the usual or normal path or form. Aberrant behavior is usually bad behavior and may be a symptom of other problems. However, in biology, the discovery of an aberrant variety of a species can be exciting news, and in medical research the discovery of an aberrant gene can lead the way to new cures for diseases.

errant \'er-ənt\ (1) Wandering or moving about aimlessly. (2) Straying outside proper bounds, or away from an accepted pattern or standard.

● Modern-day cowboys have been known to use helicopters to spot errant calves.

Errant means both "wandering" and "mistaken." A *knight-errant* was a wandering knight going about slaying dragons or rescuing damsels in distress. *Arrant* is a rarely used variant of *errant*, but we sometimes hear it in the phrase *arrant knave*, which comes from Shakespeare and refers to an extremely untrustworthy individual. More typical is the errant cloud or breeze that just happens along or the errant child that requires discipline.

erratic \i-'ra-tik\ (1) Having no fixed course. (2) Lacking in consistency.

● In the 1993 World Series, the Phillies weren't helped by the erratic performance of their ace relief pitcher, "Wild Thing."

Erratic can refer to literal "wandering." A missile that loses its guidance system may follow an erratic path, and a river with lots of twists and bends is said to have an erratic course. *Erratic* can also mean "inconsistent" or "irregular." So a stock market that often changes direction is said to be acting *erratically*. And Wild Thing's problem was erratic control: he could throw strikes but he also threw a lot of wild pitches.

erroneous \i-'rō-nē-əs\ Mistaken, incorrect.

● The chess wizard's parents formed an erroneous idea of his intelligence because he didn't talk until he was six.

Erroneous seems to be used most often with words that suggest mental activity. "Erroneous assumptions" and "erroneous ideas" are two very common phrases in English, perhaps because we suffer from so many of them. "Erroneous information" is also very common, and it leads to erroneous decisions, erroneous theories, and erroneous conclusions.

CED/CESS, from the Latin verb *cedere*, meaning "to go" or "to proceed," produces many English words, from *procession*, meaning something that goes forward, to *recession*, which is a moving back or away.

---

accede \ak-'sēd\ (1) To give in to a request or demand. (2) To give approval or consent.

• Voters tend to worry when Congress seems to be acceding to the demands of too many special-interest groups.

To accede usually means to yield, often under pressure, to the needs or requests of others. Sometimes this is a good thing, as when family members accede to the needs of others or we accede to our curiosity and take the peaceful back road to our destination. *Accede* often also implies reluctance. Patients may accede to surgery, and voters may accede to a tax increase, but eager shoppers do not accede to price reductions—they welcome them.

antecedent \ˌan-tə-'sē-dənt\ (1) A preceding event, state, or cause. (2) One's ancestor or parent.

• The harsh terms of the treaty that ended World War I are often said to have been antecedents of World War II.

Antecedents can be persons, conditions, or events that are responsible, if only in part, for a later person, condition, or event. So the rhythm-and-blues music of the 1940s and 1950s is an antecedent of today's rock and roll. And the breakup of the Soviet Union was surely an important antecedent of the war in Yugoslavia. Since our parents and ancestors are responsible for our existence, they are our own antecedents.

concession \kən-'se-shən\ (1) The yielding of a point or privilege, often unwillingly. (2) An acknowledgment or admission.

• When the company agreed to pay millions of dollars in damage claims, the payments were seen as a concession that somebody had done something wrong.

When the baseball strike of the 1980s was settled, both players and management had to make concessions. This meant that each side *conceded* (gave up or reduced) some of its demands until they reached agreement. *Concede* can also mean simply "admit." So your boss may concede that she is at fault for something, or you may have to concede that your opponent in an argument has some good points.

precedent \'pre-sə-dənt\ Something done or said that may be an example or rule to guide later acts of a similar kind.

• When Judy bought Christmas presents for all her relatives one year she claimed that it set no precedent, but it did.

The Supreme Court relies on precedents, earlier laws or decisions that provide some example or rule to guide them in the present case. Sometimes, as in the famous 1954 ruling that ordered public schools desegregated, the precedent lies in the Constitution and its Amendments.

Quizzes

A. Complete the analogy:

1. descending : ascending :: errant : _____
   a. moving b. wandering c. fixed d. straying
2. abundance : plenty :: antecedent : _____
   a. ancestor b. descendant c. relative d. protector
3. fruitful : barren :: erroneous : _____
   a. productive b. pleasant c. targeted d. correct
4. collision : hit :: concession : _____
   a. drive b. hover c. yielding d. refuse
5. stable : constant :: erratic : _____
   a. fast b. invisible c. mistaken d. unpredictable
6. swerve : veer :: accede : _____
   a. assent b. descent c. reject d. demand

7. typical : normal :: aberrant : _____
    a. burdened b. roving c. odd d. missing
8. etiquette : manners :: precedent : _____
    a. courtesy b. tradition c. rudeness d. behavior

B. Fill in each blank with the correct letter:

a. aberrant   e. erratic
b. errant   f. erroneous
c. precedent   g. antecedent
d. concession   h. accede

1. Her unfair opinion of him was based on several _____ assumptions.
2. They could find no _____ for this offense to guide them in deciding how to deal with it.
3. Doctors traced the _____ changes in his temperature to the attack of malaria.
4. Willy Loman lived the _____ life of the traveling salesman.
5. In agreeing to end the bombing, the rebels made only a single _____.
6. After repeated incidents of criminally _____ behavior, he finally got sent to jail.
7. After lengthy negotiations, the union will probably _____ to several of the company's terms.
8. She proudly claimed Booker T. Washington as her _____.

Words from Mythology and History

Augean stable \ȯ-'jē-ən-'stā-bəl\ A condition or place marked by great accumulation of filth or corruption.

● Leaders of many of the newly formed nations of Eastern Europe found that the old governments of their countries had become Augean stables that they must now clean out.

Augean stable most often appears in the phrase "clean the Augean stable," which usually means "clear away corruption" or "perform a large and unpleasant task that has long called for attention." Augeus, the mythical king of Elis, kept great stables that held 3,000 oxen and had not been cleaned for thirty years when Hercules was assigned the job. Thus, the word *Augean* by itself has come to mean "extremely difficult or distasteful," so we can also refer to Augean tasks or Augean labor, or even Augean clutter. By the way, Hercules cleaned the stables by causing two rivers to run through them.

Croesus \\'krē-səs\\ A very rich person.

● H. Ross Perot's many successful business ventures have made him an American Croesus.

Croesus most often appears in the phrase "rich as Croesus," which means "extremely rich." Bill Gates, founder of Microsoft, could fairly be called "rich as Croesus." Croesus himself was a sixth-century B.C. king of Lydia, an ancient kingdom in what is now Turkey. He conquered many surrounding regions, grew wealthy, and became the subject of many legends.

dragon's teeth \\'dra-gənz-'tēth\\ Seeds of conflict.

● We should realize that we sow dragon's teeth when we neglect the education of our children.

This term often appears in the phrase "sow dragon's teeth," which means to create the conditions for future trouble. In an ancient Greek legend, Cadmus killed a dragon and planted its teeth in the ground. Armed men immediately sprang up from where the teeth were sown and tried to kill him. The goddess Athena directed him to throw a precious stone into their midst and they proceeded to slaughter each other until only the five greatest warriors were left, and these became Cadmus's generals.

Hades \\'hā-dēz\\ The underground home of the dead in Greek mythology.

● Always careful not to offend, the angry Senator bellowed, "Who in Hades gave out this information about me?"

Hades is both the land of the dead and the god who rules there. Hades (Pluto) the god is the brother of Zeus (Jupiter) and Poseidon (Neptune), who rule the skies and the seas respectively. His own realm is Hades, the region under the earth, full of mineral wealth and fertility and home of the dead. There he rules with his wife Persephone (Proserpina). *Hades* has become a polite term for *Hell* and often appears in its place, as in the sentence "The restaurant became hotter than Hades after the air conditioner broke down."

lethargic \lə-'thär-jik\ (1) Lazily sluggish. (2) Indifferent or apathetic.

• Once again the long Sunday dinner had left most of the family feeling stuffed and lethargic.

The Greek philosopher Plato wrote that before a dead person could leave Hades to begin a new life, he or she had to drink from the River Lethe, whose name means "forgetfulness" in Greek. One would thereby forget all aspects of one's former life and the time spent in Hades (usually pretty awful, according to Plato). But our word *lethargic* and the related noun *lethargy* usually refer not to forgetting but rather to the weak, ghostly state of those who have drunk from Lethe as dead spirits—so weak that they may require a drink of blood before they can even speak.

Midas touch \'mī-dəs-'təch\ The talent for making money in every venture.

• For much of his career Donald Trump seemed to possess the Midas touch.

Midas was the legendary king of Phrygia who, when granted one wish by the god Dionysus, asked for the power to turn everything he touched into gold. When he found that even his food and drink turned to gold, he begged Dionysus to take back his gift. The moral of this tale of greed is usually ignored when the term is used today.

Pyrrhic victory \'pir-ik-'vik-tə-rē\ A victory won at excessive cost.

• The coach regarded their win as a Pyrrhic victory, as his best players sustained injuries that would sideline them for weeks.

Pyrrhic victories take their name from Pyrrhus, the king of Epirus an ancient country in northwest Greece. Pyrrhus defeated the Romans at the Battle of Ausculum (279 B.C.) but lost all of his best officers and many men. He is said to have exclaimed after the battle "One more such victory and we are lost."

stygian \'sti-jē-ən\ Extremely dark, dank, gloomy, and forbidding, like the River Styx.

• When the power went out in the building, the halls and stairwells were plunged in stygian darkness.

The word *stygian* comes from the name of the River Styx, which was the chief river of the Greek underground world of the dead and which had to be crossed in order to enter this world.

Quiz

Choose the word that does not belong:

1. lethargic   a. lazy   b. sluggish   c. energetic   d. indifferent
2. Croesus   a. rich   b. powerful   c. impoverished
     d. successful
3. Midas touch   a. talented   b. unsuccessful   c. rich
     d. prosperous
4. Pyrrhic victory   a. unqualified   b. costly
     c. dangerous   d. destructive
5. Augean stable   a. purity   b. corruption   c. filth
     d. Herculean
6. Hades   a. underworld   b. heaven   c. dead   d. eternity
7. dragon's teeth   a. dangerous   b. troublesome
     c. sensible   d. conflict
8. stygian   a. glamorous   b. gloomy   c. grim   d. dank

Review Quizzes

A. Match each word on the left to its antonym on the right:

1. antecedent   a. true
2. erroneous   b. generous
3. dissonant   c. energetic
4. lethargic   d. fill
5. symmetrical   e. admiring
6. acquisitive   f. typical
7. deplete   g. descendant
8. derogatory   h. hearable
9. inaudible   i. unbalanced
10. aberrant   j. harmonious

B. Complete the analogies:

1. arrogate : _____ :: implement : _____
   a. question / serve b. surrogate / tool c. claim / accomplishment d. arrogant / rake

2. precedent : _____ :: prerogative : _____
   a. example / privilege b. sample / rule c. governor / request d. forerunner / introduction

3. odometer : _____ :: Croesus : _____
   a. alphabet / dog b. intelligence / loyalty c. surprise / monster d. distance / wealth

4. audition : _____ :: inquisition : _____
   a. hearing / asking b. trying / cooking c. affecting / reflecting d. listening / seeing

5. ultrasound : _____ :: ultraviolet : _____
   a. loud / colorful b. inaudible / invisible c. medical / artistic d. excessive / exaggerated

6. concession : _____ :: perquisite : _____
   a. edible / necessary b. affordable / bearable c. reluctant / welcome d. appreciative / greedy

7. resonance : _____ :: replete : _____
   a. reworking / refilling b. echoing / full c. divided / united d. continuing / exhausted

8. stygian : _____ :: aberrant : _____
   a. muddy / angry b. dark / abnormal c. gloomy / bright d. light / simple

9. requisition : _____ :: errant : _____
   a. regular / stable b. demand / wandering c. refreshed / roving d. routine / usual

10. sonic : _____ :: auditory : _____
    a. sound / hearing b. jet-propelled / taped c. tonic / radial d. audible / visual

C. Fill in each blank with the correct letter:

a.	abrogate	f.	erratic
b.	tachometer	g.	Midas touch
c.	dragon's teeth	h.	accede
d.	complement	i.	Pyrrhic victory
e.	Croesus	j.	metric

1. Through shrewd investing, she had become as rich as
   _____ .

2. The French use the _____ system to calculate volume.
3. If you want respect, you must never _____ your responsibilities.
4. The triumphant corporate takeover proved to be a _____, since the debt that resulted crippled the corporation for years.
5. The children made only _____ progress because they kept stopping to pick flowers.
6. At last the teachers decided to _____ to the students' request for less homework.
7. He knew that with her mean gossip in the office she was sowing _____, but he did nothing to stop her.
8. The _____ showed that the engine was racing much too fast.
9. Fresh, hot bread is the perfect _____ to any dinner.
10. He skipped his class reunion, preferring to avoid any successful former classmates who clearly had the _____.

Unit 7

VID/VIS comes from the Latin verb *videre*, and appears in words having to do with seeing and sight. A *videotape* is a collection of *visual* images—that is, images *visible* to our eyes. But this root does not always involve eyes. To *envision* something, for instance, is to see it with your imagination.

visage \\'vi-zij\\ The face or appearance of a person.

● A kindly man, he had a bright, cheerful visage that people found attractive.

Visage is one of several words for the human face. *Countenance* and *physiognomy* are two others. *Countenance* is usually used to refer to the face as it reveals mood or character, and *physiognomy* is used when referring to the shape or contour of the face. *Visage* is a more literary term and may refer either to the shape of the face or the impression it gives or the mood it reveals. FBI Most Wanted posters seem to emphasize the threatening visages of the suspects. Unlike *countenance* and *physiognomy*, the use of *visage* is not restricted to humans. We can speak, for instance, of the grimy visage of a mining town.

vis-à-vis \\,vē-zä-'vē\\ In relation to or compared with.

● Many financial reporters worry about the loss of U.S. economic strength vis-à-vis our principal trading partners.

Vis-à-vis comes from Latin by way of French. It means literally "face-to-face"; things that are face-to-face can easily be compared or contrasted. So, for example, the Red Sox have often fared badly vis-à-vis the Yankees, and a greyhound is very tall vis-à-vis a Scottie.

visionary \\'vi-zhə-ˌner-ē\ (1) A person with foresight and imagination. (2) A dreamer whose ideas are often impractical.

• His followers regarded him as an inspired visionary; his opponents saw him as either a con man or a lunatic.

A visionary is someone who vividly imagines the future, whether accurately or not, with ideas that may either work brilliantly or fail miserably. Martin Luther King, Jr., was a visionary in his hopes and ideas for a just society; but this, like so many visions, has proved easier to *envision* than to achieve.

visitation \ˌvi-zə-'tā-shən\ (1) A visit or short stay, often for some definite, official purpose such as inspection. (2) A parent's privilege to have temporary access to or care of a child.

• The local ministers dreaded the annual visitation from the bishop's evaluation committee.

Visit and *visitation* share some meanings, since both refer to a fairly short call or stay. But *visit* is the more general word, while a visitation is normally a visit that is somehow out of the ordinary, such as by being formal or official. Faithful followers of religious leaders such as the Pope or the Dalai Lama look forward to visitations from these holy figures. Businesspeople, on the other hand, could probably do without annual visitations from the tax auditors.

SPIC/SPEC comes from the Latin verb *specere* or *spicere*, meaning "to look at or behold." Closely related is the root *specta-*, which comes from a slightly different verb and produces such words as *spectator*, *spectacles*, and *spectacular*.

auspicious \ȯ-'spi-shəs\ (1) Promising success; favorable. (2) Fortunate, prosperous.

• Martha was mildly superstitious, so breaking her mirror didn't seem an auspicious start to the day.

In ancient Rome there was an entire order of priests, the *auspices*, whose job it was to watch birds fly across the Roman sky. After noting what kinds of birds and how many had flown in which direction, they delivered prophecies according to what they had seen. For example, two eagles flying from east to west was usually considered auspicious, or favorable; two or more vultures flying west to east was *inauspicious*, unless the Romans were looking forward to a war. Thus, the auspices were birdwatchers, although not quite like birdwatchers today.

conspicuous \kən-'spi-kyủ-wəs\ Obvious or noticeable; striking in a way that attracts attention.

• Soon after the shooting, "No Trespassing" signs appeared in conspicuous colors at conspicuous locations around the preserve.

Conspicuous usually refers to something so obvious that it cannot be missed by the eye or mind. We often speak, for instance, of conspicuous bravery or conspicuous generosity. It also frequently describes something that draws attention by being unpleasant or unusual. Businesspeople try to avoid making themselves conspicuous by their clothes or their personal habits. The phrase "conspicuous consumption" is often used to describe lavish spending intended to increase one's social prestige, a well-known aspect of American life.

introspection \ˌin-trō-'spek-shən\ A looking within oneself to examine one's own thoughts and feelings.

• The poet Sylvia Plath's journals are filled with the results of her constant introspection.

Introspection is a valuable resource of writers. In her autobiography, *The Road from Coorain*, Jill Ker Conway produces a fascinating, highly *introspective* portrayal of her life's journey from an Australian sheep farm to the president's office of a major American women's college, and beyond. We learn not only what her life was like but how she felt about it along the way and also in *retrospect*— that is, looking back.

perspicacious \ˌpər-spi-'kā-shəs\ Having acute or shrewd mental vision or judgment.

• Successful poker players are usually perspicacious judges of human character.

Perspicacious is derived from the Latin word *perspicere*, meaning "to look through" or "to see clearly," so *perspicacious*, usually means having unusual power to see through or understand. You tend to admire the *perspicacity* of the person who understands what a fine human being you are. (The confusingly similar word *perspicuous* comes from the same Latin word but means "plain to the understanding" or simply "clear." A writer will strive for a perspicuous style, for example, and a lawyer will try to present perspicuous arguments to a judge.)

Quizzes

A. Fill in each blank with the correct letter:

a.	introspection	e.	visitation
b.	vis-à-vis	f.	auspicious
c.	perspicacious	g.	visionary
d.	conspicuous	h.	visage

1. When she considered Cleveland ____ other cities where she might have to live, she always chose Cleveland.
2. The couple were ____ by their absence from the meeting.
3. His plans for the new city marked him as a true ____.
4. The beautiful sunrise provided an ____ start to their camping trip.
5. She was a ____ woman of rare judgment, who always seemed to know the right thing to say in even the most delicate situation.
6. The ____ of Marlene Dietrich gazed out from movie posters throughout Europe and America in the 1930s.
7. After the confrontation, both devoted themselves to long periods of ____ to try to understand their own feelings.
8. A visit from her mother-in-law always felt like a ____ of the plague.

B. Match the definition on the left to the correct word on the right:

1.	compared to	a.	introspection
2.	shrewd	b.	visitation
3.	prophet	c.	vis-à-vis
4.	appearance	d.	auspicious
5.	self-examination	e.	perspicacious

6.	noticeable	f.	visionary
7.	favorable	g.	conspicuous
8.	official call	h.	visage

VOC/VOK, from the Latin noun *vox* and the verb *vocare*, has to do with speaking and calling and the use of the voice. So a *vocation* is a special calling to a type of work; an *evocative* sight or smell calls forth memories and feelings; and a *vocal* ensemble is a singing group.

equivocate \i-'kwi-və-,kāt\ (1) To use ambiguous language, especially in order to deceive. (2) To avoid giving a direct answer.

• As the company directors continued to equivocate, the union prepared to return to the picket lines.

Equivocate contains the root *equi*, meaning "equal." It thus suggests that whatever is said has two equally possible meanings. The person who equivocates avoids giving a clear, *unequivocal* message. Politicians are often said to equivocate, but equivocating is also typical of used-car salesmen or nervous witnesses in a courtroom. Sometimes even husbands and wives will equivocate to avoid a quarrel.

irrevocable \i-'re-və-kə-bəl\ Impossible to call back or retract.

• By throwing her hat into the presidential race, the young governor made the irrevocable decision to put her family into the public eye.

The word *irrevocable* has a legal sound to it, and in fact is often used in legal contexts. Irrevocable trusts are trust funds that cannot be dissolved by the people who create them. An irrevocable credit is an absolute obligation from a bank to provide credit to a customer. Under U.S. tax law, irrevocable gifts are gifts that are given by one living person to another and that cannot be reclaimed by the giver. But we all have had to make irrevocable decisions, decisions that commit us absolutely to something.

provoke \prə-'vōk\ (1) To call forth or stimulate a feeling or action. (2) To anger.

• Before every boxing match, Cassius Clay (Muhammad Ali) would provoke his opponent with poetic taunts.

To provoke a response is to call for that response to happen. Funny stories should provoke laughter; angry comments can provoke a fight; and taking controversial stands may provoke opposition. Something is *provocative* if it has the power to produce a response. The provocative clothing and behavior of some rock-music performers seem designed to provoke criticism as much as admiring attention.

vociferous \vō-'si-fə-rəs\ Making noisy or emphatic outcries.

• Parents at soccer games are often known to make vociferous protests when they think the referee has made a bad call.

Someone who is vociferous shouts loudly and insistently. The group U2 draws vociferous crowds whose noisy din at times makes it hard to hear the music. And as at any rock concert, there are vociferous objections when the music ends.

PHON is a Greek root meaning "sound," "voice," or "speech." It is similar to the Latin *voc* in meaning but typically means only "sound" when used in such words as *telephone* ("far sound"), *microphone* ("small sound"), or *xylophone* ("wood sound").

---

cacophony \kə-'kä-fə-nē\ Harsh or unpleasant sound.

• To some people, much recent jazz sounds more like cacophony than like real music.

Cacophony employs the Greek prefix *caco-*, meaning "bad," but not everything we call *cacophonous* is necessarily bad. Open-air food markets may be marked by a cacophony of voices but also by wonderful sights and sounds. Heavy metal is probably the most cacophonous form of modern music but it is still very popular. On the other hand, few people can really enjoy, for more than a few minutes, the cacophony of jackhammers, car horns, and truck engines that assaults the city pedestrian on a hot day in August.

phonetic \fə-'ne-tik\ Relating to or representing the sounds of the spoken language.

• Some school systems teach first-graders to read by the phonetic method.

The English alphabet is phonetic; that is, the letters represent sounds. Certain other alphabets, such as Chinese, are not phonetic, since their symbols represent ideas rather than sounds. But even in English a letter does not always represent the same sound; the "a" in *cat, father,* and *mate,* for example, represents three different sounds. Because of this, books about words often use specially created phonetic alphabets in which each symbol stands for a single sound in order to represent pronunciations. So in this book, *cat, father,* and *mate* would be *phonetically* represented as \'kat\, \'fä- thər\, and \'māt\

polyphonic \pä-lē-'fä-nik\ Referring to a style of music in which two or more melodies are sung or played against each other in harmony.

• The polyphonic chants of the monks punctuated the ceremony at important intervals.

Since *poly-* means "many," polyphonic music has "many voices." In *polyphony,* each part has its own melody. It reached its height during the 16th century with Italian madrigals and the sacred music of such composers as Palestrina, Tallis, and Byrd.

symphony \'sim-fə-nē\ A usually long and complex musical composition for orchestra.

• Beethoven, Bruckner, Mahler, and possibly Schubert completed nine symphonies each before their deaths.

Symphony includes the prefix *sym-* ("together") and thus means "a sounding together." The symphonies of Beethoven, most of which have four separate movements, are among the greatest ever composed. From the First, which is almost like the music of Mozart, to the magnificent choral Ninth, few other pieces of music compare to them in controlled intensity. "*Symphonic* poems" by such composers as Franz Liszt and Richard Strauss usually attempt to paint a picture or tell a dramatic story by means of music alone. Both require a symphony orchestra (sometimes called simply a "symphony" itself) made up of stringed, woodwind, brass, and percussion instruments.

Quizzes

A. Complete the analogy:

1. initial : beginning :: irrevocable : _____
   a. usual b. noisy c. final d. reversible
2. novel : literature :: symphony : _____
   a. dance b. poetry c. film d. music
3. soothe : quiet :: provoke : _____
   a. prevent b. project c. produce d. protect
4. multistoried : floor :: polyphonic : _____
   a. poetry b. melody c. story d. harmony
5. reject : accept :: equivocate : _____
   a. decide b. specify c. detect d. delay
6. melodic : notes :: phonetic : _____
   a. sounds b. signs c. ideas d. pages
7. monotonous : boring :: vociferous : _____
   a. vegetarian b. angry c. favorable d. noisy
8. stillness : quiet :: cacophony : _____
   a. melodious b. dissonant c. creative d. birdlike

B. Indicate whether the following pairs have the same or different meanings:

1. provoke / annoy   same ___ / different ___
2. phonetic / phonelike   same ___ / different ___
3. equivocate / refuse   same ___ / different ___
4. polyphonic / many-voiced   same ___ / different ___
5. irrevocable / unalterable   same ___ / different ___
6. cacophony / din   same ___ / different ___
7. vociferous / calm   same ___ / different ___
8. symphony / heavy metal   same ___ / different ___

CUR, from the Latin verb *curare*, means basically "care for." Our verb *cure* comes from this root, as do *manicure* ("care of the hands") and *pedicure* ("care of the feet").

---

curative \'kyùr-ə-tiv\ Having to do with curing diseases.

● As soon as the antibiotic entered his system, he imagined he could begin to feel its curative effects.

Medical researchers are finding curative substances in places that surprise them. Folklore has led to some ''new'' *cures* of old diseases, and natural substances never before tried have often proved effective. Taxol, a drug used in treating some cancers comes from the bark of a certain yew tree; the challenge now is to produce this *curative* synthetically, since natural supplies are limited.

curator \\'kyùr-,ā-tər\\ Someone in charge of something where things are on exhibit, such as a collection, a museum, or a zoo.

• Curators of zoos continually try to make the animals' surroundings more and more like their natural homes.

A curator cares for some sort of collection, usually works of art or animals. Thomas Hoving, in his years as director of the Metropolitan Museum of Art, was responsible for supervising the curators of all the separate art collections and seeing that all *curatorial* duties were carried out: acquiring new artworks, caring for and repairing objects already owned, discovering frauds and counterfeits, returning some pieces to their country of origin, and mounting exhibitions of everything from Greek sculpture to 20th-century clothing.

procure \\prō-'kyùr\\ To get possession of; obtain.

• In an era of Defense Department cutbacks, military planners have had to look for more economical ways to procure the supplies they need.

While *procure* has the general meaning of ''come into possession of,'' it usually implies that some effort is required. It may also suggest getting something through a formal set of procedures. In many business offices, there is a particular person responsible for procuring supplies, and many government agencies have formal *procurement* policies designed to prevent unauthorized spending. However, it sometimes seems that such policies cost more money to administer than they could possibly save.

sinecure \\'si-nə-,kyùr\\ A job or position requiring little work but usually providing some income.

• The job of Dean of Students at any college is no sinecure; the hours can be long and the work draining.

Sinecure contains the Latin word *sine*, "without," and thus means "without care." Many view the positions occupied by British royalty as sinecures, in which they earn enormous sums of money and inherit enormous amounts of property in return for nothing at all. But their many supporters defend them by pointing to the amount of public-service, charitable, and ceremonial work they perform, not to mention the effort they put into promoting Britain and all things British. Sinecure or not, many of us would probably like to try being king or queen for a day.

PERI usually means "going around something." With a *periscope*, you can see around corners. *Peristalsis* is the bodily function that moves food around the intestines; without it, digestion would grind to a halt. The moon's *perigee* is the point in its orbit where it is closest to the earth. The point in the earth's orbit around the sun that brings it closest to the sun is its *perihelion*.

---

perimeter \pə-'ri-mə-tər\ The boundary or distance around a body or figure.

● All along the city's perimeter the guerrillas kept up their attack night after night.

The perimeter of a prison is ringed with high walls and watchtowers, and the entire perimeter of Australia is bounded by water. To measure the perimeter of a square, multiply the length of one of its sides by four. Try not to confuse this word with *parameter*, which usually means a characteristic element or factor or a limit or boundary.

periodontal \ˌper-ē-ō-'dän-təl\ Surrounding the teeth; concerning or affecting the tissues around the teeth.

● Years of bad living had filled his teeth with cavities, but it was periodontal disease that finished them off.

There are dentists called *periodontists* who specialize in the treatment of periodontal problems. These specialists do their best to save a patient's teeth by making sure the periodontal tissues do not degenerate to the point where they can no longer hold the teeth in place. The *-odont-* root comes from the Greek word for "tooth," so the *endodontist,* unlike the periodontist, is concerned with problems inside the tooth.

peripatetic \per-ə-pə-'te-tik\ (1) Having to do with walking. (2) Moving or traveling from place to place.

• She spent her early adult years as a peripatetic musician, traveling from one engagement to another.

Peripatetic was the name given to the philosopher Aristotle and his followers, since he used to teach them while walking up and down in a covered walkway called the *Peripatos*. The word kept this sense of traveling or moving about. Johnny Appleseed is a good example of a peripatetic soul, wandering far and wide while he planted his apple trees. Today peripatetic executives and salespeople move from one job to the next and stare into laptop computers while flying from city to city.

peripheral \pə-'ri-fə-rəl\ (1) Having to do with the outer edges, especially of the field of vision. (2) Auxiliary or supplemental.

• The teacher seemed to have eyes in the back of her head, but what she really had was excellent peripheral vision and a thorough knowledge of how ten-year-olds behave.

Driving into or out of Chicago during rush hour requires excellent peripheral vision, especially when switching lanes. Peripheral vision relates to the outer area of the field of vision, where one can still detect movement and shape. Issues in a discussion may also be called peripheral—that is, not of primary importance. And *peripheral* now can act as a noun: computer peripherals are the added components that increase a computer's capacities.

Quizzes

A. Fill in each blank with the correct letter:

a. curative	e. peripheral
b. sinecure	f. perimeter
c. procure	g. peripatetic
d. curator	h. periodontal

1. The _____ benefits of antibiotics have saved many lives.
2. Testing _____ vision is part of most eye tests done in a doctor's office.

3. What he had hoped was an undemanding _____ turned out to be the hardest and most rewarding job of his career.

4. She knew she needed to put up a fence along the _____ of the garden.

5. We asked our purchasing manager to _____ new chairs for the office.

6. With tents and backpacks ready, the young couple were ready to become _____ vacationers.

7. At the museum we spoke to the _____ of African art.

8. Regular use of dental floss will prevent many kinds of _____ diseases.

B. Choose the closest definition:

1. sinecure   a. hopeful sign b. fruitless search c. careless act d. easy job

2. curator   a. doctor b. lawyer c. caretaker d. spectator

3. periodontal   a. visual b. inside a tooth c. around a tooth d. wandering

4. peripatetic   a. wandering b. unemployed c. surrounding d. old-fashioned

5. procure   a. say b. obtain c. look after d. heal

6. curative   a. purifying b. healing c. saving d. repairing

7. perimeter   a. factor b. characteristic c. supplement d. boundary

8. peripheral   a. supplementary b. around a tooth c. wandering d. dangerous

---

SENT/SENS, from the Latin verb *sentire*, meaning "to feel," or the noun *sensus*, meaning "feeling" or "sense," can signify different kinds of feeling. *Sentimental* has to do with emotions, whereas *sensual* relates more to physical *sensations*.

---

sensational \sen-'sā-shə-nəl\ (1) Exciting an intense but usually brief interest or emotional reaction. (2) Extremely or unexpectedly excellent.

• The sensational newspaper accounts of the marital problems of the royal couple fascinated many readers but made others a little uncomfortable.

The photos sent back from Jupiter by the Voyager satellite were sensational—both excellent and exciting. The murder of a pregnant woman by her husband was sensational also, although in a very different sense, since it was picked up by the tabloid press and *sensationalist* TV journalists, who thrive on such sordid tales and *sensationalize* every detail. Both stories, however, can be said to have created a *sensation*.

sentient \'sen-chənt\ Aware of and responsive to sense impressions.

• The planet Earth supports the only sentient beings that we yet know of in the universe.

Sentient describes beings that perceive and respond to sensations of whatever kind—sight, hearing, touch, taste, smell. The science of robotics is now capable of creating machines that *sense* things in much the way living beings do and respond in pretty much the same way as well; however, few of us are yet ready to refer to robots as sentient beings. Mary Shelley, in her novel *Frankenstein*, was among the first to suggest the possibility of creating sentient beings out of used parts.

sentiment \'sen-tə-mənt\ (1) A thought or attitude colored by feeling; opinion. (2) Tender feelings of affection.

• We don't care whose nephew he is; hiring decisions must be based on merit, not sentiment.

"My sentiments exactly!" expresses agreement to someone else's opinion. A sentiment is usually of gentle to moderate intensity. The refined women of Jane Austen's novels are full of sentiment that occasionally spills over into deep emotion but usually remains subdued and controlled. Similarly, a *sentimental* journey, as the old popular song suggests, satisfies feelings of longing and romantic homesickness rather than intense craving. *Sentiment* is used less today than it once was, and *sentimental* now usually means excessively emotional.

sensuous \'sen-shủ-wəs\ (1) Highly pleasing to the senses. (2) Relating to the senses.

• A chef like Craig Claiborne takes sensuous pleasure in the smell and taste of well-prepared food.

Sensuous and *sensual* are closely related in meaning but not identical. *Sensuous* usually implies gratification of the senses for the sake of aesthetic pleasure; great music, for example, can be a source of sensuous delight. *Sensual,* on the other hand, usually describes gratification of the senses or physical appetites as an end in itself; thus we often think (perhaps unfairly) of wealthy Roman aristocrats leading lives devoted to sensual pleasure.

SOPH is a Greek root from the word meaning "wise" or "wisdom." In our language, the root often appears in words where the wisdom concerned is of the "wiseguy" variety. But in words such as *philosophy* we see a more respectful attitude toward wisdom.

sophistry \'sä-fə-strē\ Cleverly deceptive reasoning or argument.

• The defendant's claim that he wasn't guilty of the crime because he didn't actually pull the trigger was dismissed as pure sophistry.

Our words *sophist* and *sophistry* come from the name of a group of Greek teachers of rhetoric and philosophy who were famous during the 5th century B.C. Originally, the Sophists represented a respectable school of philosophy and were involved in serious educational efforts. But in time they fell into disrepute and gained a reputation for their abilities to persuade more by means of clever and often misleading arguments than by the merits of their positions. It is not difficult to see the Sophists as the natural ancestors of many of today's politicians.

sophisticated \sə-'fis-tə-ˌkā-təd\ (1) Having a thorough and refined knowledge of the ways of society. (2) Highly complex or developed.

• In *Woman of the Year* Katharine Hepburn plays a sophisticated newspaperwoman who can handle everything except Spencer Tracy.

A satellite is a sophisticated piece of technology, intricate and complex and designed to accomplish difficult tasks. A sophisticated argument is thorough and well-worked-out. A sophisticated person, such as Humphrey Bogart in *Casablanca,* knows how to get around in the world and is able to get pretty much what he or she wants; such *sophistication* can produce a bored, blasé attitude, as it does with Bogie until his long-lost love appears.

sophomoric \ˌsä-fə-'mȯr-ik\ Overly impressed with one's own knowledge, but in fact undereducated and immature.

● The kids at summer camp played the usual sophomoric pranks—short-sheeted beds, salt in the sugar bowl, shaving cream on the light switch, water bucket balanced on the door.

Sophomoric seems to include the roots *soph-,* ''wise,'' and *moros,* ''fool,'' so the contrast between wisdom and ignorance is built right into the word. A high-school or college *sophomore* has delusions of wisdom—but only the seniors are truly wise, as we all know. Sophomoric behavior and sophomoric jokes are typical of those who have gotten a small taste of experience but think they have experienced a lot.

theosophy \thē-'ä-sə-fē\ A set of teachings about God and the world based on mystical insights into their nature and workings.

● She experimented with a number of beliefs, starting with theosophy and ending with a variety of Hinduism.

The best-known religious movement associated with theosophy began in the 19th century under the leadership of Helena Blavatsky. She combined elements of Platonic thought, Christian mysticism, and Hindu belief in a way she claimed had been divinely revealed to her. *Theosophical* beliefs include oneness with nature and reincarnation. The Theosophical Society, founded in 1875 to promote her beliefs, still exists, although scientific experiments had disproved many of her claims by the 20th century.

Quizzes

A. Indicate whether the following pairs of words have the same or different meanings:

1. sophisticated / worldly-wise   same __ / different __
2. sensuous / sophisticated   same __ / different __
3. theosophy / mythology   same __ / different __

4. sentiment / feeling   same __ / different __
5. sophistry / wisdom   same __ / different __
6. sentient / romantic   same __ / different __
7. sophomoric / wise   same __ / different __
8. sensational / enormous   same __ / different __

**B. Match the word on the left to the correct definition
     on the right:**

1. theosophy   a. immaturely overconfident
2. sentiment   b. outstandingly excellent
3. sensuous   c. doctrine of God and the
4. sophomoric   world
5. sophistry   d. gratifying the senses
6. sentient   e. false reasoning
7. sophisticated   f. opinion colored by
8. sensational   emotion
                       g. receiving perceptions
                       h. highly complex

Words from Mythology and History

Achilles' heel \ə-'ki-lēz-'hēl\ A vulnerable point.

• Grafton had been an excellent manager in his first years there,
but his Achilles' heel turned out to be his addiction to increasingly
damaging drugs.

When the hero Achilles was an infant, his sea-nymph mother
dipped him into the river Styx to make him immortal. But since
she held him by one heel, this spot did not touch the water and so
remained mortal and vulnerable. It was this heel where Achilles
was eventually mortally wounded. Today, the tendon that stretches
up the calf from each heel is called the *Achilles tendon*; however,
the term *Achilles' heel* is only used figuratively; thus, it can refer
to the weakest point in a country's military defenses, or a person's
tendency to drink too much, for example.

arcadia \är-'kā-dēə\ A region or setting of rural pleasure and
peacefulness.

• The Pocono Mountains of Pennsylvania are a vacationer's arcadia.

Arcadia, a beautiful rural area in Greece, became the favorite setting for poems about naive and ideal innocence unaffected by the passions of the larger world. There, shepherds play their pipes and sigh with longing for flirtatious nymphs; shepherdesses sing to their flocks, and goat-footed nature gods cavort in the fields and woods.

Cassandra \kə-'san-drə\ A person who predicts misfortune or disaster.

• The newspaper columnist was accused of being a Cassandra who always looked for the worst and predicted disaster, despite the fact that his predictions often came true.

Cassandra, the daughter of King Priam of Troy, was one of those beautiful young maidens with whom Apollo fell in love. He gave her the gift of prophecy in return for the promise of her sexual favors, but at the last minute she refused him. Though he could not take back his gift, he pronounced that no one would ever believe her predictions. Thus, her prophecy of the fall of Troy and the death of its heroes were laughed at by the Trojans. A modern-day Cassandra goes around predicting gloom and doom, like many current economists with their constant pessimistic forecasts.

cyclopean \ˌsī-klə-'pē-ən\ Huge or massive.

• The scale of the new ten-block high-rise medical center was cyclopean.

The Cyclops of Greek mythology were huge, crude giants, each with a single eye in the middle of his forehead. Odysseus had a terrible encounter with one of these creatures in his travels, and escaped being devoured only by blinding the monster with a burning stick. The great stone walls at such places as Troy, Tiryns, and Mycenae are called cyclopean because the stones are so massive and the construction so expert that it was assumed that only a superhuman race such as the Cyclops could have achieved such a feat.

draconian \drə-'kō-nē-ən\ Extremely severe or cruel.

• The new president thinks that only draconian spending limits and staff cutbacks can save the ailing company.

The word *draconian* comes from *Draco*, the name of a 7th-century B.C. Athenian legislator. Legends and stories about Draco hold that he created a very severe code of laws, which were sometimes said to have been written in blood rather than ink. Today, we use the word *draconian* in a wide variety of ways, sometimes even referring to something as minor as parking policies. (Because the word is derived from a person's name, *draconian* is often spelled with a capital *D*.)

myrmidon \'mər-mə-,dän\ A loyal follower, especially one who executes orders unquestioningly.

• Wherever the corporate tycoon went, he was surrounded by myrmidons all too eager to do his bidding.

Achilles' troops in the Trojan War, called Myrmidons, were created from ants. This insect origin explained their blind obedience to him, their willingness to carry out any order—such as refusing to fight even when it meant many lives would be lost. The Nazis expected all Germans in uniform to exhibit this same unquestioning loyalty and obedience; the postwar Nuremberg trials established the principle that the utter, unthinking obedience of a myrmidon does not excuse committing certain crimes against humanity in wartime.

nemesis \'ne-mə-səs\ A powerful, frightening opponent or rival who is usually victorious.

• During the 1970s and 1980s Japanese carmakers became the nemesis of the U.S. auto industry.

The Greek goddess Nemesis doled out rewards for noble acts and vengeance for evil ones. The Greeks believed that Nemesis did not always punish an offender right away, but might wait as much as five generations to avenge a crime. But whenever she worked, her cause was always just and her victory sure. Today, a nemesis may or may not be believed to be working justice. So most people agree that the weak economy was George Bush's nemesis in 1992, even if they voted for him.

Trojan horse \'trō-jən-'hȯrs\ Someone or something that works from within to defeat or undermine.

• Like a Trojan horse, she came back to school with a bad case of the flu that spread rapidly among the other students.

After besieging the walls of Troy for ten years, the Greeks built a huge, hollow wooden horse, secretly filled it with armed warriors, and presented it to the Trojans as a gift for the goddess Athena. The Trojans accepted the offering and took the horse inside the city's walls. That night, the armed Greeks swarmed out and captured and burned the city. A Trojan horse is thus anything that looks innocent but, once accepted, has power to harm or destroy—for example, a computer program that seems helpful but actually works to wipe out data and functions.

Quiz

Fill in each blank with the correct letter:

a.	myrmidons	e.	Achilles' heel
b.	draconian	f.	nemesis
c.	cyclopean	g.	Cassandra
d.	Trojan horse	h.	arcadia

1. The CEO expected immediate and absolute obedience from his _____, no matter what he asked.
2. Shortly after hiring him, they discovered that he was actually a _____, sent by a rival company to destroy the workers' faith in the company's plans.
3. The architect surrounded the pool and garden with a great stone wall modeled on the _____ walls of ancient Greece.
4. They considered their little corner of New Hampshire a true _____ in its freedom from the pressures of the modern world.
5. In eighth grade his _____ was a disagreeable girl named Rita who liked playing horrible little tricks.
6. In times of national crisis, each news commentator sounds more like a _____ than the next.
7. Historians point to the _____ treaty terms as one of the causes of the next war.
8. Believing the flattery of others and enjoying the trappings of power have often been the _____ of successful politicians.

Review Quizzes

A. Choose the correct synonym and the correct antonym:

1. auspicious   a. bad b. birdlike c. good d. likely
2. sensational   a. kindly b. exciting c. ordinary
      d. odoriferous
3. provoke   a. soothe b. incite c. veto d. announce
4. curative   a. drug b. poison c. recreation d. antidote
5. irrevocable   a. final b. retractable c. unbelievable
      d. vocal
6. perimeter   a. essence b. edge c. center d. spurt
7. nemesis   a. ally b. no one c. enemy d. sibling
8. sophomoric   a. silly b. sage c. cacophonous d. languid
9. Achilles' heel   a. paradise b. heroism c. immortality
      d. vulnerability
10. peripatetic   a. immobile b. exact c. wandering
      d. imprecise
11. conspicuous   a. shrewd b. invisible c. noticeable
      d. promising
12. vociferous   a. speechless b. steely c. pliant d. noisy
13. visionary   a. idealist b. cinematographer
      c. conservative d. writer
14. sentient   a. frantic b. unaware c. alert d. tranquil
15. sophisticated   a. rejected b. advanced c. worldly
      wise d. naive

B. Choose the closest definition:

1. phonetic a. called b. twitched c. sounded
      d. remembered
2. sophistry a. deception b. musical composition c. sound
      reasoning d. pleasure
3. procure a. appoint b. obtain c. decide d. lose
4. visage a. imagination b. citation c. expression
      d. depression
5. symphony a. piano recital b. complex rhythm c. unison
      chant d. orchestral composition

6. vis-à-vis a. compared to b. allowed to c. rented to
   d. talked to
7. introspection a. critical judgment b. self-examination
   c. inquisition d. detention
8. peripheral a. auxiliary b. central c. relating to the
   sun d. philosophical
9. draconian a. rustic b. massive c. disastrous d. severe
10. polyphonic a. multi-melodic b. uniformly harmonic
    c. relatively boring d. intentionally imitative
11. cyclopean a. serpentine b. gigantic c. infinitesimal
    d. circular
12. visitation a. journey b. prayer c. official visit
    d. stimulation
13. periodontal a. relating to feet b. around the sun
    c. around the teeth d. around a corner
14. curator a. caretaker b. watcher c. doctor d. purchaser
15. Cassandra a. optimist b. economist c. pessimist
    d. oculist

C. Fill in each blank with the correct letter:

a. equivocate   f. Trojan horse
b. sensuous   g. arcadia
c. cacophony   h. theosophy
d. sentiment   i. sinecure
e. myrmidon   j. perspicacious

1. The job turned out to be a _____, and no one cared if he
   played golf twice a week.
2. The huge Senate bill was a _____, filled with items that
   almost none of the senators were aware of.
3. We opened the door onto a haze of cigarette smoke and
   a _____ of music and laughter.
4. In the old book on _____ she found a philosophy very
   similar to the one she and her friends were exploring.
5. One _____ after another scurried in and out of the
   boardroom on errands for the chairman.
6. It didn't require a _____ eye to see that their marriage
   was a difficult one.

7. The letter described their new Virginia farm as a kind of _____ of unspoiled nature.
8. Whenever they asked for a definite date, he would _____ and try to change the subject.
9. She lay in the bath with her eyes closed in a kind of _____ daydream.
10. He always tried to end his letters with an appropriate _____ and a warm closing.

Unit 8

TEND/TENT, from the Latin *tendere*, meaning "to stretch, extend, or spread," can be seen most simply in the English word *tent*, meaning a piece of material stretched or extended over a frame. It can also be seen in the word *extend*, which means "to stretch forth or stretch out," and in *tendon*, the word for a tough band of tissue that stretches from a muscle to a bone.

contentious \kən-'ten-chəs\ Having a tendency to pick fights; quarrelsome.

• The school board meeting lasted late into the night as contentious parents argued over every detail of the new bus routes.

Someone who is contentious seems to enjoy arguing and sometimes goes to great lengths to start a fight. Some legislative battles in Congress seem to be caused as much by contentious politicians as by the issues involved. The word *contentious* can also mean "likely to cause an argument." Reform of the health-care system, for instance, has been a very contentious issue.

distend \di-'stend\ To swell or become expanded.

• Television viewers were shocked to see the distended bellies of the young children, usually a sign of malnutrition and starvation.

Distend is generally used in medical or technical contexts, and it usually refers to swelling caused by pressure from within. A doctor examining a patient complaining of intestinal pain will look to see if the abdomen is distended. Hoses distend and straighten when water is pumped through them.

portend \pȯr-'tend\ (1) To give a sign or warning beforehand. (2) To indicate or signify.

● Although the warm spell in February was welcome, the huge puddles by the melting snowbanks portended the spring floods that were likely to follow.

Portend comes directly from the Latin verb *portendere,* meaning "to foretell or predict," both of which suggest a stretching out into the future. Predicting often involves interpreting signs and omens. When the Cubs lose on opening day at Wrigley Field it often portends another season of heartbreak for Chicago fans. *Portend* may be used for both favorable and unfavorable outcomes, but it usually indicates a threat of evil or disaster. Some foreign-policy experts saw that the breakup of the Soviet Union portended chaos and strife for many countries in Eastern Europe.

tendentious \ten-'den-shəs\ Leaning toward a particular point of view; biased.

● In his later years, the professor wrote a series of tendentious essays attacking many modern novelists and praising authors from earlier eras.

Political speeches can often be as tendentious as they are *contentious*. Politicians will adopt a particular philosophy, and from that day on they will tend to view matters from that point of view. Facts are replaced by tendentious claims, and debates become predictable and unproductive.

PEND/PENS, meaning "to hang, weigh, or cause to hang down," comes from the Latin verb *pendere*. We find it in English in words like *pensive*, meaning "thoughtful," and *appendix,* that useless and sometimes troublesome piece that hangs from the intestine.

---

appendage \ə-'pen-dij\ (1) Something joined on to a larger or more important body or thing. (2) A subordinate body part, such as an arm or a leg.

● Wives complain justifiably when they are treated by others as mere appendages of their husbands.

Appendage refers to an attachment that is less important than the thing to which it is attached. A controversial speaker, for instance, may add a few soothing remarks as an appendage to an otherwise fiery speech. Some appendages are important in their own right, but may not be viewed that way by some people. So residents of Staten Island don't like having their borough viewed as simply an appendage of New York City. And many Canadians fear that their U.S. neighbors view Canada, despite its size, as an appendage to the United States.

expend \ik-'spend\ (1) To pay out. (2) To use up.

● The company was taking steps to limit the funds it was expending on health-care costs and disability benefits.

Expend comes straight from the Latin word *expendere,* meaning "to weigh out" or "to spend." *Expend* is close in meaning to *spend,* but it is usually used more in reference to business, industry, finance, or government, and it therefore usually also implies larger sums of money. We have a deficit in this country because government expends more dollars than it collects. In its nonfinancial sense, *expend* suggests an unnecessary waste of something. The deficit may continue because more ink and paper are expended on stories of gossip and scandal than on the day-to-day operations of government.

propensity \prə-'pen-sə-tē\ An often intense natural inclination or preference.

● In-laws have a natural propensity to offer advice, especially when it hasn't been requested.

A propensity is a leaning toward something. We have a propensity for something when we have a natural tendency or are driven by a natural appetite. Good reporters have a propensity to ask questions; good politicians have a propensity for avoiding them. Small children have a propensity for getting sticky, and, for some reason, spilled food has a propensity for landing on new ties.

stipend \'stī-pənd\ A sum of money paid at regular intervals in return for services or to cover expenses.

● David's fellowship to graduate school included a stipend to cover his basic living expenses.

A stipend is a little like a salary, but there are differences. A stipend may be intended more to cover expenses than to pay for a service. A stipend may arrive weekly or annually, but the amount of money is usually small. Stipends are normally paid to people involved in noncommercial activities, such as scholars, artists, and amateur athletes. One very generous stipend is the one paid by the MacArthur Foundation, which often runs into the hundreds of thousands of dollars, with no strings attached. The only catch is that you need to be a genius to get one.

Quizzes

A. Complete the analogy:

1. calculate : count :: expend : _____
   a. stretch b. speculate c. pay d. explode
2. distort : warp :: distend : _____
   a. swell b. notice c. display d. shrink
3. abode : dwelling :: stipend : _____
   a. study b. salary c. mortgage d. advance
4. sensational : great :: tendentious : _____
   a. opinionated b. neutral c. important d. promotional
5. imaginary : unreal :: propensity : _____
   a. idea b. opinion c. inclination d. artistry
6. passionate : loving :: contentious : _____
   a. competitive b. continuous c. collected
   d. quarrelsome
7. laugh : giggle :: portend : _____
   a. bend b. indicate c. argue d. stretch
8. passage : opening :: appendage : _____
   a. hanger b. hangar c. limb d. branch

B. Fill in each blank with the correct letter:

a. contentious	e. appendage
b. distend	f. expend
c. tendentious	g. propensity
d. portend	h. stipend

1. These departments _____ the largest amount of money on new computers.
2. The bodies of snakes _____ as they eat their prey.

---

3. The eager assistant was willing to be seen as the necessary _____ to his boss.
4. Life with a disagreeable, _____ neighbor is not easy.
5. Her unusual talent and _____ for chess was obvious before she was five.
6. The senator made a highly _____ speech about U.S. involvement overseas.
7. As part of his scholarship, he received a small _____ to cover living expenses.
8. Those dark clouds rolling in _____ bad weather to come.

PAN comes from Greek with its spelling and meaning intact. It simply means "all" in Greek; as an English prefix it can also mean "completely," "whole," or "general." A *panoramic* view is a complete view in every direction. *Panchromatic* film is sensitive to the reflected light of all colors in the spectrum. *Pantheism* is the worship of all gods. A *pantheon* is a temple dedicated to all the gods of a particular religion. A *pandemic* outbreak of a disease may not literally affect the entire human population, but enough to create catastrophic problems.

---

panacea \pa-nə-'sē-ə\ A remedy for all ills or difficulties; cure-all.

• Educational reform is sometimes viewed as the panacea for all of society's problems.

Panacea combines *pan-* and the Greek word *akos,* "remedy." A panacea is a magical medicine that can cure whatever ails you, or a magical solution that can solve a whole set of problems. But since no such medicine or solution exists, the word *panacea* almost always occurs in contexts where the writer is criticizing a single solution to an array of problems ("There is no panacea for the problems of the inner city"). *Panacea* is also applied to easy solutions to individual problems, although this use loses the original "cure-all" sense of the word. In the view of its opponents, for example, the proposed legalization of street drugs is a panacea doomed to create far more problems than it would solve.

pandemonium \ˌpan-də-'mō-nē-əm\ A wild uproar or commotion.

• Pandemonium erupted in the football stadium as the underdogs scored an upset victory in the final seconds.

In *Paradise Lost,* the fallen Satan has his heralds proclaim "A solemn Councel forthwith to be held / At Pandaemonium, the high Capital / Of Satan and his Peers." John Milton got the name for his capital of hell from linking *pan* with the Latin word *daemonium,* "evil spirit," thus indicating the place where Satan gathered together all the demons. For later writers, *pandemonium* became a synonym for hell itself, since a traditional image of hell was of a place where noise and confusion abound. *Pandemonium* also came to be used of any wicked, lawless, or riotous place. But nowadays, it is used to refer to the uproar itself rather than the place where it occurs.

panegyric \ˌpa-nə-'jir-ik\ A formal speech or statement giving high praise to someone or something.

• Lincoln's "Gettysburg Address" is as much a panegyric celebrating American democratic ideals as it is a eulogy for the brave soldiers who died on the battlefield.

American presidents at their inaugurations typically deliver a panegyric in praise of their great nation and the people who have had the wisdom to elect them. Probably few of them have realized that in delivering their praise-filled speeches before a vast throng they have remained true to our cultural roots in ancient Greece. In Athens *panēgyris* was the name for a public assembly, the word coming from *pan-* plus *agyris,* "assembly." A chosen speaker would deliver a set oration in praise of those who had served the state. With time the Greek word *panēgyrikos* shifted from meaning "of or for a festival assembly" to "a praise-filled oration." Today a panegyric need not be a public speech—many panegyrics are private or written—but the word continues to suggest praise that is elaborate, highflown, and perhaps a bit excessive.

panoply \'pa-nə-plē\ (1) A magnificent or impressive array. (2) A display of all appropriate accessory items.

• The full panoply of a royal coronation was a thrilling sight for the throngs of sidewalk onlookers and the millions of television viewers.

Panoply originally referred to the full suit of armor donned by a soldier or knight in preparation for combat. In fact, *panoply* comes from a Greek word that includes the noun *hopla*, "arms or armor." *Panoply* may refer to full ceremonial dress of any kind or to something resembling a suit of armor in being protective. More commonly, *panoply* refers to striking spectacle: the breathtaking panoply of the autumn foliage, or the stirring panoply of a military parade, for example. Or it can mean an extensive array or succession of things, as in "The display windows of the electronics store feature the complete panoply of equipment that is now thought necessary for home entertainment."

EXTRA places words outside or beyond their usual or routine territory. *Extraterrestrial* and *extragalactic* affairs take place beyond the earth or the galaxy. Something *extravagant*, such as an *extravaganza*, goes beyond the limits of reason or necessity. And of course *extra* itself is a word, a shortening of *extraordinary*, "beyond the ordinary."

---

extramundane \ˌek-strə-ˌmən-ˈdān\ Situated in or relating to a region beyond the material world.

• Communism is atheistic, and admits no extramundane authority.

Extramundane uses an older meaning of *mundane*, "relating to this world" or "earthly." The events described in Dante's 14th-century *Divine Comedy*, where the author is taken on a tour through hell, purgatory, and heaven, are entirely extramundane. At the end of his journey, in the highest heaven, he has a vision of extramundane harmony and bliss, the reward of the blessed for their holy earthly lives. As you can see, when *extra-* is a prefix it never means "extremely" (as in "Go extra slow through here") but instead always means "outside or beyond."

extrapolate \ik-ˈstra-pə-ˌlāt\ To extend or project facts or data into an area not known in order to make assumptions or to predict facts or trends.

• Economists try to predict future buying trends by extrapolating from current economic data.

Scientists worry about the greenhouse effect because they have extrapolated the rate of carbon dioxide buildup and predicted that its effect on the atmosphere will become increasingly severe. On the basis of their *extrapolations,* they have urged governments and businesses to limit factory and automobile emissions, and have cautioned that the burning and clearing of the Amazon rain forest must stop. Other scientists, extrapolating from the same conditions, trends, and data, have concluded that the greenhouse effect is less dangerous than we have been led to believe. The problem is that by the time either extrapolation is proved to be true, we may be at a point where further damage cannot be prevented. Notice that it is acceptable to speak of extrapolating existing data (to produce new data), extrapolating *from* existing data (to produce new data), or extrapolating new data (from existing data)—in other words, it isn't easy to use this word wrong.

extrovert \'ek-strə-ˌvərt\ A person mainly concerned with things outside him- or herself; a sociable and outgoing person.

• A complete extrovert, she made friends easily and lived one day at a time.

Extrovert (sometimes spelled *extravert*) means basically "turned outward"—that is, toward things outside oneself. The opposite personality type is the *introvert,* which naturally means "turned inward." Some psychologists have said that the only personality traits that can be identified in newborn infants are shyness and lack of shyness, which are rather close to *introversion* and *extroversion.*

extraneous \ek-'strā-nē-əs\ (1) Existing or coming from the outside. (2) Not forming an essential part; irrelevant.

• Your essay should be well-focused and should not contain any extraneous material.

Homework is difficult enough with extraneous distractions: the television, the radio, phone calls, or a pesky brother or sister. The library may be a good place to study since librarians try to limit extraneous noise. But even under ideal conditions, you can still be diverted by extraneous thoughts: the weather conditions, what to have for dinner, or a really good joke you heard recently.

Quizzes

A. Fill in each blank with the correct letter:

a. extrapolate
b. panoply
c. extraneous
d. panacea
e. extramundane
f. panegyric
g. extrovert
h. pandemonium

1. From these figures, economists can _____ data that shows a steady increase in employment.
2. Being a natural _____, he took to his new career as a salesman easily.
3. The new voice-mail system, with its full _____ of options, impressed the whole staff.
4. _____ broke out at the news of the victory.
5. The pope's address stressed that concern with worldly things must not lead us to forget spiritual and _____ matters.
6. He locked himself in his studio to ensure that there would be no _____ distractions.
7. She had been thinking of vitamins as a _____, but they weren't able to fight off infections.
8. Then he launched into a _____ to his father, calling him brilliant, loving, and saintly.

B. Indicate whether the following pairs of terms have the same or different meanings:

1. panacea / antibiotic   same ___ / different ___
2. pandemonium / chaos   same ___ / different ___
3. panegyric / pep talk   same ___ / different ___
4. panoply / display   same ___ / different ___
5. extrapolate / project   same ___ / different ___
6. extraneous / necessary   same ___ / different ___
7. extramundane / very ordinary same ___ / different ___
8. extrovert / schizophrenic   same ___ / different ___

PHOS/PHOT comes from the Greek word for "light." *Phos* can be seen in the word *phosphorus*, which refers generally to anything that glows in the dark and also to a particular glowing chemical element. *Phot,* the more familiar root, appears in words like *photography,* which is the use of light to create an image on film or paper.

phosphorescent \‚fäs-fə-'re-sənt\ (1) Giving off a glow that continues after an energy source has stopped transmitting energy. (2) Giving off a glow over a period of time without producing noticeable heat.

• The boat's wake glittered in the night with phosphorescent sea creatures stirred up by its passing.

The waters of the Caribbean Sea are phosphorescent in some places and glow with beautiful glimmering twinkles at night. The effect is created by tiny marine organisms that give off light in the warm tropical seas. Some minerals are naturally phosphorescent as well, and new chemical combinations can produce long-lasting *phosphorescence* without heat. One popular use is in Halloween "torches" that can be carried safely by children in costume.

photogenic \‚fō-tə-'je-nik\ Very suitable for being photographed.

• Visitors to New England are often disappointed to find that the photogenic small towns with white churches and tidy houses are actually few and far between.

Photogenic originally meant "produced by light" or "producing light" and was used mostly in scientific or technical contexts. During the 20th century *photogenic* developed its now most common sense, perhaps because the original technical meaning was simply ignored. So now we use *photogenic* to describe scenery, baby animals, and presidential candidates.

photon \'fō-‚tän\ A tiny particle or bundle of radiant energy.

• The idea that light consists of photons is difficult until you begin to think of a ray of light as being caused by a stream of very small particles.

It was Albert Einstein who first theorized that the energy in a light beam exists in small bits or particles called photons, and scientists now realize that light sometimes behaves like a wave (somewhat like sound or water) and sometimes like a stream of particles. The amazing power of lasers is the result of a concentration of photons that have been made to travel together in order to hit their target at the same time.

photosynthesis \ˌfō-tō-ˈsin-thə-sis\ The process by which green plants use light to produce organic matter from carbon dioxide and water.

● Sagebrush survives in harsh climates because it is capable of carrying on photosynthesis at very low temperatures.

The Greek roots of *photosynthesis* combine to produce the basic meaning "to put together with the help of light." Sunlight splits the water molecules held in a plant's leaves and releases the oxygen in them into the air. (Photosynthesis is what first produced oxygen in the atmosphere billions of years ago, and it is still what keeps it there.) What is left over combines with carbon dioxide to produce carbohydrates, which the plant uses as food.

LUC comes from the Latin noun *lux,* "light," and the verb *lucere,* "to shine or glitter." *Lucid* prose is clear in meaning, as if light were shining through it. *Lucifer,* a name for the devil, means "Light-bearer," the name he had before he fell from heaven.

---

elucidate \i-ˈlü-sə-ˌdāt\ To clarify by explaining; explain.

● A good doctor should always be willing to elucidate any medical jargon he or she uses.

Elucidate means "to shed light on." When you elucidate, you make transparent or clear something that was formerly murky or confusing. Carl Sagan, the astrophysicist, has a gift for elucidating to a large audience information about the objects in the universe. Through his *lucid* explanations he has made clear how stars are born and die, how the universe may have begun, and much more.

lucent \ˈlü-sənt\ (1) Giving off light. (2) Easily seen through.

• Their romance began under a lucent moon on a Mediterranean island.

Lucent is most often used in poetry or literature, where its meaning is usually close to that of *luminous*. The lucent petals of buttercups are one of the joys of a bright summer's day. Brightly polished stones have a lucent appearance. And we may even admire the lucent performance of a gifted musician.

lucubration \ˌlü-kyů-'brā-shən\ (1) Hard and difficult study. (2) The product of such study.

• By the end of the semester our professor admitted that he wasn't looking forward to reading through any more of our lucubrations on novels that no one enjoyed.

Lucubration came to mean ''hard study'' because it originally meant study done by lamplight, which in a world without electric lights was likely to be hard work. Abe Lincoln is known for having engaged in lucubration of this sort. The word has a literary feel to it and is often used with a touch of sarcasm.

translucent \tranz-'lü-sənt\ Partly transparent; allowing light to pass through but diffusing it so that objects beyond cannot be seen clearly.

• Architects have recently used industrial glass bricks in designing buildings because their translucent quality gives light but guards privacy.

Frosted glass is probably the most familiar translucent material. Stained glass is also translucent. Some red wines prove to be translucent when poured into a crystal goblet and held before a candle in a dark corner of a quiet restaurant.

Quizzes

A. **Indicate whether the following pairs have the same or different meanings:**

1. photogenic / glittering   same ___ / different ___
2. lucent / flashing   same ___ / different ___
3. photon / light particle   same ___ / different ___
4. translucent / beaming   same ___ / different ___

5.	phosphorescent / pulsing	same ___ / different ___
6.	lucubration / vacation	same ___ / different ___
7.	photosynthesis / twinkling	same ___ / different ___
8.	elucidate / explain	same ___ / different ___

B. Match the definition on the left to the correct word on the right:

1.	glowing	a.	lucubration
2.	production of organic matter	b.	phosphorescent
		c.	translucent
3.	clarify	d.	elucidate
4.	passing diffused light	e.	photogenic
5.	elemental particle	f.	photosynthesis
6.	brightly clear	g.	photon
7.	hard study	h.	lucent
8.	visually appealing		

MOR/MORT comes from the Latin *mori*, "to die," and *mort-*, the stem of *mors*, meaning "death." A *mortuary* is a place where dead bodies are kept until burial. A *postmortem* examination is one conducted on a recently dead body. And a *memento mori* (a Latin phrase meaning literally "Remember that you must die") is a reminder of death; the death's head carved onto an old gravestone is an example.

immortality \,i-,mȯr-'ta-lə-tē\ (1) Deathless or unending existence. (2) Lasting fame.

● Michelangelo achieved immortality with his painting and sculpture, Beethoven with his music.

Most of the world's religions deal with the issue of immortality and give advice on how to achieve it. For Achilles and the Greek heroes, immortality and *mortality* existed side by side: the *mortal* bodies of heroes died, but their *immortal* fame lived on in song and story.

moribund \'mȯr-ə-bənd\ (1) In the process of dying or approaching death. (2) Inactive or becoming outmoded.

• Many economists believe that America must replace its moribund smokestack industries with businesses based on new technology.

Moribund can be used in its original literal sense of "approaching death." Doctors will speak of a moribund patient going into a coma or a deep stupor. But *moribund* is much more commonly used to refer to things. When the economy goes bad, we hear about moribund mills and factories and towns, and the economy itself may be called moribund. People who worry about culture will speak of the moribund state of poetry or the moribund film industry—which may just mean they haven't seen a good movie lately.

mortician \mȯr-'ti-shən\ A person who prepares the dead for burial or cremation and manages the funeral.

• Every town needs a mortician, but the job only seems popular at Halloween.

Modern morticians employ skills somewhat different from those of Egyptian times. In ancient Egypt, morticians removed the organs and placed them in ornamental jars, drained the blood, and set the dead body in a solution to dry it out. The body was then wrapped in linen and placed in a mummy case, which was in turn placed in a tomb. The Great Pyramids were the most magnificent of the Egyptian tombs.

mortify \'mȯr-tə-,fī\ (1) To subdue or deaden (the body) especially by self-discipline or self-inflicted pain. (2) To embarrass greatly; humiliate.

• Teenagers are often mortified by their parents' attempts to act youthful.

Mortify once meant "put to death," but no longer. The "subdue or deaden" sense of *mortify* is most familiar to us in the phrase "mortifying the flesh," which refers to an old custom once followed by devout Christians, who would starve themselves, deprive themselves of every comfort, and even whip themselves in order to subdue their bodily desires. But the most common use of *mortify* today is the "humiliate" sense, and its connection with death is still apparent when we speak of "dying of embarrassment."

NEC/NIC/NOX, from the Latin verb *necare* and the noun *noxa*, have to do with killing or slaying. These roots are related to the Greek *nekros*, "corpse," found in such words as *necrology*, "a list of the recently dead," and *necromancy*, "the art of conjuring up spirits of the dead."

internecine \‚in-tər-'ne-‚sēn\ (1) Deadly; mutually destructive. (2) Involving conflict within a group.

• The downfall of the radical political group came as it succumbed to internecine struggles for power and influence.

The Latin word *internecinus* meant "to the death." An internecine battle, then, was simply a very bloody one. Over the years, the English word developed the sense of "mutually destructive." And during the 20th century the word developed its main meaning of "conflict within a group." So now internecine warfare seldom refers to bloody battles but instead to the internal bickering and fighting that go on within a political party, government, profession, or family.

necrosis \ne-'krō-səs\ The usually localized death of living tissue.

• One danger for young athletes is that prolonged use of some pain medications can cause necrosis in the kidney.

Many kinds of injuries and ailments can cause the death of bodily tissue. A heart attack can cause necrosis of heart tissue, and one stage in appendicitis is necrosis of the appendix. Cirrhosis and hepatitis can cause the liver to become *necrotic,* and other kinds of diseases can cause necrotic gallbladders, corneas, or intestines. Infections resulting from injuries can create necrotic tissue that may have to be surgically removed in order for the injury to heal.

noxious \'näk-shəs\ Harmful to or destructive of living things.

• The bombing of the World Trade Center caused noxious fumes and smoke to spread through the structure and cause injury to hundreds of people.

The Environmental Protection Agency regulates the disposal of noxious chemicals or wastes that would harm the environment or the creatures living in it. Such noxious residues of modern technological processes are proving harder and harder to get rid of safely. No one wants them nearby, and a way of making them disappear has simply not been found. The meaning of *noxious* is sometimes close to *obnoxious*, though it's not so often applied to people.

pernicious \pər-'ni-shəs\ Extremely harmful or destructive.

● The debate goes on about whether censorship or pornography has the more pernicious effect on society.

Pernicious usually implies serious harm done by an evil or corrupting force. Violence on television may have a pernicious influence on children. Welfare is seen as a pernicious institution by those who believe it discourages individual initiative. And AIDS is rightly referred to as a pernicious disease.

Quizzes

A. Complete the analogy:

1. immortality : _____ :: heaven : hell
    a. eternity b. god c. death d. life
2. necrosis : _____ :: disease : sickness
    a. medicine b. cure c. damage d. prescription
3. mortician : _____ :: physician : doctor
    a. grave digger b. gardener c. underwear
    d. undertaker
4. internecine : _____ :: international : domestic
    a. external b. extracurricular c. extroverted
    d. extraordinary
5. mortify : _____ :: appeal : request
    a. paralyze b. humiliate c. embalm d. slay
6. noxious : _____ :: successful : failing
    a. noisy b. beautiful c. beneficial d. noticeable
7. moribund : _____ :: cautious : fearful
    a. concerned b. obstinate c. grim d. obsolete
8. pernicious : _____ :: fruitful : productive
    a. healthful b. particular c. deadly d. demanding

B. Fill in each blank with the correct letter:

a. pernicious
b. internecine
c. necrosis
d. noxious

e. moribund
f. mortify
g. immortality
h. mortician

1. As the textile industry moved south, mill towns in New England became _____.

2. When fire broke out in the hallway, _____ fumes from the burning carpet filled every room.

3. Achilles chose _____ in legend over a long, happy life.

4. The police turned the body over to a _____ when they had finished their examination.

5. The doctor said he had to stop drinking to avoid further _____ of the liver.

6. Some religious zealots still engage in acts designed to _____ the flesh.

7. The _____ effects of a teacher's constant criticism may show in her students' unwillingness to volunteer in class.

8. The wise leader guarded against _____ conflict by providing many opportunities for cooperation among his followers.

Words from Mythology and History

aeolian harp \ē-'ō-lē-ən-'härp\ A box with strings that produce musical sounds when wind blows on them.

● Poets have long been fascinated by the aeolian harp because it is an instrument that produces music without a human performer.

Aeolus was the king or guardian of the winds, according to the ancient Greeks. He lived in a cave with his many, many sons and daughters, and sent forth whatever wind Zeus asked for. When Odysseus stopped there on his way home from Troy, he received a bag of winds to fill his sails. His men, however, opened the bag and released them all while he was asleep, and the raging winds blew them all the way back to their starting point. An aeolian harp produces enchanting harmonies when the wind passes over it. According to Homer, it was the god Hermes who invented the harp, by having the wind blow over the dried sinews attached to a tortoise shell.

cynosure \\'sī-nə-ˌshûr\\ (1) A guide. (2) A center of attention.

• Whenever the latest hot young rock star enters the nightclub, he becomes the cynosure of the assembled crowd.

Cynosure means "dog's tail" in Greek and Latin. In those languages it was the name for the constellation Ursa Minor, or the Little Bear, whose tail is formed by the North Star. The North Star has always been a trusty guide for travelers, especially sailors, because unlike the other stars, it always remains in the same position in the northern sky. So cynosure came to mean both "guide" and "center of attention."

laconic \\lə-'kä-nik\\ Using extremely few words.

• Male movie stars usually don't have a lot of dialogue to learn because most scripts seem to call for laconic leading men who avoid conversation.

Ancient Sparta was located in the region known as Laconia. The disciplined and militaristic Spartans were known for using no more words than they had to. So this terse, abrupt way of speaking became known as *laconic* after them and their territory.

mnemonic \\ni-'mä-nik\\ Having to do with the memory; assisting the memory.

• Sales-training courses recommend mnemonic devices as a way of remembering peoples' names.

The Greek word for memory is *mnemosyne*; something that helps the memory is therefore a mnemonic aid. Such snappy mnemonic devices as KISS (Keep It Simple, Stupid) or Every Good Boy Does Fine (for the notes on the lines of a musical staff with a treble clef) help to recall simple rules or complicated series that might otherwise slip away.

platonic \\plə-'tä-nik\\ (1) Relating to the philosopher Plato or his teachings. (2) Involving a close relationship from which romance and sex are absent.

• The male and female leads in many situation comedies keep their relationship platonic for the first few seasons, but romance almost always wins out in the end.

The philosopher Plato taught that all objects here on earth are pale imitations of their ideal form, just as a shadow is a weak imitation of the real object or a painting fails to capture true reality. This true form has come to be called the "platonic form." Plato presented his theories in a series of dramatic conversations between the philosopher Socrates and other people, which became known as the "Platonic dialogues." Because these philosophers and their students were all male, and because Socrates in the dialogues sometimes goes to great lengths to avoid committing homosexual acts, despite his desires, close but nonsexual friendship between two people who might be thought to be romantically attracted to each other is today known as platonic love or friendship.

sapphic \'sa-fik\ (1) Lesbian. (2) Relating to a poetic verse pattern associated with Sappho.

● The Roman poets Catullus and Horace composed wonderful love poems in sapphic verse.

Sappho wrote poems of passion and self-reflection, some of them directed to the women attending the school she conducted on the Greek island of Lesbos around 600 B.C. The poems were written in an original rhythmical pattern, which has become known as sapphic verse. The island of Lesbos also gave its name to lesbianism, which is sometimes called sapphic love.

Socratic \sō-'kra-tik\ Having to do with the philosopher Socrates or with his teaching method, in which he systematically questioned the student in conversation in order to draw forth truths.

● The professor fascinated some students but annoyed others with her Socratic method of teaching, which required them to listen, think, and participate in class.

Socrates lived in Greece in the 5th century B.C. He left no writings behind, so all that we know of him is through the writings of his disciple Plato. Today he is most remembered for his method of teaching by asking questions. His name survives in terms such as *Socratic induction,* which is a method of gradually arriving at generalizations through a process of questions and answers, and *Socratic irony,* in which the teacher pretends ignorance, but questions his students skillfully to make them aware of their errors in understanding.

solecism \'sō-lə-ˌsi-zəm\ (1) A grammatical mistake in speaking or writing. (2) A blunder in etiquette or proper behavior.

● The poor boy committed his first solecism immediately on entering by tracking mud over the Persian rug in the dining room.

In ancient Asia Minor, there was a city called Soloi where the inhabitants spoke Greek that was full of grammatical errors. Any lapse in grammar or in formal social behavior has hence come to be known as a solecism. Such things as saying "ain't" or "they was" or using the hostess's best bath towel to dry off the dog are solecisms. The earth won't shatter from such acts, but sometimes a few nerves will.

Quiz

Fill in each blank with the correct letter:

a. solecism   e. cynosure
b. sapphic   f. aeolian harp
c. platonic   g. mnemonic
d. Socratic   h. laconic

1. The teacher quickly learned the students' names by using her own _____ devices.
2. We all were fascinated as breezes raised a tune from the _____.
3. New Yorkers tend to think of their city as the _____ of the nation.
4. The _____ method is inappropriate for normal courtroom interrogation.
5. After encountering the fifth _____ in the report, we began to lose faith in the writer.
6. Her father-in-law was _____ in her presence but extremely talkative around his son.
7. She knew he loved her when a love poem in _____ verse appeared on her desk.
8. The dinner was good, but saying that it approached the _____ ideal of a meal was probably too much.

Review Quizzes

A. Choose the correct antonym *and* the correct synonym

1. elucidate   a. confuse b. count c. clarify d. describe
2. contentious   a. continental b. quarrelsome
    c. conscious d. agreeable
3. solecism   a. correctness b. love poem c. death wish
    d. error
4. noxious   a. harmful b. beneficial c. intrusive
    d. annoying
5. pernicious   a. dangerous b. large c. gentle
    d. impressive
6. laconic   a. glad b. quiet c. beneficial d. talkative
7. moribund   a. obsolete b. sashed c. delay d. healthy
8. distend   a. shrink b. swell c. seek d. hold
9. immortality   a. eternal damnation b. eternal flame
    c. eternal life d. eternal death
10. tendentious   a. opinionated b. suitable c. common
    d. objective

B. Indicate whether the following pairs of words have the same or different meanings:

1. mnemonic / ideal   same ___ / different ___
2. necrosis / infection   same ___ / different ___
3. extrapolate / project   same ___ / different ___
4. mortify / stiffen   same ___ / different ___
5. appendage / attachment   same ___ / different ___
6. cynosure / beacon   same ___ / different ___
7. pernicious / destructive   same ___ / different ___
8. propensity / projectile   same ___ / different ___
9. mortician / philosopher   same ___ / different ___
10. lucent / glittering   same ___ / different ___
11. phosphorescent / sea green same ___ / different ___
12. translucent / cross-lighted same ___ / different ___
13. solecism / goof   same ___ / different ___
14. elucidate / explain   same ___ / different ___
15. distend / swell   same ___ / different ___
16. lucubration / nightmare   same ___ / different ___
17. photosynthesis / reproduction same ___ / different ___

18. panacea / remedy	same ___ / different ___
19. photogenic / appealing	same ___ / different ___
20. internecine / impassioned	same ___ / different ___

C. Match the definition on the left to the correct word on the right:

1.	question-and-answer	a.	contentious
2.	elementary particle of light	b.	expend
		c.	sapphic
3.	allowance	d.	portend
4.	use up	e.	translucent
5.	argumentative	f.	platonic
6.	nonsexual	g.	photon
7.	foretell	h.	Socratic
8.	dying	i.	stipend
9.	lesbian	j.	moribund
10.	light-diffusing		

Unit 9

HER/HES, from the Latin verb *haerere*, means "to stick" or "to get stuck." This has produced words with two kinds of meaning. A word such as *adhesive* means basically "sticking," whereas a word such as *hesitate* means more or less "stuck in one place."

adherent \ad-'hir-ənt\ (1) Someone who follows a leader, a party, or a profession. (2) One who believes in a particular philosophy or religion.

● The general's adherents heavily outnumbered his opponents and managed to shout them down repeatedly.

A plan for cutting the deficit without raising taxes or reducing spending will usually attract adherents easily. In the 1992 presidential elections, Ross Perot inspired an army of enthusiastic adherents, more than any third-party candidate in U.S. history.

cohesion \kō-'hē-zhən\ The act or state of sticking together.

● Successful athletic teams usually achieve their victories through tight cohesion among the players.

Cohesion, which contains the prefix *co-*, "together," generally refers to similar things sticking together. *Adhesion*, on the other hand, usually means sticking to something of a different kind, in the way that *adhesive* tape or an *adherent* does. So a company may desire to create cohesion among its employees, and psychologists may seek to promote *cohesive* family units.

incoherent \ˌin-kō-'hir-ənt\ (1) Unclear or difficult to understand. (2) Loosely organized or inconsistent.

- She was tired of her boss's angry lectures, which usually turned into incoherent ranting and raving.

Incoherent is the opposite of *coherent,* and both commonly refer to words and thought. Just as *coherent* means well-ordered and clear, *incoherent* means disordered and hard to follow. *Incoherence* in speech may result from emotional stress, especially anxiety or anger. Incoherence in writing may simply result from poor planning; a twelve-page term paper that isn't written until the night before it is due will almost certainly suffer from incoherence.

inherent \in-'hir-ənt\ Part of something by nature or habit.

- A guiding belief behind our Constitution is that individuals have certain inherent rights that ought to be protected from governmental interference.

Inherent literally refers to something that "sticks in" or is "stuck in" something else. A plan may have an inherent flaw that will cause it to fail; a person may have inherent virtues that will bring him or her love and respect. Something inherent cannot be removed: the plan with inherent flaws may simply have to be thrown out, but the person with inherent virtues will never lose them.

FUG comes from the Latin verb *fugere,* meaning "to flee or escape." A *refugee* flees from some threat or danger to a *refuge,* which is a place that provides shelter and safety.

---

centrifugal \sen-'tri-fyü-gəl\ Moving outward from a center or central focus.

- Their favorite ride was the Round-up, in which centrifugal force flattened them against the outer wall of a rapidly spinning cage.

Part of an astronaut's training occurs in a *centrifuge,* a spinning machine that generates force equal to several times the force of gravity. The force sends the astronaut away from the machine's center; his or her sense of direction and balance as well as muscular strength thus become used to some of the centrifugal forces that will be at work during a real space mission.

fugitive \\'fyü-jə-tiv\\ A person who flees or tries to escape.

● The United States sometimes makes special allowances for refugees who are fugitives from persecution in their homelands.

The young outlaws Bonnie Parker and Clyde Barrow were high-spirited fugitives from justice for two years in the Depression era, fleeing and robbing banks across the Southwest, barely escaping the long arm of the law. Fugitives with Robin Hood-like style and glamour have always attracted interest and sympathy, especially from the poor.

fugue \\'fyüg\\ A musical form in which a theme is echoed and imitated by voices or instruments that enter one after another and interweave as the piece proceeds.

● For his debut on the new organ, the church organist chose a fugue by J. S. Bach.

Bach and Handel composed many fugues for harpsichord and organ in which the various parts (or voices) seem to flee from and chase each other in an intricate dance. Each part, after it has stated the theme or melody, apparently flees from the next part, which takes up the same theme and sets off in pursuit. Somewhat the same effect can be had by singing a round such as "Three Blind Mice" or "Row, Row, Row Your Boat."

subterfuge \\'səb-tər-ˌfyüj\\ (1) A trick designed to help conceal, escape, or evade. (2) A deceptive trick.

● The students employed every kind of subterfuge they knew to keep the substitute teacher from assigning homework.

Subterfuge contains the prefix *subter-* (related to *sub-*), meaning "under" or "secretly," so a subterfuge is something done secretly or "under the table." The spies depicted in John LeCarré's novels employ all kinds of subterfuge to accomplish their missions. The life of a spy sometimes seems appealing, but few of us have much experience with subterfuges more elaborate than claiming to have a previous engagement in order to avoid having dinner with our relatives.

Quizzes

A. Fill in each blank with the correct letter:

a. cohesion   e. centrifugal
b. fugitive   f. adherent
c. incoherent   g. subterfuge
d. fugue   h. inherent

1. The first-year students were sent off on a camping trip to create a greater sense of _____ within the class.
2. By _____ they had managed to infiltrate the enemy ranks and blow up the bridge.
3. The Christian Scientist philosophy of Mary Baker Eddy continued to attract many an _____.
4. Federal agents were pleased to have apprehended the _____.
5. By the time his fever reached 105°, the boy was mumbling _____ sentences.
6. A rock tied to a string and whirled about exerts _____ force on the string.
7. Mahatma Gandhi believed goodness was _____ in humans.
8. They chose a grand _____ by Bach as their wedding march.

B. Choose the closest definition:

1. inherent   a. part of b. inherited c. confused d. loyal
2. fugue   a. mathematical formula b. musical form
   c. marginal figure d. masonry foundation
3. adherent   a. sticker b. stinker c. follower d. flower
4. centrifugal   a. moving upward b. moving backward
   c. moving downward d. moving outward
5. cohesion   a. unity b. thoughtfulness c. uniformity
   d. thoughtlessness
6. subterfuge   a. overhead serve b. underhanded plot
   c. powerful force d. secret supporter
7. incoherent   a. attached b. constant c. controlled
   d. confused
8. fugitive   a. traveler b. sailor c. escapee d. drifter

COSM, from the Greek word meaning both "ornament" and "order," gives us two different groups of words. *Cosmetics* are the stuff we use to ornament our faces. The "order" meaning combines with the Greek belief that the universe was an orderly place, so words in this group relate to the universe and the worlds within it. *Cosmonaut,* for instance, is the word for a space traveler from the former Soviet Union.

cosmetic \käz-'me-tik\ Done or made for the sake of beauty or appearance.

• Renovating the house would involve more than just cosmetic changes such as fresh paint and new curtains.

Constant exposure to modern standards of beauty through advertisements prompts more and more people to make cosmetic changes in their appearance: a straightened nose, a lifted face, a tucked tummy. The cosmetic surgery that people undergo to achieve their new look does nothing to improve their underlying state of health. In fact, another meaning of *cosmetic* is "lacking substance, superficial." A company accused of corrupt practices may try to improve its image by making cosmetic changes, such as issuing idealistic policy statements or replacing a few guilty-looking executives.

cosmology \käz-'mä-lə-jē\ (1) A theory that describes the nature of the universe. (2) A branch of astronomy that deals with the origin and structure of the universe.

• Many New Age philosophies propose a cosmology that differs greatly from the traditional Jewish, Christian, or Islamic ways of viewing the universe.

Most religions and cultures include some kind of cosmology to explain the nature of the universe. In modern astronomy, the leading cosmology is still the Big Bang theory, which claims that the universe began with a huge explosion that sent matter and energy spreading out in all directions. One of the reasons fans watch "Star Trek" is for the various cosmologies depicted in the show, such as different conceptions of space, time, and the meaning of life.

cosmopolitan \käz-mə-'pä-lə-tən\ (1) Having international sophistication and experience. (2) Made up of persons, elements, or influences from many different parts of the world.

● New York, like most cosmopolitan cities, offers a wonderful array of restaurants featuring cooking styles from around the world.

Cosmopolitan includes the root *polit-*, meaning "citizen"; thus, someone who is cosmopolitan is a "citizen of the world." She may be able to read the morning paper in Rio de Janeiro and attend a lecture in Madrid with equal ease. And a city or a country that is cosmopolitan has aspects and elements that come from various countries.

cosmos \'käz-ˌmōs\ (1) The universe, especially when it is viewed as orderly and systematic. (2) Any orderly system that is complete in itself.

● The biologist, the philosopher, and the astronomer all try in their own ways to understand the mysteries of the cosmos.

In some of its uses, *cosmos* simply means "universe." So we can say that the invention of the telescope helped us learn more about our cosmos. But usually *cosmos* is used to suggest an orderly or harmonious universe. Thus it may be the philosopher, or even the religious mystic, that helps put us in touch with the cosmos. In a similar way, *cosmic* rays come from outer space, but cosmic questions come from human attempts to find order in the universe.

SCI comes from the Latin verb *scire*, "to know" or "to understand." This root appears in the word *science*, which refers to factual knowledge, and in *conscience*, which refers to moral knowledge. And to be *conscious* is to be in a state where you are able to know or understand.

---

conscientious \ˌkän-chē-'en-chəs\ (1) Governed by morality; scrupulous. (2) Resulting from painstaking or exact attention.

● New employees should be especially conscientious about turning in all of their assignments on time.

Conscience and *conscientious* both come from a Latin verb meaning "to be aware of guilt." A conscientious person is one with a strong moral sense and one who has feelings of guilt when he or she violates it. *Conscientious* indicates extreme care, either in observing moral laws or in performing assigned duties. A conscientious public official has a moral code that is not easily broken. A conscientious worker has a sense of duty that forces him or her to do a careful job. A conscientious report shows painstaking work on the part of the writer.

omniscience \äm-'ni-shəns\ Infinite awareness, understanding, and insight.

● It was comforting to believe in the omniscience of a Supreme Being, and it kept him on his best behavior.

Omniscience includes another root, *omni-*, from a Latin word meaning "all," and literally means "knowing all." Omniscience is usually only possible for a god or supernatural being. However, the narrator in many novels is *omniscient*—able to see everything that is happening, no matter where or when, and able to know and understand everything going on in the minds of all the characters. For ordinary mortals such omniscience may sound attractive but would probably actually be quite a burden.

prescient \'pre-shənt\ Having or showing advance knowledge of what is going to happen.

● For years she had read *The Wall Street Journal* every morning in hopes of finding prescient warnings about future crashes, crises, and catastrophes.

Like being omniscient, being truly prescient would require supernatural powers. But well-informed people may have such good judgment as to appear prescient, and *prescient* is often used to mean "having good foresight." U.S. presidents hope to have prescient advisers or, at least once in a while, to receive a prescient analysis of world and domestic affairs. Some newspaper columnists appear to be prescient in their predictions, but we may suspect that leaks rather than *prescience* are the secret.

unconscionable \ən-'kän-chə-nə-bəl\ (1) Not guided by any moral sense; unscrupulous. (2) Shockingly excessive, unreasonable, or unfair.

● The used-car dealer was convicted of rolling back odometers and other unconscionable business practices.

The word *unconscionable* comes from *conscience.* An unconscionable person is one whose conduct is not guided by conscience. Unconscionable acts are immoral. Unconscionable things are those that cannot be tolerated in good conscience. The owner of a new house may not expect perfection, but if it has an unconscionable number of defects, it's a lemon.

Quizzes

A. Complete the analogy:

1. present : absent :: prescient : _____
   a. evil b. blind c. far-sighted d. painstaking

2. cosmic : universal :: cosmetic : _____
   a. decorative b. organized c. planetary d. starred

3. bold : shy :: cosmopolitan : _____
   a. planetary b. naive c. unique d. nearby

4. shining : glowing :: conscientious : _____
   a. careful b. all-seeing c. well-informed d. scientific

5. description : illustration :: cosmology : _____
   a. sophistication b. universe c. explanation
   d. appearance

6. truth : fiction :: omniscience : _____
   a. morality b. ignorance c. foresight d. worldliness

7. woods : forest :: cosmos : _____
   a. stars b. planets c. orbits d. universe

8. solid : liquid :: unconscionable : _____
   a. orderly b. attractive c. universal d. moral

B. Match the definition on the right to the correct word on the left:

1. cosmopolitan   a. having foresight
2. omniscience   b. universe
3. cosmetic   c. universal knowledge
4. conscientious   d. sophisticated
5. unconscionable   e. for the sake of appearance
6. cosmology   f. scrupulous
7. prescient   g. inexcusable
8. cosmos   h. description of the universe

JUNCT, from the Latin verb *jungere*, means "join." A *junction* is a place where things come together. A *conjunction* is a word (such as *and* or *or*) that joins two other words or groups of words: "this *and* that," "to be *or* not to be."

adjunct \'a-ˌjəŋkt\ Something joined or added to another thing of which it is not a part.

● The technical school promised formal classroom instruction that would be a valuable adjunct to the on-the-job training and experience.

The roots of *adjunct*, which includes the prefix *ad-*, meaning "to or toward," imply that one thing is "joined to" another. A car wash may be operated as an adjunct to a gas station. Teachers often take on advising students as an adjunct to their regular classroom duties. And anyone truly interested in expanding his or her vocabulary will find that daily reading of a newspaper or magazine is a valuable adjunct to studying this book.

disjunction \dis-'jəŋk-shən\ A break, separation, or sharp difference between two things.

● The best English teachers see no disjunction between theory and practice when it comes to good writing.

A disjunction is often simply a lack of connection between two things. For example, there is frequently a disjunction between what people expect from computers and what they actually know about them. Sometimes this takes the form of an abrupt break. In this sense, Ronald Reagan's policies seemed to represent a disjunction with the politics of the previous twenty years. And sometimes *disjunction* is used to suggest that two things are very different in some important way, and so we speak of a disjunction between science and morality, between doing and telling, or between knowing and explaining.

injunction \in-'jəŋk-shən\ (1) A warning, direction, or prohibition regarding an activity. (2) A court order commanding or forbidding the doing of some act.

• Her new fitness program included no injunctions against drinking beer and wine, she was glad to see.

Injunctions can either require or forbid something. "Eat your vegetables" and "Drive safely" are orders to do something. But injunctions are more frequently prohibitions. For instance, some English teachers uphold the injunction against beginning a sentence with "and." Similarly, legal injunctions can command or forbid; an injunction may require that a contract be honored, or may forbid a strike from taking place.

junta \'hùn-tə\ A committee that controls a government, especially after a revolution.

• Hopes for democratic reforms ended when the military junta took power and closed down the country's major newspaper.

The Latin root is a little hard to see in this word, because it comes into English through Spanish. Though we may think of a junta as a group that seizes power illegally, the word basically refers to the joining together of the group; in fact, the oldest meaning of *junta* is "a council or committee for political or governmental purposes." But today it generally means a close-knit group of people who dominate a government after seizing power in a revolution. Given the way juntas come to power, it should be no surprise that most are made up of military officers and few are overly concerned with protecting human rights.

PART, from the Latin word *pars*, meaning "part," comes into English most obviously in our word *part* but also in words like *apartment, compartment*, and *particle*, all of which are parts of a larger whole.

---

impart \im-'pärt\ (1) To give from one's store or abundance. (2) To make known; disclose.

• As a dedicated teacher, her primary goal was always to impart knowledge.

When we impart something, we give a piece of it, sometimes a big piece. The yellow corn in chicken feed imparts the yellow color to chickens that eat it. A speaker's manner of delivery can impart authority to what he or she says. To impart is also to say or communicate: "He finally decided to impart his plans to his family"; "She imparted her displeasure regarding absences to her staff in no uncertain terms."

impartial \im-'pär-shəl\ Fair and not biased; treating or affecting all equally.

• Representatives of labor and management agreed to have the matter decided by an impartial third party.

To be partial toward someone or something is to be somewhat biased or prejudiced, which means that a person who is partial really only sees part of the whole picture. To be impartial is the opposite of this. The United Nations sends impartial observers to monitor elections in troubled countries. We hope that juries will be impartial when they render verdicts. Grandparents, on the other hand, are not expected to be impartial when describing the good looks of a new grandchild.

participle \'pär-tə-,si-pəl\ A word that is formed from a verb but used like an adjective.

• "Crying" in the phrase "the crying child" is a present participle; "guaranteed" in "satisfaction guaranteed" is a past participle.

English verbs can take several basic forms, which we call their principal parts: the infinitive ("to move," "to speak"), the past tense ("moved," "spoke"), the past participle ("moved," "spoken"), and the present participle ("moving," "speaking"). Past and present participles act like adjectives since they can modify nouns ("the spoken word," "a moving experience"). A grammatical error called a *dangling participle* occurs when a sentence begins with a participle that doesn't modify the subject. In the sentence "Climbing the mountain, the cabin came in view," "climbing" is a dangling participle since it doesn't modify "cabin."

partisan \'pär-tə-zən\ (1) A person who is strongly devoted to a particular cause or group. (2) A guerrilla fighter.

• The retiring Supreme Court justice was an unashamed partisan of the cause of free speech.

A partisan is one who supports one *part* or *party*. Sometimes the support takes the form of military action, as when guerrilla fighters engage in harassing government forces. *Partisan* can also be used as an adjective. In some families, the World Series can arouse partisan passions; most frequently, however, *partisan* refers to support of a political party, as in the phrase "partisan politics."

Quizzes

A. Choose the closest definition:

1. injunction   a. order b. position c. fact d. connection
2. impartial   a. fair b. biased c. accurate d. opinionated
3. adjunct   a. warning b. addition c. disclosure
      d. difference
4. participle   a. verb part b. warning c. supplement
      d. guerrilla fighter
5. junta   a. dance b. point c. group d. symphony
6. impart   a. separate b. support c. favor d. disclose
7. disjunction   a. prohibition b. break c. requirement
      d. intersection
8. partisan   a. judge b. teacher c. supporter d. leader

B. Indicate whether the following pairs of words have the same or different meanings:

1. impart / give   same __ / different __
2. junta / guerrilla   same __ / different __
3. participle / verb part   same __ / different __
4. impartial / supportive   same __ / different __
5. adjunct / supplement   same __ / different __
6. injunction / warning   same __ / different __
7. partisan / fighter   same __ / different __
8. disjunction / connection   same __ / different __

MIT/MIS, from the Latin verb *mittere*, "to send," appears in such English words as *missionary*, *missile*, and *emit*. A missionary is sent out to convert others to a new faith; a missile is sent to explode on some far spot; and to emit is to send something out.

emissary \'e-mə-ˌser-ē\ Someone sent out to represent another; an agent.

• The senior diplomat had served as a presidential emissary to many troubled regions of the world.

Like *missionaries,* emissaries are sent out on *missions.* However, emissaries are more likely to be representing governments, political leaders, or institutions other than churches. The mission of an emissary is usually to negotiate or to carry or collect information. Presidents send out emissaries to discuss peace terms. Politicians send out emissaries to lure major supporters. And advertising agencies find attractive models to act as emissaries for companies and products on television.

manumission \ˌman-yu-'mi-shən\ The act of freeing from slavery.

• Frederick Douglass, William Lloyd Garrison, and Harriet Tubman were major forces in the movement that led to the manumission of slaves in this country.

The verb *manumit* comes from a Latin verb made up of *manus,* meaning "hand," and *mittere,* which can mean both "let go" and "send." So *manumission,* like *emancipation,* suggests the "freeing of hands." *Emancipate* can mean to free from any kind of control or domination, but *manumit* and *manumission* always refer to liberation from slavery or servitude.

missive \'mi-siv\ A letter or written communication.

• We await further missives from your mother as to her health and sanity.

Missive simply means "letter," and its connection to the *mit-/mis-*root is that letters, after all, are meant to be sent. *Missive* is a rather formal word and is generally used humorously. A parent or grandparent teasing a college student for not writing home might say, "I've enjoyed your many missives," or might even begin a letter, "I hope this missive finds you in good health."

remittance \ri-'mi-təns\ (1) Money sent in payment. (2) The sending of money, especially to a distant place.

• The hardest part of April 15 is putting the remittance into the envelope with the 1040 form.

When we pay our bills and include a remittance, we are sending something back to pay for what we received. *Remittance* is a slightly formal word (in most cases, *payment* is just as good), but some bills do include the statement ''Please remit'' or ''Please enclose remittance.'' Another common use of *remittance* is for payments that workers send back to their families when they are working outside of their home countries. The economies of many poor countries rely on such remittances from workers employed in more industrialized countries.

PEL/PULS comes from the Latin verb *pellere,* meaning ''to move or drive.'' A *propeller* moves an airplane forward. When soldiers *repel* an enemy charge, they drive it back. And to *dispel* something is to drive it away.

---

compel \kəm-'pel\ To drive or urge with force.

• After learning more about the sufferings of the refugees, they felt compelled to make contributions to the relief agencies.

To compel is to drive powerfully. *Compulsion* is the noun form; in other words, a thing that compels. Most commonly a compulsion is a powerful inner urge—a *compelling* urge. You may feel compelled to speak to a friend about his drinking. But a compelling film is simply one that seems serious and important.

expel \ik-'spel\ (1) To drive or force out. (2) To force to leave, usually by official action.

• The doctor had him take a deep breath and then expel all the air from his lungs.

To expel is to drive out, and the noun associated with it is *expulsion*. *Expel* is similar in meaning to *eject*, except that *expel* suggests pushing out while *eject* suggests throwing out. Also, to expel usually means to force out permanently, whereas ejecting may only be temporary. The player ejected from the game may be back tomorrow; the student expelled from school is probably out forever.

impel \im-'pel\ To urge or drive forward by strong moral force.

● As the meeting wore on without any real progress being made, she felt impelled to stand and speak.

Impel is very similar in meaning to *compel* but suggests even more strongly an inner drive to do something, and often greater urgency in the desire to act. People who believe in civil disobedience feel impelled to resist unjust laws. True civil libertarians feel impelled to tolerate even what they intensely dislike.

repulsion \ri-'pəl-shən\ (1) The act of driving away or rejecting. (2) A feeling of great dislike; disgust.

● She overcame her feeling of repulsion long enough to notice the snake's beautiful diamond patterning.

Repulsion basically means ''driving back'' or the feeling that one wants to drive back something. So the goal of an armed attack is the repulsion of an enemy, and magnets exhibit both attraction and repulsion. But we generally use *repulsion* to mean strong dislike, which is also described by the adjectives *repellent* and *repulsive* (though *repellent* often appears in phrases like ''water-repellent''). For example, ''She considered most modern art to be meaningless and repellent,'' and ''He said that the food at college was repulsive.''

Quizzes

A. Fill in each blank with the correct letter:

a. manumission   e. expel
b. missive   f. impel
c. emissary   g. repulsion
d. remittance   h. compel

1. They knew that hunger would eventually _____ the grizzly to wake up.
2. An _____ was sent to the Duke with a new offer.
3. Children find the feeling of _____ caused by reptiles exciting.
4. Please enclose your _____ in the envelope provided.
5. Though the Senate can _____ a member for certain crimes, it has almost never been done.

6. His elegant Christmas _____ was always eagerly awaited.
7. Let your conscience _____ you to make the right choice.
8. Military victory of the Union forces was required to make _____ of the slaves a reality.

B. Match the definition on the left to the correct word on the right:

1. force by moral pressure   a. remittance
2. letter   b. compel
3. drive irresistibly   c. repulsion
4. disgust   d. manumission
5. agent   e. expel
6. payment   f. missive
7. drive out   g. impel
8. emancipation   h. emissary

Words from Mythology

arachnid \ə-'rak-ˌnid\ A member of the class Arachnida, which principally includes animals with four pairs of legs and no antennae, such as spiders, scorpions, mites, and ticks.

• My interest in arachnids began when I used to watch spiders build their gorgeous webs in the corners of the porch.

The Greek word for ''spider'' is *arachne*. According to Greek mythology, the original arachnid was a girl, Arachne. Like all good Greek girls, she spent much of her time weaving, but she made the mistake of claiming she was a better weaver than the goddess Athena. In a contest between the two, she angered the goddess by showing the gods at their worst in the pattern she wove. As punishment, Athena changed Arachne into a spider, fated to spend her life weaving.

calliope \kə-'lī-ə-pē\ A musical instrument similar to an organ in which whistles are sounded by steam or compressed air.

• The town's old calliope, with its unmistakable sound, summoned them to the fair every summer.

To the ancient Greeks, the muses were nine goddesses, each of whom was the spirit of one or more of the arts and sciences. Calliope was the muse of heroic or epic poetry and responsible for inspiring poets to write epics such as the *Iliad* and the *Odyssey*. Since these were generally sung and were usually very long, she was responsible for a great deal of musical reciting. When the hooting musical calliope was invented in America around 1855, her name seemed natural for it. Calliopes gave a festive air to river showboats; the loudest of them could supposedly be heard eight miles away. Today they are only heard on merry-go-rounds and at circuses.

dryad \'drī-əd\ A wood nymph.

● The Greeks' love of trees can be seen in their belief that every tree contained a dryad, which died when the tree was cut.

The term *dryad* comes from the Greek word for "oak tree." As the Greeks saw it, every tree (not only oaks) had a spirit. The myth of Daphne tells of a young woman who chose to become a dryad in order to escape an unwanted suitor, the god Apollo. Pursued by Apollo, she transformed herself into a laurel tree.

fauna \'fȯ-nə\ Animal life, especially the animals that live naturally in a given area or environment.

● In biology class they examined the fauna of the meadow next to the school.

Faunus and Fauna were the Roman nature god and goddess, part goat and part human, who were in charge of animals. Their helpers, who look just like them, are called *fauns*. Perhaps the most famous depiction of a faun is Debussy's orchestral work "Prelude to the Afternoon of a Faun," which was turned into a ballet by the great Russian dancer Nijinsky.

flora \'flȯr-ə\ Plant life, especially the flowering plants that live naturally in a specific area or environment.

● Scientists are busily identifying the flora of the Amazon rain forest before the rapid expansion of the commercial interests consumes it.

The Roman Flora, which means "flower," was the goddess of spring and flowering plants, especially wildflowers and plants not raised for food. She was shown as a beautiful young woman in a long, flowing dress with flowers in her hair and cascading across her shoulders. English preserves her name in such words as *floral*, *floret*, and *flourish*.

herculean \,hər-kyù-'lē-ən\ (1) Extremely strong. (2) Extremely extensive, intense, or difficult.

• The whole family now faced the herculean task of cleaning out the attic.

The hero Hercules (in Greek, Heracles) had to perform twelve enormously difficult tasks, or "labors," to pacify the wrath of the god Apollo. Any job or task that is extremely difficult or calls for enormous strength, therefore, is called herculean.

Pandora's box \pan-'dòr-əz-'bäks\ A source of many troubles.

• Raising the issue of a new tax opened a real Pandora's box of related economic problems.

The beautiful woman Pandora was created by the gods to punish the human race because Prometheus had stolen fire from heaven. As a gift, Zeus gave Pandora a box, but told her never to open it. However, as soon as he was out of sight she took off the lid, and out swarmed all the troubles of the world. Only Hope was left in the box, stuck under the lid. Anything that seems harmless but when opened or investigated brings forth problems is called a Pandora's box.

Scylla and Charybdis \'si-lə-and-kə-'rib-dəs\ Two equally dangerous alternatives.

• As always, they feel caught between Scylla and Charybdis as they try to hold down costs while still investing for the future.

Scylla and Charybdis were two monsters in Greek mythology who endangered shipping in the Strait of Messina between Italy and Sicily. Scylla, a female monster with twelve feet and six heads, each with pointed teeth, barked like a dog from the rocks on the Italian side. Charybdis lived under a huge fig tree on the Sicilian side and caused a whirlpool by swallowing the waters of the sea. Being caught between Scylla and Charybdis is a lot like being between a rock and a hard place.

Quiz

Complete the analogy:

1. hobgoblin : ghost :: dryad : _____
   a. moth b. oak tree c. nymph d. dragonfly
2. difficult : simple :: herculean : _____
   a. intense b. easy c. mammoth d. strong
3. wrath : anger :: Scylla and Charybdis : _____
   a. rage b. peril c. ferocity d. whirlpool
4. piano : nightclub :: calliope : _____
   a. organ b. circus c. church d. steam
5. canine : dog :: flora : _____
   a. oak trees b. wood nymphs c. plants d. animals
6. reptile : snake :: arachnid : _____
   a. toad b. salamander c. bird d. scorpion
7. cabinet : china :: Pandora's box : _____
   a. pleasures b. troubles c. taxes d. music
8. cattle : livestock :: fauna : _____
   a. meadows b. flowers c. wildlife d. trees

Review Quizzes

A. Choose the correct antonym:

1. impartial   a. fair b. biased c. cautious d. undecided
2. cosmopolitan   a. bored b. intelligent
   c. inexperienced d. well-traveled
3. incoherent   a. clear b. garbled c. confused d. unknown
4. manumission   a. prohibition b. blockade
   c. liberation d. enslavement
5. compel   a. drive b. prevent c. eject d. compare
6. inherent   a. native b. inherited c. acquired d. internal
7. cosmos   a. chaos b. order c. universe d. beauty
8. impart   a. send b. stick c. combine d. withhold
9. adjunct   a. added feature b. sharp break c. tight
   connection d. central core
10. repulsion   a. disgust b. attraction c. offense d. battle

B. Match the definition on the right to the correct word on the left:

1.	emissary	a.	verb part
2.	junta	b.	cause to move
3.	participle	c.	equal perils
4.	impel	d.	agent
5.	dryad	e.	letter
6.	missive	f.	attachment
7.	Scylla and Charybdis	g.	ruling group
8.	cosmetic	h.	very difficult
9.	herculean	i.	beautifying
10.	adjunct	j.	tree spirit

C. Fill in each blank with the correct letter:

a.	adherent	f.	flora
b.	centrifugal	g.	cohesion
c.	conscientious	h.	prescient
d.	arachnid	i.	disjunction
e.	remittance	j.	subterfuge

1. The candidate's wife, his staunchest _____, was overjoyed by the victory.
2. The successful stockbroker won a reputation for being _____.
3. The philosopher saw no _____ between science and morality.
4. _____ force keeps the roller-coaster cars from crashing to the ground.
5. Please send your _____ immediately or we will be forced to take legal action.
6. The plateau is home to various members of the _____ family.
7. The _____ of the family was strengthened with each reunion.
8. She won praise for her _____ handling of details.
9. We managed to get hold of tickets for the Grateful Dead concert only by _____.
10. The _____ of the West Creek Valley includes at least a dozen rare species.

Unit 10

PUT, from the Latin verb *putare*, meaning "to think, consider, or believe," has come into English in a variety of forms. A *reputation*, for example, is what others think of you; a *deputy* is someone "considered as" the person who appointed him or her.

disputatious \dis-pyù-'tā-shəs\ Inclined to argue or debate.

● Because both sides were so disputatious, it seemed as if a peace accord would never be reached.

A discussion may be called disputatious, and so may a subject about which people disagree, but normally we use the word to describe individuals. For example, Beethoven was the first composer of genius who dared to be disputatious with the European nobles who were the source of his income. Trial lawyers often cultivate a disputatious style, though at home they may argue no more than balloonists or lion tamers.

impute \im-'pyüt\ To attribute.

● The British imputed motives of piracy to American ships trying to prevent them from interfering with American trade during the War of 1812.

Imputing something to someone (or something) usually means observing something invisible in that person (or thing). We may impute meaning to a play or novel, or even to a casual remark by a friend, that was never intended. Imputing a particular character to a whole country—calling the Germans militaristic or the Italians amorous, for example—is very common but always risky. And many of us like to impute bad motives to others, while always regarding our own motives as pure.

putative \\'pyü-tə-tiv\ Generally supposed; assumed to exist.

● To strengthen the case for the defense, a putative expert took the stand.

Putative is almost always used to express doubt or skepticism about a common belief. Thus, Tintagel Castle in Cornwall, a picturesque ruin, is the putative fortress of King Arthur. The residents of New York City are *putatively* rude, neurotic, chic, and dangerous. And in the era of Senator Joseph McCarthy, the State Department became the putative home of hundreds of Communists.

reputed \ri-'pyü-təd\ Believed to be a certain way by popular opinion.

● A 15th-century Romanian prince, Vlad the Impaler, is reputed to have been the inspiration for the character Dracula.

Reputed is used constantly today by reporters, almost always to describe suspected criminals—''a reputed mobster,'' ''the reputed drug kingpin.'' But someone may equally well be reputed to have four dead husbands or a fortune in emeralds or an obsession with medieval catapults.

LOG, from the Greek word *logos,* meaning ''word, speech, reason,'' is found particularly in English words that end in -*logy* and -*logue*. The ending -*logy* often means ''the study of'': *biology* is the study of life, and *anthropology* is the study of humans. The ending -*logue* usually indicates a type of discussion: *dialogue* is conversation between two people or groups, and an *epilogue* is an author's last words on a subject.

---

eulogy \\'yü-lə-jē\ A speech in praise of someone, often someone who has died.

● At President Kennedy's funeral, Chief Justice Earl Warren delivered a moving eulogy.

Since the prefix *eu-* means ''well or good,'' a eulogy speaks well of a person or thing. A speech at a funeral or memorial service is generally called a eulogy, but you may also *eulogize* a living person. At a party you may bore everyone with your eulogies to your hometown, your dog, or your favorite vitamin.

monologue \'mä-nə-,lóg\ (1) A speech or dramatic scene spoken by one person or one actor. (2) Talk that dominates a conversation.

• Myra's loud and endless monologue about her travels was still ringing in our ears when we got home.

Dramatic monologues have often been used to let a character talk openly about himself or herself; the most famous of all is probably Hamlet's "To be or not to be." James Joyce and Virginia Woolf wrote long and memorable monologues for characters in their novels. Garrison Keillor, Lily Tomlin, and Bette Midler are present-day masters of the live comic monologue.

neologism \nē-'ä-lə-,ji-zəm\ A new word, usage, or expression.

• Such neologisms as *cyberspace* and *virtual reality* come from computer technology.

Neologisms are appearing in English all the time, originating from a variety of sources. Though -*log*- means "word" (and *neo*- means "new"), a neologism doesn't have to be an entirely new word. *Rap*, a very old word, was first used in the 1920s to mean "talk," and in the 1970s to describe a new type of "talk music," and each new use was also a neologism in its time.

genealogy \,jē-nē-'a-lə-jē\ (1) The descent of a person or family from an ancestor, or a history of such descent. (2) The study of family history.

• In ancient Rome, prominent senators could trace their genealogies almost to the founding of the city.

In 1976, Alex Haley, Jr., published a partly fictional genealogy of his family in the form of a novel. *Roots* was not only a *genealogical* work but a history of the United States and colonial slavery told from an African-American standpoint. When its television version became the hugest success in the history of television, amateur genealogy became widely popular among both white and black Americans.

Quizzes

A. Indicate whether the following pairs of words have the same or different meanings:

1. putative / supposed   same ___ / different ___
2. neologism / terminology   same ___ / different ___
3. reputed / questioned   same ___ / different ___
4. genealogy / genetics   same ___ / different ___
5. disputatious / dysfunctional same ___ / different ___
6. monologue / discussion   same ___ / different ___
7. impute / compute   same ___ / different ___
8. eulogy / praise   same ___ / different ___

B. Choose the closest definition:

1. monologue   a. speech b. drama c. catalog d. boredom
2. impute   a. imply b. revise c. attribute d. defy
3. reputed   a. rethought b. accused c. determined
      d. believed
4. neologism   a. new day b. new word c. new way
      d. new thought
5. putative   a. assumed b. appointed c. solved d. ignored
6. genealogy   a. generation b. inheritance c. family
      history d. height
7. disputatious   a. courageous b. disproved
      c. unknown d. argumentative
8. eulogy   a. high praise b. high flight c. high times
      d. high jump

TERR comes from the Latin *terra*, "earth." *Terra firma* is a Latin phrase that means "firm ground" as opposed to the swaying seas; a *terrace* is a leveled area along a sloping hill; the French call potatoes *pommes de terre*, literally "apples of the earth"; *territory* is a specific piece of land.

---

parterre \pär-'ter\ (1) A decorative garden with paths between the beds of plants. (2) The back area of the ground floor of a theater, often under the balcony.

• The city's park boasts a beautiful parterre with many varieties of roses.

Parterre comes to English by way of French, where it means "on the ground." In Shakespeare's day, the parterre of an English theater was filled with rowdy spectators whose response to the plays was noisy and often crude.

subterranean \,səb-tə-'rā-nē-ən\ Underground.

• Carlsbad Caverns National Park has a subterranean chamber over half a mile long.

A subway is a subterranean railway; a tunnel can provide a subterranean pathway; the subterranean vaults at Fort Knox hold billions of dollars of gold reserves. Throughout New England are subterranean reservoirs, called *aquifers,* that are tapped for water. The pressure is great enough to push the subterranean water to the surface once a well provides an outlet; such wells are called *artesian.*

terrarium \tə-'rar-ē-əm\ An enclosure, usually transparent, with a layer of dirt in the bottom in which plants and sometimes small animals are kept indoors.

• When no one was watching, they dropped their snake in the fifth-grade terrarium, and then waited in the hall to hear the screams.

The turtle exhibit at a zoo is often in the form of a terrarium, as are some of the exhibits at a plant conservatory. Terrariums try to create conditions as close as possible to a natural habitat. A covered terrarium can often sustain itself for months on the moisture trapped inside.

terrestrial \tə-'res-trē-əl\ Having to do with the earth or its inhabitants.

• Although a largely terrestrial bird, the roadrunner can take to wing for short periods when necessary.

Everything on or having to do with the earth is terrestrial, although from the top of Mount Everest or K2 it may not seem that way, since the air is so thin that climbers need to carry extra oxygen to breathe. Something *extraterrestrial* comes from beyond the earth and its atmosphere; though the word is probably most familiar from science fiction, *extraterrestrial* can be used to describe anything "out of this world," from moon rocks to meteors. But Mercury, Venus, and Mars are often called the terrestrial planets, since they are rocky balls somewhat like Earth rather than great globes consisting largely of gas like most of the outer planets. In another usage of the word, animals may be divided into the terrestrial (land-living) and the aquatic (water-living).

MAR, from the Latin word *mare*, meaning "sea," brings its salty tang to English in words like *marine*, "having to do with the sea," and *submarine*, "under the sea."

---

aquamarine \ä-kwə-mə-'rēn\ (1) A pale blue or greenish blue that is the color of clear seawater in sunlight. (2) A transparent gem that is blue or blue-green.

● Many of the houses on the Italian Riviera are painted aquamarine to match the Mediterranean.

Aquamarine includes the root *aqua*, "water," and accurately describes limpid, clear seawater such as laps the shores of the islands of Greece or those of the Caribbean. The semiprecious gem called aquamarine, a form of beryl, is named for its color.

marina \mə-'rē-nə\ A dock or harbor where pleasure boats can be moored securely, often with facilities offering supplies or repairs.

● The coast of Florida has marinas all along it for the use of anything from enormous powerboats to the flimsiest sailboats.

The word *marina* comes straight from Latin, where it means "of the sea." At a marina sailors can acquire whatever they need for their next excursion, or they can tie up their boats until the next weekend comes along. John D. MacDonald's detective hero Travis McGee lives on his boat in Miami and rarely leaves the marina.

mariner \'mar-ə-nər\ A seaman or sailor.

● When he signed on as a mariner, the young Ishmael never suspected that the ship would be pursuing a great white whale.

In Coleridge's *Rime of the Ancient Mariner,* an old seaman tells the story of how he shot a friendly albatross and brought storms and disaster to his ship. As punishment, his shipmates hung the great seabird around the mariner's neck and made him wear it until it rotted.

maritime \\'mar-ə-,tīm\\ (1) Bordering on or having to do with the sea. (2) Having to do with navigation or commerce on the sea.

● Canada's Maritime Provinces—New Brunswick, Nova Scotia, and Prince Edward Island—have a late spring but a mild winter as a result of the ocean.

The maritime countries of Portugal and England produced many explorers during the 16th and 17th centuries, many of whom, like Ferdinand Magellan and Henry Hudson, sailed under the flags of other countries. Magellan sailed for Spain and captained the ship that was the first to circle the world, charting many new maritime routes as it went. Hudson, funded by the Dutch, sailed up what is now called the Hudson River in New York, claiming that maritime area for the Netherlands.

Quizzes

A. Complete the analogy:

1. crepe : pancake :: parterre : _____
   a. balcony b. planet c. garden d. parachute
2. motel : motorist :: marina : _____
   a. dock b. pier c. sailor d. boat
3. aquarium : water :: terrarium : _____
   a. plants b. turtles c. rocks d. earth
4. urban : city :: maritime : _____
   a. beach b. dock c. sea d. harbor
5. aquatic : water :: terrestrial : _____
   a. sea b. land c. forest d. mountain
6. pink : red :: aquamarine : _____
   a. blue b. watery c. turquoise d. yellow
7. submarine : wet :: subterranean : _____
   a. blue b. dark c. hollow d. full
8. logger : lumberjack :: mariner : _____
   a. doctor b. lawyer c. chief d. sailor

B. **Match the definition on the left to the correct word on the right:**

1. theater area   a. mariner
2. blue-green gem   b. terrestrial
3. under the ground   c. marina
4. near the sea   d. terrarium
5. contained habitat   e. maritime
6. seaman   f. parterre
7. small harbor   g. subterranean
8. earthly   h. aquamarine

PATH comes from the Greek word *pathos*, which means "suffering." A *pathetic* sight moves us to pity. *Pathos* itself is used in English to describe the intense emotions produced by tragedy.

apathetic \a-pə-'the-tik\ (1) Showing or feeling little or no emotion. (2) Having no interest.

• His apathetic response to the victory bewildered his friends.

Apathy, or lack of emotion, is central to Albert Camus's famous novel *The Stranger,* in which the main character's indifference toward almost everything, including his mother's death, results in his imprisonment. We feel little *sympathy* for him, and may even feel *antipathy,* or dislike. The American voter is often called apathetic; of all the industrial democracies, only in America does more than half the adult population fail to vote in major elections.

empathy \'em-pə-thē\ The feeling of, or the ability to feel, the emotions and sensations of another.

• Her maternal empathy was so strong that she often seemed to be living her son's life emotionally.

In the 19th century Charles Dickens counted on producing a strong *empathetic* response in his readers so that they would be involved enough to buy the next newspaper installment of each novel. Today, when reading a novel such as *A Tale of Two Cities,* only the hardest-hearted reader does not feel empathy for Sidney Carton as he approaches the guillotine. One who *empathizes* suffers along with the one who feels the sensations directly. Empathy is similar to *sympathy,* but empathy usually suggests stronger, more instinctive feeling. We may feel sympathy, or pity, for victims of a war in Asia, but we may feel empathy for a close friend going through a divorce, even though it is a much smaller disaster.

pathology \pa-'thä-lə-jē\ (1) The study of diseases. (2) The abnormalities that are characteristic of a disease.

• Scientists understood the pathology of smallpox long before they found a vaccine to prevent it.

Based on its roots, *pathology* would mean literally "the study of suffering," but it is actually used to describe the study of diseases. Scientists have found vaccines or cures for diseases from chicken pox to diphtheria by studying their pathology. In this role, the researchers are called *pathologists*. However, a psychiatrist might speak of pathologies of behavior, meaning only that the behavior in question is abnormal.

sociopath \'sō-shē-ō-ˌpath\ A mentally ill or unstable person who acts in a way that harms people and society; a psychopath.

• Controlling its sociopaths is a goal of every society.

One of the most famous sociopaths of history was Jack the Ripper, the mysterious serial killer who murdered at least seven London prostitutes in 1888. But a sociopath doesn't have to be a murderer; almost any person who is destructive or potentially dangerous can be described as a sociopath. Today psychiatrists use the bland term "antisocial personality" in place of *psychopath* or *sociopath*.

PEN/PUN comes from the Latin words *poena,* "penalty," and *punire,* "to punish." From them come such English words as *penalty* and *repentance*; when a penalty is given to someone, it is expected that he or she will be moved to repentance.

---

impunity \im-'pyü-nə-tē\ Freedom from punishment, harm, or loss.

- Under the flag of truce, the soldiers crossed the field with impunity.

Impunity is protection from punishment, just as immunity is protection from disease. Tom Sawyer, in Mark Twain's novel, broke his Aunt Polly's rules with near impunity because he could usually sweet-talk her into forgiving him; if that failed, he had enjoyed himself so much he didn't care what *punishment* she gave him.

penal \'pē-nəl\ Having to do with punishment or penalties, or institutions where punishment is given.

- The classic novels *Les Misérables* and *The Count of Monte Cristo* portray the terrible conditions in French penal institutions in the last century.

A state or country's *penal code* defines its crimes and describes its punishments. During the 18th and 19th centuries, many countries established penal colonies, where criminals were sent as punishment. Often these were unbearably severe; but it was to such colonies that some of Australia's and the United States' early white inhabitants came, and the convicts provided labor for the European settlement of these lands.

penance \'pe-nəns\ An act of self-punishment or religious devotion to show sorrow or regret for sin or wrongdoing.

- In the Middle Ages bands of pilgrims would trudge to distant holy sites as penance for their sins.

Penance as a form of apology for a mistake can be either voluntary or ordered by someone else. Many religions include penance among the ways in which believers can show *repentance* or regret for a misdeed. The Christian season of Lent, 40 days long, is traditionally a time for doing penance.

punitive \'pyü-nə-tiv\ Giving, involving, or aiming at punishment.

- The loser in a court case is often directed to pay punitive damages, money over and above the actual cost of the harm done to the other party.

Trade sanctions, which limit one country's trade with another, are a form of punitive action that may be taken against a government for its human-rights violations or for acts of war, among other reasons. On a smaller scale, a school principal may take punitive measures against a misbehaving football team.

Quizzes

A. Fill in each blank with the correct letter:

a. impunity
b. apathetic
c. punitive
d. sociopath
e. empathy
f. penal
g. pathology
h. penance

1. Speeders seem to feel they can break the speed limit with ____.
2. Louis Pasteur studied the ____ of rabies in order to produce a vaccine.
3. In some households, grounding is a severe form of ____ action.
4. The mildest of the federal ____ institutions are the so-called "country club" prisons.
5. The ____ crowd responded to the singer with weak applause.
6. As ____ the wrongdoers were made to wash all the windows, except the one their ball had shattered.
7. Almost everyone feels some ____ for a child's misery.
8. A brutal dictator is the most destructive kind of ____.

B. Complete the analogy:

1. passionate : emotional :: apathetic : ____
   a. caring b. unjust c. indifferent d. dominant
2. fine : speeding :: penance : ____
   a. misdeed b. credit card c. fee d. behavior
3. psychology : mind :: pathology : ____
   a. suffering b. maps c. life d. disease
4. immunity : sickness :: impunity : ____
   a. death b. flood c. harm d. sleep
5. station wagon : car :: empathy : ____
   a. bus b. emotion c. idea d. pity
6. social : studies :: penal : ____
   a. violence b. attitude c. colony d. dream

---

7. composer : music :: sociopath : _____
     a. crime   b. illness   c. harmony   d. dread
8. constructive : idea :: punitive : _____
     a. place   b. damages   c. focus   d. outlet

MATR/METR comes from the Greek and Latin words for "mother." A *matron* is a mature woman with children; *matrimony* is marriage itself, traditionally a first step toward motherhood; and a *matrix* is something in which something else is embedded or takes form, like a baby.

maternity \mə-'tər-nə-tē\ The state of being a mother; motherhood.

● Some think the Mona Lisa's smile is the result of her maternity.

Maternity is used as both a noun and an adjective. *Maternity benefits* are benefits specially provided by employers for women having babies, and usually include *maternity leave,* time off work. With maternity come *maternal* feelings. All species of warm-blooded animals show maternal instincts, as do a few reptiles such as crocodiles and alligators.

matriculate \mə-'tri-kyủ-,lāt\ To enroll as a member of a group, especially a school or college.

● They matriculated together at both boarding school and college, but after college they disappeared entirely from each other's life.

Matriculate comes into English from *matrix,* which in Latin meant a female animal used for breeding purposes, or a plant that was used to produce other plants. It later acquired the meaning "list" or "register," for in ancient times a list might be thought of as the source or parent of the names appearing on it. A student who matriculates at a school basically signs up on a list of students. (And the school or college attended will become his or her *alma mater,* Latin for "fostering mother.")

matrilineal \,ma-trə-'li-nē-əl\ Based on or tracing the family through the mother.

● Many of the peoples of Ghana in Africa trace their family through matrilineal connections.

Matrilineal means basically "through the mother's line"; *patrilineal* means "through the father's line." Most families that follow the European model take the father's name and are therefore patrilineal; many other peoples follow a matrilineal pattern. Under either system (but especially the latter) there can be *matriarchs,* mothers who rule (*arch*) or head their families or descendants.

metropolitan \ˌme-trə-'pä-lə-tən\ Having to do with a large, important city and sometimes also its surrounding suburbs.

● The Los Angeles metropolitan area is among the largest in the world and continues to grow.

Metropolis means basically "mother city," and in ancient Greece a metropolis was usually the original city of a colony—thus the mother from which the colony was born, so to speak. A modern *metropolitan area* can be immense, and in poor countries everywhere peasants are flooding into metropolitan centers in search of jobs, often simply exchanging one form of poverty for another even worse form.

MONI comes from the Latin verb *monere,* "to warn" or "to scold." Warning and scolding often are rather similar, since many warnings could be called "pre-scoldings."

---

admonish \ad-'mä-nish\ To warn or criticize mildly.

● The daydreaming student was admonished by the teacher, who told him to pay attention in the future.

The Senate may admonish, or "reprimand," a senator who has misbehaved, but this is far less serious than being "condemned" or actually expelled from the Senate. An *admonition* or *admonishment* usually is less severe than a scolding; it may simply caution against something, and it can even include encouragement.

monitory \'mä-nə-ˌtȯr-ē\ Giving warning; cautionary.

● Through the fog they could hear the mournful, monitory note of the foghorn.

A professor may start class with a monitory comment about final exams. A president may make a monitory speech addressed to a country that is ignoring its trade obligations. And a pope may issue a monitory message to the world on the subject of war or morality.

monitor \'mä-nə-tər\ To keep track of or watch, usually for a special reason.

● The North's armored ship the *Monitor* was designed to monitor the South's naval activities in the coastal waters.

Monitor can be both a verb and a noun. A heart monitor monitors a patient's heartbeat and warns of any problems. A hall monitor monitors students behavior in the hallways. Both machine and human monitors observe or supervise and give warnings if something goes wrong.

premonition \ˌpre-mə-'ni-shən\ (1) A previous warning or notice; forewarning. (2) A feeling about an event or situation before it happens.

● He now remembered how the birds had been restless and noisy, as though they had felt a premonition of the coming earthquake.

A premonition is literally a forewarning. A story about Abraham Lincoln holds that he had a premonition of his death in a dream shortly before he was assassinated, but the *premonitory* dream did not prevent him from going to Ford's Theatre on April 14, 1865. John Kennedy flew to Dallas in 1963 ignoring the dark premonition expressed by the statesman Adlai Stevenson. And Martin Luther King delivered a great speech containing premonitions of his death only days before he was murdered in 1968.

Quizzes

A. Choose the closest definition:

1. matriculate   a. give birth   b. enroll   c. tickle   d. adjust
2. premonition   a. introduction   b. scolding
     c. prematurity   d. forewarning
3. matrilineal   a. through the mother's family
     b. graduating   c. adopted   d. female
4. monitory   a. monetary   b. mean   c. cautionary
     d. enthusiastic

5. metropolitan a. urban b. suburban c. rural d. oceanic
6. monitor a. think b. persuade c. avoid d. watch
7. maternity a. motherhood b. childhood c. Robin
   Hood d. sainthood
8. admonish a. praise b. arrest c. await d. scold

B. Match the definition on the left with the correct word on the right:

1.	through the female line	a.	monitor
2.	warning	b.	premonition
3.	sign up at school	c.	maternity
4.	regulate	d.	metropolitan
5.	gently correct	e.	matrilineal
6.	early suspicion	f.	matriculate
7.	motherliness	g.	admonish
8.	city	h.	monitory

Words from Mythology

cereal \'sir-ē-əl\ (1) A plant that produces grain that can be eaten as food, or the grain it produces. (2) The food made from grain.

● Rice is the main food cereal grown in Asia, whereas wheat is the main food cereal of the West.

The Roman goddess Ceres (the Greek Demeter) was a serene goddess who did not take part in the quarrels of the other gods. She was in charge of the food-giving plants, and the grains came to carry her name. Cereals of the Romans included wheat, barley, spelt, oats, and millet, but not corn (maize), which was a cereal of the Americas.

Junoesque \ˌjü-nō-'esk\ Having mature, poised, and dignified beauty.

● In 1876, as a centennial gift, the French sent to America a massive statue of a robed Junoesque figure representing Liberty.

Juno was the wife of Jupiter, the chief of the Roman gods. She was a matron, mature and well filled out. Her presence was imposing; her authority as wife of Jupiter and her power in her own right gave her particular dignity. But the younger Diana, goddess of the hunt, perhaps came closer to today's ideals of slim and athletic female beauty.

martial \'mär-shəl\ Having to do with war and military life.

• The stirring, martial strains of "The British Grenadiers" echoed down the snowy street just as dawn was breaking.

Mars was the Roman god of war and one of the patron gods of Rome itself. He was in charge of everything military, from warriors to weapons to provisions to marching music. Thus, when *martial law* is proclaimed, a country's armed forces take over the functions of the police. *Martial arts* are skills of combat and self-defense also practiced as sport. And a *court-martial* is a military court or trial.

Promethean \prə-'mē-thē-ən\ New or creative in a daring way.

• At his best, Steven Spielberg has sometimes shown Promethean originality in the special effects of his movies.

Prometheus was a Titan, a generation older than Zeus. When Zeus overthrew his own father Cronus and seized power, Prometheus fought on the side of the gods and against his fellow Titans. But when Zeus later wanted to destroy the race of humans, Prometheus saved them by stealing fire for them from the gods. He also taught them how to write, farm, build houses, read the stars and weather, cure themselves when sick, and tame animals—in short, all the arts and skills that make humans unique. So inventive was he that anything that bears the stamp of creativity and originality can still be called Promethean. But for his disobedience Zeus had him chained to a rocky cliff, where for many long centuries an eagle daily tore at his liver. Thus, any suffering on a grand scale can also be called Promethean.

Sisyphean \ˌsi-sə-'fē-ən\ Endless and difficult.

• High-school dropouts usually find getting a good job to be a Sisyphean task.

Reputedly the cleverest man on earth, Sisyphus tricked the gods into bringing him back to life after he died. For this they punished him by sending him back to the underworld, where he must eternally roll a huge rock up a long, steep hill, only to watch it roll back to where he started. Something Sisyphean demands the same kind of unending, thankless, and ultimately unsuccessful efforts.

titanic \tī-'ta-nik\ Having great size, strength, or power; colossal.

• The titanic floods of 1993 destroyed whole towns on the Mississippi River.

The ocean liner *Titanic* was named for its unmatched size and strength and its assumed unsinkability. But a truly titanic iceberg ripped a fatal hole in the great ship on its maiden voyage in 1912, and more than 1,500 people perished in the icy waters off Newfoundland. In Greek mythology, the original Titans also came to a bad end. They belonged to the generation of giant creators that produced the younger, stronger, cleverer gods, who soon overpowered and replaced them (see *Promethean* above).

Triton \'trī-tən\ (1) A being with a human upper body and the lower body of a fish; a merman. (2) Any of various large mollusks with a heavy, conical shell.

• In one corner of the painting, a robust Triton emerges from the sea with his conch to announce the coming of the radiant queen.

Triton was originally the son of the sea god Poseidon/Neptune. A guardian of the fish and other creatures of the sea, he is usually shown as hearty, muscular, and cheerful. Like his father, he often carries a trident (a three-pronged fork) and sometimes rides in a chariot drawn by seahorses. Blowing on his conch shell, he creates the roar of the ocean. As a decorative image, Tritons are simply the male version of mermaids. The handsome seashells that bear his name are the very conchs on which he blows. Triton has also given his name to the planet Neptune's largest moon.

vulcanize \'vəl-kə-,nīz\ To treat crude or synthetic rubber or plastic so that it becomes elastic and strong and resists decay.

• The native islanders had even discovered how to vulcanize the rubber from the local trees in a primitive way.

The Roman god Vulcan (the Greek Hephaestus) was in charge of fire and the skills that use fire, especially blacksmithing. When Charles Goodyear accidentally discovered how to vulcanize rubber

in 1839, he revolutionized the rubber industry. He called his process *vulcanization* because it used fire to heat the rubber (before
the addition of sulfur and other ingredients). His discovery influenced the course of the Civil War, when balloons made of this new,
stronger rubber carried Union spies over the Confederate armies.

Quiz

Fill in each blank with the correct letter:

a. Promethean   e. Sisyphean
b. titanic   f. vulcanize
c. Triton   g. cereal
d. Junoesque   h. martial

1. Doing the laundry and the ironing always seemed ____
    in their endlessness and drudgery.
2. The bout between Muhammed Ali and George Foreman
    matched one ____ champion against another.
3. The aging jazz singer acquired a certain ____ quality in
    her mature years.
4. On each arm of the great candelabra was carved a ____
    blowing on his conch.
5. Corn, unknown in ancient Europe, has become a staple
    ____ of the modern world.
6. When Goodyear discovered how to ____ rubber, he
    made Henry Ford's Model T possible.
7. Edison's mind may have been the most ____ since
    Leonardo da Vinci's.
8. The ____ arts of the Far East have become popular in
    the West as means of self-defense.

Review Quizzes

**A. Indicate whether the following pairs of words have
the same or different meanings:**

1. aquamarine / navy blue   same ___ / different ___
2. subterranean / underground   same ___ / different ___

3.	eulogy / poetry	same ___ / different ___
4.	disputatious / passive	same ___ / different ___
5.	empathy / sentimentality	same ___ / different ___
6.	Junoesque / matriarchal	same ___ / different ___
7.	Promethean / creative	same ___ / different ___
8.	penance / regret	same ___ / different ___
9.	matriculate / graduate	same ___ / different ___
10.	monitory / warning	same ___ / different ___
11.	titanic / powerful	same ___ / different ___
12.	vulcanize / organize	same ___ / different ___
13.	monitor / guard	same ___ / different ___
14.	impunity / freedom from harm	same ___ / different ___
15.	pathology / anger	same ___ / different ___
16.	metropolitan / coastal	same ___ / different ___
17.	marina / dock	same ___ / different ___
18.	putative / natural	same ___ / different ___
19.	terrarium / tank	same ___ / different ___
20.	monologue / chorus	same ___ / different ___

B. Choose the word that does not belong:

1. Sisyphean   a. difficult b. unending c. demanding
   d. rolling
2. maternity   a. femininity b. parenthood
   c. motherliness d. motherhood
3. mariner   a. sailor b. seaman c. crew member d. archer
4. cereal   a. corn b. eggplant c. rice d. barley
5. reputed   a. known b. reported c. believed d. thought
6. admonish   a. warn b. scold c. ask d. correct
7. premonition   a. sense b. proof c. omen
   d. forewarning
8. neologism   a. new theory b. new word c. new usage
   d. new phrase
9. maritime   a. coastal b. nautical c. oceangoing
   d. temperate
10. apathetic   a. concerned b. unconcerned c. uncaring
    d. indifferent

**C. Match the definition on the right to the correct word
on the left:**

1. punitive   a. fancy garden
2. martial   b. through the mother's line

3.	parterre	c.	relating to punishment
4.	sociopath	d.	antisocial person
5.	penal	e.	related to war
6.	matrilineal	f.	disciplinary
7.	terrestrial	g.	family history
8.	genealogy	h.	earthly

Unit 11

CANT, from the Latin verbs *canere* and *cantare*, meaning "sing," produces several words that come directly from Latin, and others that come by way of French and add an *h* to the root: for example, *chant* and *chantey*.

cantata \kən-'tä-tə\ A musical composition, particularly a religious work from the 17th or 18th century, for one or more voices accompanied by instruments.

• During the Baroque era, composers like Telemann composed sacred cantatas by the hundreds.

A cantata is sung, unlike a sonata, which is played on instruments only. Johann Sebastian Bach wrote the music for over 200 religious cantatas; he chose verses to set from hymns and new religious poems. His cantatas consisted of several different sections for different voices—solos, duets, and choruses. Some of his nonreligious cantatas have been performed like mini-operas.

incantation \in-ˌkan-'tä-shən\ (1) A use of spells or verbal charms spoken or sung as part of a ritual of magic. (2) A formula of words used in, or as if in, such a ritual.

• He repeated the words like an incantation: "The only way! The only way! The only way!"

Magic and ritual have always been associated with chanting and music. *Incantation* comes directly from the Latin word *incantare*, "enchant," which itself has *cantare* as a root. Incantations are often in strange languages; "Abracadabra" is a not-so-serious version of an incantation.

cantor \'kan-tər\ An official of a Jewish synagogue who sings or chants the music of the services and leads the congregation in prayer.

• The congregation waited for the cantor to begin the prayers before joining in.

The cantor is, after the rabbi, the most important figure in a Jewish worship service. The cantor not only must possess an excellent singing voice but also must know by heart long passages of Hebrew. Basically, *cantor* simply means "singer." The comedian and singer Edward Israel Iskowitz renamed himself Eddie Cantor for his chosen profession and became enormously popular on stage, screen, radio, and television for over 40 years.

descant \'des-,kant\ An additional melody sung above the principal melody.

• The soprano added a soaring descant to the final chorus that held the listeners spellbound.

The prefix *des-*, "two" or "apart," indicates that the descant is a "second song" apart from the main melody. In popular songs a descant will often be sung at the very end to produce a thrilling climax.

LUD/LUS comes from the Latin verb *ludere*, "to play," and *ludum*, "play" or "game." An *interlude* thus is something "between games" (*inter-* meaning "between"). A *delusion* or an *illusion* plays tricks on a person.

---

allude \ə-'lüd\ To refer broadly or indirectly.

• She liked to allude constantly to her glamorous past without ever filling in the details.

Literature is full of *allusions* in which the author refers to other, earlier works. In his epic religious poem *Paradise Lost,* John Milton alludes constantly to Greek and Latin literature, but also to events of his own time such as the discoveries and new countries of the Americas. Modern authors continue to use allusions in their work, and there is a constant flow of new material available to which they can allude. Music and art are almost as full of allusions as literature is.

collusion \kə-'lü-zhən\ A secret agreement or conspiracy for an illegal or deceptive purpose.

• Cuban cigars have continued to be smoked in this country in spite of the embargo against them because of collusion between Cuban cigar makers and American smugglers.

Collusion and the verb *collude* contain the prefix *col-* (from *con-*), meaning ''with''; thus, they contain the meaning ''play along with.'' A common form of collusion involves businesses within the same industry. Rather than competing fairly, businesses will sometimes collude to keep prices artificially high. This type of *collusive* behavior has been found in businesses from oil companies to private universities to major-league baseball, whose owners were fined millions of dollars for collusion in the 1980s.

ludicrous \'lü-də-krəs\ Laughable because of clear absurdity, falseness, or foolishness.

• At the rodeo, the ludicrous antics of the clown distract the angry bull and entertain the crowd.

In Hans Christian Andersen's tale ''The Ugly Duckling,'' the ducks find their bumbling, gawky baby's attempts to act like a duck ludicrous. When he grows into a swan, more graceful and elegant than they could ever hope to be, it is surprising that he himself doesn't find the waddling ducks ludicrous. Be careful when using the word: a comment like ''What a ludicrous idea!'' can be rather insulting.

prelude \'prāl-ˌyüd\ A performance, action, event, or piece of music that precedes and prepares for the more important thing that follows.

• The sound of a symphony orchestra tuning up is the *prelude* to a night of music.

A prelude (*pre-* meaning ''before'') goes before the main event, just as an *interlude* goes between sections of it. Dark clouds rolling in overhead can be the prelude to a storm. Graduation ceremonies are often called commencement (''beginning'') because they are considered a prelude to a new life.

Quizzes

A. Choose the closest definition:

1. descant   a. climb downward b. added melody
     c. supposed inability d. writing table
2. allude   a. play b. detract c. avoid d. refer
3. incantation   a. ritual chant b. ceremony c. solemn
     march d. recorded song
4. prelude   a. aftermath b. conclusion c. introduction
     d. admission
5. cantata   a. snack bar b. pasta dish c. sung
     composition d. farewell gesture
6. ludicrous   a. tough b. laughable c. simple d. ugly
7. cantor   a. singer b. refusal c. traitor d. gallop
8. collusion   a. accidental crash b. illegal cooperation
     c. new material d. magic spell

B. Indicate whether the following pairs of words have the same or different meanings:

1. ludicrous / deceptive   same ___ / different ___
2. incantation / sacred dance   same ___ / different ___
3. prelude / introduction   same ___ / different ___
4. descant / enchant   same ___ / different ___
5. allude / begin   same ___ / different ___
6. cantata / sonata   same ___ / different ___
7. cantor / conductor   same ___ / different ___
8. collusion / smuggling   same ___ / different ___

PHAN/PHEN, from the Greek verbs that mean "to appear or seem" or "to present to the mind," has to do with the way things seem or appear rather than the way they really are. From these roots come words such as *fanciful* and *fantasy*, in which the imagination plays an important part.

---

phantasm \'fan-ˌta-zəm\ An illusion or a ghost produced by imagination or creative invention.

• When night fell, his imagination filled the old, dark house with phantasms.

In Edgar Allan Poe's poem "The Raven," a weary scholar who has fallen asleep at midnight while reading strange old books talks with a phantasm, a ghastly raven that has come to tell him that he will "nevermore" meet his dead love in a Christian afterlife, since there is none. In the words of the old saying, "The sleep of reason produces monsters"—that is, phantasms.

phantasmagoria \fan-,taz-mə-'gȯr-ē-ə\ (1) A shifting succession of things seen or imagined. (2) A collection or combination of weird or imaginary things.

• Salvador Dalí's paintings offer a bizarre phantasmagoria of odd images.

To Western eyes an Arab souk, or market, can seem like a phantasmagoria of exotic items, but a Western supermarket can look equally *phantasmagorical* to a foreigner. A film or a novel can be *phantasmagoric*. The shifting content of a dream may seem like a phantasmagoria. To Sigmund Freud, these bizarre events and images had a deeper meaning: for Freud the key to a person's psychology lay in his or her *fantasies*.

phenomenon \fi-'nä-mə-,nän\ (1) A fact or event observed or known with the senses. (2) A rare, unusual, or important fact or event.

• To Noah and the others on his ark, the appearance of a rainbow was a joyous phenomenon.

Phenomena are "things" (though not generally "objects"), and sometimes "strange or unusual things." Something *phenomenal* is extraordinary, and *phenomenally* means "extremely" or "extraordinarily." Psychic phenomena, weather phenomena, social phenomena can all be either facts or events. A phenomenon is a single thing; the plural form is *phenomena*. Take care not to mix them up.

diaphanous \dī-'a-fə-nəs\ (1) Transparent. (2) Insubstantial or vague.

• The ballerinas of Tchaikovsky's *Swan Lake* wore diaphanous costumes that seemed to float.

Light mist is diaphanous, since things may be seen at least faintly through it. Gauzy fabric is diaphanous; another word for it is "sheer." A diaphanous princess might be a fantasy vision that is hardly real at all. And a diaphanous notion would be one without much real substance behind it.

VER comes from the Latin word for "truth." A *verdict* in a trial is "the truth spoken." But a just verdict may depend on the *veracity,* or "truthfulness," of the witnesses.

---

aver \ə-'vər\ To state positively as true; declare.

• The defendant averred that she was nowhere near the scene of the crime on the night in question.

You may aver anything that you're sure of. Since the word contains the "truth" root, it basically means "confirm as true." In legal situations it means to state or allege positively as a fact; thus, Perry Mason's clients aver that they are innocent, while the district attorney avers the opposite.

verify \'ver-ə-ˌfī\ (1) To prove to be true or correct. (2) To check or test the accuracy of.

• It is the bank teller's job to verify the signature on a check.

During talks between the United States and the former Soviet Union on nuclear weapons reduction, one big problem was how to verify that weapons had been eliminated. Since neither side wanted the other to know its secrets, *verification* of the facts became a difficult issue. Because of the distrust on both sides, many thought that the real numbers would never be *verifiable*.

verisimilitude \ˌver-ə-sə-'mi-lə-ˌtüd\ (1) The appearance of being true or probable. (2) The depiction of realism in art or literature.

• By the beginning of the 20th century, the leading European painters were losing interest in verisimilitude and beginning to experiment with abstraction.

From its roots, *verisimilitude* means basically "like the truth." Most fiction writers and filmmakers aim at some kind of verisimilitude to give their stories an air of reality. This doesn't mean they need to show something actually true, or even very common—just simply possible and believable. A mass of good details in a play, novel, painting, or film may add verisimilitude. A spy novel without some verisimilitude won't interest many readers, but a fantastical novel may not even attempt to seem true to life.

verity \'ver-ə-tē\ A true fact or statement.

● Ben Franklin's statement that "in this world nothing can be said to be certain, except death and taxes" is held as a verity by many.

The phrase "eternal verity" is often used to mean an enduring truth or bit of wisdom. Some eternal verities are found in proverbs, such as "Haste makes waste." The statement in the Declaration of Independence that "all men are created equal" is now held by many Americans to be an eternal verity—but few earlier governments had ever been based on such a truth.

Quizzes

A. Fill in each blank with the correct letter:

a. phenomenon	e. diaphanous
b. aver	f. verity
c. phantasmagoria	g. phantasm
d. verify	h. verisimilitude

1. They had never before seen a natural _____ like the boiling lake.
2. A week after his mother's death, he saw her _____ beckoning to him from the dock at dusk.
3. The prosecutor expected the witness to _____ that the suspect was guilty.
4. Realists in art and literature work to achieve _____ as they sense it.
5. Each candle was surrounded by the _____ fluttering wings of moths.
6. The Mardi Gras parade was a _____ of bizarre images too numerous to even take in.
7. She was never able to _____ anything he had told her.

8. Sometimes what has always seemed a _____ suddenly is shown to be false.

B. Complete the analogy:

1. believe : doubt :: aver : _____
   a. state b. mean c. deny d. subtract
2. scent : smell :: phenomenon : _____
   a. odor b. sight c. event d. sensation
3. illusion : fantasy :: verisimilitude : _____
   a. appearance b. realism c. style d. truth
4. faint : dim :: diaphanous : _____
   a. filmy b. huge c. old-fashioned d. sensational
5. loyalty : treason :: verity : _____
   a. dishonor b. hatred c. honesty d. falsehood
6. ogre : monster :: phantasm : _____
   a. surprise b. raven c. ghost d. fanfare
7. praise : ridicule :: verify : _____
   a. testify b. contradict c. establish d. foretell
8. fantasy : illusion :: phantasmagoria : _____
   a. collection b. kaleidoscope c. sideshow d. visions

TURB comes from the Latin verb *turbare,* "to throw into confusion or upset," and the noun *turba,* "crowd" or "confusion." A *disturbance,* for example, confuses and upsets normal order or routine.

---

perturb \pər-'tərb\ To upset, confuse, or disarrange.

• News of the new peace accord was enough to perturb some radical opponents of any settlements.

If the root -*turb* means basically "upset," then *perturb* means "thoroughly upset." A person in a *perturbed* state of mind is more than merely bothered. On the other hand, someone *imperturbable* remains calm through the most trying experiences.

turbine \'tər-,bīn\ A rotary engine with blades made to turn and generate power by a current of water, steam, or air under pressure.

• The power plant used huge turbines powered by water going over the dam to generate electricity.

The oldest and simplest form of turbine is the waterwheel, which is made to rotate by water falling across its blades and into buckets suspended from them. Hero of Alexandria invented the first steam-driven turbine in the 1st century A.D.; but a commercially practical steam turbine was not developed until 1884. Steam-driven turbines are now the main elements of electric power stations. Jet engines are gas turbines. A *turbojet* engine uses a turbine to compress the incoming air that feeds the engine before being ejected to push the plane forward; a *turboprop* engine uses its exhaust to drive a turbine that spins a propeller.

turbulent \'tər-byù-lənt\ (1) Stirred up, agitated. (2) Stirring up unrest, violence, or disturbance.

• The huge ocean liner *Queen Elizabeth II* has never been much troubled by turbulent or stormy seas.

Often the captain of an airplane will warn passengers to fasten their seatbelts because of upper-air *turbulence,* which can make for a bumpy ride. El Niño, a seasonal current of warm water in the Pacific Ocean, may create turbulence in the winds across the United States, affecting patterns of rainfall and temperature as well. The late 1960s are remembered as turbulent years of social revolution in America and Europe. Some people lead turbulent lives, and some are constantly in the grip of turbulent emotions.

turbid \'tər-bid\ (1) Thick or murky, especially with churned-up sediment. (2) Unclear, confused, muddled.

• The crowd's mood was restless and turbid; any spark could have turned it into a mob.

The Colorado River in spring, swollen by melting snow from the high mountains, races through the Grand Canyon, turbid and churning. A chemical solution may be described as turbid rather than clear. And your emotions may be turbid as well, especially where love is involved: What did he mean by that glance? Why did she say it like that?

VOLU/VOLV comes from the Latin verb *volvere,* meaning "to roll, wind, turn around, or twist around." From this source come words like *volume,* which was originally the name of a scroll or roll of papyrus, and *revolve,* which simply means "turn in circles."

devolution \ˌde-və-'lü-shən\ (1) The transfer of rights, powers, property, or responsibility to others, especially from the central to local government. (2) Evolution toward an earlier or lower state.

• In the 1980s there was a devolution of responsibility for education from the federal government to state and local governments.

Devolution implies moving backward. Once powers have been centralized in a unified government, giving any powers back to smaller governmental units can seem to be reversing a natural development. But we may also speak of moral devolution, such as occurred in Germany in the 1930s, when a country with an extraordinarily high culture became a brutal, aggressive, murderous dictatorship. The verb form is *devolve*. Thus, a job that your boss doesn't want to do may devolve upon you.

evolution \ˌe-və-'lü-shən\ A process of change from a lower, simpler, or worse state to one that is higher, more complex, or better.

• Thomas Jefferson and the other Founding Fathers believed that political evolution reached its highest form in democracy.

Part of the humor of *The Flintstones* is that it contradicts what is known about evolution, since humans actually *evolved* long after dinosaurs were extinct. *Evolution* can also be used more broadly to refer to technology, society, and other human creations. For example, though many people don't believe that human beings truly become better with the passing centuries, many will argue that our societies tend to evolve, producing more goods and providing more protection for more people.

voluble \'väl-yu̇-bəl\ Speaking readily and rapidly; talkative.

• He proved to be a voluble informer who would tell stories of bookies, smugglers, and hit men to the detectives for hours.

A voluble person has words "rolling" off his or her tongue. In O. Henry's famous story "The Ransom of Red Chief" the kidnappers nab a boy who is so unbearably voluble that they can hardly wait to turn him loose again.

convoluted \'kän-və-ˌlü-təd\ (1) Having a pattern of curved windings. (2) Involved, intricate.

• After 15 minutes, Mr. Collins's strange story had become so convoluted that none of us could follow it.

Convolution originally meant a complex winding pattern such as those on the brain. So a convoluted argument or a convoluted explanation is one that winds this way and that. An official form may have to wind its way through a convoluted process and be stamped by eight people before being approved. Convoluted language makes many people suspicious; as a great philosopher once said, "Anything that can be said can be said clearly."

Quizzes

A. Choose the closest definition:

1. convoluted   a. spinning b. babbling c. grinding
      d. winding
2. turbine   a. whirlpool b. engine c. headdress d. carousel
3. evolution   a. process of development b. process of
      democracy c. process of election d. process of
      elimination
4. perturb   a. reset b. inset c. preset d. upset
5. voluble   a. whirling b. unpleasant c. talkative
      d. garbled
6. turbulent   a. churning b. turning c. yearning d. burning
7. turbid   a. flat b. calm c. confused d. slow
8. devolution   a. handing down b. handing in c. turning
      up d. turning around

B. Match the word on the left to the correct definition on the right:

1. voluble   a. murky
2. turbine   b. fluent
3. evolution   c. seething
4. turbid   d. complicated
5. devolution   e. turning engine
6. perturb   f. degeneration
7. convoluted   g. disturb
8. turbulent   h. progress

FAC/FEC/FIC comes from the Latin verb *facere*, meaning "to make or do." Thus, a *benefactor* is someone who does good. To *manufacture* is to make, usually in a *factory*.

---

confection \kən-'fek-shən\ (1) A sweet food or fancy dish prepared from a variety of ingredients. (2) A piece of fine craftsmanship.

● The children's eyes grew wide with delight at the sight of the confections in the baker's window.

A confection is *confected* from several different ingredients or elements. Among the tastiest confections are the marzipan (almondpaste) creations molded and painted to look like fruit. The word can also be used to refer to any finely worked piece of craftsmanship. So the lacy box containing chocolate confections can be called a confection itself.

facile \'fa-səl\ (1) Easily accomplished. (2) Shallow, superficial.

● The principal made a facile argument for the school's policy, but no one was convinced.

A facile writer seems to write too quickly and easily, and a careful reader discovers that the writer hasn't really said very much. A facile suggestion doesn't deal with the issue in any depth, and a facile solution may be only temporarily effective.

olfactory \ōl-'fak-tə-rē\ Having to do with the sense of smell.

● The olfactory sense of some dogs is so powerful that they can smell a human under 20 feet of snow.

Olfactory includes part of the Latin verb *olere*, meaning "to smell." The tasters of great wines depend more on their olfactory sense than they do on their taste buds. The olfactory nerve, which produces the sense of smell, is closely connected to the sense of taste. Since the *gustatory* (taste) nerves can only distinguish four different tastes (salt, sweet, sour, and bitter), the rest of our taste perception is actually olfactory.

proficient \prə-'fi-shənt\ Skilled in an art, occupation, or branch of knowledge.

• She's proficient at every aspect of the job; all she lacks is imagination.

Proficiency is achieved through hard work and maybe talent as well. You may be proficient at math or proficient in three languages, or you may be a proficient swimmer. A proficient pianist plays the piano with skill. But proficiency isn't genius, and even calling someone proficient may imply that the person isn't brilliantly gifted.

UT/US comes from the Latin verb *uti,* "to use, make use of, employ," and the related adjective *utilis,* "useful, fit." It is *used* in such words as *abuse,* "improper use," and *reuse,* "to use again."

---

usufruct \'yü-zə-ˌfrəkt\ (1) The right to use or enjoy something. (2) The legal right of using or enjoying the products or profits of something that belongs to someone else.

• When they sold the land, they retained the right by usufruct to pick the apples in the orchards they had planted.

Usufruct is a concept that has come down from ancient times. The original term in Latin was *usus et fructus,* meaning "use and enjoyment." It is an interesting concept: since the original owner can devolve the responsibility of upkeep and taxes onto someone else while keeping usufruct, he or she may get the best of the deal. Usufruct rights end at a certain point, often when the user dies, and do not permit changing or damaging the property. As Thomas Jefferson said (and many environmentalists have echoed), "The earth belongs in usufruct to the living." And as the Roman philosopher Lucretius said, life itself is given to us only in usufruct.

usury \'yü-zhə-rē\ The lending of money with a fee charged for its use, especially lending for an unusually high fee.

• He responded that demanding 25 percent interest on the loan was usury.

Shylock, in Shakespeare's *The Merchant of Venice,* is accused of usury, since he has bargained to take a pound of Antonio's flesh in place of the money Antonio owes him. Since this would result in Antonio's death, it seems like an excessive and *unusual* penalty for the failure to repay a debt. To the borrower, usury seems *abusive*; to the lender, it is a fair fee for use of the money. No wonder Polonius told Laertes in *Hamlet*, "Neither a borrower nor a lender be"; the borrower becomes careless about spending and ends up at the *usurer's* mercy, and the lender often becomes resented or even hated and may lose his or her money.

utilitarian \yü-,ti-lə-'tar-ē-ən\ (1) Aiming at usefulness rather than beauty. (2) Useful for a specific purpose or end.

• Their view of life was strictly utilitarian; for them there was no room for art, pleasure, or relaxed conversation.

The Shakers, a religious group that dedicated itself to work and its work to God, had a utilitarian outlook on the design of furniture and household objects. Their finished pieces—whether tables, chairs, brooms, or baskets—are beautifully simple and very well fitted to their use. But *utilitarian* often means somewhat homely. Utilitarian architecture, such as many government housing projects, may be quite ugly, for example. If we say something has utilitarian value, however, we simply mean it is useful in some way.

utility \yü-'ti-lə-tē\ (1) Usefulness. (2) A government-regulated business providing a public service; the service it provides.

• The book was an invention of such extraordinary utility that in 2,000 years no one has improved on it.

A dog bred for utility is one intended for a particular use such as hunting or herding. It may be called a *utility* dog, just as a Jeep may be called a utility vehicle. The local electric company is one kind of company often called a utility, and the electric, gas, and water service in your home are called utilities as well.

Quizzes

A. Fill in each blank with the correct letter:

a. usufruct	e. facile
b. utilitarian	f. confection
c. utility	g. olfactory
d. usury	h. proficient

1. They kept the right to use their neighbor's dock by ____.
2. The interest rate for the loan offered by the bank amounted to sheer ____.
3. She was quick-witted but often her reasoning was ____ and not deeply thoughtful.
4. She chose an inexpensive, ____ model with no radio and no power windows.
5. Mozart was ____ at the piano by the age of 5.
6. The ____ of his 1940s typewriter was such that he never felt the need for a word processor.
7. The gown in the window was a gorgeous ____ by the designer Ariane.
8. Commuting daily through the smog-filled air, she was grateful that her ____ sense was not very keen.

B. Indicate whether the following pairs of words have the same or different meanings:

1. proficient / skillful   same ___ / different ___
2. usufruct / sweetness   same ___ / different ___
3. confection / candy   same ___ / different ___
4. utility / tool   same ___ / different ___
5. olfactory / assembly   same ___ / different ___
6. usury / customary   same ___ / different ___
7. facile / slippery   same ___ / different ___
8. utilitarian / useful   same ___ / different ___

Words from Mythology and History

muse \'myüz\ A source of inspiration; a guiding spirit.

• At 8:00 each morning he sat down at his desk and summoned his muse, and she almost always responded.

The Muses were the nine Greek goddesses that presided over the arts (including *music*) and literature. Their temple was called in Latin the *Museum*. An artist or poet such as Homer, especially when about to begin work, would call on his particular Muse to inspire him. Today a muse may be one's special creative spirit, but some artists have also chosen living human beings to serve as their muses.

iridescent \ˌir-ə-'de-sənt\ Having a glowing, rainbowlike play of color that seems to change as the light shifts.

• The children shrieked with glee as they blew iridescent soap bubbles into the gentle breeze.

Iris, the Greek goddess of the rainbow, took messages from Mount Olympus to earth, and from gods to mortals or other gods, using the rainbow as her stairway. *Iridescence* is thus the glowing, shifting, colorful quality of a rainbow, also seen in an opal, a light oil slick, a butterfly wing, or the mother-of-pearl that lines an oyster shell.

mausoleum \ˌmȯ-zə-'lē-əm\ (1) A large tomb, especially one built aboveground with shelves for the dead. (2) A large, gloomy building or room.

• The family's grand mausoleum occupied a prominent spot in the cemetery, for all the good it did the silent dead within.

Mausolus was ruler of a kingdom in Asia Minor in the 4th century B.C. He beautified the capital, Halicarnassus, with all sorts of fine public buildings, but he is best known for the magnificent monument, the Mausoleum, that was built by his wife Artemisia after his death. The Mausoleum was one of the Seven Wonders of the Ancient World. Today any large tomb can be called a mausoleum, and so can any big, dark, echoing interior space.

mentor \'men-ˌtȯr\ A trusted counselor, guide, tutor, or coach.

• This pleasant old gentleman had served as friend and mentor to a series of young lawyers in the firm.

Odysseus was away from home fighting and journeying for 20 years, according to Homer. During that time, the son he left as a babe in arms grew up under the supervision of Mentor, an old and trusted friend. When the goddess Athena decided it was time to complete young Telemachus's education by sending him off to learn about his father, she visited him disguised as Mentor and they set out together. From this, anyone such as a coach or tutor who gives another (usually younger) person help and advice on how to achieve success in the larger world is called a mentor.

narcissism \\'när-si-ˌsi-zəm\\ (1) Extreme self-centeredness or fascination with oneself. (2) Love or desire for one's own body.

• His girlfriend would complain about his narcissism, saying he spent more time looking in the mirror than looking at her.

Narcissus was a handsome youth in Greek mythology who inspired love in many who saw him. One was the nymph Echo, who could only repeat the last thing that anyone said. When Narcissus cruelly rejected her, she wasted away to nothing but her voice. Though he played with the affections of others, Narcissus became a victim of his own attractiveness. When he caught sight of his own reflection in a pool, he sat gazing at it in fascination, wasting away without food or drink, unable to touch or kiss the image he saw. When he finally died, the gods turned him into a flower, a narcissus, that stands with its head bent as though gazing at its own reflection. From this myth comes the name of a psychological disorder, narcissism, which is the excessive love of oneself, as well as a more common type of vanity and self-centeredness.

tantalize \\'tan-tə-ˌlīz\\ To tease or torment by offering something desirable but keeping it out of reach.

• The sight of a warm fire through the window tantalized the little match girl almost unbearably.

Tantalus, according to Greek mythology, killed his son Pelops and offered him to the gods in a stew for dinner. Almost all of the gods realized what was happening and refused the meal, but Demeter took a nibble out of Pelops's shoulder. The gods reconstructed Pelops, replacing the missing shoulder with a piece of ivory, and then punished Tantalus. In Hades he stands in water up to his neck under a tree laden with fruit. Each time he stoops to drink, the water moves out of reach; each time he reaches up to pick something, the branches move beyond his grasp. He is thus eternally tantalized by the water and fruit. Today anything or anyone that tempts but is unobtainable is tantalizing.

thespian \\'thes-pē-ən\\ (1) An actor. (2) Having to do with the drama; dramatic.

• In summer the towns of New England welcome troupes of thespians dedicated to presenting plays of all kinds.

Greek drama was originally entirely performed by choruses. Literary tradition says that Thespis, the Greek dramatist, was inventor of tragedy and the first to write roles for the individual actor as distinct from the chorus. Thespians fill all the roles in more modern plays. *Thespian* is also an adjective; thus, we can speak of "thespian ambitions" and "thespian traditions," for example.

zephyr \'ze-fər\ (1) A breeze from the west. (2) A gentle breeze.

• Columbus left Genoa sailing against the zephyrs that continually blow across the Mediterranean.

The ancient Greeks called the west wind Zephyrus and regarded him and his fellow winds as gods. A zephyr is a kind wind, bringer of clear skies and beautiful weather, though it may occasionally be more than a soft breeze.

Quiz

Fill in each blank with the correct letter:

a. mausoleum   e. muse
b. thespian   f. mentor
c. iridescent   g. zephyr
d. tantalize   h. narcissism

1. The couple felt timid and small inside the vast _____ where their lawyer asked them to come.
2. On fair days a gentle _____ would blow from morning until night.
3. The company president took the new recruit under her wing and acted as her _____ for the next several years.
4. He would often _____ her with talk of traveling to Brazil or India, but nothing ever came of it.
5. The puddle's surface was beautifully _____ in the slanting light.
6. After his last book of poetry was published, his _____ seemed to have abandoned him.
7. In everyone there is a bit of the _____ yearning for a stage.
8. By working as a model, she could satisfy her _____ while getting paid for it.

Review Quizzes

A. Choose the correct antonym and the correct synonym:

1. voluble   a. argumentative   b. mumbly   c. speechless   d. talkative
2. proficient   a. lazy   b. skilled   c. inept   d. professional
3. utilitarian   a. useless   b. useful   c. usual   d. unusual
4. zephyr   a. stormy blast   b. icy rain   c. light shower   d. gentle breeze
5. aver   a. reject   b. detract   c. deny   d. assert
6. diaphanous   a. broken   b. filmy   c. muddy   d. tattered
7. ludicrous   a. serious   b. ordinary   c. laughable   d. amazing
8. perturb   a. soothe   b. restore   c. park   d. upset
9. devolution   a. decay   b. turn   c. suggestion   d. improvement
10. usury   a. sending   b. lending   c. giving   d. mending
11. draconian   a. precise   b. gentle   c. harsh   d. inaccurate
12. turbulent   a. churning   b. official   c. cloudy   d. calm
13. tantalize   a. visit   b. satisfy   c. tease   d. watch
14. iridescent   a. shimmering   b. drab   c. striped   d. watery
15. mentor   a. translator   b. interpreter   c. guide   d. student
16. phantasm   a. vision   b. amazement   c. actuality   d. horror

B. Indicate whether the following pairs of terms have the same or different meanings:

1. thespian / teacher   same ___ / different ___
2. facile / nasty   same ___ / different ___
3. evolution / extinction   same ___ / different ___
4. verify / prove   same ___ / different ___
5. phenomenon / event   same ___ / different ___
6. collusion / opposition   same ___ / different ___
7. incantation / luxury   same ___ / different ___
8. turbid / muddy   same ___ / different ___
9. olfactory / smelling   same ___ / different ___
10. usufruct / right of use   same ___ / different ___

C. Fill in each blank with the correct letter:

a.   prelude   g.   confection
b.   narcissism   h.   allude
c.   descant   i.   cantor
d.   verisimilitude   j.   phantasmagoria
e.   cantata   k.   turbine
f.   verity   l.   mausoleum

1.   It was accepted as a _____ in their household that the
     future would be better than the past.
2.   They were a very attractive couple, but their _____ often
     annoyed other people.
3.   The university chorus was going to perform a Bach _____
     along with the Mozart *Requiem*.
4.   The children were invited to choose one chocolate _____
     apiece from the counter display.
5.   He began his singing career as a _____ in Brooklyn and
     ended it as an international opera star.
6.   She remembered Mardi Gras only as an endless _____ of
     swirling images.
7.   One day in the cemetery the _____ door was open, and he
     peered in with horrified fascination.
8.   She would try to _____ to the problem sometimes, but he
     never seemed to listen.
9.   The cocktail party was only a _____ to the main event,
     the awards ceremony.
10. Her films showed her own reality, and she had no
     interest in _____.
11. The roar of the _____ was so loud they couldn't hear
     each other.
12. As part of their musical training, she always encouraged
     them to sing their own _____ over the main melody.

Unit 12

UMBR, from the Latin *umbra*, "shadow," is a shady customer. The familiar *umbrella*, with its ending meaning "little," casts a "little shadow" to keep off the sun or the rain.

adumbrate \'a-dəm-brāt\ (1) To give a sketchy outline or disclose in part. (2) To hint at or foretell.

● The Secretary of State would only adumbrate his ideas for bringing peace to Bosnia.

A synonym for *adumbrate* is *foreshadow*, which means to present a shadowy version of something before it becomes reality or is provided in full. Rats scurrying off a ship were believed to adumbrate a coming disaster at sea. A bad review by a critic may adumbrate the failure of a new film.

penumbra \pə-'nəm-brə\ (1) The partial shadow surrounding a complete shadow, as in an eclipse. (2) The fringe or surrounding area where something exists less fully.

● This area of the investigation was the penumbra where both the FBI and the CIA wanted to pursue their leads.

Every solar eclipse casts an *umbra*, the darker central area in which almost no light reaches the earth, and a penumbra, the area of partial shadow where part of the sun is still visible. *Penumbra* can thus be used to describe any "gray area" where things are not all black and white. For example, the right to privacy falls under the penumbra of the U.S. Constitution; though it is not specifically guaranteed there, the Supreme Court has held that it is implied, and thus that the government may not intrude into certain areas of a citizen's private life. Because its existence is still shadowy, however, the

Court is still determining how much of an individual's life is protected by the right to privacy.

umber \\'əm-bər\ (1) A darkish brown mineral containing manganese and iron oxides used for coloring paint. (2) A color that is greenish brown to dark reddish brown.

• Van Dyke prized umber as a pigment and used it constantly in his oil paintings.

The mineral deposits of Italy provided sources of a number of natural pigments, among them umber. Since the late Renaissance, umber has been in great demand as a coloring agent. When crushed and mixed with paint it produces an olive, known as *raw umber*; when crushed and burnt it produces a darker tone, known as *burnt umber*.

umbrage \\'əm-brij\ A feeling of resentment at some slight or insult, often one that is imagined rather than real.

• She often took umbrage at his treatment of her, without being able to pinpoint what was offensive about it.

An umbrage was originally a shadow, and soon also meant a shadowy suspicion. Then it came to mean displeasure as well—that is, a kind of shadow blocking the sunlight. *Umbrage* is now generally used in the phrase "take umbrage at." An overly sensitive person may take umbrage at something as small as having his or her name pronounced wrong.

VEST comes from the Latin verb *vestire*, "to clothe" or "to dress," and the related noun *vestis*, "clothing" or "garment." *Vest* is the shortest English word we have from this root, and is the name of a rather small piece of clothing.

---

divest \dī-'vest\ (1) To get rid of or free oneself of property, authority, or title. (2) To strip of clothing, ornaments, or equipment.

• In protest against apartheid, many universities in the 1980s divested themselves of all stock in South African companies.

When it turned out that the New York Marathon had been won by fraud, the "winner" was divested of her prize. When a church is officially abandoned, it is usually divested of its ornaments and furnishings. And if you decide to move or to enter a monastery, you may divest yourself of many of your possessions.

investiture \in-'ves-tə-ˌchür\ The formal placing of someone in office.

● At an English monarch's investiture, he or she is presented with the crown, scepter, and sword, the symbols of power.

In its original meaning, *investiture* referred to clothing the new officeholder in the garments that symbolized power. The Middle Ages saw much debate over the investiture of bishops and abbots by kings and emperors. These rulers felt that high religious offices were theirs to give to whomever they chose as a reward for loyal service or as a guarantee of future support, but the popes saw these investitures as the buying and selling of church offices. The investiture struggle caused tension between popes and monarchs and even led to wars.

transvestite \tranz-'ves-ˌtīt\ A person, especially a male, who wears the clothing and adopts the mannerisms of the opposite sex.

● Gounod's opera *Romeo and Juliet* calls for a woman in the transvestite role of Romeo.

Transvestite includes the prefix *trans-*, "across," and thus means literally "cross-dresser." Today it is so acceptable for women to wear men's clothing that the word *transvestite* is generally applied only to men. In the theater, from ancient Greece to Elizabethan England, *transvestism* was common because all parts were played by men—even Juliet. Japanese Kabuki and No drama still employ transvestism of this sort.

travesty \'tra-vəs-tē\ (1) An inferior or distorted imitation. (2) A broadly comic imitation in drama, literature, or art that is usually grotesque and ridiculous.

● The senator shouted again that the new tax bill represented a travesty of tax reform.

The word *travesty* comes from the same prefix and root as *transvestite* and originally meant "to disguise." The "free elections" so often promised by military governments usually amount to a travesty of democracy—a disguise intended to fool the world. The variety show *Saturday Night Live* specializes in dramatic travesties mocking everything from political figures and issues to popular culture—"disguised" versions intended for entertainment. *Travesty* may also be a verb. Thus, Mel Brooks has travestied movies of all kinds—westerns, thrillers, and silent films, among others.

Quizzes

A. Fill in the blank with the correct letter:

a. penumbra   e. divest
b. transvestite   f. umber
c. investiture   g. umbrage
d. travesty   h. adumbrate

1. Titian employed assistants to mix the ＿＿ and other pigments for his paintings.
2. The ＿＿ of the prime minister was an occasion of pomp and ceremony.
3. Some people are quick to take ＿＿ the moment they think they have been slighted.
4. Since all the judges were cronies of the dictator, the court proceedings were a ＿＿ of justice.
5. The new director planned to ＿＿ the museum of two of its Picassos.
6. The farther away a source of light is from the object casting a shadow, the wider will be that shadow's ＿＿.
7. The young model became a notorious success when she was discovered to be a ＿＿.
8. The increasing cloudiness and the damp wind seemed to ＿＿ a stormy night.

B. Match the definition on the left to the correct word on the right:

1. resentment   a. penumbra
2. brownish color   b. travesty
3. installing in office   c. transvestite
4. cross-dresser   d. adumbrate
5. imitation   e. divest
6. get rid of   f. umbrage
7. near shadow   g. investiture
8. partially disclose   h. umber

THE/THEO comes from the Greek word meaning "god." *Theology* is the study of gods or religion. *Monotheism* is the worship of a single god; someone who is *polytheistic,* however, worships many gods.

apotheosis \ə-ˌpä-thē-'ō-səs\ (1) Transformation into a god. (2) The perfect example.

● After his assassination Abraham Lincoln underwent an apotheosis that transformed the controversial politician into a saintly father of democracy.

The word *apotheosis* has the prefix *apo-,* "relating to"; thus, it suggests a human who has become godlike. In Greek mythology, very few humans were *apotheosized,* but Heracles (Hercules) was one who made the grade, and there are pictures painted on ancient vases showing the big party the rest of the gods held for him when he joined them after his apotheosis. Any great classic example of something can be called its apotheosis; a collector might state, for example, that the Duesenberg Phaeton was the apotheosis of the touring car.

atheistic \ˌā-thē-'is-tik\ Denying the existence of God or divine power.

● The atheistic Madalyn Murray O'Hair successfully sought the removal of prayer from American public schools in the 1960s.

In the Roman Empire, early Christians were said to be atheistic because they denied the existence of the gods of the pantheon. The Christian church, once established, in turn condemned the unconverted Romans as *atheists* because they did not believe in the Christian God. *Atheism* is different from *agnosticism,* which claims that the existence of any higher power is unknowable.

pantheistic \ˌpan-thē-'is-tik\ (1) Seeing the power of God in all the natural forces of the universe. (2) Worshiping all gods of all creeds and cults.

● Her personal religion was almost pantheistic; she saw the holy books of Hinduism and the rituals of Caribbean folk religion as expressions of the same essential truths.

Pan means "all"; thus, *pantheistic* refers to "all gods," or alternatively to "god in all things." Originally each Roman god and goddess had a temple where sacrifices were offered and sacred objects were stored. But there came a time when too many gods demanded attention, so only a big temple in honor of the entire group would do. Thus, the great temple known as the *Pantheon* was dedicated to all the gods. (These days, *pantheon* can also refer to a group of historical superstars in any one area—the pantheon of basketball or of literature, for example.)

theocracy \thē-'ä-krə-sē\ (1) Government by officials who are regarded as divinely inspired. (2) A state governed by a theocracy.

• The ancient Aztecs lived in a theocracy in which guidance came directly from the gods through the priests.

The ancient state of Israel and its related state of Judah were *monotheistic* (one-god) theocracies; the ancient state of the Aztecs in Mexico was a *polytheistic* (multi-god) theocracy, as was that of the ancient Sumerians. All four seem to have agreed that the power of the ruling god or gods was most forceful in high places. The Sumerians and Aztecs built enormous pyramidlike temples; the Jews sought divine guidance on mountaintops. Modern-day theocracies are rare; Iran has been the best-known recent *theocratic* government.

DE/DIV comes from two related Roman words, *deus,* "god," and *divus,* "divine." *Deism,* a philosophy that teaches natural religion, emphasizes morality, and denies that the creator god interferes with the laws of the universe, was the basic faith of many of America's Founding Fathers.

---

deity \'dē-ə-tē\ A god or goddess.

• The many-armed deity Kali, wife of Shiva, is the Hindu goddess of death.

The ancient Greek deities had special cities and places they protected in return for sacrifices and prayers and special celebrations in their honor. Athena was the deity in charge of Athens; Hera was responsible for Sparta and Argos, and Apollo for Delphi. Each deity also had responsibility for a specific function or area of life: Athena for weaving and other crafts, Hera for marriage, and Apollo for the lives of young men, music, and *divination* (foretelling the future).

deus ex machina \'dā-əs-‚eks-'mä-ki-nə\ (1) In Greek and Roman drama, a god who enters above the stage by means of a crane and decides the play's outcome. (2) A person or thing that appears suddenly and solves an apparently unsolvable problem.

● Pinned down by enemy fire, the soldiers had nearly given up hope when a helicopter appeared like a deus ex machina.

Deus ex machina means literally "the god from the machine," referring to the crane that held the god over the stage. A character in a mystery who appears from out of nowhere with the solution near the end could be called a deus ex machina; however, dedicated mystery readers have contempt for such solutions.

divinatory \də-'vi-nə-‚tór-ē\ Seeking to foresee or foretell the future, usually by interpreting signs or asking for supernatural help.

● Astrologers today claim to use divinatory methods handed down from the ancient Egyptians and Babylonians.

Throughout history, divinatory practices that seek to reveal the future have been popular. In Roman times, a *diviner* known as a "haruspex" would search the guts of sacrificed animals to foretell coming events. The flights of birds were interpreted by a type of *divination* known as "augury." Tarot cards, séances, Ouija boards, and palm readings continue to be used by people hoping to *divine* (predict) the future.

divinity \də-'vi-nə-tē\ (1) The state of being a god or goddess. (2) A god or goddess; a deity.

● Some early Christian sects, such as the Arians, questioned the actual divinity of Jesus Christ.

In the 5th century A.D., the Roman Empire was on the verge of collapse. Many Roman senators claimed that the divinities that had always protected the city had abandoned them because so many people worshiped a new divinity, the Christian God. In defense, St. Augustine wrote *The City of God*, arguing that all earthly cities must pass, and that only the one true Divinity is eternal.

Quizzes

A. Fill in each blank with the correct letter:

a.	pantheistic	e.	deity
b.	deus ex machina	f.	apotheosis
c.	atheistic	g.	divinatory
d.	divinity	h.	theocracy

1. There around the temple stood idols of all the gods of this _____ religion.
2. The psychic's _____ powers were regarded by her clients as astounding.
3. His well-known _____ beliefs meant the young politician could hope for only limited success.
4. There above the stage appeared Apollo, the _____, to solve the dilemma.
5. Being inducted into the Hall of Fame is as close as a modern ballplayer can come to _____.
6. She addressed her prayer to whatever _____ chose to listen.
7. When the young man's followers proclaimed his _____, the believing Christians were shocked.
8. The high priest in this medieval _____ was equivalent to a dictator.

B. Match the word on the left to its definition on the right:

1.	deity	a.	state ruled by religion
2.	pantheistic	b.	dramatic device
3.	apotheosis	c.	supreme being
4.	divinity	d.	nonbelieving
5.	atheistic	e.	godliness
6.	divinatory	f.	accepting all gods
7.	theocracy	g.	prophetic
8.	deus ex machina	h.	perfect example

DEMO comes from the Greek word meaning "people." A *demagogue* leads the people, usually into trouble, by lying and appealing to their prejudices.

demographic \‚de-mə-'gra-fik\ Having to do with the study of human populations, especially their size, growth, density, and patterns of living.

● The government used the latest demographic figures to decide how much money to spend on education.

Demographic analysis, the statistical description of human populations, is a tool used by government agencies, political parties, and manufacturers of consumer goods. Polls conducted on every topic imaginable, from age to toothpaste preference, give the government and corporations an idea of who the public is and what it needs and wants. The government's census, which is conducted every ten years, is the largest demographic survey carried out in this country.

endemic \en-'de-mik\ (1) Found only in a given place or region. (2) Often found in a given occupation, area, or environment.

● Malaria is a disease that is endemic in tropical regions around the world.

Endemic means literally "in the population." Since the panda is found in the wild exclusively in central China and eastern Tibet, scientists say that it is "endemic to" those areas or that they are "endemic areas" for the panda. But the word can also mean simply "common" or "typical," so we can say that colds are "endemic in" nursery school and that love of Barbie dolls is "endemic among" young American girls.

pandemic \‚pan-'de-mik\ Widespread and affecting a large portion of the people.

● The worldwide AIDS pandemic may eventually prove to be the most deadly such event in human history.

Pandemic is a stronger version of *epidemic*. In a pandemic outbreak, practically everyone may be affected. In 1348 a pandemic plague called the Black Death struck Western Europe and killed 25 million people. In 1918 a *pandemic* of influenza killed 20 million people around the world. Pandemic smallpox repeatedly swept through the world's populations until the 1970s, even though a vaccine had existed since 1798. When the Beatles first visited the United States in the early 1960s, they were greeted by pandemic "Beatlemania," a mild form of musical insanity.

demotic \di-'mä-tik\ Popular or common.

• Because of television, the demotic language and accents of the various regions of this country are becoming more and more similar.

Demotic describes what is done by ordinary people as a group. It often describes their speech—demotic Californian is different from demotic Texan, for example. The most demotic dress in America is probably blue jeans and sneakers, and those who wear them can be said to have demotic taste in fashion.

POPUL comes from the Latin word meaning "people," and in fact forms the basis of the word *people* itself. *Popular* means not only "liked by many people" but also "relating to the general public." *Popular culture* is thus the culture of the general public. And the *population* is the people of an area.

---

populist \'pä-pyə-list\ A believer in the rights, wisdom, or virtues of the common people.

• He decided that he would campaign as a populist in order to appeal to his working-class voters.

The word *populist* first appeared in the 1890s with the founding of the Populist Party, which stood primarily for the interests of the farmers against the big-money interests. In later years *populism* came to be associated with the white working class as well. Populism can swing from liberal to conservative. It sometimes has a religious tendency; it usually is not very interested in international affairs; it has sometimes been unfriendly to black interests; and it is often anti-intellectual. But the *populist* style always shows its concern with Americans with average incomes as opposed to the rich and powerful.

populace \'pä-pyu̇-ləs\ (1) The common people or masses. (2) Population.

• Perhaps Henry Ford's major achievement was to manufacture a car that the entire populace could afford—the Model T.

Franklin D. Roosevelt's famous radio "Fireside Chats" were designed to address the entire populace in a familiar way. He used the talks to *popularize* his economic programs and to give heart to the populace as they struggled through the Great Depression.

populous \'pä-pyù-ləs\ Numerous, densely settled, or having a large population.

• Though often ignored by Americans, Indonesia is the fourth most populous country in the world.

Modern Mexico City is the world's most populous city; its metropolitan area has about 25 million people. But even when Cortés came to the nearby Aztec city of Tenochtitlán in 1519, he found one of the largest cities in the world at that time. However, when he conquered the city in 1521 it wasn't nearly so populous, since European diseases had greatly reduced the population. (Avoid confusing *populous* and *populace*, which are pronounced exactly the same.)

vox populi \'väks-'pä-pyü-,lï\ Popular sentiment or opinion.

• Clever politicians always listen to the vox populi and adjust their opinions or language to get the voters on their side.

Vox populi is Latin for "the voice of the people." It comes from the old saying "Vox populi, vox Dei," or "The voice of the people is the voice of God"—in other words, the people are always right. In a democracy the vox populi is often regarded as almost sacred. We hear the vox populi loud and clear at every election, and by means of opinion polls we continue to hear it on every imaginable issue, from the President's personal affairs to U.S. military action overseas.

Quizzes

A. Choose the closest definition:

1. pandemic   a. isolated   b. widespread   c. present
       d. absent
2. populace   a. politics   b. numerous   c. masses
       d. popularity

3. endemic   a. common   b. absent   c. infectious
   d. occasional
4. demotic   a. devilish   b. common   c. cultural   d. useful
5. populous   a. well-liked   b. foreign   c. numerous
   d. obscure
6. demographic   a. describing politics   b. describing
   populations   c. describing policies   d. describing
   epidemics
7. populist   a. communist   b. campaigner   c. socialist
   d. believer in the people
8. vox populi   a. public policy   b. public survey   c. public
   opinion   d. public outrage

**B. Indicate whether the following pairs of words have
the same or different meanings:**

1. demotic / common   same ___ / different ___
2. populist / politician   same ___ / different ___
3. endemic / typical   same ___ / different ___
4. populace / popularity   same ___ / different ___
5. demographic / phonetic   same ___ / different ___
6. vox populi / mass sentiment   same ___ / different ___
7. pandemic / infectious   same ___ / different ___
8. populous / well-loved   same ___ / different ___

POLIS/POLIT comes from the Greek word for "city." "City-states" operated much like separate nations in ancient Greece, so all their *politics* was local, like all their public *policy*, and even all their *police*!

---

acropolis \ə-'krä-pə-ləs\ The high, fortified part of a city, especially an ancient Greek city.

• On the Athenian Acropolis, high above the rest of the city, stands the Parthenon, a temple to the goddess Athena.

Acropolis includes the root *acro-*, meaning "high." South American cities often contain a section on high ground that has been walled and built up so that the city can be defended. This fortified hill gives the defenders an automatic advantage over their attackers. In Europe, an acropolis often consisted of a walled castle inside which the population of the city and the surrounding area could retreat in case of attack. The Greeks and Romans included in their acropolises temples to the city's most important gods.

megalopolis \me-gə-'lä-pə-ləs\ (1) A very large city. (2) A thickly populated area that includes one or more cities with the surrounding suburbs.

● With its rapid development, the southern coast of Florida around Miami quickly became a megalopolis.

A "large city" named Megalopolis was founded in ancient Greece to help defend Arcadia against Sparta. Today Megalopolis has only about 5,000 people. The megalopolis on the eastern U.S. seaboard that stretches from Boston to Washington, D.C., however, now is the home of almost 50 million people. The densely populated cities seem to flow into each other all along the coast. It is projected that this megalopolis will only grow as time goes on.

politic \'pä-lə-,tik\ (1) Cleverly tactful. (2) Wise in promoting a plan or plan of action.

● Anger is rarely a politic approach to seeking agreement, since it usually comes across as rude and self-righteous.

Once teenagers learn to drive, they quickly learn the politic way to ask for the car—that is, whatever gets the keys without upsetting the parents. It is never politic to ask for a raise when the boss is in a terrible mood. As these examples show, *politic* can be used for many such situations that have nothing to do with public *politics*.

politicize \pə-'li-tə-,sīz\ To give a political tone or character to.

● By 1968 the Vietnam War had deeply politicized most of the college campuses.

Sexual harassment was once seen as a private matter, but in recent years it has been thoroughly politicized. A number of the women who have politicized it may themselves have been politicized by it—that is, may have started to think in a *political* way because of it. Václav Havel was an *unpolitical* playwright who became politicized by events and ended up as president of the Czech Republic.

CIRCU/CIRCUM means "around" in Latin. So *circumnavigate* is "to navigate around," often describing a trip around the world, and *circumambulate* means "to walk around." A *circuit* can be a tour around an area or territory, or the complete path of an electric current.

---

circuitous \sər-'kyü-ə-təs\ (1) Having a circular or winding course. (2) Not forthright or direct in action.

• Some philosophers arrive at their conclusions by circuitous reasoning that most people can barely follow.

Circuitous is often the opposite of *direct*. A circuitous path is no shortcut: twisting and turning and cutting back on itself, it is the kind of route one would expect to find in the mountains. A lawyer may use circuitous arguments when defending an unsavory client. A clever businessman may use circuitous methods to raise the money for a real-estate deal. (Sometimes *circuitous* may even be a bit like *dishonest*.)

circumference \sər-'kəm-frəns\ (1) The perimeter or boundary of a circle. (2) The outer boundary or surface of a shape or object.

• To calculate the approximate circumference of a circle, multiply its diameter by 3.14.

Circumference means literally "carrying around"—that is, around the boundary of a circle or other geometric figure. Attempts have been made to measure the circumference of the earth since the time of Aristotle. Columbus believed one such calculation, and it led him to think he could reach China by sailing west more quickly than by sailing east. His measurement was wrong, calculating the Earth's circumference about a quarter too small, and many later attempts continued to produce different measurements for the earth's circumference.

circumspect \'sər-kəm-ˌspekt\ Careful to consider all circumstances and possible consequences; cautious.

• She never rushed into any decision but was instead always circumspect and thoughtful.

Since *-spect* comes from the Latin word for "look," *circumspect* basically means "looking around" yourself before you act. Being a doctor or a banker has traditionally called for a circumspect personality. In most dictatorships, authors must be circumspect in what they write, since any lack of *circumspection* could land them in prison, or worse.

circumvent \'sər-kəm-,vent\ (1) To make a circuit around. (2) To manage to get around, especially by clever means.

● We circumvented the traffic jam on the highway by using the back roads.

Achilles' mother, Thetis, hoped to circumvent the prophecy that Achilles would die in a war against Troy, so she disguised the boy as a woman among the women of his uncle's household. But clever Odysseus, recruiting for the Greek army, arrived disguised as a peddler, and among the jewelry pieces he displayed to the women he laid a sword. When Achilles ignored everything but the sword, he was found out and had to go to war. Though he was the best warrior on either side, Achilles could not circumvent his eventual fate, and was killed by Paris with a poison arrow to his heel.

Quizzes

A. Fill in each blank with the correct letter:

a. circumspect   e. acropolis
b. megalopolis   f. circumvent
c. circumference   g. politic
d. politicize   h. circuitous

1. She was ____ enough with the chairman to get the bill through the committee.
2. Only the Tokyo-Yokohama metropolitan area rivals the ____ of the East Coast.
3. The doctors were ____ about the prime minister's condition that morning.
4. Her clever attempts to ____ the official procedures failed miserably.
5. The entire ____ of the estate was lined with tall oaks.

6. The directions they were given were inaccurate, so their route turned out to be a ____ one.

7. In times of danger, the entire populace retreated to the ____.

8. They believed that if they could ____ the peasants they could force the government to resign.

B. Match the word on the left to the correct definition on the right:

1.	politicize	a.	high fortified area
2.	megalopolis	b.	make political
3.	circumspect	c.	avoid
4.	circumvent	d.	chain of cities
5.	politic	e.	outside
6.	acropolis	f.	cleverly tactful
7.	circumference	g.	careful
8.	circuitous	h.	roundabout

Animal Words

aquiline \\'a-kwə-ˌlīn\\ (1) Relating to eagles. (2) Curving like an eagle's beak.

• To judge from the surviving busts of noble Romans, many of the men had strong aquiline noses.

Aquiline, from the Latin word meaning "eagle," is most often used to describe a nose that has a broad curve and is slightly hooked, like a beak. The word for eagle itself, Aquila, has been given to a constellation in the northern hemisphere. The aquiline figure on the U.S. seal brandishes the arrows of war and the olive branch of peace.

asinine \\'a-sə-ˌnīn\\ Foolish, brainless.

• He's not so great when he's sober, but when he's drunk he gets truly asinine.

The donkey or *ass* has often been accused of stubborn, willful, and stupid behavior lacking in logic and common sense. Asinine behavior exhibits similar qualities. Idiotic or rude remarks, aggressive stupidity, and general immaturity can all earn someone (usually a man) this description. If you call him this to his face, however, he might behave even worse.

bovine \'bō-,vīn\ (1) Relating to cows and oxen. (2) Placid, dull, unemotional.

• The veterinarian specialized in bovine diseases.

Bovine comes from the Latin word for "cow." The goddess Hera, the wife of Zeus, is called "cow-eyed," and Zeus fairly melts when she turns those big bovine eyes on him. But *bovine* is normally used either technically, when discussing cows—"bovine diseases," "bovine anatomy," and so on—or to describe a human personality. However, it can be a rather unkind way to describe someone.

canine \'kā-,nīn\ Relating to dogs or the dog family; doglike.

• Throughout the election, her husband's almost canine devotion helped her survive the tough criticism of her opponents.

Dogs are not always given credit for their independence, but they are prized for their talents and their intelligence. And canine devotion and loyalty are legendary; in the old *Lassie* and *Rin-Tin-Tin* television series, there would be at least one heroic act of devotion per show.

feline \'fē-,līn\ (1) Relating to cats or the cat family. (2) Like a cat in being sleek, graceful, sly, treacherous, or stealthy.

• The performers moved across the high wire with feline grace and agility.

Cats have always provoked a strong reaction from humans. The Egyptians worshiped them and left thousands of feline mummies and idols as evidence. In the Middle Ages, felines were feared as agents of the devil; they were thought to creep around silently at night doing evil and caring not at all for anything except themselves. (Notice that *feline* is also a noun.) Felines from lions and tigers down to domestic cats are smooth, silent, and often sleepy; feline independence, feline treachery, and feline slyness are other traits that some have seen in these mysterious creatures.

leonine \'lē-ə-,nīn\ Relating to lions; lionlike.

• As he conducted, Leonard Bernstein would fling his leonine mane wildly about.

The Latin word for "lion" is *leon*, so the names Leon, Leo, and Leona all mean "lion" as well. A leonine head usually has magnificent hair, like a male lion's mane, and someone may give an impression of leonine power or splendor. But the leonine character in *The Wizard of Oz* is notably lacking in the courage for which members of its family are famed.

porcine \'pȯr-,sīn\ Relating to pigs or swine; piglike.

• After a lifetime of overeating, his shape was porcine; unfortunately, his manners were also.

Whether deservedly or not, pigs don't enjoy a very flattering image, and they are rarely given credit for their high intelligence. While *porcine* is not as negative a term as *swinish*, it may describe things that are fat, greedy, pushy, or generally piggish—but primarily fat. Porky Pig and Miss Piggy are not porcine in their behavior, only in their appearance—that is, pink and pudgy.

vulpine \'vəl-,pīn\ (1) Relating to foxes; foxlike. (2) Sneaky, clever, or crafty; foxy.

• One glance at the vulpine faces of the two bond traders was enough to convince him of their true character.

Foxes may have beautiful coats and tails, but they are almost impossible to keep out of the henhouse. No matter how secure the place seems to be, their vulpine craftiness will find a way in. People who display the same kind of sneaky cleverness, especially in their faces, are also called vulpine.

Quiz

Fill in each blank with the correct letter:

a.	leonine	e.	canine
b.	aquiline	f.	feline
c.	porcine	g.	vulpine
d.	asinine	h.	bovine

1. Collies and chow chows often have splendid, _____ neck ruffs.
2. The dancer performed the piece with _____ grace.
3. Proud of the _____ curve of his nose, the silent-film star presented his profile to the camera at every opportunity.
4. The slick fellow offering his services as guide had a disturbingly _____ air about him.
5. Soldiers are expected to show _____ loyalty to their unit and commander.
6. The job applicant's _____ manner suggested a lack of ambition.
7. Jeff and his crowd were in the balcony, throwing down cans and being generally _____.
8. The _____ landlord climbed the stairs slowly, gasping for breath, with the eviction notice in his hand.

Review Quizzes

A. Choose the closest definition:

1. vulpine   a. reddish b. sly c. trustworthy d. furry
2. circumspect   a. boring b. long-winded c. roundabout d. cautious
3. politic   a. governmental b. voting c. tactful d. clumsy
4. populous   a. numerous b. populated c. popular d. common
5. atheistic   a. without a clue b. faithful c. disbelieving d. without a doubt
6. endemic   a. local b. neighborly c. sensational d. foreign
7. circuitous   a. electrical b. mountainous c. indirect d. round
8. feline   a. sleek b. clumsy c. crazy d. fancy
9. pantheistic   a. of one god b. disbelieving c. nonreligious d. accepting all gods
10. deity   a. discussion b. decision c. psychic d. god
11. pandemic   a. widespread b. infectious c. hideous d. frightening
12. megalopolis   a. monster b. dinosaur c. huge city d. huge mall

13. demotic   a. reduced b. common c. upper-class
    d. demented
14. divinity   a. prophecy b. mortality c. prayer
    d. godliness
15. circumvent   a. surround b. circle c. get around
    d. discuss
16. divest   a. add on b. take off c. take in d. add up

B. Fill in each blank with the correct letter:

a. populist   f. apotheosis
b. demographic   g. bovine
c. theocracy   h. populace
d. investiture   i. politicize
e. aquiline   j. circumference

1. The _____ of the great Albert Einstein seemed to occur
    while he was still living.
2. All the _____ surveys show that the U.S. population is
    growing older.
3. Nothing ever seemed to disturb her pleasant but _____
    manner.
4. The younger ones stood around the _____ of the room
    while the older ones sat in the center.
5. The _____ of the society's new leader was a secret and
    solemn event.
6. With his _____ nose, he looked like a member of the
    ancient Roman senate.
7. By that fall they had managed to _____ the factory
    workers around the issue of medical benefits.
8. He was a _____ in his style, though he actually had a
    great deal of money.
9. The _____ of the country is mostly composed of three
    ethnic groups.
10. In a _____, the legal punishments are often those called
    for in the holy books.

**C. Match the word on the left to the correct definition
on the right:**

1. porcine   a. half-shadow
2. divinatory   b. doglike

3.	asinine	c.	brownish coloring
4.	penumbra	d.	public opinion
5.	leonine	e.	cross-dresser
6.	umber	f.	unforeseen explanation
7.	vox populi	g.	uncouth
8.	deus ex machina	h.	plump
9.	transvestite	i.	like a lion
10.	canine	j.	prophetic

Unit 13

CORD, from the Latin word for "heart," turns up in many common English words. For example, the word *concord* (which includes the prefix *con-*, "with") means literally that one heart is *with* another heart, and thus that they are in agreement. So *discord* (with its prefix *dis-*, "apart") means "disagreement" or "conflict."

accord \ə-'kȯrd\ (1) To grant. (2) To be in harmony; agree.

• For the cast's brilliant performance of the play, the audience accorded them a standing ovation.

A new federal law may accord with—or be in *accordance* with—the guidelines that a company has already established. The rowdy behavior of the hero Beowulf accords with Norse ideals of the early Middle Ages, but would not be in accordance with the ideals of another young Danish lord of a later century, Shakespeare's Prince Hamlet.

concordance \kən-'kȯr-dəns\ An index of the important words in a book or in an author's works, with the passages in which they occur.

• A concordance to Shakespeare's plays makes it easy to find all the places he used the word *bodkin*.

A literary concordance lists all the places a given word appears in a work. *Concordance* resembles *concord,* but the "agreement" here is in the way that all the passages use the identical word. All concordances produced before the recent past had to be done by hand, and often were the work of several lifetimes. (Just imagine putting together a concordance for the Bible by hand.) Now, a computer with CD-ROM can search a book or an author's works in a flash, but concordances in book form are still valuable for many purposes.

cordial \\'kȯr-jəl\ (1) Warm, friendly, gracious. (2) Something that warms and revives, especially a liqueur.

• After the meeting, the president extended a cordial invitation to everyone for coffee at her own house.

Anything that is cordial comes from the heart. A cordial greeting or cordial relations (for example, between two countries) are warm and honest without being passionate. A cordial or liqueur, such as crème de menthe or Drambuie, is alcoholic enough to warm the spirits and the heart.

discordant \dis-'kȯr-dənt\ Being at odds, conflicting, not in harmony.

• The one discordant note came from the only vegetarian present, who would not eat the main course, roast beef.

Drawing up a peace treaty may require that the parties to the treaty resolve their discordant aims. Even among allies, *discord* is not always absent. Stalin's goals after World War II did not at all *accord* with those of Russia's allies—England, America, and France; his discordant demands led to the division of Europe for almost half a century. The opinions of Supreme Court justices are frequently discordant. The discordant ethnic groups in the old Yugoslavia were controlled only by the iron hand of Marshal Tito.

CULP comes to English from the Latin word for "guilt." A *culprit* is someone who is guilty of a crime, though his or her *culpability*, or guilt, should not be assumed before it is proved.

---

culpable \\'kəl-pə-bəl\ Deserving to be condemned or blamed.

• The company was found guilty of culpable negligence in allowing the chemical waste to leak into the groundwater.

A mother always thinks she knows which children are culpable when the cookie jar has been raided: their *culpability* is usually written all over their faces. *Culpable* is probably more commonly used in law than in everyday speech and writing.

exculpate \'ek-skəl-ˌpāt\ To clear from accusations of fault or guilt.

• The alleged mastermind of the plot managed to exculpate herself with an airtight alibi.

Exculpate comes to mean "to clear from guilt" through the prefix *ex-*, meaning "out of" or "away from." A suspected murderer may be exculpated by the confession of another person. The word has an extended meaning as well, referring to moral guilt or responsibility. In America a criminal is not exculpated because of a harsh childhood, but may be if found insane.

inculpate \in-'kəl-ˌpāt\ To accuse or incriminate; to show evidence of someone's involvement in a fault or crime.

• It was his own father who finally inculpated him, though without intending to.

Inculpate is the opposite of *exculpate,* but less often used. By inculpating someone else, an accused person may manage to exculpate himself. Through plea bargaining, the prosecution can often encourage a defendant to inculpate his friends in return for a lighter sentence.

mea culpa \ˌmā-ə-'kùl-pə\ An admission of personal fault or error.

• The principal said his mea culpa at the school board meeting, but not all the parents accepted it.

Mea culpa, "through my fault," comes from the prayer of confession in the Catholic Church. Said by itself today, it means "I apologize" or "It was my fault." But it is also a noun. A book may be a long mea culpa for the author's past treatment of women, or an oil company may issue a mea culpa after a tanker runs aground.

Quizzes

A. Choose the closest definition:

1. exculpate a. convict b. prove innocent c. suspect
    d. prove absent
2. discordant a. unpleasant b. relieved c. unlimited
    d. conflicting
3. culpable a. disposable b. refundable c. guilty
    d. harmless
4. cordial a. hateful b. friendly c. fiendish
    d. cool
5. inculpate a. incorporate b. resist c. incriminate
    d. offend
6. concordance a. index b. digit c. list
    d. disagreement
7. mea culpa a. rejection b. apology c. admission
    d. forgiveness
8. accord a. harmonize b. accept c. distress d. convince

**B. Match the definition on the left to the correct word
    on the right:**

1. accuse   a. accord
2. excuse   b. concordance
3. agreement   c. mea culpa
4. heartfelt   d. discordant
5. grant   e. culpable
6. blamable   f. cordial
7. disagreeing   g. inculpate
8. confession   h. exculpate

DIC, from *dicere*, the Latin word meaning "to speak," says a lot.
A *contradiction* (with the prefix *contra-*, "against") speaks against
or denies something. A *dictionary* is a treasury of words. And *dic-
tion* is another word for speech.

---

edict \'ē-ˌdikt\ (1) An official announcement that has the force of
a law. (2) An order or command.

• In 1989 an edict by the leader of Iran pronouncing a death sentence on a British novelist stunned the world.

Edicts are few and far between in a democracy, since very few important laws can be made by a president or prime minister acting alone. But when a crisis arose in the Roman Republic, the senate would appoint a dictator to rule by edict. The dictator could make decisions quickly, and his edicts could be issued faster than the senate could act. When the crisis was over, the edicts were revoked and the dictator usually retired from public life.

interdiction \\ˌin-tər-'dik-shən\\ (1) An edict prohibiting something. (2) The destruction of or cutting off of an enemy's line of supply.

• U.S. forces repeatedly tried to halt the North Vietnamese by interdiction of their supplies.

An interdiction comes between and forbids or takes. From 1920 to 1933 the 18th Amendment attempted to *interdict* the production and drinking of alcohol. But such an interdiction proved useless; Americans of all social classes and every degree of respectability refused to give up their beloved beverages, and all attempts to interdict the supply by the "Untouchable" Eliot Ness and other government agents could not stop the flow of illegal moonshine and bathtub gin.

jurisdiction \\ˌj u̇r-is-'dik-shən\\ (1) The power or right to control or exercise authority. (2) The territory where power may be exercised.

• Unluckily for the defendants, the case fell within the jurisdiction of the federal court rather than the more tolerant state court.

Gods and goddesses often intervened in the areas under their jurisdiction. Apollo, whose jurisdiction included archery, guided the arrow that killed Achilles in the Trojan War. Poseidon, angered at the blinding of his son the Cyclops, punished Odysseus with hard wanderings over the sea, where he had final jurisdiction. Today questions of jurisdiction are generally technical legal matters— questions about which law-enforcement agency can get involved, which court will hear the case, and so on—but matters that may be all-important in the final outcome of legal cases.

malediction \ˌma-lə-'dik-shən\ A curse.

• In the story of Sleeping Beauty, the evil fairy hurls a malediction at the infant princess, foretelling that she will prick her finger and die.

Maledictions, "evil sayings," are used less commonly in many cultures than they used to be. The Romans had a malediction for every purpose. They inscribed these curses on lead tablets and buried them in the ground. Archaeologists have found maledictions cursing the person who stole someone's lover, the person who stole prize apples, and the person who cursed the curser. Maledictions may call for every punishment imaginable, from sickness to injury and even death.

GNI/GNO comes from a Greek and Latin verb meaning "to know" (and led to the word *know* itself). In the group of words built from this root, you may *recognize* ("know again") some and be *ignorant* of ("not know") others. An *agnostic* is someone who claims that whatever is divine cannot be known. An *ignoramus* is a person who knows absolutely nothing.

---

cognitive \'käg-nə-tiv\ (1) Having to do with the process of knowing, including awareness, judgment, and understanding. (2) Based on factual knowledge that has been or can be gained by experience.

• A child is not a computer; a third-grader's cognitive abilities are highly dependent on his or her upbringing and happiness.

Cognitive skills and knowledge involve the ability to acquire factual information, often the kind of knowledge that can easily be tested. *Cognition* is thus distinguished from social, emotional, and creative development and ability.

diagnosis \ˌdī-əg-'nō-səs\ (1) The identification of a disease by its symptoms. (2) An investigation of and conclusion about a situation or problem.

• However, according to Marianne's diagnosis the company's problem was its managers, not its workers.

A diagnosis identifies a disease or problem through its physical evidence. One of the most useful new *diagnostic* tools is MRI, or "magnetic resonance imaging," which allows doctors to see what is going on in the soft tissue, such as muscle, cartilage, and brain, that X rays see right through. With MRI, *diagnosticians* can be far more accurate in their diagnoses. (Notice how this plural is formed.)

incognito \\,in-,käg-'nē-tō\ In disguise or with one's identity concealed.

● Katherine Ann Power, an activist and bank robber, lived incognito for 23 years before giving herself up in 1993.

In the famous myth of Baucis and Philemon, Zeus and Hermes visit a village incognito to test the villagers. The seemingly poor travelers are turned away from every household except that of Baucis and Philemon. This elderly couple, though very poor themselves, provide the incognito gods with a feast. When the gods finally reveal themselves, the couple is rewarded for their hospitality, and the rest of the village is destroyed for their lack of it.

prognosis \präg-'nō-səs\ (1) The chance of recovery from a given disease or condition. (2) Forecast or prophecy.

● The prognosis for a patient with chicken pox is usually excellent; the prognosis for someone with liver cancer is terrible.

Prognosis contains the prefix *pro-*, meaning "before." It is thus "knowledge beforehand," based on the normal course of events in similar situations. Economists try to *prognosticate,* or predict, what the economy will do, based on the trends they see and their knowledge of where such trends tend to lead. A prognosis of recovery and growth is obviously much better than one of recession and stagnation.

Quizzes

A. Fill in each blank with the correct letter:

a.	diagnosis	e.	interdiction
b.	malediction	f.	incognito
c.	cognitive	g.	edict
d.	jurisdiction	h.	prognosis

1. Psychology is not entirely a _____ science, since it deals with behavior as well as the mind.
2. Belief in the power of a _____ to harm has faded with the advances of science and growing rejection of superstition.
3. Movie stars often go out in public _____, in faded sweatshirts, worn-out pants, and sunglasses.
4. When their dictatorial grandfather issued an _____, everyone obeyed it.
5. The electrician made a quick _____ and fixed the heater by replacing a faulty switch.
6. The _____ for the world's climate in the next century is uncertain.
7. An _____ of their supply lines by enemy mortars on the surrounding hills meant the loyalists would have to find new routes.
8. The judge refused to consider two elements in the case, saying that they lay outside his _____.

B. Indicate whether the following pairs of words have the same or different meanings:

1. diagnosis / analysis   same ___ / different ___
2. cognitive / digestive   same ___ / different ___
3. interdiction / prohibition   same ___ / different ___
4. malediction / curse   same ___ / different ___
5. incognito / hospitable   same ___ / different ___
6. jurisdiction / power   same ___ / different ___
7. prognosis / prophecy   same ___ / different ___
8. edict / order   same ___ / different ___

APT/EPT, from *aptare*, "to fit," and *aptus*, "fit," is endlessly *adaptable*, changing itself to fit many words and purposes. You are *apt*, or "likely," to come upon them when you least expect, so *adept* are they at fitting in.

---

adaptation \a-ˌdap-'tā-shən\ Adjustment to conditions of an environment, or to a new or different use.

• Humans have undergone many adaptations since the first hominids roamed the land.

Adaptation usually makes survival or success more likely. There are moths in England that were once light gray; on the bark of a tree they were practically invisible to birds looking for food. During the Industrial Revolution in England, when factory smoke turned the trees black with grime, the light-colored moths became clearly visible and were eaten. As the years passed, the moths went through a protective adaptation and became black or dark gray like the trees, and once again invisible to the birds.

aptitude \\'ap-tə-ˌtüd\\ (1) Natural tendency, talent, or ability. (2) Ability to learn.

• She longed to learn to play piano but feared she had no aptitude for music.

Most students applying for college take both aptitude tests and achievement tests. Aptitude tests claim to measure how much you are able to learn, and achievement tests how much you have already learned. That is, a math achievement test should require that you have memorized formulas and complex operations, whereas a math aptitude test should require only that you show you can work quickly and intelligently with basic operations. Many aptitudes, both physical and mental, show up clearly in children by the age of 3 or 4.

adept \\ə-'dept\\ Expert or highly skilled.

• The dollmaker was astonishingly adept at painting the features of famous dancers on her little porcelain heads.

Charlie Chaplin was adept at far more than acting, directing, and screenwriting; he was an acrobat of professional quality, and songs he wrote became popular hits. Most of us would settle for being adept in only a couple of areas.

inept \\i-'nept\\ Foolish, incompetent, bungling.

• The government's inept handling of the whole affair led to its defeat in the next election.

Inept is the opposite of *adept*. Inspector Clouseau has been the image of *ineptitude* for a generation of moviegoers, who may have caught a glimpse of themselves in his dignified but hopeless incompetence.

ART comes from the Latin word for "skill." Until a few centuries ago, almost no one made a strong distinction between skilled craftsmanship and what we would call "art." *Art* could also mean simply "cleverness." The result is that this root appears in some words where we might not expect it.

artful \'ärt-fəl\ (1) Skillful. (2) Wily, crafty, sly.

● It was an artful solution: each side was pleased with the agreement, but the lawyer himself stood to make the most money off of it.

A writer may produce an artful piece of prose, one that is clearly and elegantly written. The same writer, however, could also make an artful argument, one that leaves out certain details and plays up others so as to make a stronger case. In the first instance, the writer's work is well-crafted; in the second, he or she is instead crafty. (Try not to use *artful,* however, when you really mean "artistic.")

artifact \'är-ti-,fakt\ A usually simple object, such as a tool or ornament, made by human workmanship or modification.

● Archaeologists have found many artifacts that help us understand how the early Anasazi people of the Southwest lived.

One of the things that makes humans unique is their ability to make and use tools. These tools and the objects made with them are artifacts, a word that literally means "made with skill." Human cultures in all eras, from the Stone Age onward, have left behind artifacts from which we can learn about their lives.

artifice \'är-tə-fəs\ (1) Clever skill. (2) A clever trick.

● By his cunning and artifice, Iago convinces Othello that Desdemona has been unfaithful.

Artifice combines the same roots as *artifact,* but usually suggests something deceptive or tricky or at least highly *artificial.* Simplicity, honesty, and genuineness are the opposites of artifice, which is related to disguise, fantasy, and complexity. Starting with the Puritans, America has traditionally prided itself on its lack of artifice, seeing a character like Huckleberry Finn as an image of the essential American. But artifice is often in the eye of the beholder, and the book *Huckleberry Finn* is itself filled with literary artifice.

artisan \'är-tə-zən\ A skilled worker or craftsperson.

● At the fair, they saw examples of the best carving, pottery, and jewelry by local artisans.

In the Middle Ages artisans organized themselves into guilds. In every city each group of artisans, such as the weavers or carpenters, had its own guild. The guilds set wages and prices for the artisans' wares, and also protected them from competing artisans who did not belong. Guilds existed in some European countries until the 19th century. In America, however, most artisans have always been fiercely independent.

Quizzes

A. Complete the analogy:

1. sensation : feeling :: aptitude : _____
   a. amount b. emotion c. talent d. article

2. mournful : sad :: artful : _____
   a. clever b. doleful c. fake d. creative

3. strong : weak :: adept : _____
   a. skilled b. easy c. inept d. unjust

4. physician : doctor :: artisan : _____
   a. plumber b. nurse c. teacher d. craftsperson

5. life : death :: adaptation : _____
   a. sensation b. excitement c. stagnation d. rejection

6. labor : strength :: artifact : _____
   a. skill b. statuette c. remains d. trick

7. clumsy : grace :: inept : _____
   a. honesty b. competence c. stupidity d. ignorance

8. confession : true :: artifice : _____
   a. skill b. honest c. false d. ridiculous

B. Match the definition on the left to the correct word on the right:

1. skilled craftsman   a. artful
2. natural talent   b. artifice
3. skillfully sly   c. adaptation
4. expert   d. inept
5. slyness   e. artisan
6. process of change   f. aptitude
7. man-made object   g. adept
8. awkward   h. artifact

CAD/CID/CAS all comes from the same Latin verb, *cadere*, meaning "to fall, fall down, drop," or from the related noun *casus*, "fall or chance." An *accident* happens to you out of the blue. By *coincidence*, things fall together in a pattern. *Casual* dress is what you put on almost by chance. A *cascade* is a rushing down of something.

---

cadaver \kə-'da-vər\ A dead body, especially one that is to be dissected; a corpse.

• The cadaver she was given to work on was an unclaimed homeless woman and came from the Manhattan morgue.

The mystery writer P. D. James always produces a cadaver with a tale that must be unraveled by her sleuth, Adam Dalgliesh. And occasionally one of her living characters may have gaunt, *cadaverous* features, such as hollow cheeks and sunken eyes, which resemble the features of a corpse.

casualty \'ka-zhù-wəl-tē\ A person, especially a military person, or a thing that is injured, lost, or destroyed; a victim.

• When the platoon limped back to camp, they learned that Lieutenant Steiger had been a casualty of a land mine.

The casualty count in a war includes the dead, the wounded, and the seriously ill. In the American Civil War, for instance, deaths represented only about half of the total casualties—and most of the deaths resulted from infection and disease rather than from battle wounds alone. We may also use the term less literally. For example, if a woman's new husband doesn't get along with her best friend, the friendship may become a casualty of the marriage.

decadent \'de-kə-dənt\ (1) Self-indulgent. (2) Decaying or declining.

• The French Empire may have been at its most decadent just before the French Revolution.

Many of the rich people of ancient Rome lived decadent lives, full of every sort of excess imaginable, as their empire fell apart. No expense was spared to bring exotic delicacies to their tables, from African ostrich eggs to snow from the Alps—in the days before refrigeration! And Rome's emperors were often part of the problem. Commodus, the 18-year-old bodybuilder son of the emperor, was leading his troops against the barbarians on the frontier when he heard his father had died, and raced immediately back to Rome to take up a life of pleasure and *decadence*.

recidivism \ri-'si-də-,vi-zəm\ A tendency to fall back into earlier habits or modes of behaving, especially criminal habits.

• Recidivism among smokers who try to quit is very high.

Recidivism means literally "a falling back," and usually implies "into bad habits." Though the criminal justice system tries to reduce the rate of recidivism among criminals, most released prisoners return to a life of crime as *recidivists*.

CIS comes from the Latin verb meaning "to cut, cut down, or slay." An *incisor* is one of the big front biting teeth; beavers and woodchucks have especially large ones. A *decision* "cuts off" previous discussion and uncertainty.

---

concise \kən-'sīs\ Brief and condensed, especially in expression or statement.

• Professor Childs's exam asked for a concise, one-page summary of the causes of the American Revolution.

Most students, and many adults, think that adding unnecessary sentences with long words will make their writing more impressive. But in fact almost every reader values *concision*: concise writing is usually easier to read, better thought out, and better organized—that is, simply better writing.

excise \'ek-ˌsīz\ To cut out, especially surgically.

• The ancient Minoans from the island of Crete apparently excised the hearts of their human sacrifices.

Excise takes part of its meaning from the prefix *ex-*, "out." A writer may excise long passages of a novel to reduce it to a reasonable length, or merely excise sections that may give offense. A surgeon may excise a large cancerous tumor, or make a tiny *excision* to examine an organ's tissue.

incisive \in-'sī-siv\ Impressively direct and decisive.

• A few incisive questions were all that was needed to expose the weakness in the prosecutor's case.

To *incise* is to cut into; an incisive remark, then, "cuts into" the matter at hand. A good news analyst makes incisive comments about the story he or she is following, shedding light on the situation. A good movie critic *incisively* remarks on a film's strengths and weaknesses, helping us decide whether or not to see it.

precision \pri-'si-zhən\ (1) Exactness of definition or statement. (2) Accuracy of performance or measurement.

• Only slowly did he learn to speak with precision, to find the exact words for everything in place of the crude, awkward language of his friends.

The weather can never be predicted with absolute precision. Modern technology such as computer models and satellite photos help forecasters to be more *precise* than ever before, but there are so many factors involved in making the weather that any forecaster always runs the risk of being *imprecise*.

Quizzes

A. Fill in each blank with the correct letter:

a. casualty   e. concise
b. decadent   f. excise
c. cadaver   g. incisive
d. precision   h. recidivism

1. Ms. Raymond's report on her trip up the Amazon is _____ but fascinating.

2. They were a _____ crowd; rich and idle, they spent their days taking drugs and their nights hunting for pleasure in the clubs.

3. The medical students were assigned in threes to work on each _____.

4. The reporter was known for remarks that were so _____ that his interviewees were often embarrassed.

5. The first American _____ of the Revolutionary War may have been the black soldier Crispus Attucks.

6. _____ among chocolate lovers who try to limit their intake is appallingly high.

7. Before eating an apple, some people carefully _____ the brown spots.

8. What the tipsy darts players lacked in _____ they made up for in enthusiasm.

B. Choose the closest definition:

1. precision   a. accuracy b. beauty c. conciseness
      d. dependence

2. decadent   a. rotten b. generous c. self-indulgent d. ten years long

3. excise   a. tax b. examine c. refuse d. cut out

4. recidivism   a. backsliding b. backstabbing
      c. backscratching d. backslapping

5. incisive   a. damaging b. direct c. dirty d. definite

6. casualty   a. serious remark b. serious outlook c. serious condition d. serious injury

7. concise   a. short b. sure c. shifting d. sharp

8. cadaver   a. victim b. suspect c. corpse d. detective

Animal Words

apiary \ˈā-pē-ˌer-ē\ A place where bees are kept for their honey.

● An apple orchard is an excellent site for an apiary, since the bees keep the apple trees productive by pollinating them.

The social life in an apiary is strange and marvelous. The queen bee, who will become the mother of an entire colony, is created by being fed "royal jelly" in her larval stage. The tens of thousands of worker bees are underdeveloped females; only a handful of the bees are male, and they do no work at all. The workers defend the hive by kamikaze means, stinging any intruder and dying as they do so.

caper \ˈkā-pər\ (1) A playful leap. (2) A prank or mischievous adventure.

● For their caper in the girls' bathroom, all three seniors were suspended for a week.

Caper in Latin means "a male goat." Anyone who has watched a young goat frolic in a field or clamber onto the roof of a car knows the kind of crazy fun the English word *caper* is referring to. A *capriole* is a backward kick done in midair by a trained horse. *Capricorn,* or "horned goat," is a constellation and one of the signs of the zodiac.

equestrian \i-ˈkwes-trē-ən\ Having to do with horseback riding.

● The equestrian acts, in which bareback riders performed daring acrobatic feats atop prancing horses, were her favorites.

The word *equestrian* comes from *equus,* Latin for "horse." War memorials often show great commanders in equestrian poses. In these sculptures the man always sits nobly upright, but the horse's stance varies. Depending on whether the rider was killed in battle or survived, was victorious or defeated, the horse stands with four, three, or two hooves on the ground. Equestrian statues have been popular through the centuries because until this century almost every commanding officer was trained in equestrian skills and combat.

lupine \\'lü-ˌpīn\\ Like a wolf; wolfish.

•, They heard the resonant voices of a lupine chorus howling most of the night.

Lupine comes from *lupus,* the Latin word for "wolf," and the related adjective *lupinus,* "wolfish." Dogs often exhibit lupine behavior, since many of them are descended from wolves. Lupine groups have a highly organized social structure, in which leaders and followers are clearly distinguished, and dogs often show these lupine patterns when living in groups. *Lupine* is also a noun, the name of a well-known flower, which was once thought to drain, or "wolf," the soil of its nutrients.

lycanthropy \\lī-'kan-thrə-pē\\ The taking on of the form and behavior of a wolf by means of magic or witchcraft.

• The 1941 film *The Wolf Man* starred Lon Chaney, Jr., as a man cursed with lycanthropy.

For centuries a belief in lycanthropy has been part of the folk culture of lands where wolves exist. The word comes from the joining of two Greek roots—*lyc,* meaning "wolf," and *anthrop,* meaning "man." A victim of this enchantment is a *lycanthrope,* or werewolf. When the moon is full, the animal part of his nature takes over and he is transformed into a wolf, only much more bloodthirsty. The lycanthrope preys on humans, especially babies and buried corpses, and can even cause lycanthropy in others by biting them.

ornithologist \\ȯr-nə-'thä-lə-jist\\ A person who studies birds.

• John James Audubon, the great painter of the birds of early America, was also a writing ornithologist of great importance.

Ornithologist comes from two Greek roots, *ornith-,* meaning "bird," and *log-,* meaning "study." Roger Tory Peterson's numerous field guides have long been some of the amateur ornithologist's most useful tools.

serpentine \\'sər-pən-ˌtīn\\ Like a snake or serpent in shape or movement; winding.

• The Great Wall of China, the greatest construction of all time, wends its serpentine way for 1,200 miles.

A snake moves by curving and winding along the ground. Roads through the Pyrenees, the mountains that separate Spain from France, tend to be serpentine, curving back and forth upon themselves on the steep slopes. (*Serpentine* has many other meanings as well; it can describe human character or physique, for example, and it is also the name for a soft green mineral and for party streamers.)

simian \'si-mē-ən\ Having to do with monkeys or apes; monkeylike.

● In mid-afternoon the pale youth could be seen watching the simian antics in the Monkey House with strange intensity.

The Latin word for "ape" is *simia*, which itself comes from *simus*, "snub-nosed." Not only monkeys and apes can be simian. A human baby may cling to her mother in a simian way; a person may have a simian style of eating a banana; kids may display simian agility as they play on the jungle gym; and a grunt may be simian even when made by a human.

Quiz

Indicate whether the following pairs have the same or different meanings:

1. equestrian / horselike   same ___ / different ___
2. ornithologist / studier of birds   same ___ / different ___
3. lupine / apelike   same ___ / different ___
4. apiary / monkey colony   same ___ / different ___
5. lycanthropy / werewolfism   same ___ / different ___
6. caper / leap   same ___ / different ___
7. simian / clumsy   same ___ / different ___
8. serpentine / steep   same ___ / different ___

Review Quizzes

A. Fill in each blank with the correct letter:

a. artisan   k. recidivism
b. edict   l. cadaver
c. equestrian   m. inculpate

d. artifact
e. discordant
f. casualty
g. cognitive
h. apiary
i. exculpate
j. inept

n. serpentine
o. interdiction
p. precision
q. artifice
r. aptitude
s. prognosis
t. simian

1. The farmer tended his ___ lovingly and gathered delicious wildflower honey every year.

2. In trying to ___ herself, she only made herself look guiltier.

3. The enemy's ___ of supplies left the city helpless.

4. Though he showed astonishing mathematical ___ as a child, he spent his life as a salesman.

5. They arrived in time to see the top riders compete in the championship ___ event.

6. The doctor's ___ is guarded, but she is cautiously optimistic that recovery will be complete.

7. Fortunately, the accident caused only one minor ___.

8. We made our way slowly along the ___ course of the lazy river.

9. Each side's anger at the other has set a sadly ___ tone for the negotiations.

10. We set the clock with great ___ on the first day of every new year.

11. The thief tried hard to ___ as many of his friends in the crime as he could.

12. These beautiful handblown goblets were obviously made by a talented ___.

13. The final ___ from the presidential palace commanded every citizen to wear a baseball cap at all times.

14. The child scrambled over the wall with ___ agility.

15. As a baby, he was unusually quick to develop ___ skills.

16. She found a small clay ___ in the shape of a bear at the site of the ancient temple.

17. The local mechanics are ___ or dishonest or both, so I don't recommend them.

18. There bobbing by the wharf was a ___, the remains of a man in a white suit.

19. He used every ____ imaginable to hide his real age from the television cameras.
20. The rate of ____ for those imprisoned for felonies is alarmingly high.

B. Choose the correct synonym and the correct antonym:

1. accord   a. give one's due b. give one's heart
       c. withhold what is earned d. withhold approval
2. malediction   a. prayer b. benediction c. oath d. curse
3. artful   a. lovely b. sly c. talented d. honest
4. decadent   a. decaying b. ten-year c. twelfth d. growing
5. cordial   a. amorous b. hostile c. terrific d. heartfelt
6. incognito   a. indoors b. in disguise c. as oneself
       d. as you were
7. incisive   a. toothed b. sharp c. toothless d. dull
8. concise   a. lengthy b. wide c. dated d. brief
9. culpable   a. doleful b. stentorian c. guilty d. innocent
10. adept   a. changed b. skilled c. clumsy d. unwell

C. Choose the closest definition:

1. ornithologist   a. student of fish b. student of words
       c. student of birds d. student of wolves
2. mea culpa   a. through my eyes b. through my fault
       c. through my door d. through my work
3. lupine   a. foxy b. horselike c. sheepish d. wolfish
4. adaptation   a. process of going b. process of change
       c. process of mending d. process of canning
5. jurisdiction   a. area of power b. area of coverage
       c. area of damage d. area of target
6. excise   a. take out b. hold out c. cut out d. fold out
7. concordance   a. index b. bible c. glossary d. contents
8. lycanthropy   a. sorcery b. monstrosity c. vampirism
       d. werewolfism
9. diagnosis   a. identification b. symptoms c. disease
       d. treatment
10. caper   a. wolf b. goat c. dance d. prank

Unit 14

CRYPT/CRYPH comes from the Greek word for "hidden." To *encrypt* a message is to encode it—that is, to hide its meaning in code language. A medical term beginning with *crypto-* always means there is something hidden about the condition.

apocryphal \ə-'pä-krə-fəl\ Of doubtful genuineness or authenticity.

● Jason's story, they now realized, was completely apocryphal, though he himself may have believed it.

Both the Old and the New Testaments sometimes include books that have a doubtful status, since the leaders of the Jewish and Christian religions have determined that they aren't completely deserving of being included with the official scriptures. These documents are known as the *Apocrypha*; the root here suggests that the Apocrypha's origins are somewhat hidden and so not reliable. Today anything fake or counterfeit that is claimed to be genuine, such as the supposed diaries of Adolf Hitler in the 1980s, can be called apocryphal.

cryptic \'krip-'tik\ (1) Mysterious; puzzlingly short. (2) Acting to hide or conceal.

● Louisa threw Philip a cryptic look whose meaning he couldn't be sure of.

Until the writing on the Rosetta Stone was finally translated in the early 19th century, Egyptian hieroglyphic writing was entirely cryptic, its meaning hidden from the modern world. In the same way, a cryptic comment or remark or look is one whose meaning is unclear and perhaps even mystifying. Cryptic coloring among plants and animals acts like camouflage; some moths, although very tasty to blue jays, are *cryptically* colored to look like bugs that the jays consider inedible.

cryptography \krip-'tä-grə-fē\ (1) Secret writing. (2) The encoding and decoding of messages.

• The instructions for the missile launch are translated into code by the cryptography team.

During World War II, cryptography became an extremely complex science for both the Allied and Axis powers. The Allies managed to get their hands on the Axis machine designed to produce unbreakable codes; the Axis *cryptographers,* on the other hand, never managed to crack the Americans' ultimate code—the Navajo language. In the age of computers, cryptography has become almost unbelievably complex; it is widely used in peacetime in such areas as banking telecommunications.

crypt \'kript\ A room completely or partly underground, especially under the main floor of a church; a room or area in a large aboveground tomb.

• His old nightmare was of being locked in a crypt with corpses as his only companions.

Hidden under the main floor of a great church is often a large room, the centerpiece of which may be a tomb. Many European churches were built over the tomb of a saint or other religious figure; the great St. Peter's Church in the Vatican is an example. A large mausoleum, or aboveground tomb, may contain crypts or small chambers for individual coffins.

AB/ABS comes to us from Latin, and means "from," "away," or "off." *Abuse* is the use of something in the wrong way. To *abduct* is to "lead away from" or kidnap. *Aberrant* behavior is behavior that "wanders away from" what is usually acceptable. But there are so many words that include these roots, it would be *absurd* to try to list them all here.

---

abscond \ab-'skänd\ To depart in secret and hide.

• We discovered the next morning that our guest had absconded with the family silver during the night.

In J.R.R. Tolkien's novel *The Hobbit,* Bilbo Baggins absconds from Gollum's caves with the ring he has found, the ring Gollum calls ''my precious''; the results of his theft and absconding are detailed in the three-volume *Lord of the Rings*. Wagner's massive four-part opera *The Ring of the Nibelung* similarly begins with a dwarf absconding with gold which he turns into a magic ring. Absconding from a problem is often only a temporary relief from it; a young couple might abscond from their parents to get married, but sooner or later they must face those parents again.

abstemious \ab-'stē-mē-əs\ Restrained, especially in the consumption of food or alcohol.

• By living an abstemious life they managed to stay very healthy and to save enough money to take a trip every few years.

Many monks of the 14th century were held to the Rule of St. Benedict, which demand an abstemious life of obedience and poverty. But not all monks could maintain such abstemious habits. Chaucer's *Canterbury Tales* contains a portrait of a monk who is anything but abstemious: for instance, although monks were supposed to follow a vegetarian diet, he is an enthusiastic hunter who loves a fat swan best. He justifies breaking the Rule by saying that it is old, and he's just keeping up with modern times.

abstraction \ab-'strak-shən\ The consideration of a thing or idea without associating it with a particular example.

• All her ideas sounded like abstractions, since in fact she had no experience of actual nursing at all.

Abstract art is art that makes little attempt to show physical objects as they are usually seen. The roots of the word mean ''to pull or draw away''; therefore, an abstract design distances itself from any particular object. Theories are often abstractions, especially when they ''pull back'' to take a broad view and try to apply to or explain everything of a certain kind—for example, all governments, all molecules, or all rock singers.

abstruse \ab-'strüs\ Hard to understand; deep or complex.

● The professor helpfully filled the blackboard with abstruse calculations, but they only served to confuse the class more.

Very often scientific writing is filled with an abstruse special vocabulary, or jargon, which is necessary for exact and precise descriptions. Unfortunately, the language of a science like quantum physics can make an already difficult subject even more abstruse to the average person. Luckily, there are books available that untangle the *abstrusities* in this and other sciences, and explain those difficult ideas in plain, everyday terms.

Quizzes

A. Match the definition on the left to the correct word on the right:

1. mysterious   a. apocryphal
2. code writing   b. abstraction
3. fake   c. abscond
4. difficult   d. cryptic
5. tomb   e. abstruse
6. theory   f. crypt
7. self-controlled   g. cryptography
8. flee   h. abstemious

B. Fill in each blank with the correct letter:

a. cryptic   e. cryptography
b. abscond   f. abstemious
c. abstraction   g. apocryphal
d. crypt   h. abstruse

1. Many an explorer believed the _____ stories of the City of Gold and died hunting for it.
2. His answer was so short and _____ that I have no idea what he meant.
3. The great, echoing _____ of St. Stephen's Cathedral could have held hundreds of people.
4. That is merely an _____; in the real world, things work very differently.

---

5. The _____ vocabulary of the literature professor led many students to drop her class.
6. He led an _____ life these days and rarely thought of his former high living.
7. Their _____ hadn't been revised in years, and there were worries about the security of their data.
8. The bride is so shy that her mother fears she'll _____ from the reception.

PED comes from the Greek word for "child" this time. See also its "foot" meaning in Unit 4. The two usually aren't hard to tell apart—but don't mistake a *pediatrician* for a *podiatrist*.

pedagogy \'pe-də-ˌgō-jē\ The art or profession of teaching; the study of teaching.

• His own pedagogy shows great style and imagination but received little recognition.

To the Greeks, a *pedagogue* was a slave who escorted boys to school and back, taught them manners, and offered extra help with their studies after school. In time the word came to mean simply "teacher." It has an antique ring to it, so it often means a stuffy, boring teacher. *Pedagogy* doesn't have much of that ring to it. It usually means "methods of teaching," while *pedagogic* training usually includes classroom practice.

encyclopedic \in-ˌsī-klə-'pē-dik\ (1) Of or relating to an encyclopedia. (2) Covering a wide range of subjects.

• The *Jeopardy* champion displayed her encyclopedic knowledge with great success.

In Greek, *paidaea* meant "child-rearing" or "education," and *kyklios* meant "circular" or "general"; thus, an encyclopedia is a work broad enough to provide a kind of general education. The *Encyclopaedia Britannica* is a huge work that covers nearly every field of human knowledge. Some dictionaries are also encyclopedic, since they give extended information about history, technology, science, and so on. But *encyclopedic* doesn't have to refer to books: a rock-and-roll radio station may have an encyclopedic collection of popular music, for example.

pediatrician \‚pē-dē-ə-'tri-shən\ A doctor who specializes in the diseases, development, and care of children.

• A child usually sees a pediatrician until he or she turns 15.

Pediatrics is a fairly new medical specialty; up until about a hundred years ago children were considered small adults and given the same medical treatment, only milder. Benjamin Spock was America's most famous pediatrician through the middle of this century; his book *Baby and Child Care* changed the way people looked at raising children.

pedant \'pe-dənt\ (1) A formal, unimaginative teacher. (2) A person who shows off his or her learning.

• At one time or another, every student encounters a pedant who makes even the most interesting subject tedious.

It is not always easy to tell a *pedantic* teacher from one who is simply thorough. Half of *pedantry* is in the minds of the students. A pedant need not be a teacher; anyone who displays his or her knowledge in a boring manner can qualify.

NASC/NAT/NAI comes from the Latin verb *nasci*, meaning "to be born." Words that have come directly from Latin carry the root *nasc-* or *nat-*, but those that took a detour through French bear a telltale *nai-*—words like *renaissance*, "rebirth," or *naive*, "unsophisticated."

cognate \'käg-‚nāt\ (1) Related or alike by nature. (2) Related because descended from the same language.

• The Italian word *ostinato* has its English cognate in *obstinate*; both come from the Latin word *obstinatus*.

The prefix *co-*, "with," gives *cognate* the meaning "born with" and therefore "related to." This relationship applies to people as well as to words. Your relatives on your mother's side are your cognate relatives; the ones on your father's side are called *agnate*, with a basic meaning of ''born to.''

innate \i-'nāt\ (1) Present from birth onward; inborn. (2) Part of the essential nature of something.

• The plan has innate problems that are going to make it unworkable.

What is innate in individuals, and in the human race in general, is a constant source of disagreement. No amount of education or experience alone could produce an Isaac Newton or a W.B. Yeats, and the athletic achievements of Michael Jordan or Chris Evert Lloyd required great innate ability. But even the most *natural* geniuses or athletes must work to develop their capacities, no matter how great their *native* talent may be.

nascent \'na-sənt\ Coming or having just come into being.

• The children excitedly watched the nascent butterfly emerge from its chrysalis and begin to stretch its crumpled wings.

With the breakup of the former Soviet Union, the many nascent independent governments in Eastern Europe have had to cope with *renascent* nationalism within their borders, with every ethnic group wanting its own nation. We actually speak of nascent ideas or thoughts or social creations more often than of nascent animals.

renaissance \‚re-nə-'säns\ (1) Rebirth or revival. (2) The period of European history between medieval and modern times, from about the 14th to the 17th century, which saw a revival of classical culture, a flowering of the arts and literature, and the beginnings of modern science.

• Rembrandt van Rijn, the Dutch painter, was one of the greatest artists produced by the European Renaissance.

The Renaissance is known chiefly for the discoveries of its explorers, the masterpieces its artists created, and its important scientific advances. Galileo made detailed observations of sunspots and the moons of Jupiter, and Copernicus identified the Earth as a planet revolving around the sun—ideas that were considered dangerous at the time. But we may also speak of a modern-day renaissance (uncapitalized)—for example, a renaissance of folk music or of weaving. The *cognate* word *renascence* is sometimes used as an alternative form.

Quizzes

A. Indicate whether the following pairs of words have the same or different meanings:

1. nascent / preexisting   same __ / different __
2. encyclopedic / narrow   same __ / different __
3. renaissance / rebirth   same __ / different __
4. cognate / related   same __ / different __
5. pediatrician / foot doctor   same __ / different __
6. innate / inborn   same __ / different __
7. pedagogy / teaching   same __ / different __
8. pedant / know-it-all   same __ / different __

B. Match the definition on the left to the correct word on the right:

1. thorough   a. renaissance
2. beginning   b. pediatrician
3. boring teacher   c. cognate
4. related   d. encyclopedic
5. present from birth   e. nascent
6. education   f. pedant
7. revival   g. innate
8. children's doctor   h. pedagogy

FER, from the Latin verb *ferre,* means "to carry." If you *refer* to an incident in your past, you "carry back" to that time. And *transfer* means "to carry across."

---

deferential \ˌde-fə-'ren-chəl\ Showing respect or esteem.

● Wherever the chairman goes, he receives deferential treatment from his hosts.

As we all know, young people should always *defer* (that is, yield or submit) to their elders and betters, who deserve *deference* and appreciate manners that are properly deferential. Unfortunately, deference from young people isn't what it used to be. (We can also defer, or "put off," a decision until another time, but this meaning isn't found in *deferential*.)

fertile \'fər-təl\ (1) Bearing great quantities of fruit or imaginative ideas; productive or inventive. (2) Able to support abundant plant growth.

• Unfortunately, those with the most fertile minds often seem to have the most personal problems.

A fertile imagination and a fertile field are both very productive. The first might bring forth a whole new world, like J.R.R. Tolkien's Middle Earth; the second might bring forth enough corn for an entire town. But both have to be tended and nurtured in order to *confer* their benefits. *Fertile* and *infertile, fertility* and *infertility* often refer to the ability to bear children as well.

inference \'in-frəns\ (1) A conclusion arrived at from facts or statements taken as true. (2) A guess or assumption made on the basis of little or no evidence.

• Trial lawyers try to present evidence in such a way that the jury can draw from it only the inference that favors their client.

Inferences are risky. In the myth of Pyramus and Thisbe, an inference leads to disaster. When these two lovers are supposed to meet, Pyramus arrives late to find a lion and a bloodstained garment. From this he *infers* that Thisbe has been killed, and, unable to bear it, he kills himself. But Thisbe has only been hiding, and when she finds the dead Pyramus she kills herself in grief. (Shakespeare makes a humorous scene out of this story in *A Midsummer Night's Dream*. But his *Romeo and Juliet* tells the story of two lovers who die as the result of a very similar inference.)

proliferate \prə-'li-fə-ˌrāt\ To grow or increase by rapid production of new units; to multiply.

• Imitators of Ernest Hemingway began to proliferate as soon as he achieved success and popularity.

The literal meaning of *proliferate* is "to bear offspring," and all other usages begin with this. In "The Sorcerer's Apprentice" the apprentice learns how to order the first broom to multiply itself *prolifically*, but not how to command it to stop. Brooms proliferate wildly, each carrying buckets of water that soon flood the sorcerer's studio.

TRANS comes from Latin to indicate movement "through, across, or beyond" something. *Translation* carries the meaning from one language to another. A television signal is sent or *transmitted* through the air (or a cable) to your set. When making your way through a city on public *transportation*, you may have to *transfer* from one bus or subway across to another.

---

transfiguration \trans-ˌfi-gyə-ˈrā-shən\ A change in form or appearance; a glorifying spiritual change.

• Being in love caused a complete transfiguration of her personality.

The transfiguration of Christ from human to divine form, as his apostles watch, is related in the books of Matthew and Mark. From this Biblical origin, *transfiguration* and *transfigure* developed their general meaning, "a transformation" and "to transform." Ebenezer Scrooge undergoes a transfiguration from mean-spirited miser to loving benefactor by the end of *A Christmas Carol*. A face may be transfigured by joy, and an "ugly duckling" child may be slowly transfigured into a radiant beauty.

transfuse \trans-ˈfyüz\ (1) To spread into or throughout; to permeate. (2) To transfer into a vein of a person or animal.

• There was considerable excitement about the new president, who everyone expected to transfuse new life into the institution.

When blood *transfusions* were first attempted by Europeans in the early 1600s, they were met with skepticism. The established practice was to bleed patients, not transfuse them with blood. Some patients were transfused with animal blood, and so many died because of the procedure that it was outlawed in most of Europe by 1700. Not until 1900 were the major blood groups (A, B, AB, and O) recognized, making transfusions safer and more effective.

transient \'tran-chē-ənt\ (1) Not lasting long; short-lived. (2) Passing through a place and staying only briefly.

• They ran an inn in Vermont that was popular with the transient tourists who passed through the state to see the autumn foliage.

A summer job on a farm is transient work, lasting only as long as the growing season. A brief visit to a town on your way somewhere else is a transient visit. A transient mood is one that passes quickly. Doctors speak of transient episodes of dizziness or weakness, which vanish without a trace. *Transient* is also a noun, used for a person who passes through a place, staying only briefly. The hoboes and tramps of earlier years were some of our most colorful transients.

transcendent \tran-'sen-dənt\ (1) Exceeding or rising above usual limits; surpassing, supreme. (2) Beyond comprehension; beyond ordinary experience or material existence.

• Despite the chaos around her she remained calm, with a transcendent smile on her face.

In the Middle Ages the authority of the Pope was considered transcendent in Europe, above the power of kings and emperors, but in the 16th century the *transcendence* of the Papacy was challenged by Martin Luther and Henry VIII of England. A transcendent experience is one that takes you out of yourself and convinces you of a larger life or existence. In this sense, it means something close to "supernatural" or "spiritual."

Quizzes

A. Fill in each blank with the correct letter:

a.	transfiguration	e.	deferential
b.	proliferate	f.	transient
c.	transfuse	g.	inference
d.	fertile	h.	transcendent

1. Copies of American blue jeans seem to ＿＿ in all parts of the world.
2. He lived a ＿＿ existence, spending more nights in airport hotels than at home.
3. The private assumed her usual ＿＿ attitude toward the lieutenant.

4. Waiting for the nurse to _____ her, she couldn't remember the accident clearly.

5. They had witnessed a complete _____, as a poor flower vendor became a lady of society.

6. The _____ Connecticut River valley is famous for its tobacco crops.

7. In search of a _____ experience, she had entered a monastery in Tibet.

8. Please don't draw the wrong _____ from what I've said about the building plans.

B. Match the word on the left to the correct definition on the right:

1.	fertile	a.	supreme
2.	transcendent	b.	implied conclusion
3.	deferential	c.	glorification
4.	transfiguration	d.	productive
5.	proliferate	e.	multiply
6.	transient	f.	yielding
7.	inference	g.	passing
8.	transfuse	h.	transfer

PON/POS, from the Latin verb *ponere*, means "put" or "place." You *expose* film by "placing it out" in the light. You *oppose* an *opponent* by "putting yourself against" him or her. You *postpone* a trip by "placing it after" its original date.

---

component \kəm-'pō-nənt\ A separate part of a whole; an ingredient or element.

• All the components of the agreement were in place, but the owner still hadn't given her final approval.

A component is what is "put together with" other parts to make a whole. A stereo system is made up of different components—tuner, cassette deck, CD player, phonograph, and speakers—each of which fills its own different function in the overall system. The components of a crime bill would include sections on sentencing and parole, prisons, the judicial system, and so on. But the pieces of a jigsaw puzzle may be too similar to be called components.

disposition \\,dis-pə-'zi-shən\\ (1) Tendency, inclination. (2) Basic outlook or attitude.

• It was his classmates' disposition to argue about everything that convinced him he didn't want to be a lawyer after all.

Animals and people may have sweet or sour dispositions, or personalities. Some of them also may share the tendency, or disposition, to eat greedily, to yawn loudly, or to dash about making odd noises. But many humans have a disposition to gossip, to tell stupid jokes, and to think gloomy thoughts about the future, which your dog may not have.

repository \\ri-'pä-zə-,tȯr-ē\\ A place or container where something is stored.

• The 98-year old Miss Sarah turned out to be a repository of lore about the glory days of Beale Street.

A vault or safe is the most secure repository for valuable possessions such as jewelry or money. A book may be a repository of wisdom. A mine is a repository of mineral resources like raw diamonds or gold ore. In all of these lie *deposits* that have been "replaced," and there they *repose* until disturbed.

superimpose \\,sü-pər-im-'pōz\\ To put or place one thing over something else.

• With the transparent sheet, the teacher superimposed national boundaries on an outline of the continent of Africa.

Using "mirror shots," with semitransparent mirrors set at 45° angles to the scene, filmmakers used to superimpose shadowy images of ghosts or scenes from a character's past onto scenes from the present. In a similar way, in your own papers you may try to superimpose your own obsession with cockroaches or Wallace Beery onto every historical or economic or literary subject, to the bafflement of your professors.

TEN/TIN/TAIN, from the Latin verb *tenere* and the related word *tenax,* basically means "hold" or "hold on to." A *tenant* is the "holder" of an apartment, house, or land, but not necessarily the owner. A *lieutenant* governor may "hold the position" or "serve in lieu" of the governor when necessary.

---

abstinence \'ab-stə-nəns\ Holding oneself back voluntarily from indulging an appetite or craving.

• Burned out by too many wild nights, she moved to the country and took up a life of abstinence.

Today we usually speak of abstinence from alcohol, rich foods, or sex. But religious beliefs lead many to *abstain* from much more, and abstinence can become a way of life. Certain religious sects may demand abstinence from such things as meat, dancing, and colorful clothing.

tenacious \tə-'nā-shəs\ Stubborn or persistent in clinging to a thing.

• He was known as a tenacious reporter who would stay with a story for months, sometimes risking his health and even his life.

Success requires a tenacious spirit and a drive to achieve. Nowhere is this more apparent than in the entertainment business. Thousands of actors and actresses work *tenaciously* to have a career in the movies. But without beauty or talent, *tenacity* isn't always rewarded, and only a few become stars.

tenable \'te-nə-bəl\ Capable of being held or defended; reasonable.

• She was depressed for weeks after her professor said that her theory wasn't tenable.

Tenable means "holdable." If you hold an opinion but good evidence appears that completely contradicts it, your opinion is no longer tenable. If your own evidence is shown to be false, it ceases to be tenable evidence. So the old ideas that cancer is infectious or that leeches can cure your whooping cough and criminal insanity are now probably *untenable*.

sustenance \'səs-tə-nəns\ (1) Something that gives support or strength. (2) Food, nourishment.

● Napoleon's invading army, forced to turn back from Moscow by the terrible Russian winter, ended up eating its horses when all other sustenance ran out.

Sustenance holds us up from underneath (the prefix *sus-* being a form of *sub-*, meaning "under"). Sustenance can be either physical or emotional. So a big Sunday dinner with your family can provide you with sustenance of both kinds.

Quizzes

A. Choose the closest definition:

1. disposition   a. temperature b. personality c. anger
      d. riddance
2. tenacious   a. sticking b. intelligent c. loving d. helping
3. superimpose   a. surpass b. put into c. place over
      d. amaze
4. abstinence   a. self-help b. self-will c. self-service
      d. self-restraint
5. repository   a. tomb b. storage container c. office
      d. library
6. tenable   a. decent b. tough c. reasonable
      d. controllable
7. component   a. part b. whole c. some d. all
8. sustenance   a. substance b. apartment c. clothing
      d. nourishment

B. Indicate whether the following pairs have the same or different meanings:

1.	component / ingredient	same ___ / different ___
2.	sustenance / support	same ___ / different ___
3.	repository / return	same ___ / different ___
4.	abstinence / absence	same ___ / different ___
5.	superimpose / offend deeply	same ___ / different ___
6.	tenacious / sensible	same ___ / different ___
7.	disposition / nature	same ___ / different ___
8.	tenable / unlikely	same ___ / different ___

Number Words

MONO is Greek for "one" or "only." So a *monorail* is a railroad that has only one rail, a *monotonous* voice seems to have only one tone, and a *monopoly* puts all ownership in the hands of a single company, eliminating any competition.

---

monogamous \mə-'nä-gə-məs\ Being married to one person or having one mate at a time.

• Geese, swans, and many other birds are monogamous and mate for life.

American marriage is by law monogamous; people are permitted to have only one spouse (husband or wife) at a time. There are cultures with laws that permit marriage to more than one person at a time, or *polygamy*. Some Islamic countries permit polygamy, as do some African tribes. In this country the Mormons were *polygamous* until 1890, when they were forced to practice *monogamy* by the unsympathetic federal government.

monograph \'mä-nə-,graf\ A scholarly essay written on a single small topic and published separately.

• Her paper on the slang used by southern college students was printed as a monograph.

A monograph usually takes the form of a book, but a smallish book. The contents discuss a single area or subject. The subjects of monographs tend to be specialized—for example, *A Statistical Study of the Graphic System of Present-Day American English*.

monolithic \,mä-nə-'li-thik\ (1) Appearing to be a huge, featureless, often rigid whole. (2) Made up of material with no joints or seams.

• The sheer monolithic rock face of El Capitan looks impossible to climb, but its cracks and seams are enough for experienced rock climbers.

Monolithic combines *mono-* with *lith,* "stone," and *monolith* in its original sense means a huge stone like those at Stonehenge. Just as the face of a cliff can be monolithic, so can any huge or imposing institution. The former U.S.S.R. seemed monolithic and indestructible to the West, but the monolith crumbled with the breakup of the Soviet Union into independent republics. To a lone individual, a huge corporation or a government bureaucracy may seem equally monolithic.

monotheism \\'mä-nō-thē-ˌi-zəm\\ The worship of a single god.

• Christian monotheism finally triumphed in the Roman Empire in A.D. 392, when worship of all the pagan gods and goddesses was forbidden.

The monotheism of the ancient Hebrews had to combat the *polytheism* (worship of many gods) of the surrounding peoples from the earliest times. As the Bible relates, several times in their history the Hebrews turned away from their *monotheistic* religion and accepted foreign gods, such as those imported by King Solomon. Their own God would then punish them, and the people of Israel would return to monotheism.

UNI comes from the Latin word for "one." A *uniform* is a single design worn by everyone. A *united* group has one single opinion or forms a single *unit*. A *unitard* is a one-piece combination leotard and tights, very good for skating, skiing, dancing—or riding a one-wheeled *unicycle*.

---

unicameral \\ˌyü-ni-'ka-mə-rəl\\ Having only one lawmaking chamber.

• China has a unicameral system of government; a single group of legislators meets to make its laws.

Unicameral means "one-chambered," and the term is generally used only to describe a governing body. Our federal legislature, like those of most democracies, is *bicameral,* with two legislative (lawmaking) bodies—the Senate and the House of Representatives. Except for Nebraska, all the state legislatures are also bicameral. But nearly every city is governed by a unicameral council.

unilateral \\ˌyü-ni-'la-tə-rəl\\ (1) Done by one person or party; one-sided. (2) Affecting one side of the body.

• The Japanese Constitution of 1947 includes a unilateral rejection of warfare as an option for their country.

The United States announced a unilateral nuclear-arms reduction in the early 1990s. Such a reduction never occurred in the previous decades, when only *bilateral* ("two-sided") negotiations—that is, negotiations with the Soviet Union—ever resulted in reductions. *Multilateral* agreements, such as those reached at the great Earth Summit in Rio de Janeiro in 1992, may involve most of the world's nations.

unison \\'yü-nə-sən\\ (1) Perfect agreement. (2) Sameness of musical pitch.

• Unable to read music well enough to harmonize, the village choir sang only in unison.

This word usually appears in the phrase "in unison," which means "together, at the same time" or "at the same musical pitch." Music of the early Middle Ages was written to be sung in unison, which can sound strange to modern ears used to hearing rich rhythms and harmonies. An excited crowd responding to a speaker may shout in unison, and a group of demonstrators may chant in unison.

unitarian \\,yü-nə-'ter-ē-ən\\ Relating or belonging to a religious group that believes that God exists only in one person and stresses individual freedom of belief.

• With his unitarian tendencies, he wasn't likely to get into fights over religious beliefs.

Unitarianism, originally a sect of Christianity believing in a single or *unitary* God, grew up in 18th-century England and developed in America in the early 19th century. By rejecting the idea of the three-part Trinity—God as father, son, and holy ghost—they denied that Christ was divine and thus cannot truly be considered Christian. In this century it joined with the *Universalist* Church, a movement founded on a belief in *universal* salvation—that is, the saving of every soul from damnation after death. Both have always been liberal and fairly small; today they count about half a million members.

Quiz

Fill in each blank with the correct letter:

a. monotheism   e. unitarian
b. unilateral   f. monograph
c. monolithic   g. unicameral
d. unison   h. monogamous

1. The President is allowed to make some _____ decisions without asking Congress's permission.
2. The relationship was unbalanced: she was perfectly _____, while he had two other women in his life.
3. In rejecting a _____ legislature, America seemed to follow Britain's lead.
4. The steep mountain face looked _____ and forbidding.
5. As a strict Catholic, she found _____ beliefs unacceptable.
6. Most religious groups in this country practice one or another form of _____.
7. She ordered a brief _____ on the subject of the origin of the thoroughbred.
8. The children recited the Halloween poems in _____.

Review Quizzes

A. Choose the correct synonym for the following:

1. fertile   a. green b. productive c. barren d. bare
2. unilateral   a. one-sided b. sideways c. complete d. multiple
3. abstinence   a. self-love b. self-restraint c. self-criticism d. self-indulgence
4. innate   a. natural b. acquired c. genuine d. official
5. repository   a. bedroom b. storeroom c. bank window d. dispensary
6. cryptography   a. gravestone writing b. physics writing c. code writing d. mathematical writing
7. sustenance   a. subtraction b. nourishment c. poison d. addition
8. deferential   a. respectful b. shy c. outgoing d. arrogant

9. monotheism   a. nature worship   b. worship of one god   c. worship of pleasure   d. sun worship
10. abscond   a. steal   b. discover   c. retire   d. flee
11. transcendent   a. supreme   b. beautiful   c. heroic   d. intelligent
12. inference   a. conclusion   b. claim   c. concept   d. refusal
13. transient   a. flowing   b. passing   c. intense   d. speeding
14. pedagogy   a. study   b. teaching   c. research   d. child abuse
15. nascent   a. dying   b. lasting   c. eating   d. beginning
16. unison   a. solitude   b. harmony   c. collection   d. agreement
17. proliferate   a. survive   b. prosper   c. multiply   d. die off
18. crypt   a. code   b. granite   c. tomb   d. church
19. superimpose   a. increase   b. lay over   c. improve   d. excel
20. monogamous   a. with one spouse   b. without a spouse   c. with several spouses   d. with someone else's spouse

B. Fill in each blank with the correct letter:

a. renaissance   f. abstraction
b. pediatrician   g. tenacious
c. monograph   h. disposition
d. unitarian   i. transfuse
e. transfiguration   j. abstruse

1. In the 1990s there has been a ＿＿ of interest in goddess worship.
2. Tuesday the baby sees the ＿＿ for its immunizations and checkups.
3. His ＿＿ had gotten so bad that he found himself snapping angrily at his friends.
4. The anemia was serious enough that they had to ＿＿ him with two pints of blood.
5. The notion of a savior was foreign to his ＿＿ beliefs.
6. The ＿＿ promised by their leader failed to occur on the predicted day.
7. The speech contained one ＿＿ after another, but never a specific example.

8. She would occasionally publish a short ____ on the results of her recent research.

9. The sick child's ____ grip on life was their only hope now.

10. The researcher's writing was ____ but it was worth the effort to read it.

C. Indicate whether the following pairs of words have the same or different meanings:

1. component / part   same __ / different __
2. pedant / pupil   same __ / different __
3. cryptic / tomblike   same __ / different __
4. monolithic / tedious   same __ / different __
5. abstemious / self-controlled   same __ / different __
6. cognate / related   same __ / different __
7. apocryphal / sacred   same __ / different __
8. tenable / reasonable   same __ / different __
9. unicameral / one-chambered   same __ / different __
10. abstruse / deep   same __ / different __

Unit 15

TERM/TERMIN comes from the Latin verb *terminare,* "to limit, bound, or set limits to," or the related noun *terminus,* a "limit or boundary." In English, those boundaries or limits tend to be final: to *terminate* a sentence or a meeting or a ballgame means to end it, and a *term* goes on for a given amount of time and then ends.

---

indeterminate \in-di-'tər-mə-nət\ Not precisely determined; vague.

• The law allowed for indeterminate sentences for certain unusual classes of offenders.

A mutt is usually the product of indeterminate breeding, since at least the father's identity is generally a mystery. An art object of indeterminate origins is normally less valued than one with a maker's name on it. If negotiations are left in an indeterminate state, nothing has been decided.

interminable \in-'tər-mə-nə-bəl\ Having or seeming to have no end; tiresomely drawn out.

• Their appeals to their audiences for money are so interminable that there's barely time for the sermons.

Nothing is literally endless except maybe the universe and time itself. So *interminable* as we use it is always an exaggeration. On an unlucky day you might sit through an interminable lecture, an interminable meeting, and an interminable film—all in less than 24 hours.

terminal \'tər-mə-nəl\ (1) Forming or relating to an end or limit. (2) Fatal.

● She knows these are the late stages of a terminal illness, and has already drawn up a will.

A terminal illness ends in death; with terminal boredom you are "bored to death." For some, a high-school diploma is their terminal degree; others finish college before *terminating* their education. A bus *terminal* should be the endpoint of a bus line; a computer terminal was originally the endpoint of a line connecting to a central computer. A terminal ornament may mark the end of a building, and terminal punctuation ends this sentence.

terminology \,tər-mə-'nä-lə-jē\ The words with specialized or precise meanings used in a field or subject.

● Civil engineers use a technical terminology that is like a foreign language to an outsider.

Terms—that is, specialized words or expressions—tend to have precise boundaries of meaning. Each field has its own terminology, or "jargon," which helps those who work in the field communicate with each other quickly and accurately. But the expert's workaday language is often the layperson's *terminological* hell.

VINC/VICT comes from the Latin verb *vincere*, which means "to conquer" or "to overcome." The *victor* defeats an enemy, whether on a battlefield or a football field. To *convince* someone that you're right is a *victory* of another kind.

---

evince \i-'vins\ To be outward evidence of; show or reveal.

● As a witness she evinced honesty and dignity, and the jury was favorably impressed.

A man may evince interest in a woman by casting glances, making small talk, and generally hanging around, or by even more obvious tactics. A novelist's writing may evince concern for refugees or the elderly. A country may evince a desire for closer relations by arranging a ping-pong competition, as China did with the United States in 1971.

invincible \in-'vin-sə-bəl\ Incapable of being conquered or overcome.

● The supposedly invincible Spanish Armada was defeated by a fleet of small English ships in 1588.

Antaeus, a giant and son of Poseidon, was invincible so long as he remained in contact with the ground. But his *invincibility* crumbled when he challenged Hercules to wrestle and Hercules held the giant over his head, thereby defeating his "invincible" foe.

provincial \prə-'vin-chəl\ (1) Having to do with a province. (2) Lacking polish, culture, and broad experience.

● They were both by now sick of Chicago and would gladly have exchanged the fast life for more provincial pleasures.

A *province* is an administrative section of a larger state or country. The word comes from Roman times. The Romans gained territory by conquest, and a conquered area might become a province. (There is still some question about how the word was actually formed.) The areas usually set up a local or provincial government. Life in these provinces was not as fancy as life at Rome, just as life in the rural, provincial parts of any country is not as polished or refined as life in its cities.

victimize \'vik-tə-ˌmīz\ To make a victim of; trick, deceive, or injure.

● Like most tourists there, we were victimized by the local merchants and guides.

A *victim* is the person who is victimized. Robin Hood and his band of merry men victimized the rich in order to give to the poor—but the rich noblemen and churchmen had gotten that way by victimizing the poor in the first place. Physical and emotional *victimization* by one's parents when young is a complaint heard often today from "adult children."

Quizzes

A. Choose the closest definition:

1. evince   a. reveal b. throw out c. eject d. overcome
2. interminable   a. remarkable b. unthinkable
      c. reliable d. eternal

3. terminology   a. instruction b. design c. vocabulary
    d. technology
4. provincial   a. professional b. global c. local d. national
5. invincible   a. unsuitable b. impossible
    c. inflammable d. unconquerable
6. terminal   a. fatal b. technical c. verbal d. similar
7. indeterminate   a. lengthy b. uncertain c. unending
    d. likely
8. victimize   a. conquer b. applaud c. deceive d. invite

B. Fill in each blank with the correct letter:

a. invincible   e. indeterminate
b. terminology   f. evince
c. victimize   g. terminal
d. interminable   h. provincial

1. Her manners were a bit rough and _____, but charming.
2. All day long, reports came in of people the con man had
    tried to _____.
3. We waited anxiously for the mare to _____ signs of
    giving birth.
4. The students generally find the _____ of psychology
    fairly easy to learn and use.
5. He was a man of _____ age, and mysterious in other
    ways as well.
6. Don't you ever have those great days when you feel
    absolutely _____?
7. He gave _____ lectures, and I usually dozed off in the
    middle.
8. Last week we assumed his condition was _____; today no
    one is making predictions.

SPHER comes from the Greek word for "ball," and it appears
in words for things that have something round about them. A ball
is itself a *sphere*. The *stratosphere* and the *ionosphere* are parts of
the *atmosphere* that encircles the earth.

stratosphere \\'stra-tə-ˌsfir\\ (1) The part of the earth's atmosphere
that extends from about seven to about 31 miles above the surface.

(2) A very high or the highest region.

• In the celebrity stratosphere she now occupied, a fee of two million dollars a film was a reasonable rate.

The stratosphere (*strato-* simply means "layer" or "level") lies above the earth's weather and mostly changes very little. About 20 miles above the earth's surface it contains the ozone layer, which shields us from the sun's ultraviolet radiation except where it has been harmed by manmade chemicals. The levels of the *atmosphere* are marked particularly by their temperatures; the *stratospheric* temperature hovers around 32°—very moderate considering that temperatures in the *troposphere* below may descend to about -70° and in the *ionosphere* above may rise to 1000°.

biosphere \'bī-ə-ˌsfir\ (1) The part of the world in which life can exist. (2) Living things and their environment.

• The moon has no biosphere, so an artificial one would have to be constructed for any long-term stay.

The *lithosphere* is the solid surface of the earth (*lith-* means "rock"); the *hydrosphere* is the earth's water (*hydro-* means "water"), including the clouds and water vapor in the air; the *atmosphere* is the earth's air (*atmos-* means "vapor"). The term *biosphere* can include all of these and the 10 million species of living things they contain. The biosphere recycles its air, water, organisms, and minerals constantly to maintain an amazingly balanced state; human beings should probably do their best to imitate it. Though the word has a new sound to it, it was first used a hundred years ago.

hemisphere \'he-mə-ˌsfir\ Half a sphere, especially half the global sphere as divided by the equator or a meridian.

• Sailors who cross the equator from the northern to the southern hemisphere for the first time are given a special initiation.

Hemisphere includes the prefix *hemi-,* meaning "half." The northern and southern hemispheres are divided by the equator. The eastern and western hemispheres aren't divided so exactly; usually the eastern hemisphere includes all of Europe, Africa, and Australia and almost all of Asia, and the western hemisphere contains North and South America and a great deal of ocean.

spherical \\'sfir-ə-kəl\\ Relating to a sphere; shaped like a sphere or one of its segments.

• The girls agreed that the spacecraft had been perfectly spherical and deep blue, and that its alien passengers had resembled large cockroaches.

Something spherical is like a *sphere* in being round, or more or less round, in three dimensions. Apples and oranges are both spherical, though never perfectly round. A *spheroid* has a roughly spherical shape; an asteroid is often a spheroid, fairly round but lumpy.

VERT/VERS, from the Latin verb *vertere*, means "to turn" or "to turn around." An *advertisement* turns your attention to a product or service. *Vertigo* is the dizziness that results from turning too rapidly or that makes you feel as if everything else is turning.

divert \\dī-'vərt\\ (1) To turn from one purpose or course to another. (2) To give pleasure to by distracting from burdens or distress.

• The farmers successfully diverted some of the river water to irrigate their crops during the drought.

The Roman circus was used to provide *diversion* for its citizens—and sometimes to divert their attention from the government's failings as well. The diversion was often in the form of a fight—men pitted against lions, bears, or each other—and the audience was sure to see blood and death. A *diverting* evening in the 1990s might instead include watching several murders on a movie screen.

perverse \\pər-'vərs\\ (1) Corrupt; improper; incorrect. (2) Stubbornly or obstinately wrong.

• The unsuspected murderer had apparently felt a perverse desire to chat with the police.

The 12th-century citizens of Paris thought keeping a cat or taking a bath without clothes on were perverse—that is, satanic or ungodly. But this is an older meaning; today *perverse* usually means somehow "contradictory" or "opposed to good sense." Someone who loves great art but collects cheap figurines may admit to having perverse tastes. To desire a stable life but still go out on drinking binges could be called acting *perversely* or even self-destructively. Don't confuse *perverse* with *perverted*, which today tends to mean "having strange sexual tastes." And likewise avoid confusing their noun forms, *perversity* and *perversion*.

avert \ə-'vərt\ (1) To turn away or aside (especially one's eyes). (2) To avoid or ward off; prevent.

● General Camacho's announcement of lower food prices averted an immediate worker's revolt.

Sensitive people avert their eyes from gory accidents and scenes of disaster. But we also speak of averting the disaster itself. Negotiators may avert, or avoid, a strike by all-night talks, and leaders may work to avert a war in the same way. In the Cuban missile crisis of 1962 it seemed that worldwide nuclear catastrophe was narrowly (or barely) averted. *Aversion* means "dislike or disgust"—that is, your feeling about something you don't want to look at.

versatile \'vər-sə-təl\ (1) Turning easily from one skill to another. (2) Having many uses.

● The versatile Gene Kelly acted, sang, and directed—and dazzled America with his dancing.

The horse was the most versatile and valuable asset of the armies of Attila the Hun. A Hun could stay in the saddle for weeks at a time, opening a vein in the horse's neck to suck the blood for food. The Huns made a kind of liquor from mare's milk. Extra horses were stampeded in battle to create *diversions*. Relying on this *versatility*, Attila and the Huns conquered much of eastern and central Europe in the 5th century.

Quizzes

A. Complete the analogy:

1. pint : quart :: hemisphere : _____
   a. ocean b. continent c. sphere d. globe
2. reasonable : sensible :: perverse : _____
   a. mistaken b. stupid c. contrary d. unlikely
3. forest : trees :: stratosphere : _____
   a. gases b. clouds c. planets d. altitude
4. accept : agree :: divert : _____
   a. distress b. amuse c. differ d. disturb

5.   escape : flee :: avert : _____
        a. prevent b. throw c. entertain d. alarm
6.   cube-shaped : square :: spherical : _____
        a. global b. oval c. curved d. circle
7.   flexible : stretchable :: versatile : _____
        a. well-rounded b. similar c. skilled d. trained
8.   atmosphere : stratosphere :: biosphere : _____
        a. recycling b. hydrosphere c. energy d. earth

**B.   Match the word on the left to the correct definition
on the right:**

1.   avert
2.   spherical   a.   with many uses
3.   divert   b.   upper atmosphere
4.   hemisphere   c.   wrongheaded
5.   versatile   d.   avoid
6.   biosphere   e.   half-sphere
7.   stratosphere   f.   entertain
8.   perverse   g.   globelike
                                  h.   life zone

MORPH comes from the Greek word for "shape." *Morph* is
itself an English word with a brand-new meaning; by morphing,
filmmakers can now alter photographic images or shapes digitally,
making them move or transform themselves in astonishing ways.

amorphous \ə-'mȯr-fəs\ Without a definite shape or form;
shapeless.

• The sculptor took an amorphous lump of clay and molded it
swiftly into a rough human shape.

A new word may appear to name a previously amorphous group
of people, as the word *yuppie* did in 1983. An amorphous but terrifying thing may loom in a nightmare. In all the Greek myths of
the creation the world begins in an amorphous state, just as at the
beginning of the Bible "the earth was without form, and void."

anthropomorphic \ˌan-thrə-pə-'mȯr-fik\ (1) Having or described as having human form or traits. (2) Seeing human traits in nonhuman things.

- The old, diseased tree had always been like a companion to her, though she knew her anthropomorphic feelings about it were sentimental.

Anthropomorphic means a couple of different things. In its first sense, an anthropomorphic cup would be a cup in the shape of a human, and an anthropomorphic god would be one that looked and acted like a human. All the Greek and Roman gods are anthropomorphic, for example, even though Socrates and even earlier Greeks believed that their fellow Greeks had created their gods in their own image rather than the other way around. In its second sense, the animal characters in *Aesop's Fables* are anthropomorphic since they all have human feelings and motivations though they don't look like humans. When the fox calls the grapes sour simply because they are out of reach, it is a very human response. At least 3,000 years after Aesop, *anthropomorphism* is still alive and well, in the books of Beatrix Potter, George Orwell's *Animal Farm*, and hundreds of animated cartoons and comic strips.

metamorphosis \,me-tə-'mȯr-fə-səs\ (1) A physical change, especially one supernaturally caused. (2) A developmental change in an animal that occurs after birth or hatching.

- Day by day we watched the gradual metamorphosis of the tadpoles into frogs.

Many myths end in a metamorphosis. As Apollo is chasing the nymph Daphne, she calls on her river-god father for help and he turns her into a laurel tree to save her. Out of anger and jealousy, the goddess Athena turns the marvelous weaver Arachne into a spider that will spin only beautiful webs. But rocks may also *metamorphose*, or undergo metamorphosis; coal under great pressure over a long period of time will become diamonds. And the transformation of caterpillars into butterflies is the most famous of natural metamorphoses.

morphology \mȯr-'fä-lə-jē\ (1) The study of the structure and form of plants and animals. (2) The study of word formation.

- Her biology term paper discussed the morphology of three kinds of seaweed.

Morphology contains the root *log-*, "study." *Morphologists* study plants and animals and use the information to classify species. In language, morphology considers where words come from and why they look as they do.

FORM is the Latin root meaning "shape" or "form." Marching in *formation* is marching in ordered patterns. A *formula* is a standard form for expressing information, such as a recipe or a rule written in mathematical symbols.

---

conform \kən-'fòrm\ (1) To be similar or identical; to be in agreement or harmony. (2) To follow ordinary standards or customs.

• Ignoring all pressure to conform, she would stride with her goats through the fields at sunset, her hair wild and her long skirts billowing.

Employees must usually conform with company procedures. A certain philosophy may be said to conform with American values. A Maine Coon cat or a Dandie Dinmont terrier must conform to its breed requirements in order to be registered for breeding purposes. A *nonconformist* ignores society's standards or deliberately violates them, and laughs at the whole idea of *conformity*. (Note that "conform to" and "conform with" are both correct, though "conform to" is more common.)

formality \fòr-'ma-lə-tē\ (1) An established custom or way of behaving that is required or standard. (2) The following of formal or conventional rules.

• The bride and groom wanted a small, intimate wedding without all the usual formalities.

Formal behavior follows the proper *forms* or customs, and *informal* behavior ignores them. The formality of a dinner party is indicated by such formalities as invitations, required dress, and full table settings. Legal formalities may turn out to be all-important even if they seem minor. America requires fewer formalities than many other countries (in Germany you may know people for years before using their first names, for example), but even in relaxed situations Americans may be observing invisible formalities.

formative \'fôr-mə-tiv\ (1) Giving or able to give form or shape; constructive. (2) Having to do with important growth or development.

• She lived in Venezuela during her formative years and grew up speaking both Spanish and English.

Whatever gives shape to something else may be called formative; thus, for example, the Grand Canyon was a product of the formative power of water. But it usually applies to nonphysical shaping. An ambitious plan goes through a formative stage of development. America's formative years included experimentation with various forms of government. And the automobile was a huge formative influence on the design of many of our cities.

format \'fôr-ˌmat\ (1) The shape, size, and general makeup of something. (2) A general plan, arrangement, or choice of material.

• The new thesaurus would be published in three formats: as a large paperback, as a hardcover book, and as a CD-ROM.

TV news shows seem to change their formats, or general form, as often as their anchorpeople. The situation comedy is even called a format. The format of a book or newspaper page is its design or layout.

Quizzes

A. Indicate whether the following pairs of words have the same or different meanings:

1. formative / form-giving   same ___ / different ___
2. morphology / shapeliness   same ___ / different ___
3. conform / agree   same ___ / different ___
4. anthropomorphic / man-shaped   same ___ / different ___
5. format / arrangement   same ___ / different ___
6. amorphous / shapeless   same ___ / different ___
7. formality / convention   same ___ / different ___
8. metamorphosis / hibernation   same ___ / different ___

B. Fill in each blank with the correct letter:

a. morphology   e. conform
b. formative   f. amorphous

---

c. metamorphosis   g. formality
d. format   h. anthropomorphic

1. The newspaper's new ＿＿ led the public to expect
    stories of glamour and scandal.
2. The job description seemed a bit ＿＿, and she
    wondered what she would really be doing.
3. While on the base, you are expected to ＿＿ with all
    official rules and regulations.
4. He sees many ＿＿ traits in his dogs, but he thinks that
    one of them may be a space alien.
5. He seemed to undergo a complete ＿＿ from child to
    young adult in just a few months.
6. The new couple found the ＿＿ of the dinner a little
    overwhelming.
7. He had spent his life on the ＿＿ of a single genus of
    dragonfly.
8. Among her ＿＿ influences she included her favorite
    uncle, her ballet classes, and the Nancy Drew series.

DOC/DOCT comes from the Latin *docere*, which means "to
teach." A *doctor* is a highly educated person capable of instructing
others in the *doctrines*, or basic principles, of his or her field—
which is not necessarily medicine.

doctrine \'däk-trən\ (1) Something that is taught. (2) An official
principle, opinion, or belief.

• According to the 19th-century doctrine of papal infallibility, the
pope's formal statements on matters of faith and morals must be
regarded as the absolute truth.

The original doctrines were those of the Catholic Church, especially as taught by the so-called *doctors* (or religious scholars) of
the Church. Other systems, organizations, and governments have
taught their own doctrines. Traditional psychiatrists may still follow the doctrines of Sigmund Freud. Old and established legal
principles are called legal doctrine. Communist doctrine was often
regarded as almost sacred. In
1823 the Monroe Doctrine stated that the United States opposed
European influence in the Americas, and in 1947 the Truman Doc-

trine held that America would support free countries against enemies outside and inside.

docile \'dä-səl\ Easily led, tamed, or taught; obedient.

● Training a dog is much easier if the animal has a docile temperament to start with.

A docile patient obeys all doctors and nurses, takes the prescribed medication, and doesn't nag anyone with questions. A docile labor force doesn't make demands or form unions. A docile population is easily led by even bad leaders. And a docile spouse does what he or she is told.

doctrinaire \‚däk-trə-'nar\ Tending to apply principles or theories without regard for practical difficulties or individual circumstance.

● She avoided taking a doctrinaire approach to teaching; education theories didn't always match the reality of instructing 25 lively students.

Someone doctrinaire sticks closely to official doctrines or principles. A doctrinaire judge will give identical sentences to everyone found guilty of a particular crime. A doctrinaire feminist will treat all men as if they were identical. A doctrinaire free-market economist will call for a single solution for the economic problems in all countries, regardless of their social and cultural history.

indoctrinate \in-'däk-trə-‚nāt\ (1) To teach, especially basics or fundamentals. (2) To fill someone with a particular opinion or point of view.

● The sergeants had six months to indoctrinate the new recruits with army attitudes and discipline.

Indoctrinate simply means ''brainwash'' to many people. But its meaning isn't always so negative. Every society indoctrinates its young people with the values of their culture. In the United States we tend to be indoctrinated to love freedom, to be individuals, and to work hard for success, among many other things. A religious cult may indoctrinate its members to give up their freedom and individuality and to work hard only for its leader's goals. *Indoctrination* in these opposite values leads many to regard cults as dangerous.

TUT/TUI, from the Latin verb *tueri*, originally meant "to look at," but the English meaning of the root gradually came to be "to guide, guard, or teach." A *tutor* guides a student (or *tutee*) through a subject, saving the most careful tutoring for the most difficult areas.

intuition \ˌin-tù-'wi-shən\ (1) The power of knowing something immediately without mental effort; quick insight. (2) Something known in this way.

• She scoffed at the notion of "women's intuition," special powers of insight and understanding that only women are supposed to have.

Intuition is very close in meaning to *instinct*. The moment someone enters a room you may feel you know *intuitively* or instinctively everything about him or her. Highly rational people may try to ignore their intuition and insist on being able to explain everything they think. Artists and creative thinkers, on the other hand, tend to rely on their intuitive sense of things. Intuition can be closely related to their imagination, which seems to come from somewhere just as mysterious.

tuition \tù-'wi-shən\ (1) The act of teaching; instruction. (2) The cost of or payment for instruction.

• As Kara happily flipped through her college catalogs, her parents looked on in dismay, mentally calculating the total tuition costs.

The sense of *tuition* meaning "teaching" or "instruction" is mostly used in Britain today. In America *tuition* almost always means the costs charged by a school, college, or university. In the mid-1990s it was possible to receive an education through college for less than $20,000; but it was also possible to spend about $200,000 in tuition and fees for a boarding-school and college education.

tutelage \'tü-tə-lij\ Instruction or guidance of an individual; guardianship.

• Under the old man's expert tutelage, they learned how to carve and paint realistic decoys.

Tutelage usually implies specialized and individual guidance. Alexander the Great was under the tutelage of the philosopher Aristotle between the ages of 13 and 16, and his *tutor* inspired him with a love of philosophy, medicine, and science. At 16 he commanded his first army, and by his death 16 years later he had founded the greatest empire ever seen. But it's not so easy to trace the effects of the brilliant tutelage he had received in his youth.

tutorial \tü-'tòr-ē-əl\ (1) A class for one student or a small group of students. (2) An instructional program that gives information about a specific subject.

• Students tend to learn more in a tutorial than they do in a large class.

Tutorials with live tutors are useful for both advanced students and struggling ones. Most computer programs include electronic tutorials to help the user get used to the program, leading him or her through the different operations to show what the program can do. But a difficult program might still require a real-life tutor to be fully understood.

Quizzes

A. Choose the closest definition:

1. docile   a. tame b. learned c. taught d. beloved
2. tuition   a. requirement b. instruction c. resolution d. housing
3. indoctrinate   a. medicate thoroughly b. research thoroughly c. instruct thoroughly d. consider thoroughly
4. tutelage   a. responsibility b. protection c. instruction d. safeguard
5. doctrine   a. solution b. principle c. religion d. report
6. tutorial   a. small class b. large class c. night class d. canceled class
7. doctrinaire   a. by the way b. by the by c. by the rule d. by the glass
8. intuition   a. ignorance b. quick understanding c. payment d. consideration

---

B. **Match the word on the left to the correct definition on the right:**

1. indoctrinate
2. tutelage
3. doctrine
4. tutorial
5. doctrinaire
6. intuition
7. docile
8. tuition

a. instruction costs
b. easily led
c. fill with a point of view
d. insight
e. guardianship
f. teaching
g. individual instruction
h. rigidly principled

Number Words

DI/DUO, the Greek and Latin prefixes meaning "two," show up in both technical and nontechnical terms. A *duel* is a battle between two people. A *duet* is music for a *duo*, or a pair of musicians. If you have *dual* citizenship, you belong to two countries at once. Most birds are *dimorphic*, with feathers of one color for males and another color for females.

dichotomy \dī-'kä-tə-mē\ (1) A division into two often contradictory groups. (2) Something with qualities that seem to contradict each other.

• With her first job she discovered the dichotomy between the theories she'd been taught and the realities of professional life.

In the modern United States there is a dichotomy between life in a big city and life in the country, big-city life being fast-paced and often dangerous, and country life being slow-moving and usually safe. But the dichotomy is nothing new: the Roman poet Horace was complaining about it in the 1st century B.C. Among other eternal dichotomies, there is the dichotomy between wealth and poverty, between the policies of the leading political parties, between a government's words and its actions—and between what would be most fun to do right this minute and what would be the mature and sensible and intelligent alternative.

diplomatic \‚di-plə-'ma-tik\ (1) Relating to negotiations between nations. (2) Tactful.

• In his dealings with my cranky old Aunt Louisa, Alex was always diplomatic, and she was very fond of him.

The path from *di-*, "two," to *diplomatic* is a winding one. A Greek *diploma* was an official document folded in two and sealed, or a passport. So *diplomacy* came to mean the international carrying and exchanging of such documents for the purpose of negotiation. *Diplomats* are famous for their tact and sensitivity (and sometimes their insincerity), so it's natural that *diplomatic* should apply to social behavior as smooth and sensitive as an ambassador's.

duplex \'dü-‚pleks\ (1) Having two principal elements; double. (2) Allowing electronic communication in two directions at the same time.

• Their splendid duplex apartment had a panoramic view of Paradise Park.

Duplex can describe a confusing variety of things, depending on the technical field. Most of us use it as a noun: a *duplex* generally is either a two-family house or a two-story apartment. In computer science and telecommunications, duplex (or *full-duplex*) communication can go in both directions at once, while *half-duplex* communication can go only one way at a time. In other areas, translate *duplex* as "double" and see if the sentence makes sense.

duplicity \dù-'pli-sə-tē\ Deception by pretending to feel and act one way while acting in another.

• By the time Jackie's duplicity in the whole matter had come to light, she had moved leaving no forwarding address.

The Greek god Zeus often resorted to duplicity to get what he wanted, and most of the time what he wanted was some woman. His duplicity usually involved a disguise: he appeared to Leda as a swan, and to Europa as a bull. Sometimes he had to be *duplicitous* to get around his wife Hera. After he had had his way with Io and was about to get caught, he turned her into a cow to avoid Hera's wrath.

BI/BIN also means "two" or "double." A *bicycle* has two wheels; *binoculars* consist of two little telescopes; *bigamy* is marriage to two people at once. A road through the middle of a neighborhood *bisects* it into two pieces.

bipartisan \ˌbī-'pär-tə-zən\ Involving members of two political parties.

• The President named a bipartisan commission of four Republicans and three Democrats to look into the issue.

Since the United States has a two-party system of government, legislation often must have some bipartisan support in order to pass into law. Bipartisan committees review legislation, compromising on some points and removing or adding others in order to make the bill more agreeable to both parties and make bipartisan support more likely.

binary \'bī-nə-rē\ (1) Consisting of two things or parts; double. (2) Involving a choice between two alternatives.

• The Milky Way contains numerous binary stars, each consisting of two stars orbiting each other.

Binary has many uses, most of them in technical terms. Most computers, for example, are based on the binary number system, in which only two digits, 0 and 1, are used. (0 stands for a low-voltage impulse and 1 stands for a high-voltage impulse.) All their information is kept in this form. The word "HELLO," for example, looks like this: 1001000 1000101 1001100 1001100 1001111.

biennial \ˌbī-'e-nē-əl\ (1) Occurring every two years. (2) Continuing or lasting over two years.

• The great biennial show of new art usually either puzzled or angered the critics.

Biennial conventions, celebrations, competitions, and sports events come every two years. *Biennials* are plants that live two years, bearing flowers and fruit only in the second year. In contrast, *semiannual* means "twice a year." But no one can agree whether *biweekly* means "twice a week" or "every two weeks," and whether *bimonthly* means "twice a month" or "every two months.'' Maybe we should stop using both of them until we can decide.

bipolar \‚bī-'pō-lər\ Having two opposed forces or views; having two poles or opposed points of attraction.

● Our bipolar earth spins on an axis that extends between the North and the South Pole.

Magnets are always bipolar: one pole attracts and the other repels or drives away. The Cold War arms race was bipolar, since it mainly involved the opposing powers of the United States and Russia. Evolutionism and creationism are bipolar views on the history of life, the two major opposing beliefs on the subject in America. And manic-depressive illness, in which the person swings between the two extremes of high excitation and deep depression, is now often called *bipolar disorder*.

Quiz

Fill in each blank with the correct letter:

a.	bipolar	e.	diplomatic
b.	duplex	f.	binary
c.	biennial	g.	dichotomy
d.	duplicity	h.	bipartisan

1. The new law was written in a thoroughly ＿＿ way, and so passed through Congress easily.
2. In response to his angry questions she gave ＿＿ but vague answers.
3. Powerful drugs like lithium are often prescribed for ＿＿ depression.
4. A liar's ＿＿ usually catches up with him sooner or later.
5. The ＿＿ number system is at the heart of the modern technological revolution.
6. His father found there was a painful ＿＿ between the tidy instructions and the messy assembly.
7. They shared the modest ＿＿ with another family of four.
8. Every two years we get to hear Mildred McDermot sing ''Moonlight in Vermont'' at the ＿＿ town picnic.

Review Quizzes

A. Fill in each blank with the correct letter:

a.	anthropomorphic	k.	provincial
b.	doctrine	l.	versatile
c.	tuition	m.	conform
d.	interminable	n.	intuition
e.	duplex	o.	indeterminate
f.	binary	p.	bipartisan
g.	formative	q.	metamorphosis
h.	biennial	r.	diplomatic
i.	doctrinaire	s.	tutelage
j.	spherical	t.	hemisphere

1. This marble was limestone before it underwent ＿＿＿.
2. The computer works by making choices between ＿＿＿ opposites.
3. The main piano competition is ＿＿＿, but there are smaller ones on the off-years.
4. The number of places open is still ＿＿＿, but probably about 20 or 30.
5. Your equipment doesn't ＿＿＿ to our specifications, so we regret that we can't place an order.
6. My attitudes may be ＿＿＿ but my ambitions are global.
7. I had an ＿＿＿ wait in the doctor's office and didn't get home until 6:00.
8. The young woman's ＿＿＿ told her this was a friendship she would treasure forever.
9. Hoping for a ＿＿＿ career, she took three languages in college.
10. With her talent for singing, dancing, and playing piano, she was a ＿＿＿ performer.
11. The governor named a ＿＿＿ committee to keep the issue as nonpolitical as possible.
12. After this ＿＿＿ payment there's only one more year before she graduates, thank God.
13. The ＿＿＿ was roomy, but the other family made a great deal of noise.
14. Under the great man's ＿＿＿, the young composer learned how to develop his ideas into full-fledged sonatas.

15. As a practicing Catholic, she thought frequently about the church ____ that life begins at conception.
16. Michelangelo's great painting shows an ____ God touching Adam's finger.
17. A ____ interpretation of these rules will leave no room for fun at all.
18. My trip to Australia was the first time I had left this ____.
19. I'd like you to write an essay about the person who had the greatest ____ influence on your thinking.
20. The inside of the ____ stone was a hollow lined entirely with purple cyrstals.

B. Choose the correct synonym and the correct antonym:

1. invincible   a. vulnerable   b. unbreakable   c. inedible   d. unconquerable
2. divert   a. please   b. entertain   c. bore   d. send
3. amorphous   a. beginning   b. shapeless   c. shaping   d. formed
4. terminal   a. first   b. final   c. highest   d. deathlike
5. duplicity   a. desire   b. two-facedness   c. honesty   d. complexity
6. formality   a. convention   b. black tie   c. rationality   d. casualness
7. evince   a. hide   b. reveal   c. conquer   d. defy
8. dichotomy   a. operation   b. negotiation   c. contradiction   d. agreement
9. docile   a. rebellious   b. angry   c. passive   d. soft
10. perverse   a. brilliant   b. reasonable   c. amazing   d. bizarre

C. Choose the closest definition:

1. format   a. design   b. formality   c. formation   d. concept
2. biosphere   a. life cycle   b. environment   c. stratosphere   d. evolution
3. morphology   a. study of structure   b. study of woods   c. study of butterflies   d. study of geometry
4. avert   a. embrace   b. prevent   c. assert   d. escape

5. bipolar   a. depressed b. monopolistic c. opposing
   d. two-handed
6. indoctrinate   a. teach b. demonstrate c. infiltrate
   d. consider
7. terminology   a. study b. specialty c. jargon d. symbols
8. victimize   a. suffer b. agonize c. harm d. complain
9. tutorial   a. penalty b. teacher c. classroom d. lesson
10. stratosphere   a. cloud level b. spherical body
    c. atmospheric layer d. ozone depletion

Unit 16

TOP comes from *topos*, the Greek word for "place." A *topic* is the subject of a paper or discussion. Its root originally meant "commonplace"—that is, a common subject.

ectopic \ek-'tä-pik\ Occurring or originating in an abnormal place.

• A pacemaker was installed to correct the patient's ectopic heartbeat.

Ectopic is a medical word that means "out of place." An ectopic heartbeat originates in an abnormal area of the heart. An ectopic kidney is located in an abnormal position. But *ectopic* most commonly describes a pregnancy in which the fertilized egg begins to develop in an area outside the uterus, such as in a fallopian tube.

topical \'tä-pə-kəl\ (1) Designed for local application to or treatment of a bodily part. (2) Referring to the topics of the day.

• If the topical ointment doesn't work on the rash, the doctor will prescribe an antibiotic pill.

Like a topical medicine, a topical reference or story applies to something specific, focusing on a topic that is currently in the news. Comedians often use topical humor, making jokes about the latest political scandal or a currently popular movie. Topical humor has a short lifespan, though, because the news keeps changing and new hot topics keep coming along to replace the old ones.

topiary \'tō-pē-,er-ē\ Relating to the art of shaping trees or shrubs into odd or ornamental shapes.

• Beyond the house was a topiary garden with shrubs shaped like barnyard animals.

The art of *topiary* has been known since the 1st century A.D., and is supposed to have been invented by a friend of the Roman Emperor Augustus. In modern topiary gardens, trees and shrubs are carefully cut and pruned and trained into odd shapes. Sometimes topiary effects mimic the shapes of people or animals. Topiary art differs from other forms of sculpture in two important ways—it requires constant pruning, and the sculpture eventually dies.

topography \tə-'pä-grə-fē\ (1) The art of showing the natural and man-made features of a region on a map or chart. (2) The features of a surface, including both natural and man-made features.

• Planning the expedition involved careful study of the region's topography.

Topography combines *top-* with *graph-*, a root meaning ''write'' or ''describe.'' The topography of the Sahara Desert features shifting sand dunes and dry, rocky mountains. A *topographical* map shows the contours and surface features of a region. Engineers planning a new road through a hilly area use topographical maps and charts to help in choosing the best route.

CENTR/CENTER comes from the Greek *kentron* and the Latin *centrum*, meaning ''sharp point'' or ''exact middle of a circle.'' A *centrifuge* is a spinning machine that throws things outward from the *center*; the apparent force that pushes them outward is called *centrifugal* force.

---

eccentric \ik-'sen-trik\ (1) Not following an established or usual style or conduct. (2) Straying from a circular path; off-center.

• The woman who collected dozens of stray cats was considered eccentric but harmless by her neighbors.

An eccentric wheel spins unevenly. An eccentric person, like an eccentric wheel, is a little off-center. Most *eccentricities* are harmless to others, and some may even do some good. For instance, riding a bicycle to work rather than driving a car might be considered eccentric by some people, but it's good exercise and it cuts down on pollution. People who are called *eccentrics* are often just ahead of their time.

epicenter \'e-pi-ˌsen-tər\ (1) The location on the earth's surface directly above the focus of an earthquake. (2) The center or focus of activity.

• The destruction caused by Mexico City's earthquake was extensive because the city was at the quake's epicenter.

The meaning of *epi-* in *epicenter* is "over," so the epicenter of an earthquake lies over the center or "focus" of the quake. *Epicenter* can also refer to the centers of things that may seem in their own way as powerful—though not as destructive—as earthquakes. Wall Street, for example, might be said to lie at the epicenter of the financial world.

egocentric \ˌē-gō'sen-trik\ Overly concerned with oneself; self-centered.

• He was a brilliant but egocentric artist who would talk only about his own life and work.

Ego means "I" in Latin. To an egocentric person, *I* is the most important word in the language. Great artists and writers are often *egocentrics*. Such people are hard to live with, but their *egocentricity* is often forgiven, being seen as an unfortunate side effect of their talent.

ethnocentric \ˌeth-nō-'sen-trik\ Marked by or based on the attitude that one's own group is superior to others.

• Some people were angry at what they saw as an ethnocentric bias in the way the film portrayed immigrants.

The Greek word *ethnos* means "nation." An ethnocentric person feels that his or her own nation or group is the cultural center of the world. *Ethnocentricity* shows itself in a lack of respect for other ways of life. The so-called "Ugly American" has an ethnocentric attitude toward foreign countries and cultures.

Quizzes

A. Fill in each blank with the correct letter:

a. epicenter   e. topography
b. ectopic   f. egocentric
c. ethnocentric   g. topical
d. topiary   h. eccentric

1. His remarks showed an ____ bias against foreign cultures.
2. The ____ of a river valley often includes a wide, fertile floodplain.
3. The earth's orbit around the sun is ____ rather than perfectly circular.
4. An ____ pregnancy is an unusual event that may create complications.
5. The doctor prescribed a ____ ointment for her to apply to the poison ivy.
6. There's nothing wrong with liking yourself so long as you don't become ____.
7. We had great fun walking through the ____ garden identifying the different shapes.
8. Luckily, the quake's ____ was far away from any human settlement.

B. Match the word on the left to the correct definition on the right:

1. topical   a. central point
2. egocentric   b. centered on one's own
3. topiary   group
4. ethnocentric   c. away from its usual place
5. topography   d. self-centered
6. eccentric   e. of current interest
7. ectopic   f. ornamentally pruned
8. epicenter   g. placed off-center
                    h. landscape features

DOM comes from the Latin *domus*, "house," or *dominus*, "master." A *domain* is the area where a person has authority or is *dom-*

inant. Unfortunately, dominant people can also be *domineering,* seeing themselves as the masters of those they live and work with.

---

predominant \prē-'dä-mə-nənt\ Greater in importance, strength, influence, or authority.

● The predominant color of the desert landscape was a rusty brown.

Something predominant stands out above all the rest. The predominant theme in an essay is the one that *predominates*—the main idea that the writer wants to express. An individual's predominant motive for wanting a larger vocabulary may be to get a better job, or perhaps simply to be a better-educated person—and the positive effects of a large vocabulary on one's romantic life are well-known.

domicile \dä-mə-ˌsīl\ A dwelling place or home; a residence.

● The neighborhood had about 20 modest domiciles with well-tended lawns and tidy flower beds along the front walks.

A domicile is a home; people live in it and usually take care of it. A domicile is also a legal residence, the address from which one registers to vote, licenses a car, and pays income tax. Wealthy people may have several homes in which they live at different times of the year, but only one of those homes is their official domicile for all legal purposes.

domination \ˌdä-mə-'nā-shən\ (1) Supremacy or power over another. (2) The exercise of governing or controlling influence.

● The region was under the domination of a single nation, even though it had not yet invaded its neighbors.

The total domination of Europe has never been achieved: the Roman Empire could never fully dominate the northern Germanic tribes; Napoleon couldn't conquer Spain; and although Adolf Hitler was *dominant* over most of the continent, he never managed to overpower England. The domination of popular music by rock and roll, however, was obvious by the end of the 1950s. And the domination of modern thought by science may have occurred many decades earlier, according to some thinkers.

dominion \də-'min-yən\ (1) An area over which one rules; domain. (2) Supreme authority.

● The Roman Empire had dominion over the entire Mediterranean, and called it *mare nostrum,* "our sea."

To rule an area is to have dominion over it. The area itself may also be known as a dominion. In the days of the British Empire, England had dominion over many countries throughout the world. A country like Canada, although completely independent, is still part of the British Commonwealth and was until recently officially known as the Dominion of Canada.

HABIT/HIBIT comes from the Latin *habere,* "to have" or "to hold." A *habit,* bad or good, has a hold on you. To *prohibit* is to "hold back" or prevent.

---

exhibitionist \ek-sə-'bi-shə-nist\ Someone who acts to attract attention.

● Most great performers have more than a touch of the exhibitionist about them.

To make an *exhibition* of yourself is to act in a way that makes you the center of attention in a public place—something that an exhibitionist loves to do. Calling someone an exhibitionist is usually meant as a criticism, but *exhibitionism* is not always such a bad thing. Today's *exhibitionist* class clown may be tomorrow's stand-up comic.

habitation \ha-bə-'tā-shən\ (1) The act of living in a place or occupying it. (2) A dwelling place or residence; a settlement or colony.

● The swamps of southern Florida are fit for habitation by alligators but not really by humans.

A town or village is one kind of habitation, and an individual house in that town or village is another kind. The shelter and warmth provided by the house make it a *habitat* suitable for habitation by people—specifically by those who *inhabit* it.

habitual \hə-'bi-chü-wəl\ (1) Practiced or done on a regular basis. (2) Like a habit; usual or customary.

• Even after she'd retired from work, she kept up her habitual practice of rising at the crack of dawn.

Habitual gambling, drinking, smoking, or overeating are a few of life's hazards; in each case the *habit* represents a kind of addiction. Habitual criminals seem to be addicted to crime. But other habits may be desirable; keeping a habitual work schedule is usually essential to a productive life.

inhibit \in-'hi-bət\ (1) To hold in check or restrain. (2) To prevent or slow down an activity or occurrence.

• The cast she had to wear for six weeks after the accident inhibited her movements up and down stairs.

Oil inhibits rust. Some gardeners use chemicals to inhibit the growth of weeds; others use natural means. Fear of being taken for a fool can inhibit the partygoer who feels an urge to put a lampshade on his head and dance on a coffee table. Everyone has *inhibitions,* internal controls that keep them from doing or saying something harmful or embarrassing, and even confident people can feel inhibited when they find themselves among strangers.

Quizzes

A. Choose the closest definition:

1. domination   a. name b. control c. attraction
      d. movement
2. habitation   a. custom b. limit c. dwelling d. chewing
3. domicile   a. imbecile b. ridicule c. home d. supremacy
4. inhibit   a. live in b. laugh at c. restrain d. retrain
5. dominion   a. weakness b. kingdom c. game d. habit
6. habitual   a. customary b. concise c. ordinary
      d. gnawing
7. predominant   a. longest b. lightest c. strongest
      d. earliest
8. exhibitionist   a. show-off b. shower c. showtime
      d. showdown

B. Complete the analogy:

1. exhibit : display :: inhibit : _____
   a. reveal b. try c. hold back d. push out
2. occasional : sometimes :: habitual : _____
   a. rarely b. never c. once d. frequently
3. persuasion : influence :: domination : _____
   a. household b. country c. command d. outlaw
4. transportation : bus :: habitation : _____
   a. tree b. river c. blanket d. house
5. nest : bird :: domicile : _____
   a. frog b. raccoon c. human d. termite
6. thrower : catcher :: exhibitionist : _____
   a. clown b. actor c. audience d. exhibitor
7. controversy : argument :: dominion : _____
   a. attitude b. difference c. realm d. country
8. larger : smaller :: predominant : _____
   a. secondary b. necessary c. primary d. demanding

PRO comes from Greek and Latin, where it means "before," "forward," or "for." As a prefix, it can also mean "earlier than," "front," or "in front of." A lifetime of anger or bitterness can *proceed,* or "come forth," from an unhappy childhood. An ambitious army officer expects to be *promoted,* or "moved forward," rapidly. Those who *provide* for the future by laying away money are "looking ahead."

---

procrastinate \prō-'kras-tə-ˌnāt\ To put off intentionally the doing of something that ought to be done.

● Every year the Mortons procrastinate about preparing their tax returns, and before they know it April 15th is breathing down their necks.

The wise Lord Chesterfield, in one of his letters to his son, advised, "No idleness, no laziness, no *procrastination*; never put off till tomorrow what you can do today." But the motto of the *procrastinator* was expressed by the writer Matthew Browne as "Never do today what you can / Put off till tomorrow." *Procrastinate* has at its root the Latin word *cras,* "tomorrow." Those who procrastinate, however, are apt to delay and postpone far longer than tomorrow if at all possible.

prodigious \prə-'di-jəs\ (1) Arousing amazement or wonder. (2) Extraordinary in size, amount, or extent; enormous.

• Tom's demonstrations of his prodigious memory for baseball trivia were a source of amazement to his friends.

Prodigious and its parent *prodigy* come from the Latin word *prodigium,* meaning "omen" or "monster." Omens—signs of things to come—can be pretty strange occurrences, and with time *prodigious* came to be applied to anything that was strange or weird. It now describes something unusually large or amazing. Someone who wolfs down huge amounts of food is said to have a prodigious appetite. Science-fiction writer Isaac Asimov's literary output was prodigious almost beyond belief: he wrote hundreds of books.

prophylaxis \prō-fə-'lak-səs\ Treatment aimed at preserving health and preventing the spread of disease.

• Where rabies is concerned, prophylaxis in the form of the vaccination of domesticated animals is vastly preferable to the standard postinfection treatment.

Prophylaxis contains the Greek root *phylact-,* meaning "guard." A *prophylactic* measure such as washing the hands before meals tends to guard against disease. Before the polio vaccines became available, prophylaxis against polio included avoiding crowds and public swimming pools, especially during the summer. These days the best known kind of *prophylactic* is used to prevent sexually transmitted diseases; but prophylactic measures only work when people use them.

propitious \prə-'pi-shəs\ (1) Being a sign of good things to come; promising success. (2) Likely to produce good results.

• The ongoing surge in economic growth makes this a propitious time for launching a new business.

Propitious comes from joining *pro-* to the Latin verb *petere,* "to seek." In classical times, one sought the assistance of the gods to ensure the success of something; and the word *propitious* still implies that a thing's successful outcome is in the hands of fate or some higher power. If the omens are propitious, your new business will succeed, your proposal of marriage will be accepted, and your bald spot will disappear after one application of the new miracle lotion you purchased from a television shopping network.

RETRO means "back," "behind," or "backward" in Latin. *Retro* is itself a fairly new word in English, meaning "nostalgically old-fashioned" usually when describing styles or fashions. A nation *retrocedes* a territory by giving it back to the country it originally belonged to.

---

retroactive \ˌre-trō-'ak-tiv\ Intended to apply or take effect at a date in the past.

• The fact that the tax hike was retroactive annoyed the public the most.

We normally think of time as constantly moving forward. Since *retroactive* seems to defy time's forward movement, retroactive taxes, laws, and regulations are often seen as particularly obnoxious and unfair. One fairly recent tendency has been to judge people and events of the past in terms of present-day morality and attitudes. Such retroactive judgments are seen by some as evidence that modern society is overly self-impressed and ignorant of history.

retrofit \'re-trō-ˌfit\ To furnish something with new or modified parts or equipment that was optional or unavailable at the time of manufacture.

• The office building has been retrofitted with air-conditioning, but the result has been a mixed success.

The concept of retrofitting became an urgent necessity during World War II, when weapons technology was advancing at a feverish pace and planes and ships were becoming outdated even before their construction was complete. The only solution was to retrofit the completed craft with the technology-of-the-week. Retrofitting was revived on a massive scale during the energy crisis of the 1970s, when *retrofit* came to be applied to the new features added to old houses to make them more energy-efficient. In more recent years, buildings have had to be retrofitted to make them accessible to wheelchair users and other disabled persons.

retrogress \\re-trō-'gres\\ To return to an earlier and usually worse or more primitive state.

• According to the tests, the sophomores had actually retrogressed in the course of spring term.

Retrogress is the opposite of *progress*. It usually implies an unexpected or undesirable decline from a higher or advanced level. During the extreme conditions of total war, the whole of a society can seem to retrogress to a primitive state. In certain social situations, adolescents can retrogress to an infantile level of maturity. The increasing number of people who are poor or homeless can be seen as evidence of a kind of social *retrogression*.

retrospective \\re-trə-'spek-tiv\\ A generally comprehensive exhibition or performance usually covering an artist's output to date.

• A retrospective covering the photographer's entire career is forcing critics to revise their earlier assessments of her status as an artist.

A retrospective is a look back at an artist's career. The word *retrospective* is rooted in the Latin verb *specere*, "to look." The subject of a retrospective is usually an older living artist or one who has recently died. Galleries honor photographers, film festivals honor directors and actors, and concert organizations honor composers. A retrospective frequently produces appreciation of an artist's achievement.

Quizzes

A. Fill in each blank with the correct letter:

a.	retrospective	e.	prodigious
b.	procrastinate	f.	retrogress
c.	retrofit	g.	prophylaxis
d.	propitious	h.	retroactive

1. The museum is honoring the acclaimed sculptor with a _____ that covers his 50 years as an artist.
2. A team of hungry football players can eat _____ quantities of food.

3. The school is planning to _____ the old gym with all-new equipment.
4. It is easy to _____ about picking up your room; the mess will still be there whenever you get around to it.
5. It didn't take long for the survivors of the jungle plane crash to _____ to a barely civilized state.
6. The lengthening of human lifespans is due to _____ as much as to miracle drugs and surgical advances.
7. Although the tax increase was not passed until June, its effect was _____ to the first of the year.
8. The moment right after a victory is the most _____ time to ask the coach to cancel the next day's practice.

B. Match the word on the left to the correct definition on the right:

1.	retrogress	a.	enormous
2.	propitious	b.	effective as of earlier
3.	retrospective	c.	promising
4.	retrofit	d.	put off
5.	procrastinate	e.	review of a body of work
6.	prophylaxis	f.	revert to an earlier state
7.	retroactive	g.	disease prevention
8.	prodigious	h.	modernize

TEMPOR comes from the Latin *tempus,* meaning "time." The Latin phrase *tempus fugit* means "time flies," an observation that somehow seems more true during summer vacation than in the dead of winter. A *temporary* repair is meant to last only a short time. The *tempo,* or speed, of a country-and-western ballad is usually different from that of a heavy metal song.

---

contemporary \kən-'tem-pə-ˌrer-ē\ (1) Occurring or existing during the same period of time. (2) Having to do with the present period; modern or current.

● The couple filled their new house with fashionable contemporary furniture.

Contemporary can be confusing because of its slightly different meanings. It usually means "modern" or "new"; but it also refers to things from the same era as certain other things. And it is also a noun: Jane Austen's *contemporaries* included William Blake and William Wordsworth, for example. MTV brings us the latest in contemporary music, even though some of it is played by musicians who may be *contemporaneous* with the parents of most of its audience.

extemporaneous \ek-ˌstem-pə-'rā-nē-əs\ (1) Composed, performed, spoken, or done on the spur of the moment; impromptu or improvised. (2) Carefully prepared but delivered without notes.

• It was once common for people to make extemporaneous speeches, recite poetry, and give little solo song recitals after dinner.

Some people claim there is a difference between *extemporaneous* and *impromptu*, saying that an extemporaneous speech is planned beforehand but not written down, while an impromptu speech is genuinely unprepared or "off-the-cuff." But the two words are often used as though they were identical. The ability to speak well *extemporaneously* used to be an important talent for politicians, but now they have "spin doctors" who can follow their remarks with an explanation of what they really meant to say.

temporal \'tem-pə-rəl\ (1) Having to do with time as opposed to eternity; having to do with earthly life as opposed to heavenly existence. (2) Having to do with time as distinguished from space.

• The quick passing of the seasons as we grow older makes us feel the fleeting nature of temporal existence.

Temporal existence is often contrasted with spiritual existence, which many religions teach is eternal. The American system of government features a separation of church and state—that is, a separation of spiritual and temporal authority. But such separation is a relatively new development. In past centuries, the Roman Catholic Church exerted temporal authority in many parts of Europe, and the Church of England has always been headed by the temporal ruler of Great Britain.

temporize \'tem-pə-ˌrīz\ (1) To act in a way that fits the time or occasion; to give way to current opinion. (2) To draw out discussions to gain time.

● The legislature was accused of temporizing while the budget deficit continued to worsen.

People are not usually admired for temporizing. A political leader faced with a difficult issue may temporize by talking vaguely about possible solutions without actually doing anything. The point of such temporizing is to avoid taking definite—and possibly unpopular—action, in hopes that the problem will somehow go away. But the effect is usually just to make matters worse.

CHRON comes from the Greek word for "time." A *chronicle* records the events of a particular time. A *chronometer* is a device for measuring time, usually one that's more accurate (and more expensive) than an ordinary watch or clock.

---

anachronism \ə-'na-krə-ˌni-zəm\ (1) The error of placing a person or thing in the wrong time period. (2) A person or thing that is out of its own time.

● A Model T Ford putt-putting down the highway at 25 miles per hour was an anachronism by 1940.

Shakespeare's productions were full of anachronisms. All the characters, even Romans and Greeks, were dressed in the clothes of Shakespeare's time; and *Macbeth,* set in the 11th century, contains *anachronistic* references to clocks and cannons, things the real Macbeth would have known nothing about. Anachronisms of another sort seem to belong in the past. Manual typewriters and slide rules may seem to be anachronistic in these days of computers and calculators, and a person who prefers to do things the old-fashioned way is also sometimes described as an anachronism.

chronic \'krä-nik\ (1) Lasting a long time or recurring frequently. (2) Always present; constantly annoying or troubling; habitual.

● The children briefly stopped their chronic bickering when they were given ice-cream cones.

Chronic coughing goes on and on; chronic lateness occurs day after day; chronic lameness never seems to get any better. Unfortunately, situations that are chronic almost always seem to be unpleasant. We don't hear about chronic peace, but we hear about chronic warfare. And we rarely speak of chronic health, but often of chronic illness.

chronology \krə-'nä-lə-jē\ (1) A sequence of events in the order they occurred. (2) A table, list, or account that presents events in order.

● She kept a journal throughout her trip in order to have an accurate record of its chronology afterward.

Chronology means literally "the study of time." History is much more than a simple chronology of events, but keeping events in *chronological* order is an important first step. World War I and the conditions following it preceded and contributed to World War II; tracking the chronology of the events surrounding these wars helps historians to understand the conditions that caused them.

synchronous \'siŋ-krə-nəs\ (1) Happening or existing at exactly the same time; simultaneous. (2) Recurring or acting at exactly the same intervals.

● The theory depended on whether the chemical appeared in synchronous deposits worldwide seven million years ago.

Communications satellites are usually put into a synchronous (or *geosynchronous*) orbit, circling the earth once every 24 hours and so appearing to hover over a single spot on the surface. This type of *synchronized* movement is important, since you have to know where to aim your satellite dish. *Synchronous* is also much used in the computer field, where it refers to the use of a simple timing signal that permits very rapid exchange of data between computers.

Quizzes

A. Complete the analogy:

1. antique : ancient :: contemporary : _____
   a. simultaneous b. modern c. fragile d. warped
2. foreigner : import :: anachronism : _____
   a. antique b. novelty c. watch d. eyesore

3. argue : agree :: temporize : _____
   a. discuss b. negotiate c. conclude d. grow cold
4. drama : scenes :: chronology : _____
   a. events b. clock c. length d. sequence
5. sudden : expected :: extemporaneous : _____
   a. sudden b. rehearsed c. off-the-cuff d. off-the-wall
6. infrequent : occasional :: chronic : _____
   a. short b. surprising c. continuous d. noisy
7. temporary : enduring :: temporal : _____
   a. modern b. existing c. arising d. eternal
8. amorphous : shapeless :: synchronous : _____
   a. simultaneous b. in sequence c. out of order
   d. always late

B. Match the word on the left to the correct definition on the right:

1. chronic
2. temporal
3. anachronism
4. extemporaneous
5. synchronous
6. temporize
7. chronology
8. contemporary

a. current
b. order of events
c. ongoing
d. happening at the same time
e. talk to fill time
f. unplanned
g. measurable by time
h. something from the past

Number Words

TRI means "three," whether derived from Greek or Latin. A *tricycle* has three wheels. A *triangle* has three sides and three angles. And a *triumvirate* is a board or government of three people.

triceratops \trī-'ser-ə-,täps\ One of a group of large dinosaurs that lived during the Cretaceous period and had three horns, a bony crest or hood, and hoofed toes.

● The triceratops probably used its horns for defense against the attacks of meat-eating dinosaurs.

Triceratops means literally "three-horned face," referring to the two horns above the eyes and the smaller third horn on the snout. The triceratops was one of the last dinosaurs to evolve and also one of the last to become extinct. It could reach lengths of 30 feet and could stand nearly eight feet high. Despite its ferocious looks and its two sharp three-foot-long horns, the triceratops was actually a vegetarian.

tricolor \'trī-,kə-lər\ (1) Having three colors. (2) A national flag that has three colors arranged in three equal horizontal or vertical bands.

• Many collies are tricolor dogs, even though their name actually means "black."

The French flag is tricolor, as are the Italian, Irish, German, Dutch, and Belgian flags. The colors vary, as do the direction of the stripes. The American flag is *tricolored*, but it is not a true, three-striped tricolor since it has 13 stripes and many stars as well.

trident \'trī-dənt\ (1) A three-pronged spear carried by various sea gods in mythology. (2) Any three-pronged spear.

• Neptune, Roman god of the sea, carries a large trident and is often wreathed in seaweed.

A trident has three teeth or prongs, as the root *dent*, "tooth," tells us. The trident has long been used to spear fish in different parts of the world, but it has also been used as a weapon. A type of Roman gladiator called a *retiarius* carried one. Matched against a man with a sword, the retiarius would try to snare his opponent with a net and then spear his helpless foe.

trilogy \'tri-lə-jē\ A series of three creative works that are closely related and develop a single theme.

• Tolkien's trilogy, *The Lord of the Rings*, has become a well-loved classic.

A trilogy has three parts. Authors have chosen to create trilogies to allow themselves to develop a more complex story or cover a longer span of time. Dozens of tragic trilogies were written for the Greek stage. The three *Star Wars* movies of George Lucas are an example of a film trilogy.

trimester \trī-'mes-tər\ (1) A period of about three months, especially one of three such periods in a human pregnancy. (2) One of three terms into which an academic year is sometimes divided.

● Many women experience morning sickness in the first trimester of pregnancy.

Semester, which comes from the Latin words for ''six'' and ''month,'' has come to mean half an academic year when the year is divided into two segments; a trimester is one-third of an academic year that is divided into three segments. Usually, though, a semester is not six months long, and an academic trimester is not three months long; the lengths are approximate. In a human pregnancy, a trimester is approximately three months long, representing one-third of the total nine months that a pregnancy normally lasts.

trinity \'tri-nə-tē\ (1) *capitalized*: The unity of Father, Son, and Holy Spirit as three persons in one God in Christian belief. (2) A group of three people.

● Understanding the concept of the Holy Trinity is fundamentally important for any Catholic.

The nature of the Trinity or Holy Trinity has caused centuries of argument and division within the Christian faith. In general use, *trinity* usually keeps some of its religious sense; for example, a group of three foreign leaders forming what is seen as a dangerous alliance might be referred to as an ''unholy'' trinity.

triptych \'trip-tik\ (1) A picture or carving made in the form of three panels side by side. (2) Something composed or presented in three sections.

● The Renaissance produced many beautiful triptychs portraying religious scenes that are still used as altarpieces.

Triptych contains the root *-ptyche,* the Greek word for ''fold.'' A painted or carved triptych has three hinged panels; the two outer panels fold in toward the central one. A literary or musical triptych, on the other hand, is like a trilogy, with three closely related parts that tell a single story or develop a single set of themes.

trivial \'tri-vē-əl\ (1) Commonplace or ordinary. (2) Of little value or importance.

● She was so caught up in the trivial details of the trip that she hardly noticed the beautiful scenery.

Trivial comes from a Latin word meaning "crossroads"; it probably came to mean "commonplace" from the notion that anything found at a crossroads is pretty common. A trivial conversation can be conversation that is both commonplace and useless. But a trivial reason for not going on a date ("I have to wash my hair") can hide a reason that is not so trivial ("I can't stand the sight of you"). To *trivialize* something is to treat it as if it didn't matter, as if it were just another *triviality*.

Quiz

Choose the closest definition:

1. trimester   a. a three-masted sailing ship b. a period of about three months c. a three-cornered hat d. a three-minute egg
2. trivial   a. crossed b. indented c. unimportant d. found
3. tricolor   a. three-striped flag b. three-headed monster c. three-footed booby d. three-month delay
4. trinity   a. romantic triangle b. three-part recipe c. group of three d. triplets
5. trident   a. three-toothed hag b. three-pronged spear c. triple portion d. threesome
6. trilogy   a. three-person conversation b. three-hour nap c. three-volume story d. three-ton truck
7. triceratops   a. three-foot alligator b. three-set tennis match c. three-topped tree d. three-horned dinosaur
8. triptych   a. three-week travel voucher b. three-part painting c. three-phase rocket d. three-handed clock

---

Review Quizzes

A. Fill in each blank with the correct letter:

a. prodigious
b. topical
c. contemporary

d. temporize
e. inhibit
f. synchronous

g.	topiary	n.	eccentric
h.	epicenter	o.	retroactive
i.	dominion	p.	extemporaneous
j.	chronic	q.	predominant
k.	habitual	r.	domicile
l.	retrofit	s.	propitious
m.	trivial	t.	trilogy

1. To her, the opinions of her employees were never _____ or unimportant.

2. Many people are criticized for being _____ watchers of television.

3. England, though a small nation, once had _____ over a great empire.

4. There are medications that _____ the body's allergic response to things like ragweed pollen.

5. Sheila is still waiting for a _____ time to ask for a raise.

6. It cost millions to _____ the airplane with the latest navigational instruments.

7. The dancers were well-rehearsed and their movements were beautifully _____.

8. When the third volume of her _____ was published, her fans snapped it up eagerly.

9. Before beginning to drill, the dentist applies a _____ anesthetic.

10. Even though he's skinny, Roger is known for his _____ appetite.

11. The doctor told him his condition was _____ and untreatable but not life-threatening.

12. Because he had left his notes at home, he had to give an entirely _____ lecture.

13. The book was criticized for having too many subjects and no _____ theme.

14. The city maintains a small _____ garden full of trees and bushes in all sorts of shapes.

15. The problem won't go away no matter how long you _____ and stall for time.

16. It isn't fair to make _____ judgments about the moral values of historical figures.

17. His habit of wearing purple socks and white sneakers to the office was considered harmlessly _____.

18. You can have several homes, but only one legal ___.
19. We spent Sunday afternoon looking at the museum's collection of recent ___ art.
20. Her casual remark landed her at the ___ of a real controversy.

B. Choose the closest definition:

1. egocentric   a. group-centered   b. centered on the mind   c. self-centered   d. mentally ill.
2. habitation   a. place to live   b. usual behavior   c. greediness   d. slowness
3. retrospective   a. backward glance   b. exhibit of an artist's work   c. illusion of depth   d. difference of opinion
4. anachronism   a. electronic clock   b. literary theory   c. chronological error   d. current topic
5. triceratops   a. winged dragon   b. dinosaur   c. three-part work   d. climbing gear
6. tricolor   a. black, tan, and white   b. banded carpet   c. patriotic   d. deceptive
7. temporal   a. religious   b. ideal   c. time-related   d. durable
8. procrastinate   a. put down   b. put off   c. put up   d. put away
9. ectopic   a. amazing   b. current   c. reserved   d. out of place
10. triptych   a. three-part painting   b. triple window   c. computer switch   d. multi-volume work

C. Match each word on the left to the correct definition on the right:

1.	prophylaxis	a.	land's features
2.	exhibitionist	b.	group-centered
3.	retrogress	c.	three-pronged spear
4.	domination	d.	one who shows off
5.	chronology	e.	group of three
6.	ethnocentric	f.	go backward
7.	trimester	g.	order of events
8.	topography	h.	school-year term
9.	trinity	i.	preventive treatment
10.	trident	j.	control

Unit 17

ANIM comes from the Latin *anima*, meaning "breath" or "soul," and it generally describes something that is alive or lively. An *animal* is a living, breathing thing. *Animism* is the belief that *inanimate* things have a spirit and an awareness.

animated \\'a-nə-ˌmā-təd\\ (1) Full of life; lively, vigorous, active. (2) Seeming or appearing to be alive.

• Her gestures as she talked were so animated that even people across the room would watch her.

Animated cartoon characters have been "given life" by film techniques, though the *animation* of drawings actually goes back to handheld toys in the 1830s. A child watching the cartoon may also be animated—squealing, laughing, and jumping around. Protest groups, hockey fans, and rock-concert audiences all tend to be animated in their own ways.

magnanimous \\mag-'na-nə-məs\\ (1) Showing a lofty and courageous spirit. (2) Generous and forgiving.

• She was magnanimous in victory, saying she'd been lucky to win and praising her opponent's effort.

Magnanimity is the opposite of pettiness. Its basic meaning is "greatness of spirit." A truly magnanimous person can lose without complaining and win without gloating. Angry disputes can sometimes be resolved when one side makes a magnanimous gesture toward the other.

animosity \\ˌa-nə-'mä-sə-tē\\ Ill will or resentment.

• Legend has it that the animosity between the Greeks and the Trojans began with the stealing of Helen from her husband.

In parts of the world where communist governments have fallen, old animosities that had been hidden for years have resurfaced and have led to terrible violence and bloodshed. Forms of government may change, but the deep animosity that exists between certain ethnic and religious groups sometimes seems as if it will last forever.

inanimate \i-'na-nə-mət\ (1) Not alive; lifeless. (2) Not lively; dull.

• Rodin's sculptures are so expressive that, although inanimate, they seem full of life and emotion.

Everything in the world is either *animate*, "alive," or *inanimate*, "not alive." The couch you sit on while you watch TV is an inanimate object, as is your footrest, your bag of snacks, and your remote control. Spend too much time on that couch and you risk becoming a "couch potato." (A potato is an inanimate object.)

FIG comes from the Latin verb *fingere*, which means "to shape or mold," and the related noun *figura*, meaning "a form or shape." A *transfiguration* changes the shape or appearance or nature of something. A *disfiguring* injury changes the shape of part of the body.

---

configuration \kən-₁fi-gyù-'rā-shən\ An arrangement of parts or elements; shape, design.

• The decorator changed the configuration of the office so that people would have more privacy at their desks.

Configuration is used constantly in many technical fields, where it often might be replaced by *arrangement, shape,* or *design.* James Watson and Francis Crick won a 1962 Nobel Prize for their description of the double-helix configuration of the DNA molecule. Since then, much research has been done into what different configurations within the DNA strands mean and what they control, and genetic engineers have tried to *configure* DNA in new ways to prevent or treat diseases.

effigy \\'e-fə-jē\ An image of a person, especially a crude representation of a hated person.

• The night before the big game, an effigy of the rival coach was burned on a huge bonfire.

It was the practice of the Egyptians to bury an effigy of a dead person along with that person's body. The idea was that if anything happened to the person's body in the afterlife, the effigy could be used as a spare. *Effigy* now usually refers to crude stuffed figures of the kind that get burned and hanged by angry protestors and unruly college students.

figment \\'fig-mənt\ Something made up or imagined.

• His preference for Cindy is a figment of your imagination; believe me, he barely knows she exists.

A figment is formed from imaginary elements. Daydreams are figments; nightmares are figments that can seem very real. When Orson Welles produced the radio play ''The War of the Worlds'' in 1938, he caused a panic among thousands of people who didn't realize the invasion by Martians was just a figment of the author's imagination.

figurative \\'fi-gyů-rə-tiv\ (1) Representing form or figure in art. (2) Saying one thing in terms normally meaning or describing another thing.

• The Renaissance saw an enormous development in the realistic techniques of figurative sculpture.

Words and phrases can have both literal and figurative meanings. We can literally close the door to a room, or we can *figuratively* close the door to further negotiations—that is, refuse to take part in them. Figurative language can help make what we say more memorable so long as we don't overdo it or ''go overboard.'' Figurative language includes *figures* of speech such as similes, metaphors, and symbols. As you've surely noticed, a great many of the definitions in this book show a word's figurative meaning (often something nonphysical) along with its literal meaning (which is often physical).

Quizzes

A. Fill in each blank with the correct letter:

a. inanimate   e. figment
b. figurative   f. magnanimous
c. animated   g. configuration
d. effigy   h. animosity

1. The _____ form of the dog lay stretched in front of the fire for hours.
2. They ran test after test to find the most effective _____ for the new airplane's wings.
3. Inviting her former rival to take part in the conference was a _____ gesture.
4. Don't tell him, but his popularity is just a _____ of his imagination.
5. Shakespeare uses _____ language constantly to enrich the speech in his plays.
6. Over lunch they had an _____ discussion about the race for senator.
7. The best negotiators try to reduce any intense _____ between feuding partners.
8. Every Halloween they set a crude _____ of a farmer on their porch, though they never really knew why.

B. Indicate whether the following pairs of terms have the same or different meanings:

1. figment / fruitcake   same ___ / different ___
2. animosity / hatred   same ___ / different ___
3. figurative / symbolic   same ___ / different ___
4. magnanimous / petty   same ___ / different ___
5. effigy / bonfire   same ___ / different ___
6. animated / lively   same ___ / different ___
7. configuration / list of parts   same ___ / different ___
8. inanimate / not alive   same ___ / different ___

ANN/ENN comes from Latin *annus* and means "year." An *annual* event occurs yearly. A wedding or birthday *anniversary* is

an example, although the older you get the more frequent they seem
to be.

---

superannuated \ˌsü-pər-ˈan-yü-ˌwā-təd\ (1) Outworn, old-fashioned, or out-of-date. (2) Forced to retire because of old age or
infirmity.

• He called himself a car collector, but his backyard looked like a
cemetery for superannuated clunkers.

A superannuated car is too old and broken-down to be used any-
more. A superannuated style is out-of-date—its time has come and
gone. A superannuated person is literally someone who is "too
old" and has had to retire. More often, though, *superannuated*
describes people who seem somehow to belong to the past. So we
might speak of superannuated hippies, for example, or describe
adults who never seem to have grown up as superannuated
teenagers.

annuity \ə-ˈnü-ə-tē\ Money that is payable yearly or on some
regular basis; a contract providing for such payment.

• Through her working career she invested regularly in annuities
that would support her after retirement.

Annuities are handy things to have when you retire, since they
provide an income on an *annual* basis or more frequently. Most
company pensions are doled out in the form of annuities, and
sweepstakes jackpots may also come as annuities. Most other annuities are contracts with life-insurance companies that specify that
payments begin at retirement.

millennium \mə-ˈle-nē-əm\ (1) A period of time lasting 1,000
years; the celebration of a 1,000-year anniversary. (2) A period of
great happiness and perfection on earth.

• Classical Greek culture flourished in the first millennium B.C.

Some religions talk of a coming millennium when evil will be
banished from the earth and all will live in peace and happiness.
The members of these religions, who expect this millennium to
arrive soon and who keep themselves in a constant state of pre-
paredness, are called *millenarians* or *millennialists*. Their belief is
often based on the prophecies in the biblical Book of Revelation.

perennial \pə-'re-nē-əl\ (1) Enduring or continuing without interruption; perpetual or constantly recurring. (2) Present at all times of the year; continuing to grow for several years.

• "Rudolph the Red-Nosed Reindeer" is a perennial favorite around Christmastime.

A perennial garden is full of plants like delphiniums and asters that continue to bloom year after year; *annual* plants, by contrast, grow for only a single season and so must be replanted *annually*. Evergreens are *perennially* green and are perennial favorites for wreaths and holiday decorations. In a similar way, street crime is now a perennial political issue, and a perennial candidate may ride back into the political arena year after year announcing that he's the only one who can lick it.

EV comes from the Latin *aevum,* "age" or "lifetime." This root occurs in only a few English words, but it is related to the Greek *aion,* "age," from which we get the English word *eon,* meaning a very long period of time.

coeval \kō-'ē-vəl\ Having the same age or lasting the same amount of time; contemporary.

• Homer's *Iliad* and *Odyssey,* probably written around 800 B.C., are coeval with parts of the Hebrew Bible.

Coeval usually describes things that existed together for a very long time or that originated at the same time in the distant past. Astronomers might speak of one galaxy as being coeval with another. A period in the history of one civilization might be coeval with a similar period in another. *Coeval* is also used as a noun, usually referring to a person. Two artists who lived and worked at the same time might be described as coevals.

longevity \län-'je-və-tē\ (1) A long duration of life. (2) Length of life; long continuance.

• Picasso had a career of remarkable longevity, producing plentifully until his death at 91.

The longevity of the average American is increasing—from about 45 years in 1900 to about 75 years today—as medicine advances and we learn to live healthier lives. But the most impressive human longevity is nothing compared to that of the bristlecone pine, a kind of tree found in the western United States that is known to live for 5,000 years.

medieval \ˌmē-dē-'ē-vəl\ (1) Relating to the Middle Ages of European history, from about A.D. 500 to 1500. (2) Extremely out-of-date.

• The cathedral at Chartres in France is a masterpiece of medieval architecture.

The medieval period is often thought of as the age of knights in armor, damsels in distress, and towering castles. But in reality it was a time of violence, famine, plague, and superstition, dominated by rulers who often represented all that is bad in human nature. *Medievalists* study both Middle Ages: the ideal world of the medieval writers and poets, as well as the real history in which life was often nasty, brutish, and short.

primeval \prī-'mē-vəl\ (1) Having to do with the earliest ages; primitive or ancient. (2) Existing from the beginning.

• When settlers first came to North America, they found primeval forests, seemingly untouched by human influence.

Primeval suggests the earliest periods in the earth's history. Myths are often stories of primeval beings. According to scientists, life on earth began in the protein-rich primeval seas. The decomposition of plankton there produced our petroleum, and coal developed from the slow decomposition of plant matter in the primeval swamps.

Quizzes

A. Choose the closest definition:

1. perennial a. flowerlike b. excellent c. everlasting
   d. thorough
2. longevity a. length b. long life c. longitude d. longing
3. superannuated a. amazing b. huge c. aged d. perennial

4. coeval   a. ancient b. simultaneous c. same-sized
     d. continuing
5. millennium   a. thousand b. century c. era
     d. a thousand years
6. annuity   a. annual event b. annual payment c. annual
     income d. annual garden
7. medieval   a. antiquated b. middle-aged c. romantic
     d. knightly
8. primeval   a. wicked b. elderly c. primitive d. muddy

**B. Match the definition on the left to the correct word
on the right:**

1. ancient   a. perennial
2. of the same age   b. longevity
3. yearly payment   c. primeval
4. era of earthly paradise d. coeval
5. of the Middle Ages   e. millennium
6. worn out   f. annuity
7. length of life   g. medieval
8. continuing   h. superannuated

CORP comes from *corpus,* the Latin word for "body." A *corporation* is one kind of body, a *corpse* is another, and a *corps,* such as the Marine Corps, is yet another.

---

corporeal \kȯr-'pȯr-ē-əl\ Having or relating to a physical body; substantial.

• Artists have always portrayed angels as corporeal beings, usually with actual wings.

Corporeal existence has always been opposed to *spiritual* existence in the history of Christianity. Some religious groups have insisted that corporeal existence is contaminated with evil and that believers must control their physical desires in order to achieve godliness. In legal use, *corporeal* describes physical property such as houses or cars, as opposed to something valuable but nonphysical like a good reputation.

corpulent \'kȯr-pyu̇-lənt\ Having a large, bulky body; fat.

• Robert had been a "fat man" when he was poor, but after he made his fortune he became a "corpulent gentleman."

The Duchess of Windsor may have said you can never be too rich or too thin, but that is a narrowly modern point of view. In earlier times in Europe, being corpulent was considered a sign of wealth and well-being, as demonstrated by the *corpulence* of many European kings. Still today, corpulence is thought to be superior to thinness in many of the world's cultures.

corporal \'kȯr-pə-rəl\ Relating to or affecting the body.

• She was reminded that shaking a child was now regarded as unacceptable corporal punishment in the public-school system.

The adjective *corporal* today usually appears in the phrase "corporal punishment," which means "bodily punishment." This used to include such acts as mutilation, branding, imprisonment, and even death. But today execution comes under the separate heading of "capital punishment," which originally involved losing your head (*capit-* meaning "head"). The milder forms of corporal punishment are used by most American parents and were once common in schools as well. *Corporal* occasionally is used in other ways: in the traditional church, the corporal works of mercy include seven helpful acts such as sheltering the homeless and burying the dead. (The military rank of corporal actually comes from *caporal*, which has the same root as *capital*.)

incorporate \in-'kȯr-pə-ˌrāt\ (1) To blend or combine into something already existing to form one whole. (2) To form or form into a corporation.

• The most recent edition of the dictionary incorporates thousands of new words and meanings.

A chef might come up with a new item she wants to incorporate into a menu. It might involve incorporating exotic ingredients into a pasta recipe. Making the recipe could require incorporating those ingredients—mixing them together—into a smooth paste. And if the new recipe becomes a hit, her restaurant could be so successful that she would build a new one and *reincorporate* as a new legal *corporation*!

TANG/TACT comes from the Latin verb *tangere,* "to touch." A person who shows *tact* has a delicate touch when it comes to dealing with other people. To make *contact* is to touch or "get in touch."

intact \in-'takt\ Untouched by anything that harms; entire, uninjured.

• The garage was damaged by the storm, but the house itself came through it intact.

Intact literally means "untouched." You may have heard that no one in a town was untouched—that is, everyone was affected negatively—by a school-bus disaster. But a community might not even remain intact, or whole, after a hurricane. You'd be lucky if a vase you dropped remained intact. And you'd be very fortunate if your health remained intact after 20 years of smoking.

tactile \'tak-təl\ (1) Able to be perceived by touching. (2) Relating to the sense of touch.

• He always enjoyed the tactile sensation of running his hand over the lush turf.

The blind rely on their tactile sense to read braille. The braille alphabet uses one to six raised dots in various combinations to represent different letters. Those skilled at reading braille have such highly developed tactile abilities that they can identify each letter the instant their finger comes into *contact* with the dot pattern.

tangential \tan-'jen-chəl\ Touching lightly; incidental.

• As far as Katherine was concerned, everything else was tangential to her own plans.

Someone who starts talking about one thing and gets sidetracked has gone off on a *tangent.* (In geometry, a tangent is a straight line that touches a curve at a single point.) The new subject is tangential to the first subject—it "touches" it lightly and moves off in a different direction. A few of the people we meet truly enter our lives, but most acquaintances remain only tangential.

tangible \'tan-jə-bəl\ Able to be perceived, especially by touch; physical, substantial.

● The snow was tangible evidence that winter had really come.

Something that's literally tangible can be touched. A rock is tangible, and so is a broken window; if the rock is lying next to the window, it could be tangible evidence of vandalism. We might also say that the tension in a room is tangible—that is, we feel it so strongly that it seems "touchable." But tension, like hope, happiness, and hunger, is literally *intangible*—it's real enough, but it can't be touched.

Quizzes

A. Fill in each blank with the correct letter:

a. incorporate   e. corporeal
b. tangible   f. tangential
c. corporal   g. intact
d. tactile   h. corpulent

1. The question was _____ to the main subject, but he answered it anyway.
2. The flogging of sailors was once a common form of _____ punishment in the British navy.
3. The district attorney felt there wasn't enough _____ evidence for an airtight case.
4. Years of too many table scraps had made the family dog _____.
5. Brain surgeons need to develop a very delicate _____ sense.
6. Wanda used an electric mixer to _____ the new ingredients into the smooth paste.
7. The theme of the sermon was that we should care more for the spiritual than for the _____ world.
8. To everyone's surprise, Paul came through the ordeal with his health and good humor _____.

B. Indicate whether the following pairs of terms have the same or different meanings:

1. corpulent / boring   same ___ / different ___
2. tangential / touching lightly   same ___ / different ___
3. incorporate / leave out   same ___ / different ___
4. intact / partial   same ___ / different ___

5.	corporeal / substantial	same ___ / different ___
6.	corporal / military	same ___ / different ___
7.	tactile / sticky	same ___ / different ___
8.	tangible / touchable	same ___ / different ___

CODI/CODE comes from the Latin *codex*, meaning "trunk of a tree" or "document written on wooden tablets." A *code* can be either a set of laws or a system of symbols used to write messages. To *encode* a message is to write it in code. A genetic code, transmitted by genes, is a set of instructions for everything from blood type to eye color.

---

codex \'kō-ˌdeks\ A book in manuscript or handwritten form, especially a book of Scripture, classics, or ancient texts.

• There on the shelves of the monastery library they saw codex after codex, all carefully copied and illustrated by hand.

In the Middle Ages, before Gutenberg invented the printing press, all books were in codex form. These manuscripts in book form themselves replaced the older scrolls, or rolls. Because they had to be hand-copied, there were limited copies of any single book, and sometimes only a single copy. These codices (note this unusual plural form) were usually written on parchment, the skin of a sheep or goat prepared in a special way. The earliest surviving codex may date from the 1st century A.D.

codicil \'kä-də-səl\ (1) An amendment or addition made to a will. (2) An appendix or supplement.

• With the birth of each new grandchild, the old man added a new codicil to his will.

A codicil is literally a little *codex,* a little bit of writing on a small piece of writing material. It is used to add to or change something about a larger piece of writing. Codicils to a will can change the terms of the original will completely; in mystery novels, such changes have been known to cause a murder, the destruction of the will, and sometimes both. In real life codicils are not usually quite that exciting.

codify \'kä-də-,fī\ To arrange according to a system; classify.

● In about A.D. 534, the Emperor Justinian codified the laws of the Roman Empire in a single document called the Codex Justinianus.

One sense of *code* is "a systematic statement of a body of law." Laws that have been included in such a statement have been codified. The rules of baseball differed greatly from one place to another until they were codified by Alexander Cartwright in 1845. They haven't changed much since, though we don't know what Cartwright would say about the designated hitter.

decode \di-'kōd\ (1) To put a coded message into an understandable form. (2) To find the underlying meaning of; decipher.

● The Allies were able to decode many important secret messages sent by the Germans and Japanese in World War II.

Decode is usually used to mean "take out of *code* and put into understandable language." Decoding secret, *encoded* messages is always an important part of international spying, and last-minute decoding of crucial information often plays a dramatic part in spy novels and movies. Literature and dreams can also be decoded. Psychoanalysts try to decode the images that the unconscious mind creates in dreams to understand the emotions that lie behind those images.

SIGN comes from the Latin noun *signum*, "sign or mark." An architect's *design* marks out the pattern for a building; if the owner *designates* that design as the one he wants, he so indicates by putting a *signature*, his own special mark, on an agreement.

---

assignation \,a-sig-'nā-shən\ (1) The act of assigning. (2) An agreement about the time and place for a meeting, especially a secret meeting.

● His political career was somewhat damaged when it was learned he had made repeated assignations with the wife of a foreign diplomat.

Men and women who have affairs usually have to make assignations with their lovers. Any prearranged meeting can be an assignation, but the term almost always carries the suggestion that something fishy is going on. When two unmarried people get together it's a date, but when one of them is married it becomes an assignation.

resign \ri-'zīn\ (1) To give up a position or office. (2) To accept something as unavoidable.

• By the last quarter the fans were resigned to losing, but two miraculous touchdowns snatched victory from the jaws of defeat.

The Latin *resignare* meant originally "to cancel" or "give up"— that is, to "sign away" something. So "surrender" or "give up" is the basic meaning of the English word as well. Just as you may give up or surrender your job to someone else, you may admit defeat at the hands of something bigger, or give yourself up to it— you may in fact be resigned to losing your job! An older person may have a general air of *resignation* after having resigned herself to too many defeats over a long lifetime.

signatory \'sig-nə-ˌtȯr-ē\ A person or government that signs an agreement with others; especially a government that agrees with others to abide by a signed agreement.

• More than a dozen countries were signatories to the agreement setting limits on fishing in international waters.

A signatory puts his or her *signature* on a document that is also *signed* by others. In 1215 the English barons revolted against King John and forced him to join them as a signatory to the Magna Carta. This agreement *assigned* the barons clear rights, restated their obligations to the King, and limited the King's power over them. King John was an unwilling signatory, never fully *resigned* to the barons' terms. This has been called the first step toward democracy in the English-speaking countries, though it did nothing at all for the common people.

signet \'sig-nət\ (1) A seal used instead of a signature to give personal or official authority to a document. (2) A small engraved seal, often in the form of a ring.

• The early American colonies had charters confirmed with the king's signet.

Signets have been used for thousands of years. The design of a signet is personalized for its owner, and no two are alike. The ancients used signets to mark their possessions and to sign contracts. In later years signets were used to stamp a blob of hot wax sealing a folded secret document so that it couldn't be opened and read without the design being broken. The Pope still wears a signet, called the Fisherman's Ring, which is carved with a figure of St. Peter encircled with the Pope's name. After a Pope's death, the ring is destroyed and a new one is made for the new Pope.

Quizzes

A. Choose the closest definition:

1. codify a. conceal b. list c. disobey d. interpret
2. signet a. stamp b. gold ring c. Pope's sign d. baby swan
3. codicil a. small fish b. one-tenth c. amendment to a will d. legal objection
4. assignation a. signature b. assassination c. secret lover d. appointment
5. resign a. accept b. appoint c. assign d. arrest
6. codex a. private seal b. handwritten book c. secret letter d. coded message
7. signatory a. document b. agreement c. banner d. cosigner
8. decode a. explain b. conceal c. symbolize d. disguise

B. Match the word on the left to the correct definition on the right:

1. resign	a.	interpret
2. codex	b.	addition
3. signatory	c.	give up
4. decode	d.	engraved seal
5. signet	e.	old type of book
6. codify	f.	signer
7. assignation	g.	organize laws
8. codicil	h.	secret meeting

Number Words

QUADR/QUART comes from Latin words meaning "four" or "fourth." In English, a *quart* is one-fourth of a gallon, just as a *quarter* is one-fourth of a dollar. A *quadrangle* has four sides but is not necessarily square; *quadruplets* are four babies born at the same time.

---

quadrennial \kwä-'dre-nē-əl\ (1) Happening every four years. (2) Lasting for four years.

• American presidents are elected on a quadrennial schedule, the elections being held every leap year.

The Olympic Games occur *quadrennially* in summer and winter versions. The World Cup in soccer, the greatest single sporting competition in the world, is also a quadrennial event. High school usually only takes a *quadrennium* to complete, though it might seem to take a millennium.

quadrille \kwä-'dril\ A square dance popular in the 18th and 19th century, made up of five or six patterns for four couples; music for this type of dance.

• Quadrilles were very popular at the balls of the South before the Civil War.

The quadrille, named for its four couples, seems to have begun as a French country dance. In the 18th century it was picked up by the French nobility; as performed by elegantly dressed aristocrats, it became slow and formal. It crossed the Channel to England, and from there crossed to New England, where it turned back into a dance for the common people. As the American square dance it became lively again, and now employed a "caller" to make sure everyone remembered the steps.

quadriplegic \,kwä-drə-'plē-jik\ Paralyzed in both arms and both legs.

• A motorcycle accident in her teens had killed her boyfriend and left her a quadriplegic.

Though *paraplegics* have lost the use only of their legs, quadriplegics are paralyzed in all four limbs. Today voice-activated computerized wheelchairs help the quadriplegic get around, houses can be equipped with similar systems to operate lights and appliances, and monkeys are now trained to help quadriplegics with everyday tasks, increasing the independence of those afflicted with *quadriplegia*.

quartile \'kwȯr-ˌtīl\ One of four equal groups each containing a quarter of a statistical population.

• The schools in our town always average in the lowest quartile in both reading and math achievement.

A quartile is essentially a *quarter* of a specific group that has been tested or evaluated in specific ways. The first quartile scores highest, the second quartile next highest, and so on. For achievement and proficiency tests, the first quartile is the place to be; for blood pressure or cholesterol, the fourth quartile is a healthier standing.

TESSAR/TETR comes from the Greek word for "four." A *tessera* is the small and usually four-sided piece of rock or tile used to make mosaics. *Tessellation* is the technique of making mosaic, or of covering a surface with identical shapes that fit exactly without covering or overlapping each other; a floor covered with square tiles is a simple example.

---

tetracycline \ˌte-trə-'sī-ˌklēn\ A yellow crystalline antibiotic effective against a wide range of organisms.

• He was sent home with a prescription for tetracycline and some advice about how to avoid catching the infection again.

Antibiotics work against bacteria and other tiny organisms that sometimes infect the body, though not against viruses of any kind. Tetracycline, which comes from a kind of soil bacteria, is one of the most used of the antibiotics. It can be effective against acne, Lyme disease, chlamydia, cholera, ricketts, and various lung and eye infections, among other things. Its name means "four-ringed''—that is, it consists of four fused hydrocarbon rings. Most chemical names are made up of a series of Greek and Latin roots strung together.

tetrahedron \\,te-trə-'hē-drən\ A solid shape formed by four flat faces.

• Box kites are often made with tetrahedrons rather than squares or triangles.

The simplest tetrahedron is made of four equal-sided triangles: one is used as the base; and the other three are fitted to it and each other to make a kind of pyramid. The pyramids of Egypt, however, are not tetrahedrons: with a square base and four triangular faces, this shape is five-sided.

tetralogy \te-'tra-lə-jē\ A set of four connected literary, artistic, or musical works.

• *The Raj Quartet*, Paul Scott's long and complex tetralogy of India, was made into a highly praised television series.

Vivaldi's *Four Seasons* can be called a tetralogy, since it is a set of four violin concertos, one for each season of the year. Eight of Shakespeare's history plays are often grouped into two tetralogies. Wagner's great *Ring of the Nibelung,* an opera tetralogy based on Norse mythology, contains about 18 hours of music. But we have no complete examples of the original tetralogies, sets of four plays performed together in ancient Athens. The first three were always tragedies; the last was a wild comedy.

tetrapod \'te-trə-,päd\ A vertebrate with two pairs of limbs.

• His special study was the great seismosaurus, probably the largest tetrapod—and the largest land animal—that ever lived.

The earliest tetrapods (or ''four-footed'' animals) were mammal-like reptiles that evolved before the rise of the dinosaurs and ranged from mouse-sized to cow-sized. Today the tetrapods include the reptiles, the amphibians, the birds, and the mammals—including humans. Though they don't include the fish, it is quite possible that our own limbs began as paired fins hundreds of millions of years ago.

Quiz

Match the definition on the left to the correct word on the right:

1. four-sided solid   a. quadriplegic
2. square dance   b. tetralogy
3. one-fourth of a group   c. quadrennial
4. four connected works   d. tetrapod
5. paralyzed in four limbs   e. quartile
6. four-year   f. tetrahedron
7. antibiotic   g. quadrille
8. four-limbed animal   h. tetracycline

Review Quizzes

A. Choose the correct synonym and the correct antonym:

1. decode   a. translate b. recover c. encode d. transmit
2. animated   a. colorful b. lifeless c. smiling d. vigorous
3. tangible   a. readable b. touchable c. eternal
                 d. nonphysical
4. animosity   a. affection b. mammal c. dedication
                 d. hatred
5. corpulent   a. slim b. spiritual c. overweight d. bodily
6. figurative a. modeled b. literal c. painted d. symbolic
7. corporal   a. military b. bodily c. nonphysical
                 d. reasonable
8. perennial   a. two-year b. lasting c. temporary
                 d. flowering
9. longevity   a. anniversary b. shortness c. uncertainty
                 d. permanence
10. primeval   a. recent b. antique c. ancient d. swamplike

B. Fill in each blank with the correct letter:

a. magnanimous   d. intact
b. signatory   e. quadriplegic
c. corporeal   f. effigy

g.	inanimate	n.	quartile
h.	tactile	o.	tetrapod
i.	millennium	p.	coeval
j.	tetrahedron	q.	tetracycline
k.	medieval	r.	superannuated
l.	codex	s.	incorporate
m.	figment	t.	assignation

1. She meditated in order to forget her _____ being and to focus entirely on her spiritual self.

2. The year 2000 marks the start of the third _____ A.D.

3. In _____ times, lords built castles to protect themselves and their people.

4. Every large land animal is a _____, as is every bird.

5. He was a truly _____ man—kind, generous, and well-loved.

6. The two had agreed on a time and place for their _____, but only one could come.

7. In his report he hoped to _____ all the research he had been doing for the last year.

8. In the rare-book room of the library, the scholar found another _____ containing three long poems in Old English.

9. A grade-point average that falls in the top _____ earns a student special privileges.

10. A _____ can be a strong and stable structure, since it is made of four triangles.

11. For the homecoming celebration, we made an _____ of our opponents' mascot and draped it in black.

12. The cat can lie absolutely _____ for hours in the morning sun.

13. Each _____ to the environmental treaty agreed to a set of strict new policies.

14. The life of a _____ is not always as restricted as it once was.

15. Being blind, his _____ sense was extremely well-developed.

16. It was a terrible experience, but they came through it with their sense of humor _____.

17. The rain you thought you felt must be a _____ of your imagination.

18. Every piece of furniture in the office looked worn-out and _____.

19. That tree was planted when I was born, so it and I are _____.

20. Penicillin and _____ are among the most useful of the antibiotics.

C. Match the definition on the left to the correct word on the right:

1. incidental   a. configuration
2. will addition   b. tetralogy
3. four-year   c. annuity
4. arrangement   d. quadrennial
5. regular payment   e. codify
6. formal dance   f. quadrille
7. four-part work   g. tangential
8. seal   h. signet
9. give up   i. codicil
10. classify   j. resign

Unit 18

CAPIT, from the Latin word for "head," *caput*, turns up in some pretty important places. The *captain* of a ship is the head of the whole operation; the *capital* of a state or country is the seat of government, where the head of state is located. A *capital* letter stands head and shoulders above a lowercase letter, as well as at the head of a sentence.

capitalism \'ka-pə-tə-,li-zəm\ An economic system based on private ownership, private decisions, and open competition in a free market.

● In the 1980s, the leaders of the free world had faith that capitalism and a free-market economy would solve all our problems.

Capitalism works by encouraging competition in a fair and open market. It is practiced enthusiastically by *capitalists,* people who use capital—that is, goods or money—to increase production and make more goods and money. Capitalism is often said to run in opposition to communism. Where a *capitalist* economy encourages private actions and ownership, a communist system calls for public ownership and control by the state. *Capital* (wealth that is used to produce more wealth) is now flowing into formerly communist countries to help them develop a capitalist economy.

capitulate \kə-'pi-chə-,lāt\ To surrender or stop resisting; give up.

● When the students had worked hard, the teacher would sometimes capitulate to their pleas and not assign any homework.

Capitulation may refer to surrender on the battlefield, as when the Saxons of northwest Germany capitulated to Charlemagne in the

8th century. In modern life, a company's managers may capitulate to the demands of striking workers when they realize that further resistance is useless.

decapitate \di-'ka-pə-,tāt\ (1) To cut off the head; behead. (2) To destroy or make useless.

• The huge harvesting machine decapitated every stalk of wheat in the field.

Decapitation is a quick and, in theory, fairly painless way to go, so it was once considered a privileged form of execution suitable only for nobles like the unfortunate wives of Henry VIII. Common people were executed by hanging or other, more gruesome means. The invention of the guillotine in the 18th century was partly for the purpose of making decapitation available to people of all classes.

recapitulate \,rē-kə-'pi-chə-,lāt\ To repeat or summarize the most important points or stages.

• At the end of his talk, the President carefully and clearly recapitulated the main points in order.

Recapitulation usually involves the gathering of the chief (or "head") ideas in a brief summary, just as *capitulation* originally meant material organized under headings. But a recapitulation may be a complete restatement as well. In many pieces of classical music, the recapitulation, or *recap,* is the long final section of a movement where the earlier music is restated in the main key.

ANTHROP comes from the Greek word for "human being." An *anthropomorphic* god, such as Zeus or Athena, basically looks and acts like a human. People often *anthropomorphize* their pets, seeing them as small, furry human beings rather than as animals.

---

anthropoid \'an-thrə-,pȯid\ Any of several large, tailless apes.

• Chimpanzees, gorillas, orangutans, and gibbons are all classified as anthropoids.

The word *anthropoid* means literally "resembling a human being." Anthropoid apes are so called because they resemble humans more closely than do other primates, such as monkeys and lemurs.

anthropology \ˌan-thrə-'pä-lə-jē\ The science and study of human beings.

• By studying the cultures of primitive peoples, anthropology helps us to have a better understanding of our own culture.

Anthropologists, those who study the whys and wherefores of human existence, look not only at the tribes of the remote Amazon but also at the neighborhoods of Brooklyn or Santa Monica. Every group and every culture is material for anthropology, which clearly takes an *anthropocentric*, or "human-centered," view of the world.

misanthropic \ˌmi-sən-'thrä-pik\ Hating or distrusting humans.

• Few characters in literature are more misanthropic than Ebenezer Scrooge, who cares for nothing but money.

Jonathan Swift, the author of *Gulliver's Travels,* was famous for the *misanthropy* of his satiric writing, but despite his apparent misanthropic attitude, he was loved by the people of Ireland. One third of his income was given to charity, and another third was saved and used to found a hospital—certainly not the acts of a true *misanthrope*.

philanthropy \fə-'lan-thrə-pē\ (1) Effort to promote human welfare. (2) An act or gift aimed at helping others.

• His philanthropy was so welcome—this year he had given a new hospital wing—that no one cared to inquire how he had made his money.

Philanthropy is a demonstration of human kindness. *Philanthropic* organizations like the International Red Cross are devoted to helping people in need. Such organizations are often created by wealthy *philanthropists* who want to see their money used for a good purpose. But philanthropic gestures can be large or small, and may be gifts of money or time or assistance; all they need do is help others in some way.

Quizzes

A. Fill in each blank with the correct letter:

a. misanthropic   e. recapitulate
b. capitalism   f. anthropology
c. philanthropy   g. decapitate
d. capitulate   h. anthropoid

1. Our team had to ____ to theirs, conceding victory despite our best efforts.
2. Through ____ we learn about the great variety that can be found in human cultures.
3. The economies of much of the world run on the principles of ____.
4. The gorilla is classified as an ____ because of its relatively close resemblance to humans.
5. The guillotine was used in France to ____ criminals before capital punishment was outlawed there.
6. The bitter and ____ old man was disliked by all his neighbors.
7. The sports reports quickly ____ the highlights of recent games.
8. The wealthy family's ____ made it possible for the homeless shelter to add ten more beds.

B. Match the word on the left with the correct definition on the right:

1. recapitulate   a. free-market system
2. misanthropic   b. charitable act
3. capitalism   c. surrender
4. anthropoid   d. summarize
5. decapitate   e. hating humans
6. anthropology   f. study of cultures
7. capitulate   g. ape
8. philanthropy   h. behead

CUMB/CUB can be traced to the Latin verb stems *cumb-*, "to lie down," and *cub-*, "to lie." A *cubicle* was originally a small room for sleeping ("lying down") that was separated from a larger room, though now it can be any small area set off by partitions, as in an office. An *incubus* is an evil male spirit that was once believed to seek out women in order to "lie on" them in their sleep.

---

incumbent \in-'kəm-bənt\ (1) Imposed as a duty. (2) Holding a specified office or position.

• The incumbent senator was so popular that it was hard to find anyone willing to run against him.

When something is our duty we say that it is incumbent upon us to do it—it is a burden that has been laid on us and cannot be ignored. An incumbent officeholder "lies" in office and will have to be removed from that office by anyone else who wants it. Political *incumbency* is very important in any election, since people tend to vote for the person already in office no matter how much they may complain about officeholders in general.

incubate \'in-kyů-ˌbāt\ (1) To sit on eggs or other materials or to keep them warm artificially so that they will hatch or develop or react. (2) To develop an idea.

• The display of chicks hatching out of incubated eggs is always a big attraction at the fair.

Incubating something means keeping it in an environment that allows it to develop. For eggs, this means a nest with a warm mother bird's body; for a chemical reaction, it means conditions having the proper temperature and mixture; for an idea, it means a state of unhurried thoughtfulness. An *incubator* is a mechanical device that substitutes for a nesting hen, but no mechanical device has been invented that serves as an incubator for ideas.

recumbent \ri-'kəm-bənt\ Leaning, resting, or lying down as if resting.

• It was a large recumbent statue of Buddha, who looked soft, relaxed, and feminine.

The ancient Greeks and Romans took their meals in a recumbent posture, lying on a low couch. For the Greeks, the meal was a time of relaxation and self-improvement in the form of poetry reading and philosophical discussions. For the Romans, the meal was often a time for gorging themselves on large amounts of food and wine. The Romans may have found their *recumbency* at meals necessary; if you ate that much, you'd need to lie down too.

succumb \sə-'kəm\ (1) To give in to greater strength or force or overpowering appeal or desire. (2) To die.

● We finally succumbed to the lure of the irresistible chocolate cake.

One can succumb to a cold or to a pleading request or to a yearning for ice cream—anything that proves too strong to be resisted. And everyone eventually will succumb to death. From its root, *succumb* means literally to "lie down," but in a strong or final way.

DYNAM comes from Greek and means "to be able" or "to have power." *Dynamite* has enough power to blow up the hardest granite bedrock. A *dyne* is a unit used in measuring force. An instrument that measures force is called a *dynamometer*.

---

dynamic \dī-'na-mik\ (1) Relating to physical force or energy. (2) Continuously and productively active and changing; energetic or forceful.

● They liked to keep the situation dynamic by shaking things up every so often.

Dynamic is the opposite of *static*, which means "not moving or active." So all living languages, for example, are dynamic rather than static, changing from year to year even when they don't appear to be. A bustling commercial city like Hong Kong is dynamic, constantly changing and adapting. And *dynamic* would describe stars of unusual energy and inventiveness like Whoopi Goldberg and Robin Williams.

dynamo \dī-nə-ˌmō\ (1) A power generator. (2) A forceful, energetic person.

● Even as they entered the power plant, the roar of the water covered the sound of the immense dynamos.

The dynamos of a power plant are usually enormous mechanisms driven by water or steam which turn mechanical energy into electricity. A human dynamo is a person who seems to have unlimited energy. The legendary Fiorello La Guardia, the mayor of New York from 1934 to 1945, had the forcefulness and vigor to match an intensely *dynamic* city like New York.

dynasty \'dī-nə-stē\ (1) A line of rulers from the same family. (2) A group, family, or team that keeps its powerful position for a long time.

● Ancient Egypt was ruled by one dynasty after another for over 3,000 years.

In the histories of countries like Egypt and China, the rulers are organized by dynasties. The recorded history of these countries extends for thousands of years, and many of the ruling dynasties stayed in power for many generations. For example, the Shang dynasty of China lasted nearly 600 years. But today any sports team that wins a championship two years in a row is likely to be called a dynasty.

hydrodynamic \,hī-drō-dī-'na-mik\ Having to do with the science that studies fluids in motion and the forces that act on bodies surrounded by fluids.

● Building levees to contain a flood presents complicated hydrodynamic problems.

The Bernoulli principle, which is basic to *hydrodynamics,* says that the faster a fluid substance flows, the less outward pressure it exerts. It shows the close relationship between *hydrodynamics* and *aerodynamics* (which deals with the movement of air and other gases), since it can partly explain how air will "lift" an airplane by the way it flows over the wings. Hydrodynamics is used today even in studying the surface of the planets and even the stars. In informal speech *hydrodynamic* often means "hydrodynamically efficient."

Quizzes

A. Choose the closest definition:

1. dynamo   a. powerhouse b. force unit c. time interval d. power outage
2. incumbent   a. coming in b. retiring c. holding office d. standing up

3. dynasty   a. glamorous clan b. ruling family c. great
      wealth d. powerful leader
4. succumb   a. rest b. enchant c. approach d. give up
5. incubate   a. brood b. store c. lie down d. sleep
6. hydrodynamic   a. relating to moving fluids b. water-
      resistant c. relating to boats d. relating to water
7. recumbent   a. tired again b. lying down
      c. vulnerable d. not straight
8. dynamic   a. explosive b. energetic c. excited
      d. dangerous

**B. Indicate whether the following pairs have the same or
     different meanings:**

1.	hydrodynamic / tidal	same ___ / different ___
2.	incubate / develop	same ___ / different ___
3.	recumbent / resting	same ___ / different ___
4.	dynasty / saga	same ___ / different ___
5.	incumbent / falling down	same ___ / different ___
6.	dynamo / generator	same ___ / different ___
7.	succumb / resist	same ___ / different ___
8.	dynamic / electric	same ___ / different ___

GRAD comes from the Latin noun *gradus,* "step" or "degree,"
and the verb *gradi,* "to step, walk." A *grade* is a step up or down
on a scale of some kind. A *gradual* change takes place in small
steps. The *gradient* of a steep slope might be 45 *degrees.*

degrade \di-'grād\ (1) To lower in status or level. (2) To bring
into disrepute or corrupt morally or intellectually.

• They had feared for years that television was degrading the
intellectual capacity of their children.

In Shakespeare's *King Lear,* the old king is degraded by the daughters he has given his kingdom to. He finds it *degrading,* for
instance, when the number of his guards is reduced from 100 to
25. His *degradation* seems complete when in his madness, he is
reduced to living in the wilderness.

gradation \grā-'dā-shən\ (1) A series made up of successive stages. (2) A step in an ordered scale.

● In the fall, the leaves show gradations of color from deepest red to brightest yellow.

In the Boy Scouts, gradations of rank move upward from Tenderfoot to Eagle Scout. A violin or a voice can produce gradations of musical pitch too small to appear in written music. And social life has always been a matter of gradations. In the 18th century Jonathan Swift could even write of "the several kinds and gradations of laughter, which ladies must daily practice by the looking-glass."

graduate \'gra-jù-₁wāt\ (1) To separate into degrees, grades, classes, or intervals. (2) To receive an academic degree or diploma; to pass from one stage to another.

● You'll need to use a graduated cylinder for this experiment, because exact measurements are crucial.

To graduate from a school means to obtain a new degree (*degree* originally means "step") and pass on to a new stage. But you may graduate to a new stage of life when you marry, get a new job or job title, or buy a house. Our graduated income tax also rises by steps; it is intended to take not simply more money but a larger percentage of the income of those with high incomes than of those with low incomes.

retrograde \'re-trō-₁grād\ (1) Moving or performed in a direction that is backward or opposite to the usual direction. (2) Moving toward a worse or earlier state.

● She knew her artistic tastes were retrograde, but she still loved scenes of quiet country life the most.

Retrograde describes backwardness of one kind or another. An idea or policy might be called retrograde if it seems to look backward or to be a step in the wrong direction. A retrograde view of women might be one that saw them basically as housekeepers. Retrograde art might look like art from the 1940s or the 1890s. Mars and Jupiter show retrograde (that is, backward) motion at some stages of their orbits, though this has to do with the way we see those orbits from the earth and not with any real backward movement.

LAT comes from a Latin verb that means "to carry or bear." From this root come *relation* and *relative,* a person you are *related* to, whether you like it or not. You might be *elated,* or "carried away by joy," to get free tickets to a rock concert, but your elderly relative might not share your *elation.*

collate \kō-'lāt\ (1) To assemble pages in the proper order. (2) To collect, compare, and arrange data.

• The larger photocopiers collate and staple automatically.

The everyday meaning of *collate* today is to assemble pages mechanically. But we also often speak of collating information—that is, gathering it, comparing it carefully, and putting it into a new form. Collating electronically usually means combining two or more sets of data into a new set in a new order.

prelate \'pre-lət\ A member of the church with high rank.

• A dutiful prelate tries to visit all area churches every year.

A prelate is literally someone who has been raised up or "carried forward." In the Roman Catholic Church, the term applies to a number of high-ranking members of the clergy, including arch-bishops, bishops, and abbots.

relativity \,re-lə-'ti-və-tē\ A theory that says that mass and energy are equivalent and that a moving object will experience changes in mass, size, and time which are related to its speed.

• The theory of relativity changed the way people looked at the world; where there were once absolutes, now everything is relative.

Albert Einstein's special theory of relativity explores the *relation-ships* between space and time and between energy and matter, rela-tionships that had hardly been dreamed of by earlier scientists. The theory includes the famous equation $E = mc^2$, "Energy equals mass times the speed of light squared." Many of the predictions made by the general theory of relativity have been confirmed experimentally.

correlate \'kȯr-ə-,lāt\ To connect in a systematic way; establish the mutual relations of.

• Eric's main task in running the research project was to correlate the activities in the lab and in the field.

We correlate one thing with another when we connect them in a clear way or when we show their *relationship*. Numerous studies have shown a *correlation* between smoking and cancer. A scientist might correlate the findings of previous researchers, setting them forth in a way that shows how they are *related*.

Quizzes

A. Choose the closest definition:

1. correlate a. carry over b. show a relationship c. get along d. compare
2. degrade a. reduce in size b. raise in esteem c. lower in rank d. increase in importance
3. collate a. arrange in order b. distribute c. review d. produce
4. graduate a. go to school b. measure exactly c. increase in size d. rise to a higher stage
5. prelate a. high church official b. foremost player c. important officer d. graduate degree
6. gradation a. program in a series b. stage in a series c. eventual decline d. definite improvement
7. relativity a. galactic travel b. altered speed of light c. relationship between mass, energy, and time d. relationship of human races
8. retrograde a. moving in reverse b. grading again c. primitive d. switching grades

B. Fill in each blank with the correct letter:

a. collate   e. retrograde
b. gradation   f. prelate
c. correlate   g. graduate
d. degrade   h. relativity

1. Einstein's special theory of _____ gave science a whole new world of problems to solve.
2. Each subtle _____ of color seemed more beautiful as the sun slowly set.
3. An archbishop is a high-ranking _____ of the church.

---

4. The new prime minister decided to _____ the income tax for the sake of fairness.

5. To _____ the research materials will require at least a month.

6. This turned out to be a _____ step, and they never really recovered from it.

7. The new study will _____ the findings of several previous studies.

8. Apologize for your mistake, but don't _____ yourself.

CRIT comes from a Greek verb that means "to judge" or "to decide." A film *critic* judges a movie and tells us what is good or bad about it. Her *critical* opinion may convince us not to go, or we may overlook any negative *criticism* and see it anyway.

criterion \krī-'tir-ē-ən\ A standard by which a judgment or decision is made.

● In the NFL, the ultimate criterion for judging a team's excellence is its ability to win the Super Bowl.

A criterion or several *criteria* (the plural form) serve as guidelines. You must meet certain criteria in order to graduate. Your work must meet certain criteria in order to be acceptable. One of the criteria for success in many fields is a good vocabulary!

hypercritical \ˌhī-pər-'kri-tə-kəl\ Overly critical.

● Teachers have to correct their students' mistakes without seeming to be hypercritical.

Constructive criticism can be helpful. If your aunt asks you what you think of her new experimental meatloaf and you say it needs a pinch of oregano, you're being constructive. If you say she should cut down on the sawdust next time, however, you're being hypercritical.

critique \kri-'tēk\ (1) A judgment or evaluation, especially a rating or discussion of merits and faults. (2) To review or criticize.

● The students offered gentle critiques of each other's reports.

Critique is both a noun and a verb. Often writers and artists will form groups solely to critique each other's work, hoping that these critiques will help them improve.

hematocrit \hi-'ma-tə-ˌkrit\ (1) An instrument for measuring the relative amounts of plasma and corpuscles in blood. (2) The ratio of red blood cells to whole blood as determined by a hematocrit.

● The hematocrit is one of the most frequently used diagnostic aids.

The hematocrit is used to separate a sample of blood into its different parts—the red blood cells, white blood cells, and plasma. An abnormal proportion of red blood cells is a good early indicator of many diseases.

JUR comes from the Latin verb *jurare*, "to swear or take an oath," and the stem of the noun *jus*, "right or law." A *jury*, made up of *jurors*, makes judgments based on the law. A personal *injury* caused by another person is "not right."

---

abjure \ab-'jür\ (1) To give up or reject by oath. (2) To abstain or hold back from.

● The Spanish Inquisition forced many Jews to abjure their religion.

To abjure means literally "to swear away." After the holidays, many people abjure all sweets and fattening foods. This *abjuration* is not usually accompanied by an oath, but it is often a vow to oneself. *Abjure* is often confused with another similar verb, *adjure*, which means "to command solemnly as if under oath." A judge might adjure a criminal to rehabilitate himself; but it is up to the criminal to abjure a life of crime.

perjury \'pər-jə-rē\ The voluntary breaking of an oath to tell the truth; false swearing.

● He was convicted of perjury for having lied under oath about his business dealings.

The prefix *per-* in the Latin verb *perjurare* means "in a harmful way." A witness who *perjures* himself or herself in a court of law does harm to the truth by knowingly telling a lie. *Perjurious* testimony is a serious criminal offense.

jurisprudence \ˌjür-is-ˈprü-dəns\ (1) A system of law, or the functioning of that system. (2) The philosophy behind a body of law.

• As a young lawyer his heroes were the crusaders of 20th-century jurisprudence, especially William O. Douglas and Thurgood Marshall.

Felix Frankfurter had a lasting effect on American jurisprudence. He began his career as a government prosecutor. He later became a professor of law, especially interested in the *jurisprudential* philosophy and principles upon which our system of jurisprudence is based. As advisor to Franklin Roosevelt and later as a Supreme Court justice, he continued to refine and apply his concepts of jurisprudence.

objurgate \ˈäb-jər-gāt\ To scold harshly.

• The judge objurgated the convicted accountant for his part in the crime.

An *objurgation* in a court of law would probably come with a severe penalty. *Objurgate* is more often used, however, to describe criticism or scolding that has no legal authority, but that is unusually harsh or violent in tone.

Quizzes

A. Indicate whether the following pairs have the same or different meanings:

1. objurgate / praise   same ___ / different ___
2. hematocrit / test tube   same ___ / different ___
3. jurisprudence / legal philosophy same ___ / different ___
4. hypercritical / untruthful   same ___ / different ___
5. perjury / testimony   same ___ / different ___
6. criterion / standard   same ___ / different ___
7. abjure / reject   same ___ / different ___
8. critique / evaluation   same ___ / different ___

B. Fill in each blank with the correct letter:

a. hematocrit   e. abjure
b. jurisprudence   f. hypercritical
c. criterion   g. perjury
d. objurgate   h. critique

1. He never learned how to make his criticism seem constructive rather than ____.
2. We could not ____ responsibility for the incident, since it was our fault.
3. The judges gave a thorough and helpful ____ of each contestant's work.
4. Although her own philosophy of ____ was very liberal, her interpretation of the law while serving as a judge was restrained.
5. What shall we use as the basic ____ for this award?
6. The old gentleman tends to ____ his grandson unmercifully for the little sins of childhood.
7. The ____ showed an abnormal ratio of red blood cells.
8. She committed ____ when she swore on the witness stand that she had spent the night alone at home.

Number Words

PENT comes from the Greek word for "five." The *Pentagon* in Washington, headquarters of the Defense Department, has five sides like any other pentagon. A *pentatonic* scale in music has five pitches, rather than the seven in a major or minor scale.

pentathlon \pen-'tath-,län\ An athletic contest in which each athlete competes in five different events.

• The modern pentathlon includes swimming, cross-country running, horseback riding, fencing, and target shooting.

The Greek word *athlos* means "contest or trial." *Pentathletes,* those who compete in the pentathlon, have to be in excellent condition. The ancient Greek pentathlon tested warriors' skills in sprinting, long jumping, javelin throwing, discus throwing, and wrestling. Women now compete in a pentathlon consisting of hurdles, shot put, high jump, long jump, and 800-meter run.

Pentateuch \'pen-tə-,tük\ The first five books of the Old Testament, traditionally said to have been written by Moses.

• He did his graduate work on Genesis, the first book of the Pentateuch.

Pentateuch means simply "five books." In Greek, the Pentateuch (which Jews call the Torah) includes the books of Genesis, Exodus, Leviticus, Numbers, and Deuteronomy. Among these are some of the oldest and most famous stories in the Bible, including the story of Moses, and some of the oldest codes of law, including the Ten Commandments given to Moses on Mount Sinai.

pentameter \pen-'ta-mə-tər\ A line of poetry consisting of five metrical feet.

• Shakespeare's tragedies are written mainly in blank verse, which is unrhymed iambic pentameter.

In a line of poetry written in perfect iambic pentameter, there are five unstressed syllables, each of which is followed by a stressed syllable. Each pair of syllables is a metrical foot called an *iamb*. Much of the greatest poetry in English has been written in iambic pentameter. Robert Frost's line "I'm going out to clean the pasture spring" is an example of it, whereas his "Whose woods these are I think I know" is an example of iambic *tetrameter,* with only four accented syllables.

pentagram \'pen-tə-,gram\ A five-pointed star usually made by connecting alternate points with a straight line and sometimes used in magic or occult practices.

• Many people believe in the positive effects that come from crystals, meditation, and pentagrams.

The five-pointed stars used in magic and occultism are pentagrams, *pentacles,* or *pentangles*. Children draw them all the time without thinking of them as anything but stars. With one point upright, the pentagram is said to be connected with protection from demons and devils; with two points upright, it is said to signify devil worship.

QUINT comes from the Latin word meaning "five." *Quintuplets* are babies that come in sets of five. A *quintessence* is literally the "fifth essence," the fifth and highest element of ancient and medieval philosophy, which was supposed to be in the celestial bodies.

quincentennial \ˌkwin-sen-'te-nē-əl\ A 500th anniversary, or the celebration of such an event.

• In 1992, we celebrated the quincentennial of Christopher Columbus's first voyage to America.

The United States is such a young country that it will be quite some time before we reach our quincentennial as a nation: 2276 A.D., to be exact. Some cities will celebrate their quincentennials long before that, but even St. Augustine, Florida, our oldest city, has to wait until 2065. The rest of us can look forward happily to our national *tricentennial* and then our *quadricentennial*.

quintessential \ˌkwin-tə-'sen-chəl\ Representing the essence or the perfect or typical example of something.

• He felt that steak, eggs, and home fries were the quintessential Sunday breakfast.

Throughout the Middle Ages and the Renaissance, Virgil was thought of as the quintessential poet. Dante made Virgil his guide through hell in the *Inferno,* which itself could be called the *quintessence* of medieval literature. And John Milton, the quintessential English epic poet, modeled his *Paradise Lost* on Virgil's *Aeneid.*

quintet \kwin-'tet\ (1) A musical piece for five instruments or voices. (2) A group of five, such as the performers of a quintet or a basketball team.

• The team's five starters are considered one of the most talented quintets in professional basketball.

A classical quintet is usually written for strings (usually two violins, two violas, and a cello) or woodwinds (flute, oboe, clarinet, bassoon, and horn). But brass quintets (two trumpets, horn, trombone, and tuba) have become popular in North America recently. One of the most common rock-and-roll lineups—two guitars, a bass, a keyboard, and drums—is also a quintet. And the Temptations were an immensely popular vocal quintet.

quintile \'kwin-,tīl\ One or another of the values that divide a tested population into five evenly distributed classes; one of those classes.

● The center's tests put their one-year-old high in the fifth quintile for motor skills.

Americans love statistics about themselves and use them for everything from income to ice cream consumption to trash production. Each of these ratings can be divided into quintiles; the fifth or lowest quintile would include the 20 percent of the population who make the least money or eat the least ice cream or generate the least trash, and the first quintile would include the 20 percent who make, eat, or generate the most.

Quiz

Match the definition on the left to the correct word on the right:

1. occult symbol   a. quintet
2. most typical   b. quintile
3. event with five contests c. Pentateuch
4. 500th birthday   d. pentathlon
5. composition for five   e. quincentennial
6. poetic rhythm   f. pentagram
7. first books of the Bible g. quintessential
8. one fifth of a group   h. pentameter

Review Quizzes

A. Choose the correct synonym and the correct antonym:

1. degrade   a. praise b. outclass c. lose d. lower
2. capitulate   a. nod b. yield c. resist d. fall in
3. hypercritical   a. pretended b. complimentary
       c. underdeveloped d. overly harsh
4. recumbent   a. sleeping b. lying c. bent d. standing
5. retrograde   a. failing b. forward c. sideways
       d. backward

6. abjure   a. take up b. damn c. swear off d. include
7. succumb   a. savor b. give in c. hold over d. hold out
8. misanthropic   a. humanitarian b. wretched
     c. antisocial d. monumental
9. objurgate   a. swear b. praise c. scold d. lead away
10. philanthropy   a. selfishness b. culture c. scholarship
     d. generosity

B. Fill in each blank with the correct letter:

a. decapitate	i. recapitulate
b. anthropology	j. incubate
c. dynamic	k. dynasty
d. graduate	l. prelate
e. correlate	m. hematocrit
f. incumbent	n. pentathlon
g. pentagram	o. quintet
h. quintile	

1. During the 25th _____, Egypt was ruled by Nubians from farther up the Nile River.
2. She had the boys _____ the glass tube to make a simple rain gauge.
3. The teacher was careful to _____ her main points at the end of each class.
4. He felt it was _____ upon him as a citizen to vote in every election.
5. The _____ had risen to his high position after many years in the church.
6. The author attempts to _____ data from several different fields.
7. The concert included a string _____ by Beethoven.
8. He spent a year in Nepal working toward his doctorate in _____.
9. The _____ showed no sign of disease.
10. Their standard practice was to lop off the hands of minor offenders and _____ serious criminals.
11. The test results placed her in the highest _____ of the population.
12. By all accounts, he was a _____ and forceful individual.
13. The hen wanted to _____ all the eggs, but we took two of them from under her.

14. In her room they found a _____ on a strange altar.
15. He has qualified for the _____ and may win several of the competitions.

C. Choose the closest definition:

1. anthropoid   a. tapirs and antelopes   b. cats and dogs
   c. chimpanzees and gorillas   d. salamanders and
   chameleons
2. gradation   a. step in a series   b. show in a series
   c. novel in a series   d. speech in a series
3. quintile   a. fifteenth   b. five-spot   c. group of five   d. one
   fifth
4. quintessential   a. fifth   b. being   c. typical   d. important
5. Pentateuch   a. New Testament books   b. five-sided
   figure   c. Old Testament books   d. five-pointed star
6. capitalism   a. free-enterprise system   b. common-
   property state   c. socialist democracy   d. free-love zone
7. dynamo   a. explosive   b. missile   c. generator   d. electric
   weapon
8. quincentennial   a. 5th anniversary   b. 15th
   anniversary   c. 50th anniversary   d. 500th anniversary
9. pentameter   a. five-line stanza   b. five-word sentence
   c. five-beat verse   d. five-sided shape
10. relativity   a. space-time theory   b. blood relationship
    c. connection theory   d. association
11. criterion   a. dinosaur   b. mourning   c. criticism   d. gauge
12. jurisprudence   a. legal philosophy   b legal agreement
    c. senior judge   d. cautious ruling
13. collate   a. photocopy   b. order   c. organize   d. delay
14. perjury   a. panel   b. cursing   c. misleading   d. lying
15. critique   a. mystique   b. commentary   c. argument
    d. defense

Unit 19

BIO comes from the Greek word for "life." It forms the base for many English words: a *biosphere* is a body of life forms in an environment; *biology* is the study of all living forms and life processes; and *biotechnology* uses the knowledge acquired through biology.

biodegradable \bī-ō-di-'grä-də-bəl\ Able to be broken down into harmless substances by microorganisms or other living things.

• Though the advertisements promised that the entire package was biodegradable, environmentalists expressed their doubts.

Several useful word elements combine to create the word *biodegradable*. The root *grad*, "to step or move," is joined with the prefix *de-* "downward," and the resulting compound is then linked with *bio-* to create our word for things that can be broken down into basic substances through normal environmental processes. Ecologically conscious consumers are likely to prefer such environmentally friendly products as biodegradable detergents and trash bags.

bionic \bī-'ä-nik\ (1) Relating to the application of biological data to engineering. (2) Having normal powers, abilities, or performance improved by electronic or mechanical devices.

• Bionic limbs, feet, and hands are becoming realities, not just television fantasies.

The science of *bionics* uses knowledge about how biological systems work to help solve engineering problems. In popular use, the adjective *bionic* usually refers to artificial limbs or other bodily parts that work as much like real ones as possible. A perfect bionic arm would move and function as easily as a real arm. We're still a long way from seeing bionic limbs as good as that, but progress is being made, and the lives of many people have already been improved as a result.

biopsy \\'bī-,äp-sē\\ The removal and examination of tissue, cells, or fluids from a living body.

• Everyone felt relieved when the results of the biopsy showed the tumor was benign.

The matter examined in a biopsy is always taken from a living organism. Biopsies have become best known as a means of detecting cancer, but cardiologists also do biopsies of heart muscle to investigate suspected heart disease, and obstetricians do biopsies on pregnant women to test for fetal disorders. The fact that a biopsy does no harm to the patient is one of its virtues.

symbiosis \\,sim-bē-'ō-səs\\ (1) The close living together of two different forms of life in a way that benefits both. (2) A cooperative relationship between two people or groups.

• The lichen that grows on rocks is produced by the symbiosis of a fungus and an alga, two very different organisms.

The prefix *sym-*, "with," in *symbiosis* produces the notion of cooperation. The *symbiotic* relationship between an alga and a fungus results in a creation—lichen—that neither organism could achieve on its own. Symbiotic associations are not limited to the botanical world. Entertainment celebrities exist in symbiosis with the press that swarms about them. Neither group could exist, let alone flourish, without the other.

GEN *generates* many English words. Their basic meaning is "come into being" or "be born." The root occurs in *gene*, the most fundamental of biological architects, and in *genealogy*, the study of family roots.

---

carcinogenic \\,kär-sə-nō-'je-nik\\ Producing or causing cancer.

• Although Barbara knows all too well that the tobacco in cigarettes is carcinogenic, she's too addicted to quit.

It sometimes seems as if the list of carcinogenic substances gets longer every day. A substance such as a food additive that has been in common and widespread use for years may unexpectedly show signs of *carcinogenicity* in laboratory experiments. When that happens, the suspected *carcinogen* will often have to be withdrawn from the market. If the substance is a building material like asbestos, it may also have to be physically removed from homes and other buildings.

congenial \kən-'jē-nē-əl\ (1) Similar in outlook, temperament, and tastes. (2) Suited to one's taste or nature.

• Brenda has high hopes of finding a congenial roommate—a quiet nonsmoker who enjoys classical music.

An old sense of the word *genius* is "spirit." *Congenial* is formed from *com-*, "with, together," and *genius*. It can describe two people who share the same spirit, who go together well. We might speak of the *congeniality* of a person who seems to get along well with everyone. A place or situation can also be described as congenial or *uncongenial*, depending on whether or not it suits our tastes.

indigenous \in-'di-jə-nəs\ (1) Originating in and found naturally occurring in a particular area or environment. (2) Inborn or native.

• The Amazon rain forest abounds in indigenous plants whose medicinal value is just now being discovered by scientists.

Long before the arrival of the Europeans, the indigenous peoples of the Americas had developed highly complex societies. Some Native American peoples, such as the Hohokam and the Pueblos, lived with each other in what are known as *heterogeneous* ("of mixed origin") communities. Other native peoples, such as the Apache and Sioux, kept entirely to themselves, living in *homogeneous* ("of the same kind") societies. Whatever the type of society formed, the Native Americans generally had an indigenous respect for the land they inhabited, a mostly unspoiled wilderness.

generic \jə-'ner-ik\ (1) Not specific; general. (2) Not protected by a trademark.

• Consumers can often save money by buying generic products instead of brand-name goods.

Animals and plants have generic names indicating the *genus*, or *general* group, to which a particular species belongs. A generic product, such as a drug, has no brand name and can be less costly than the same product sold by a well-known manufacturer. A plain box of generic laundry detergent may not look like much, but it probably has much the same ingredients as the expensive brand-name box that features a chorus line of dancing socks on its cover. Anything that is interchangeable can be called generic: for example, the hero in a typical romance.

Quizzes

A. Fill in each blank with the correct letter:

a. generic	e. biopsy
b. symbiosis	f. congenial
c. carcinogenic	g. bionic
d. biodegradable	h. indigenous

1. She found the café highly ____ and would sit there for hours.
2. Scientists are working on new ____ devices to enable amputees to walk more easily.
3. It is obviously best to avoid the insecticides that are known to be ____.
4. Just about everything in our bodies is ____ except the fillings in our teeth.
5. The doctor ordered a ____ of the suspicious-looking patch of skin.
6. They had been married 50 years, and the ____ of their relationship appeared complete.
7. Potatoes and pumpkins were ____ to the New World, although now the potato is a staple of the European diet.
8. Once a new drug's patent has run out, the ____ copies flood the market.

B. Indicate whether the following pairs have the same or different meanings:

1. congenial / friendly	same ___ / different ___	
2. biopsy / life story	same ___ / different ___	

3.	indigenous / foreign	same ___ / different ___
4.	biodegradable / readily broken down	same ___ / different ___
5.	carcinogenic / cancer-causing	same ___ / different ___
6.	symbiosis / shared existence	same ___ / different ___
7.	generic / general	same ___ / different ___
8.	bionic / fantastic	same ___ / different ___

FUNG/FUNCT comes from the Latin verb *fungi*, "to perform, carry out, or undergo." A car that is *functional* is able to perform its *function* of providing transportation. A functional illiterate is a person who manages to get by in society without the reading and writing skills possessed by most other members of the society.

malfunction \,mal-'fəŋk-shən\ To fail to operate in the normal or usual manner.

• The car skidded off the road when the brakes malfunctioned.

Machines usually work, but their parts wear out eventually, and if those parts aren't replaced, sooner or later any machine will malfunction. A malfunctioning switch might keep us from turning on a light. A malfunctioning heart valve might require surgical replacement with an artificial valve.

functionary \'fəŋk-shə-,ner-ē\ (1) Someone who performs a certain function. (2) Someone who holds a position in a political party or government.

• He was one of a group of party functionaries assigned to do the dirty work of the campaign.

Functionary has negative overtones. It refers especially to a person of lower rank, with little or no authority, who must carry out the orders of a superior. *Functionary* is a close synonym of *bureaucrat,* another word often used negatively, and both are often preceded by words like *petty* or *obscure*. *Functionary* can also refer to the world beyond government and offices. Characters in a play might be called functionaries if it is obvious that the sole reason for their existence is to serve the function of providing a plot twist.

fungible \'fən-jə-bəl\ Being such that one part or amount is interchangeable with or may be substituted for another equal part or amount in satisfying an agreement.

• Coal, grain, and lumber are all fungible commodities; art is not.

Fungible is a term that comes to us from civil law. A farmer under contract to supply 5,000 bushels of wheat may fulfill this obligation with any 5,000 bushels of wheat since for the purpose of the contract one bushel of wheat is just like any other bushel of wheat—wheat is a fungible commodity. When we lend a friend 20 dollars we expect to get the money back, but we do not expect to get the very same 20-dollar bill back. Any combination of bills or coins totaling 20 dollars will do, since currency is fungible.

perfunctory \pər-'fəŋk-tə-rē\ (1) Shallow, routine, mechanical. (2) Lacking in interest or enthusiasm.

• She gave her husband a perfunctory kiss and dashed out the door to catch the train.

Perfunctory includes the prefix *per-*, "through," to produce a sense that suggests "getting through with" something. When we do something in a perfunctory manner, we are just trying to get through with it. Bored actors who have performed a play more times than they care to remember are likely to give a perfunctory performance. A reluctant dishwasher who would rather be doing something else will give the pots and pans a perfunctory wash and dry. A teacher who has lost all interest in her subject is probably going to be the most perfunctory of lecturers.

MUT comes from the Latin *mutare*, "to change." Plenty of science-fiction movies have been made on the subject of weird *mutations*, changes in normal people or animals that end up causing no end of death and destruction. More often than not, it is some mysterious or alien force that causes the unfortunate victim to *mutate*.

---

commutation \ˌkäm-yù-'tā-shən\ (1) The replacement or substitution of one form of charge or payment for another. (2) The change of a penalty or punishment to a milder form.

• Feeling that the prisoner had been punished enough, the governor agreed to a commutation of the life sentence to time served.

Commutation combines the meaning of the root *mut-* with the prefix *com-,* "with," to produce a word having "exchange" as its basic meaning. A commutation is an exchange or substitution of one thing for another. When you agree to accept an item of value in place of a monetary payment for a service, you are agreeing to a commutation. When a chief executive substitutes a life sentence for the death sentence originally handed down by a court, he is *commuting* the original sentence. When a person *commutes* between a suburb and a city, she is "exchanging" one location for another.

immutable \i-'myü-tə-bəl\ Not able or liable to change.

• Early philosophers believed that there was an immutable substance at the root of all existence.

When the negative prefix *im-* is added to *mutable,* "changeable," we get its opposite. People deeply in love may describe their love as immutable, for they truly believe that it will never change. In a constantly changing world, people hunger for things as immutable as the laws of nature, and may observe an immutable moral code and set of values. Unfortunately, *immutability* is not a basic quality of many things in this world.

permutation \pər-myu̇-'tā-shən\ (1) Transformation. (2) A change in the order of a set of objects; rearrangement, variation.

• Their relationship seemed to go through an endless series of permutations.

When the prefix *per-,* "through" or "thorough," is added to *mutation,* the result is *permutation,* "a thorough change." The word usually implies a change produced by rearranging the existing parts rather than by introducing new parts. With their daily diet of dalliance and deceit, soap operas love permutations; the cast of regulars is constantly being rearranged into new pairs and even triangles.

transmute \trans-'myüt\ (1) To change in shape, appearance, or nature, especially for the better; to transform. (2) To experience such a change.

• Alchemists of the Middle Ages believed they could find a way to transmute lead into gold.

A *transmutation* changes something over into something else. In the "Myth of Er" at the end of Plato's *Republic*, human souls are transmuted into the body and existence of their choice. Having learned from their last life what they do not want to be, many choose transmutation into something they think they would like better. A meek man chooses to be transmuted into a tyrant, a poor man into a rich (but miserable) man, a farmer into a dashing (but short-lived) warrior, and so on. Very few seem to have learned anything from their former life that will make their choice a real improvement.

Quizzes

A. Choose the closest definition:

1. fungible   a. identical b. unique c. exchangeable
      d. defective
2. permutation   a. perversion b. rearrangement
      c. deviation d. inflation
3. functionary a. bureaucrat b. hard worker c. activist
      d. executive
4. transmute   a. reconsider b. send away c. silence
      d. convert
5. perfunctory   a. perfect b. mechanical c. thorough
      d. persuasive
6. immutable   a. unchangeable b. immature c. noisy
      d. defiant
7. malfunction   a. work slowly b. work improperly
      c. work evilly d. work mechanically
8. commutation   a. driving b. train ride c. replacement
      d. review

B. Complete the analogies:

1. hostile : friendly :: immutable : _____
      a. changeable b. decaying c. breathable d. out of date
2. silent : audible :: perfunctory : _____
      a. driven b. shallow c. careful d. relaxed

---

3. communication : speech :: commutation : _____
   a. carpool b. reservation c. exchange d. permanence
4. essential : necessary :: fungible : _____
   a. unnecessary b. interchangeable c. enjoyable
   d. profitable
5. chaos : disorder :: permutation : _____
   a. addition b. multiplication c. change d. removal
6. drone : hive :: functionary : _____
   a. anthill b. stadium c. vacation d. corporation
7. transmit : send :: transmute : _____
   a. transit b. transform c. transfer d. transport
8. misbehave : scold :: malfunction : _____
   a. function b. fix c. exchange d. rearrange

FRAG/FRACT comes from the Latin verb *frangere*, "to break or shatter." A *fraction* is one of the pieces into which a whole can be broken; recipes typically call for *fractional* parts of a stick of butter or a cup of flour. The dinnerware on which food is served is often *fragile* or easily broken. A person whose health is easily broken might be described as *frail*.

---

fractious \'frak-shəs\ (1) Apt to cause trouble or be unruly. (2) Stirring up quarrels; irritable.

● Shopping with a fractious child is next to impossible.

A fractious person is one whose self-control is easily broken. A fractious machine is one whose tendency toward breakdowns is likely to cause its operator to have one as well. A fractious horse is simply one that has not been properly broken or trained.

fragmentary \'frag-men-ˌter-ē\ Consisting of broken or disconnected parts; incomplete.

● Scholars have long speculated about the contents of the missing portions of the fragmentary Shakespeare manuscript.

To *fragment* a cookie means to break it up into pieces or *fragments*. Evidence that is fragmentary, or incomplete, may not be enough to present a clear picture. Anthropologists found only fragmentary fossil evidence of one of the earliest "humans" yet discovered, but the evidence was enough for them to determine what "Lucy" probably looked like.

infraction \in-'frak-shən\ The breaking of a law or a violation of another's rights.

• The school dealt with most minor infractions of the rules through the dean's office.

Infraction is usually applied to the breaking of a law, rule, or agreement. A priest might be guilty of an infraction of canon law; a nation might be charged with an infraction of an international treaty. *Infringement* more often refers to a violation of a right or privilege. Use of another's writings without permission may be an infringement of the copyright.

refraction \ri-'frak-shən\ (1) Deflection of a ray of light or wave of energy as it passes at an angle from one substance into another in which its speed is different. (2) The apparent distortion of an object when viewed through a transparent substance such as glass or water.

• The light refraction made it look as if the spoon in the water glass was bent.

The root of *refraction* is seen in the notion that the path of a ray of light or wave of energy is "broken" when it is deflected or turned. The effects of refraction can be seen in a rainbow, which is formed when light rays passing into (and reflecting out of) water droplets are bent at different angles depending on their color, so that the light separates into bands of color. The amount of refraction depends on the angle and the type of matter; refraction can occur even when passing through different kinds of air.

TELE has as its basic meanings "distant" or "at a distance." A *telescope* looks at faraway objects, a *telephoto* lens on a camera magnifies distant objects for a photograph, and a *television,* for better or worse, allows us to watch things taking place far away.

---

telegenic \,te-lə-'je-nik\ Well-suited to appear on television, especially by having an appearance and manner attractive to viewers.

• To be an anchorperson on the evening news, it is almost as important to have a telegenic face as it is to understand current events.

The word *telegenic* is a blend of "*tele*vision" and "photo*genic.*" With the supreme importance of TV cameras in politics, politicians are finding they need to be telegenic in order to have a successful political career. Not only people but events can be described as telegenic; but a telegenic event is often a human tragedy, such as fire or earthquake or flood, that happens to broadcast well and capture the interest of the viewers.

teleological \ˌtē-lē-ə-'lä-ji-kəl\ Showing or relating to design or purpose, especially in nature.

• Many naturalists object to the teleological view that sees everything in nature as part of a grand design or plan.

Teleology has the basic meaning "the study of ends or purposes." A *teleologist* attempts to understand the purpose of something by looking at its results. A philosopher who believes in teleological ethics argues that we should judge whether an act is good or bad by seeing if it produces a good or bad result. A teleological explanation of evolutionary changes claims that all such changes occur for a definite purpose.

telemetry \tə-'le-mə-trē\ (1) The science or process of measuring such things as pressure, speed, or temperature, sending the result usually by radio to a distant station, and recording the measurements there. (2) The information or data transmitted in this way.

• The telemetry of the satellite went dead, and the scientists no longer knew where it was or what had happened to it.

Telemetry is used to obtain data relating to the internal functioning of, for example, missiles, rockets, unmanned planes, satellites, and probes. It provides data on such factors as position, altitude, attitude, and speed as well as conditions like temperature, air pressure, wind speed, and radiation. Astronauts on the space shuttle are monitored with telemetry that measures and transmits readings on their blood pressure, respiration, and heart rates. This same kind of telemetry is used by biologists to study animals in the wild.

telepathic \,te-lə-'pa-thik\ Communicating from one mind to another through extrasensory means, with no visible connection between the two.

● She never thought of herself as telepathic, but she awoke with a start when her brother died at 2:00 A.M. 1000 miles away.

Telepathy or "mind reading" is very difficult to prove scientifically. A common test of telepathic ability involves an experimenter, a subject, and a deck of cards that show different geometric shapes. The experimenter pulls a card and looks at it, and the person being tested attempts to see what is on the card *telepathically,* by reading the experimenter's mind. But years of research have failed to prove telepathic ability; the results are rarely better than those produced by random guessing. Still, most Americans continue to believe in telepathy, and millions claim to have had telepathic experiences.

Quizzes

A. Fill in each blank with the correct letter:

a. telepathic	e. infraction
b. fractious	f. teleological
c. telegenic	g. refraction
d. fragmentary	h. telemetry

1. Details about her dream were _____ and incomplete.
2. The philosopher's argument was _____ in that it looked for a design or purpose in natural phenomenon.
3. The ship's _____ crew was threatening mutiny throughout the trip.
4. She anticipated my thoughts so well it almost seemed as if she had _____ powers.
5. The goldfish bowl on the windowsill produced a _____ of the incoming sunlight.
6. The biologists used _____ to track the migration habits of the caribou.
7. That last _____ of the rules cost their team 15 yards.
8. Some newscasters seem to have been hired for nothing more than their _____ smiles.

B. **Match each word on the left to the correct definition on the right:**

1. telepathic
2. refraction
3. telemetry
4. fragmentary
5. telegenic
6. fractious
7. teleological
8. infraction

a. incomplete
b. quarrelsome
c. mind-reading
d. distortion
e. violation
f. well-suited to television
g. long-distance measurement
h. relating to design or purpose

PHIL comes from the Greek word meaning "love." In *philosophy*, it is joined with *sophia*, "wisdom," so philosophy means literally "love of wisdom." When joined with *biblio-*, "book," the result is *bibliophile*, or "lover of books." *Philadelphia*, containing the Greek word *adelphos*, "brother," is the city of "brotherly love." To live up to the name, its inhabitants should all be committed to *philanthropy*, or goodwill toward their fellow human beings (*anthrōpos* being Greek for "human being.").

oenophile \'ē-nə-ˌfīl\ A person with an appreciation and usually knowledge of fine wine.

● As an amateur oenophile, he was glad to give advice about wines to his friends.

The root *oeno-* comes from the Greek word meaning "wine." The oenophile should be distinguished from the *oenologist*, or "student of wine," who has a technical knowledge of the cultivation of wine grapes and of the whole winemaking process. An oenophile's knowledge is apt to be limited mostly to the finished product. Oenophiles may not know how to make a great wine, but they know one when they taste it.

philatelist \fə-'la-tə-list\ A person who collects or studies stamps.

● The U.S. Postal Service issues first-day covers of each new stamp design especially for philatelists.

The first postage stamps were made available on May 1, 1840, in England. It didn't take long for the hobby of stamp collecting to arise. The earliest known reference to *philately* is from a London newspaper advertisement in 1841, where a young lady let it be known that she was "desirous of covering her dressing room with cancelled postage stamps." Modern philatelists are more likely to put the stamps they collect in special albums.

philology \fə-'lä-lə-jē\ (1) The study of literature and related subjects, including the use of language in literature. (2) The study of language and especially of historical development in languages.

• Philology naturally includes both literature and language, for the study of one without the other is hard to imagine.

Philology literally means "love of words," *logos* being Greek for "word" or "speech." *Philology* is now rarely used in its literary sense, except in the titles of scholarly journals that date to the 19th century. *Philology* and *philologist* are now more likely to be applied to linguistics, the study of speech and language. But what student of literature is not also a lover of words?

philter \'fil-tər\ (1) A potion or charm believed capable of arousing passion. (2) A magical potion.

• In Shakespeare's *A Midsummer Night's Dream*, the mischievous Puck possesses a philter that, when sprinkled on a sleeper's eyelids, will cause that person to fall in love with the first object beheld upon awakening.

Tales in which a philter caused two people to fall in love were common in the Middle Ages. Such a potion, the very root of which is "love," was a handy way to explain forbidden passion of the kind that occurred in many medieval legends. In some accounts of King Arthur's adventures, for example, a philter is responsible for sparking the love between Arthur's queen, Guinevere, and Sir Lancelot.

NEG and its variants *nec-* and *ne-* are the prefixes of denial or refusal in Latin. The Latin verb *negare*, "to say no," is the source of our English verb *negate*. A *negative* is something that denies, contradicts, refuses, or reverses.

abnegation \ab-ni-'gā-shən\ Denial, especially self-denial.

• It may be impossible for a child to understand the value of abnegation while standing in front of a bowl of candy.

Abnegation, with the help of the prefix *ab-*, "away from," calls up an image of pushing oneself away from forbidden fruit. This is not always easy to do, as we all know. Periods of abnegation and fasting are included in the yearly calendar of many religions. The Christian season is Lent, for example, and Muslims practice abnegation during the month of Ramadan.

negligible \'ne-gli-jə-bəl\ So small as to be neglected or disregarded.

• The weather forecast sounded bad, but the amount of snow turned out to be negligible.

Negligible comes from the same Latin verb as *neglect*, so something that's negligible is literally "neglectable." *Negligibility* can be good or bad. An accident that results in negligible damage to your car is not so bad. But if movie studios show a negligible amount of interest in your script for a new blockbuster action film about a young couple struggling to improve their vocabulary, that's not so good.

renegade \'re-nə-ˌgād\ (1) A person who deserts one cause, faith, or loyalty for another. (2) An individual who refuses to behave according to law or convention.

• As a renegade from liberalism, the neoconservative mocked all his former beliefs.

Renegade was originally applied to a Christian who became a Muslim. Eventually it came to mean anyone who leaves one faith or cause for another. A renegade can also be someone who denies the authority of law or society. In the Old West, Native Americans who refused to accept the authority of the territorial government and to live on their assigned reservations were called renegades. Today one doesn't even have to break the law to be a renegade. Someone refusing to go along with the dictates of designers might be called a fashion renegade.

renege \ri-'neg\ (1) To deny or take back. (2) To go back on a promise or commitment.

● If his partners renege at this point, the whole project will probably fall through.

A person who reneges is refusing to honor his or her word. To renege on a bet is to refuse to pay up when you lose. History is full of promises and commitments and treaties reneged. The United States' dealings with Native Americans over a period of about 300 years add up to a sad history of reneging on formal treaties.

Quizzes

A. Choose the closest definition:

1. philology   a. study of cigars b. study of trees c. study of language d. study of love
2. negligible   a. small b. correctable c. noteworthy d. considerate
3. oenophile   a. pig lover b. book lover c. word lover d. wine lover
4. renegade   a. restorer b. rebel c. reformer d. realist
5. philatelist   a. stamp collector b. gem collector c. wine collector d. coin collector
6. abnegation   a. abundance b. abruptness c. self-denial d. self-satisfaction
7. philter   a. healing lotion b. sieve c. car part d. love potion
8. renege   a. repeat b. go back on c. renegotiate d. overturn

B. Indicate whether the following pairs have the same or different meanings:

1. renegade / loyalist   same ___ / different ___
2. philatelist / postman   same ___ / different ___
3. philter / strainer   same ___ / different ___
4. renege / return   same ___ / different ___
5. oenophile / wine expert   same ___ / different ___
6. abnegation / absence   same ___ / different ___
7. philology / study of stamps same ___ / different ___
8. negligible / unimportant   same ___ / different ___

Number Words

DEC comes from both Greek and Latin and means "ten." A *decade* lasts for ten years; a *decahedron* is a geometrical shape with ten sides; and the *decimal* system is based on 10.

---

decalogue \'de-kə-ˌlóg\ (1) *capitalized:* The Ten Commandments. (2) Any basic set of rules that is enforced with authority.

• The health club's rules governing use of the pool read like a decalogue.

In *decalogue* the root *deca-* is combined with *logos,* Greek for "word" or "speech." According to the Bible, the original Decalogue, the Ten Commandments, was handed to Moses by God atop Mount Sinai. In Judeo-Christian tradition, the Ten Commandments are regarded as laws handed down from the highest authority and as the foundation of morality.

decathlon \di-'kath-ˌlän\ An athletic contest made up of ten parts.

• The United States has dominated the Olympic decathlon for its whole modern history.

The decathlon consists of ten separate competitions: 100-meter run, 400-meter run, 1500-meter run, 110-meter high hurdles, javelin throw, discus throw, shot put, pole vault, high jump, and long jump. The decathlon tests an array of major athletic skills; the winner is truly an all-around athlete. The word itself means "ten contests," from *deca-* and *athlon,* "contest." Its roots lie in ancient Greece, where such competitions were based on the skills needed in battle.

decibel \'de-sə-bəl\ A unit based on a scale ranging from 0 to about 130 used to measure the loudness of sound, with 0 indicating the least perceptible sound and 130 the average level that causes pain.

• The decibel level in the room was so high you couldn't hear yourself think.

The *bel* in *decibel* honors the inventor of the telephone, Alexander Graham Bell. The decibel readings of some everyday sounds make for interesting comparisons. Whispers and rustling leaves usually register under 20 decibels. The average level of conversation is about 50 decibels. Noisy factories or office machinery will likely have decibel levels of 90 to 100. In the category of deafening sounds, between 100 and 120 decibels, we find elevated trains, thunder, artillery—and rock concerts.

decimate \'de-sə-ˌmāt\ (1) To kill one man in every ten. (2) To reduce drastically or destroy most of.

• Before modern medicine, diphtheria and typhoid could decimate the populations of entire towns and cities.

Commanders in the Roman army took discipline seriously. Mutiny in the ranks was dealt with by selecting by lot one soldier in every ten and then executing the unfortunate winners of this gruesome lottery. The earliest recorded uses of *decimate* in English are mainly historical references to this Roman practice. Today, however, *decimate* is common only in its later sense describing great loss of life or a serious or catastrophic reduction in number. Aerial bombardment can decimate whole sections of a city. A wave of layoffs can decimate a company's workforce. The populations of some of Africa's greatest wild animals have been decimated by poaching.

CENT means "one hundred," from the Latin *centum*. Our dollar is made up of a hundred *cents;* other monetary systems use *centavos* or *centimes* as the smallest coin. A *centipede* has what appears to be a hundred pairs of legs, though the actual number varies greatly. But there really are a hundred years in a *century*.

centenary \sen-'te-nə-rē\ A 100th anniversary or the celebration of it; a centennial.

• The company is celebrating the centenary of its founding with a lavish banquet.

Centenary, like its cousin *centennial,* is used to refer to two distinct things. A centenary is, first of all, an anniversary. The year 1995 may mark the centenary of a town's founding. The year-long calendar of public events that the town sponsors for the occasion is also called the centenary, the celebration of the anniversary. A new centenary comes every hundred years. A town celebrating its 300th anniversary is observing its third centenary. The year 1992 was the fifth centenary of the sighting of the New World by Columbus.

centigrade \'sen-tə-ˌgrād\ Relating to a temperature scale in which 0° is the freezing point of water and 100° is its boiling point.

• The normal temperature of a human body is 37° centigrade.

The centigrade scale is essentially identical to the Celsius scale; it is the standard scale by which temperature is measured in most of the world. Anders Celsius of Sweden first devised the centigrade scale in the early 18th *century*. But in his version, 100° marked the freezing point of water, and 0° its boiling point. Later users found it less confusing to reverse these two. To convert Fahrenheit degrees to centigrade, subtract 32 and multiply by 5/9. To convert centigrade to Fahrenheit, multiply by 9/5 and add 32.

centimeter \'sen-tə-ˌmē-tər\ A length measuring 1/100th of a meter, or about 0.39 inch.

• There are 2.54 centimeters in an inch, 30.48 centimeters in a foot.

In the metric system, which is used in most countries of the world, each basic unit of measure of length, area, or volume can be divided into centimeters. A meter consists of 100 centimeters, a square meter consists of 10,000 square centimeters, and a cubic meter consists of 1,000,000 cubic centimeters.

centurion \sen-'chủr-ē-ən\ The officer in command of a Roman century, originally a troop of 100 soldiers.

• Centurions and their centuries were the backbone of the great Roman armies.

A centurion was roughly equivalent to a captain in today's U.S. Army, and a century was approximately an army company. Centurions play a role in the New Testament; Jesus performs a miracle for a centurion, and in later years St. Paul is arrested by centurions.

Quiz

Fill in each blank with the correct letter:

a. centurion   e. decathlon
b. decimate   f. centimeter
c. centigrade   g. Decalogue
d. decibel   h. centenary

1. A noise measuring only one ＿＿ is almost too soft to be heard.
2. Training for a ＿＿ requires regular practice at all sorts of running, jumping, and throwing.
3. Most towns in the United States have long since celebrated their ＿＿.
4. The ＿＿ in the Old Testament is matched by the Beatitudes in the New Testament.
5. Rain is likely to become snow at about 0° ＿＿.
6. An earthquake can easily ＿＿ the buildings of an entire city.
7. The legion commanders decided that each ＿＿ should divide up the food within his own century.
8. In Paris last week's rainfall measured under a ＿＿.

Review Quizzes

A. Choose the correct synonym and the correct antonym:

1. immutable a. unalterable b. transformable c. inaudible d. audible
2. perfunctory a. lengthy b. superficial c. hollow d. meaningful
3. permutation a. sameness b. splendor c. disorder d. rearrangement
4. fungible a. irreplaceable b. similar c. exchangeable d. enjoyable
5. fractious a. smiling b. peaceable c. angry d. troublesome
6. generic a. general b. large c. inexpensive d. specific

7. infraction   a. lawful act b. arrest c. piece d. trespass
8. indigenous   a. poor b. unnatural c. native d. alien
9. fragmentary   a. incomplete b. poorly remembered
     c. whole d. explosive
10. congenial   a. unfriendly b. sociable c. respectable
     d. dark
11. abnegation   a. position b. self-indulgence c. self-
     denial d. refusal
12. symbiosis   a. musical instrument b. independence
     c. community d. interdependence
13. renegade   a. barrier b. loyalist c. deserter d. violator
14. decimate   a. destroy b. pair up c. multiply d. remove
15. renege   a. afford b. honor c. flee d. deny

B. Fill in each blank with the correct letter:

a. commutation   i. refraction
b. functionary   j. telepathic
c. telegenic   k. malfunction
d. carcinogenic   l. oenophile
e. philology   m. biopsy
f. biodegradable   n. decathlon
g. decibel   o. centurion
h. centenary

1. This bag is made of _____ plastic that will quickly decay.
2. The accident was caused by a _____ of the hydraulic
   system.
3. Tobacco is well-known to be a _____ substance.
4. After years of tasting and testing, he declared himself a
   full-fledged _____.
5. That music might sound better if the sound were turned
   down a _____ or two.
6. Which of the ten events in the _____ is your favorite?
7. The _____ of light in a glass of water distorts things
   when you look through it.
8. Doctors recommended a _____ in case the X ray hadn't
   picked up something.
9. A minor _____ in the company handled such complaints.
10. The experiment showed that her claim to have _____
    powers was false.

11. How old will you be when I celebrate my _____?
12. He was successful in radio but not _____ enough to succeed on television.
13. The _____ and his soldiers had proved themselves skilled fighters in the battles on the eastern frontier.
14. The study of literature and word use was traditionally known as _____.
15. After having reviewed the new evidence that had come to light, the governor announced a _____ of the sentence.

C. Indicate whether the following pairs of terms have the same or different meanings:

1.	transmute / endanger	same ___ / different ___
2.	bionic / artificial	same ___ / different ___
3.	telemetry / space travel	same ___ / different ___
4.	centimeter / thousandth of meter	same ___ / different ___
5.	philatelist / dancer	same ___ / different ___
6.	teleological / sensible	same ___ / different ___
7.	decalogue / rules	same ___ / different ___
8.	negligible / ignorable	same ___ / different ___
9.	philter / shield	same ___ / different ___
10.	centigrade / temperature scale	same ___ / different ___

Unit 20

NOM comes from the Latin word for "name." A *nominee* is "named"—or *nominated*—to run for or serve in office. A *binomial* ("two names") is the scientific name for a species; the domestic cat, for example, has the binomial *Felis catus*. A *polynomial*, with "many names," is an algebraic equation involving several terms.

ignominious \ig-nə-'mi-nē-əs\ (1) Marked with shame or disgrace; dishonorable. (2) Humiliating or degrading.

• For the Greek heroes, nothing was worse than dying an ignominious death at the hands of an enemy.

The *ig-* in *ignominious* is akin to the negative prefix *in-*; when joined to the root *nom-,* it indicates the "namelessness" that goes with shame or dishonor. A person who suffers an ignominious fate has lost the opportunity to make a name for himself; he dies nameless and forgotten. In the former Soviet Union, party leaders who fell out of favor, even if they avoided being imprisoned or executed, became nonpersons. Their names were removed from official records and history books and were never mentioned again. They were treated as if they simply had never existed.

misnomer \mis-'nō-mər\ A wrong name, or the use of a wrong name.

• Calling the aboriginal peoples of the western hemisphere "Indians" was one of the great misnomers in recorded history.

History abounds in misnomers. Historians have long noted that the Holy Roman Empire was neither holy, Roman, nor an empire. The Battle of Bunker Hill was actually fought on nearby Breed's Hill. That high-water mark of 1960s counterculture, the Woodstock Festival, was actually held near Bethel, New York. The Pennsylvania Dutch are actually of German ancestry. Koala bears are not bears—they are marsupials. In the world of food, the honor for most memorable misnomer probably goes to the Rocky Mountain Oyster. As naive diners have sometimes discovered too late, they're not really oysters.

nomenclature \'nō-mən-ˌklā-ˌchu̇r\ (1) A name or designation, or the act of naming. (2) A system of terms or symbols used in biology, where New Latin names are given to kinds and groups of animals and plants.

• Naming newly discovered plants or animals requires close study of the system of nomenclature.

The word *nomenclature* includes part of the Latin word *calatus*, "called." Every field has a distinctive nomenclature, or set of terms, and its own system for applying it. Automobile manufacturers have long relied on the animal kingdom, so parking lots *nominally* resemble zoos filled with Jaguars, Cougars, Lynxes, Impalas, Broncos, Mustangs, and Eagles. The U.S. space program has borrowed from classical mythology such heroic names as Mercury, Gemini, Apollo, and Saturn. Nomenclature has reached new heights of creativity in particle physics. There the elementary particles known as quarks, which are believed to come in pairs, have acquired such names as "up" and "down," "top" and "bottom," "strange" and "charm"; in an alternative nomenclature, top and bottom quarks are also known as "truth" and "beauty"—which is all most of us know about quarks and all we need to know.

nominal \'nä-mə-nəl\ (1) Existing in name or form only and not in reality. (2) So small as to be unimportant; trifling or insignificant.

• The actor was the nominal author of the book of memoirs, but 90 percent of the writing was the ghostwriter's own prose.

Nominal derives from the Latin *nominalis*, "of a name." Something nominal exists only in name and not in substance. In a constitutional monarchy the nominal ruler is the king or queen, but the real power is in the hands of the elected prime minister. In the case of the United Kingdom, the British monarch is also the nominal head of the Church of England. Those baptized in the Church who are still not really churchgoers might be called nominal Christians.

Other things are said to be nominal when they are small in comparison to their actual value. As a favor, one might sell a friend a good piece of furniture for a nominal amount. The charge for a visit to a health maintenance organization might be a nominal $3.00, since the actual cost of the visit is mostly covered by the annual fee paid by the patient's employer.

PATER/PATR, from both the Greek and the Latin word for "father," is the source of many English words. A *patriarchy* is a society or institution in which ultimate authority rests with the father or with the men of the family. A *patron* is one who assumes a fatherly role toward an institution or project, typically giving moral and financial support.

---

expatriate \ek-'spā-trē-ət\ (1) Living in a foreign land. (2) One living in a foreign land.

● As he got to know his fellow expatriates in Morocco, he found himself wondering what had made them leave America.

The word *expatriate* combines the prefix *ex-*, "out of" or "away from," with the Latin word *patria*, "fatherland." A famous colony of expatriates was the group of writers and artists who gathered in Paris between the world wars. Their number included the Americans Ernest Hemingway, F. Scott Fitzgerald, and Gertrude Stein. Expatriates differ from exiles or emigrants in that their residence abroad is usually voluntary and extended but not permanent, and they generally retain their original national identity. Later expatriates include the novelists Aleksandr Solzhenitsyn, originally from Russia, and Gore Vidal, an American living in Italy. Often expatriates end their self-imposed exiles and, like Solzhenitsyn, *repatriate* themselves.

paternalistic \pə-,tər-nə-'lis-tik\ Tending to supply the needs of or regulate the activities of those under one's control.

● Some still accused the university of being too paternalistic in regulating student living arrangements.

A paternalistic person or institution often seeks to control all aspects of the life of those under its control. For that reason, *pater-*

nalistic often has a negative sound. While the paternalistic authority often acts out of the best intentions, its control is regarded as excessive. A paternalistic employer may provide such benefits as cheap housing and a cafeteria, but may also have strict rules regarding personal appearance and against marriages within the company. *Paternalism* was once common at colleges and universities, but a changing society has largely put an end to that.

patrician \pə-'tri-shən\ A person of high birth or of good breeding and cultivation; an aristocrat.

• They passed themselves off as patricians, and no one looked too closely at where their money came from.

Patrician originally meant a descendant of one of the original citizen families of ancient Rome. Until about 350 B.C. only descendants of one of those families could hold the office of senator, consul, and pontifex (a member of a council of priests). Later, the word was applied to members of the nobility created by the Roman emperor Constantine. As time went by, other nobles, such as those in medieval Italian republics and in German city-states, also came to be known as patricians. Today a person of noticeably refined and cultured tastes, whether actually of high birth or not, is often called a patrician. The actress Grace Kelly was much admired for her *patrician* beauty even before she became Princess Grace of Monaco. She may have been the daughter of a one-time bricklayer, but her classic features were worthy of ancient Rome's finest sculptors.

patrimony \'pa-trə-ˌmō-nē\ Property or anything else passed down from one's father or ancestors; heritage.

• Conservationists regard wilderness areas as part of our national patrimony, which we must pass on to future generations as we found them.

Patrimony originally referred to a landed estate inherited from one's father or other ancestor. While such patrimonies still exist for the lucky few, there are other kinds as well. The patrimony of many an old town along the Eastern seaboard is often its fine collection of houses dating from the 18th and 19th centuries. Many European countries realize that their art and archeological treasures, amassed over hundreds or thousands of years, are part of an irreplaceable cultural patrimony that should be guarded and preserved at all costs.

Quizzes

A. Fill in each blank with the correct letter:

a. patrician
b. misnomer
c. expatriate
d. nominal

e. ignominious
f. paternalistic
g. nomenclature
h. patrimony

1. We pay a _____ fee each time we use the swimming pool.
2. The company's policies regarding dress and conduct are rather _____.
3. "Friend" is a _____ for Charlotte; "rival" is more like it.
4. The prodigal son entirely squandered his _____ even before he inherited it.
5. The first attempts to launch rockets ended in _____ failure.
6. These days, there are _____ Americans living in every part of the world.
7. The _____ applied to newly identified plants must follow a strict set of rules.
8. His family and upbringing were _____, but he still considered himself a man of the people.

B. Match the word on the left to the correct definition on the right:

1. paternalistic
2. nomenclature
3. patrimony
4. misnomer
5. expatriate
6. nominal
7. ignominious
8. patrician

a. wrong name
b. aristocrat
c. exercising fatherly authority
d. heritage
e. naming system
f. disgraceful
g. in name only
h. living abroad

LEGA comes from the Latin *legare,* meaning "to appoint" or "to send as a deputy." A *legation* consists of a group sent on a special mission, especially a diplomatic mission to a foreign country. A *legatee,* on the other hand, is the person appointed to receive a *legacy* or inheritance.

delegation \‚de-li-'gā-shən\ A group of people chosen to represent the interests or opinions of others.

• Each of the American colonies sent a delegation to the Continental Congress.

A delegation differs from a *legation* in that the members of a delegation are usually not charged with a specific mission but merely with the overall task of representing the interests of a body of people, often at a conference during an assembly's regular session. It is assumed that the delegation will discuss and vote on questions regarding the welfare of those not in attendance. The delegation of laymen to a religious conference is responsible for expressing laymen's concerns, just as the delegation of laymen to a medical convention may want to make sure that the rights and needs of patients are not ignored.

legacy \'le-gə-sē\ (1) Something left to a person in a will. (2) Something handed down by an ancestor or predecessor or received from the past.

• The Stradivarius family of violin makers left a priceless legacy of remarkable instruments.

A legacy is basically a gift, such as money or other personal property, that is bestowed by the terms of a will—usually a substantial gift that needs to be properly managed. But the rights and opportunities that women enjoy today can be called the living legacy of the early suffragists and feminists. And much of Western civilization—law, philosophy, aesthetics—is the undying legacy of ancient Greece.

legate \'le-gət\ An official representative, such as an ambassador or envoy.

• Every significant European power sent legates of some kind to the international peace conference.

A legate usually acts alone, while a *delegate* acts as part of a group. The Vatican sends Papal legates to represent the Pope's point of view in negotiations. Such negotiations may be diplomatic or church-related; there must be legates prepared to handle both, since the Vatican is both the headquarters of the Roman Catholic Church and a politically independent state.

relegate \'re-lə-ˌgāt\ (1) To remove or assign to a less important place. (2) To refer or hand over for decision or for carrying out.

• As first-year students, we were relegated to the back of the line so all the older classes could eat first.

Originally *relegate* meant to send into exile, or banish. When you relegate an old sofa to the basement—a less important place than the living room—you are sending it to home-decorating Siberia. When a chief executive is confronted with an insignificant or troublesome matter, he immediately relegates it—or delegates it—to an underling or to the ever-popular "committee for further study."

GREG comes from the Latin *grex*, "herd" or "flock." Bees, wolves, people—any creatures that like to live together in flocks or herds—are gregarious animals. People who greatly enjoy companionship, who are happiest when part of a rowdy herd, are highly gregarious.

---

aggregate \'a-grə-gət\ A collection or sum of units or parts.

• The aggregate of incriminating details unmistakably pointed toward a conviction.

Aggregate comes from the Latin verb *aggregare*, "to add to." An aggregate is often an example of something being greater than the sum of its parts. While the lies of a habitual liar may be individually insignificant, the aggregate of lies may be great enough to destroy all credibility. No individual element in a person's background would necessarily assure a criminal career, but the aggregate of factors may make a life of crime seem unavoidable. *Aggregate* is often used in the phrase "in the aggregate," as in the sentence "The well-rounded student's achievements were, in the aggregate, sufficiently impressive to merit a scholarship."

congregation \ˌkän-gri-'gā-shən\ (1) A gathering of people especially for worship or religious instruction. (2) The membership of a church or synagogue.

• That Sunday the minister delivered an especially inspirational sermon to the congregation.

Congregation reinforces the notion of togetherness by adding the prefix *con-*, "with," to the root. *Congregate* can often suggest a spur-of-the-moment or informal flocking together. A crowd quickly congregates at the scene of an accident. Domestic animals tend to congregate during a storm. Under military rule people are often forbidden from congregating on street corners. But a congregation is usually a group that has gathered for a formal purpose.

egregious \i-'grē-jəs\ Standing out, especially in a bad way; flagrant.

• Many of the term papers contained egregious grammatical errors.

Egregious would mean literally "out of the herd." An egregious person or thing possesses some quality that sets him or it apart from others. Originally, the distinguishing quality was something good. But by the 16th century *egregious* had taken a U-turn, and the word was applied to something that was outrageously bad. This is today the most common sense. An egregious fool is one who manages to outdo run-of-the-mill fools. Egregious rudeness sets a new standard for unpleasant salesclerks.

segregate \'se-grə-ˌgāt\ (1) To separate from others or from the general mass; isolate. (2) To separate along racial lines.

• Scientists now believe that they have segregated the gene that causes the birth defect.

To the root *greg, segregate* adds the prefix *se-*, "apart." Thus, when one segregates something, one sets it apart from the herd. The word typically means separating something undesirable from the healthy majority. In prisons, hardened criminals are segregated from youthful offenders. Lepers were once commonly segregated from the general population because they were thought to be highly infectious. During the apple harvest, damaged fruit is segregated from the main crop and used for cider. The opposite of *segregate* is often *integrate*.

Quizzes

A. Complete the analogy:

1. habit : custom :: legacy : _____
   a. descendant b. tradition c. transit d. deputy
2. obedient : tame :: egregious : _____
   a. crowded b. uncrowded c. gross d. fair
3. governor : executive :: legate : _____
   a. letter b. priest c. deputy d. bandit
4. faithful : disloyal :: aggregate : _____
   a. individual b. together c. plural d. many
5. flock : group of sheep :: delegation : _____
   a. group of candidates b. group of worshipers c. group of runners d. group of representatives
6. tear : mend :: segregate : _____
   a. mix b. sort c. send away d. refine
7. revise : amend :: relegate : _____
   a. vanish b. banish c. tarnish d. varnish
8. location : place :: congregation : _____
   a. birds b. whales c. group d. temple

B. Fill in each blank with the correct letter:

a. congregation
b. relegate
c. segregate
d. delegation

e. legacy
f. aggregate
g. legate
h. egregious

1. The child tried to hide his mistake with an _____ lie.
2. The king's _____ carried word of the victory back to the royal court.
3. Battlefield medics were forced to _____ the hopeless cases from the other casualties.
4. Their parents left them a _____ of hard work and happiness.
5. Taken in the _____, these statistics are very disturbing.

6. At the conference a carefully chosen ____ presented its views to the president.

7. The ____ grew silent as the first strains of the wedding march sounded.

8. There in the corner, where the shopkeeper had decided to ____ him, sat a stuffed bear with a mournful face.

FLU/FLUCT comes from the Latin verb *fluere,* "to flow." A *flume* is a narrow gorge with a stream flowing through it. A *fluent* speaker is one from whom words *flow* easily. Originally, *influence* referred to an invisible *fluid* that was believed to flow from the stars and to affect the actions of humans.

---

affluence \'a-ˌflü-əns\ An abundance of material wealth.

• The affluence of the city's northern suburbs is indicated by the huge houses there.

Affluence comes from the Latin verb *affluere,* "to flow abundantly." The basic meaning is that someone or something blessed with affluence has received an incoming tide or deluge of something. Since the *affluent* residents of suburbs generally work in the central city, the wealth of a metropolitan area can often be said to *flow* in one direction—out.

effluent \'e-ˌflü-ənt\ Something that flows out; polluting waste material discharged into the environment.

• The effluent from the mill had long ago turned this once-beautiful stream into a foul-smelling open-air sewer.

Effluent comes from the Latin verb *effluere,* "to flow out." An effluent can be a branch of a river or lake that flows out of the main body of water. But nowadays *effluent* is more commonly used of wastes that pour into our water and air. Smoke, liquid industrial refuse, and raw sewage (a pleasant thought indeed) can all be referred to as effluents.

fluctuation \ˌflək-chù-'wā-shən\ (1) An uncertain shifting back and forth. (2) An ebbing and flowing in waves.

• The wide fluctuations in the stock market had many small investors worried.

Fluctuate implies constant, irregular, and generally unpredictable changes that resemble the movement of waves but often lack their regular movement. A patient in the emergency room may have a rapidly fluctuating pulse and blood pressure. A manic-depressive person suffers from disturbing and unpredictable fluctuations in mood. The wild fluctuations in the careers of actors and singers probably account for their many neuroses.

mellifluous \me-'li-flŭ-wəs\ Flowing like honey or sweetened as if with honey.

• The actor's rich, mellifluous voice is familiar to us from voice-overs for commercials, station breaks, and documentaries.

The word *mellifluous* contains the root *mel-*, "honey." *Mellifluous* usually applies to sound. Many of Ravel's and Debussy's compositions have a dreamy, mellifluous quality. But the word can also be used of sweet things: Each fall the beekeepers extract the mellifluous golden liquid from their hives.

PREHEND/PREHENS comes from the Latin verb *prehendere*, "to seize." It is the root of such English verbs as *apprehend* and *comprehend*. For some derivatives of words formed from this root, the *d* is changed to an *s*, as in *apprehensive* and *comprehensive*.

apprehensive \ˌa-pri-'hen-siv\ Looking at the future with anxiety or alarm.

• She was extremely apprehensive about her first day at the new school.

To *apprehend* is to seize completely, in either a physical or an intellectual sense. To apprehend a thief is to seize and arrest him. To apprehend danger is to become aware of it, to "grasp" it mentally. *Apprehension* of an upcoming event is regarding it with anxiety, dread, or fear, after having grasped all the unpleasant possibilities. While apprehension can be crippling, often a person who is apprehensive simply has a firm grasp of an unfortunate situation.

comprehend \,käm-pri-'hend\ (1) To grasp the meaning of; understand. (2) To take in or include.

● In the days following the dropping of the atomic bomb on Hiroshima, few people comprehended the fact that the nuclear age had arrived.

The prefix *com-*, "with," emphasizes the notion of union or inclusion. So to comprehend is to grasp with the mind the complete nature or meaning of something. This clear and complete mental grasp is what often distinguishes *comprehend* from *understand*: you may understand the instructions in a handbook without comprehending their purpose. *Comprehend* also has a second meaning. A person's notion of good manners may comprehend (that is, include) more than simple table etiquette. To some people, true courage comprehends much more than physical bravado or showing off.

prehensile \prē-'hen-səl\ Adapted for grasping, especially by wrapping around.

● In her nightmare, prehensile tentacles encircled her limbs and probed her features.

Howler monkeys are among the American monkeys with prehensile tails. Famous for their ear-splitting howls, these monkeys can wrap their tails around a nearby branch and use their prehensile feet and hands for lobbing a coconut or picking lice from their fur.

reprehensible \,re-pri-'hen-sə-bəl\ Deserving stern criticism or blame; culpable.

● Whether or not he ever broke the law, Jack's treatment of Lenore was thoroughly reprehensible.

In *reprehensible* the prefix *re-*, "back," is added to the root, so *reprehend* means literally "to hold back." To reprehend is to express disapproval of something after first reserving judgment—a wise practice indeed. *Reprehensible* usually is applied to things, not people—the sin and not the sinner. Thus, a U.S. senator can be censured for reprehensible conduct, and opponents of blood sports find bullfighting morally reprehensible.

Quizzes

A. Choose the closest definition:

1. apprehensive   a. greedy b. grasping
    c. understanding d. fearful
2. fluctuation   a. wavering b. waving c. weaving
    d. woven
3. reprehensible   a. understandable b. worthy of blame
    c. worthy of return d. inclusive
4. comprehend   a. take b. understand c. compress
    d. remove
5. mellifluous   a. flowing slowly b. flowing outward
    c. flowing smoothly d. flowing downward
6. effluent   a. waste b. waist c. trash d. air
7. prehensile   a. able to peel b. able to swing c. able to
    howl d. able to grasp
8. affluence   a. suburb b. excess c. wealth d. mall

**B. Indicate whether the following pairs of words have
the same or different meanings:**

1. prehensile / dropping   same ___ / different ___
2. mellifluous / smooth   same ___ / different ___
3. reprehensible / unusual   same ___ / different ___
4. effluent / pollutant   same ___ / different ___
5. comprehend / include   same ___ / different ___
6. fluctuation / stability   same ___ / different ___
7. apprehensive / arresting   same ___ / different ___
8. affluence / wealth   same ___ / different ___

TEMPER comes from the Latin verb *temperare*, "to moderate
or keep within limits" or "to mix." It comes into English in words
like *temperature*. *Tempered* (as in tempered steel) means "to
harden by reheating and cooling in oil or water." *Tempered* enthusiasm, similarly, is enthusiasm that has cooled a bit.

---

intemperate \in-'tem-pə-rət\ Not moderate or mild; excessive,
extreme.

● Connoisseurs of wine and scotch are almost never intemperate drinkers.

The addition of the prefix *in-*, ''not,'' to *temperate* produces a word of opposite meaning. Someone or something intemperate rejects moderation in favor of excess. A religious fanatic is likely to preach with intemperate zeal. A mean-spirited theater critic will be intemperate in her criticism of a new play and will fill her review with intemperate language. *Intemperate* also refers specifically to the excessive use of intoxicating liquors. Someone who never knows when to stop consuming alcohol is an intemperate drinker.

temper \'tem-pər\ To dilute, qualify, or soften by the addition of something more agreeable; to moderate.

● A wise parent tempers discipline with love.

In Latin, *temper* means ''to mix'' or ''to keep within limits,'' and the same meaning is carried over into English. When one tempers something, one mixes it with some balancing quality or substance so as to avoid anything extreme. Thus, one tempers justice with mercy, enthusiasm with caution, and honesty with tact.

tempera \'tem-pə-rə\ A painting medium usually consisting of pigment mixed with a water-soluble binding substance such as eggwhite.

● Many of the finest Renaissance paintings, including those by Giotto and Botticelli, are done in tempera.

The name *tempera* refers to the mixing of pigment with the binding material. Tempera was the chosen medium for easel paintings and altarpieces for perhaps two hundred years. This preference for tempera lasted until the 15th century, when oily ingredients began to be used by many painters. Oils proved both more versatile and more durable than egg-based tempera, and their arrival resulted in the disappearance of tempera until modern times. Edvard Munch's famous painting ''The Scream'' is a modern example of tempera.

temperance \'tem-prəns\ (1) Moderation in satisfying appetites or passions. (2) The drinking of little or no alcohol.

● Buddhism teaches humankind to follow ''the middle way''—that is, temperance in all things.

Since *temperance* means "moderation," you might assume that with reference to alcoholic beverages, *temperance* would automatically mean their moderate consumption, or "social drinking." But historically temperance has usually meant the prohibition of all alcoholic drink (except perhaps for the well-known "medicinal purposes"). To temperance leaders such as Carry Nation, the safest form of alcoholic consumption was no alcohol at all. Starting in Kansas and eventually going national, Carry led immoderate hatchet-swinging attacks, known as "hatchetations," on saloons. National prohibition did eventually come—and go—but it was largely through the efforts of more temperate reformers.

PURG comes from the Latin verb *purgare*, "to clean or cleanse." An *unexpurgated* version of Ovid's *Metamorphoses* has not been cleansed of its vulgar or "dirty" sections. *Purging* literature of passages that might harm youthful readers has kept many an editor occupied; even in ancient times, some of Ovid's poetry was carefully *purged*.

---

expurgate \'ek-spər-ˌgāt\ To cleanse of something morally harmful or offensive; to remove objectionable parts from.

● In high school, my English class had to make do with an expurgated edition of Chaucer's *Canterbury Tales*.

To *expurgate* means "to purify" or "to clean out," as the prefix *ex-*, "out of," indicates. *Expurgation* has a long and questionable history. Perhaps history's most famous *expurgator* was the English editor Thomas Bowdler, who in 1818 published the *Family Shakespeare*, an expurgated edition of Shakespeare's plays that omitted or amended passages "which cannot with propriety be read aloud in a family." Today the term *bowdlerize* is a synonym of *expurgate*.

purgative \'pər-gə-tiv\ (1) Cleansing or purifying, especially from sin. (2) Causing a significant looseness of the bowels.

● Many a lazy afternoon in the orchard has led to the discovery of the purgative effect of too many apples.

Purgative can be used as a noun as well as an adjective. For centuries, doctors prescribed purgatives (that is, laxatives) for all kinds of ailments, not knowing anything better to do. Physical cleansing has always reminded people of emotional and spiritual cleansing, as expressed in the saying "Cleanliness is next to godliness." So we speak of confession having a purgative effect on the soul, for example. According to popular psychology, expressing your anger is purgative; but in fact it may generally be no better for your emotional life than taking a laxative.

purgatory \\'pər-gə-ˌtȯr-ē\\ (1) According to Roman Catholic doctrine, the place where the souls of those who have died in God's grace must pay for their sins through suffering. (2) A place or state of temporary suffering or misery.

• For both of them, filled with anxiety and foreboding, the long, sleepless night felt like purgatory.

Purgatory is the place where the soul is cleansed of all impurities, as Dante described in his poem *The Divine Comedy*. Today *purgatory* can refer to any place or situation in which suffering and misery are felt to be sharp but temporary. Waiting to hear the results of a test can be a purgatory. An endless after-dinner speech can make an entire roomful of people feel as if they are in purgatory.

purge \\'pərj\\ (1) To clear of guilt or sin. (2) To free of something unwanted or considered impure.

• During the 1930s Stalin and his henchmen purged the Soviet communist party of thousands of disloyal members, both actual and merely suspected.

In some cultures and situations, a ritual bath or prayer may be enough to purge guilt or evil spirits. But the Minoans who lived on Crete thousands of years ago may have used human sacrifice as a way of *purging* the entire community, which is fine for the community but rough on the victims. In many cultures, people periodically purge themselves physically by taking strong laxatives; this used to be a popular springtime ritual, and herbal *purgatives* were readily available. (At certain times of day, anyone watching television ads would think our whole nation was completely devoted to this practice.)

Quizzes

A. Fill in each blank with the correct letter:

a.	intemperate	e.	purgatory
b.	expurgate	f.	temper
c.	temperance	g.	purgative
d.	purge	h.	tempera

1. For a sick person, waiting for medical test results can feel like ___.

2. Don thinks we had better ___ our enthusiasm for this scheme with a large dose of skepticism.

3. When taken in moderate quantities, the ___ effects of bran can be healthful.

4. The widow leapt to her feet and launched into a shockingly ___ tirade at the jury.

5. Filmmakers must sometimes ___ entire scenes from their films to receive an acceptable rating.

6. Her eternal watchword was ___; no one ever saw her upset, worn out, angry, or tipsy.

7. Concerned about the union movement that was starting there, the president considered trying to ___ the entire department.

8. The poster paints we use today are a modern form of the ___ used by Renaissance painters.

B. Match the definition on the left to the correct word on the right:

1.	place of misery	a.	tempera
2.	unrestrained	b.	purge
3.	remove offensive material	c.	temperance
4.	mix or moderate	d.	purgative
5.	purifying	e.	temper
6.	moderation or abstinence	f.	expurgate
7.	remove impure elements	g.	intemperate
8.	egg-based paint	h.	purgatory

Number Words

MILL means either "one thousand" or "a thousandth." A *millennium* is a thousand years, and a *million* is a thousand thousands. But a *milligram* is a thousandth of a gram, a *milliliter* a thousandth of a liter, and a *millimeter* a thousandth of a meter.

millefleur \mēl-'flər\ Having a pattern of small flowers and plants all over.

• She was painstakingly embroidering a millefleur pattern on a casing for a pillow.

Millefleur came into French from Latin *mille florae* ("a thousand flowers") and from French directly into English. In some of the famed Unicorn Tapestries at The Cloisters Museum in New York, the unicorn appears at various stages of his mythological career—frolicking, relaxing, hunted, and caught—against a millefleur background. Many of the flowers and plants forming the pattern play symbolic parts in the unicorn myth and in other medieval tales.

millenarianism \,mi-lə-'ner-ē-ə-,ni-zəm\ (1) Belief in the 1000-year era of holiness foretold in the Book of Revelation. (2) Belief in an ideal society to come, especially one brought about by revolution.

• Millenarianism is one of the future-oriented beliefs common in the New Age movement.

Originally the *millennium* was specifically the thousand years prophesied in the biblical Book of Revelation, when holiness will prevail on earth and Jesus Christ will preside over all. Later, *millennium* was extended to mean any period—always in the future—marked by universal happiness and human perfection. The history of Christianity is filled with episodes in which members of sects were certain that the biblical millennium was arriving and gathered together to await it. Some nonreligious millenarians have also believed in a future utopia, one marked by human perfection. Although they usually regard this utopia as certain, they generally have been willing to help it along by working for a political, social, or economic revolution. The millennium is always approaching; to date it has not arrived.

millipede \'mi-lə-ˌpēd\ Any of a class of many-footed insects that have a cylindrical, segmented body with two pairs of legs on each segment, and, unlike centipedes, no poison fangs.

• As they turned over rocks and bricks in their search for the lost bracelet, millipedes of various sizes went scurrying off.

Millipedes would have a thousand legs if their structure were true to their name. But in fact they have far fewer. Even so, a millipede in motion is a sight to ponder: how can it possibly coordinate all those legs so that it doesn't trip over itself? Like some tiny conga line or bunny hop, it scuttles away to a rhythm only it can hear.

millisecond \'mi-lə-ˌse-kənd\ One thousandth of a second.

• The life of a lightning bolt is measured in milliseconds.

A millisecond isn't long enough for the blink of an eye, but it may determine the winner of a swim race or a hundred-yard dash. With the ever-increasing speed of modern technology, even a millisecond seems a little sluggish. Computer operations are now measured in nanoseconds—that is, billionths of a second.

HEMI/SEMI means "half." *Hemi-* comes from Greek, *semi-* from Latin. A *hemisphere* is half a sphere, and a *semicircle* is half a circle. (The French prefix *demi-*, which probably developed from Latin as well, also means "half"—as in *demitasse*, a little after-dinner coffee cup half the size of a regular cup.)

---

semitone \'se-mē-ˌtōn\ The tone at a half step.

• The ancient piano in the great music room had been allowed to fall terribly out of tune, with every note at least a semitone flat.

A semitone (sometimes called a *half tone* or *half step*) is the interval from a white key to a neighboring black key on the piano keyboard—for example, from G to G-sharp or from G to G-flat. In an octave (from G to the next G above, for instance), there are twelve semitones. Semitones are the smallest intervals that are used intentionally in almost any of the music you will normally hear. Two semitones equal a *whole tone*—the interval from G up to A or from G down to F, for example.

semicolon \'se-mē-ˌkō-lən\ The punctuation mark ; , used chiefly to separate major sentence elements such as independent clauses.

● Some young vandal had done a search-and-replace on Mr. Marsh's computer file; in place of every semicolon was the mysterious message *"Hendrix RULES!"*

The semicolon was introduced into modern type by an Italian printer around 1566. But it is actually the same symbol as the ancient Greek question mark and is thus older than the colon, which first appears around 1450. Don't mix the two up. A colon introduces something: usually a list, sometimes a statement. A semicolon separates two independent but related clauses; it may also replace the comma to separate items in a complicated list.

hemiplegia \he-mi-'plē-jə\ Total or partial paralysis of one side of the body that results from disease of or injury to the motor centers of the brain.

● There was disagreement among the therapists about how reversible Yolanda's hemiplegia might be.

Hemi-, unlike *semi-*, almost always appears in scientific or technical words, including medical terms such as hemiplegia. A *hemiplegic,* like a paraplegic (who has lost the use of both legs), has usually suffered brain damage, often from a wound, hemorrhage, or blood clot. Other conditions that affect one side of the body are *hemihypertrophy* (excessive growth on one side), *hemiatrophy* (wasting), and *hemiparesis* (weakness or partial paralysis).

semiconductor \ˌse-ˌmē-kən-'dək-tər\ A solid that conducts electricity like a metal at high temperatures and insulates like a nonmetal at low temperatures.

● Silicon, the most widely used semiconductor, has formed the basis for a revolution in human culture.

A semiconductor is a crystal material whose ability to conduct electricity rises as its temperature goes up and can be varied by adding small amounts of impurities. A manufactured chip of the semiconductor silicon, less than half an inch square, may contain hundreds of thousands of transistors that can serve control and memory functions when installed in a computer, automobile, calculator, VCR, or microwave oven.

Quiz

Fill in each blank with the correct letter:

a. millefleur	e. semicolon
b. semiconductor	f. millenarianism
c. millisecond	g. hemiplegia
d. semitone	h. millipede

1. _____ is expected to increase dramatically as the end of this millennium approaches.
2. In most integrated circuits, silicon is used as the _____.
3. Her fascination with insects began with her study of a _____ and its many legs.
4. Unable to reach the high note, the soprano asked her pianist to play the whole piece a _____ lower.
5. For the baby's room they chose wallpaper with a dainty _____ design.
6. A childhood disease had resulted in the crippling _____ that had confined him to a wheelchair for ten years.
7. The difference between first and second place was a matter of a mere _____.
8. The meaning of a clause rarely hinges on whether it ends with a colon or a _____.

Review Quizzes

A. Complete the analogy:

1. repulsive : attractive :: ignominious : _____
   a. favorite b. honorable c. horrible d. disgraceful
2. obnoxious : pleasant :: egregious : _____
   a. boring b. bothersome c. noticeable
   d. inconspicuous
3. milliliter : volume :: millisecond : _____
   a. distance b. weight c. time d. mass

4. enthusiastic : eager :: intemperate : ____
   a. calm b. amused c. restrained d. uncontrolled
5. cancer : tumor :: hemiplegia : ____
   a. paralysis b. swelling c. blood clot d. left side
6. erase : delete :: expurgate : ____
   a. confess b. read c. censor d. scrub
7. smug : self-satisfied :: apprehensive : ____
   a. shy b. mild c. wary d. involved
8. recession : decline :: fluctuation : ____
   a. tide b. uncertainty c. steadiness d. flow
9. abandon : leave :: relegate : ____
   a. consider b. represent c. assign d. design
10. matrimony : marriage :: patrimony : ____
    a. fatherhood b. inheritance c. property d. divorce

B. Choose the closest definition:

1. patrician a. highly cultivated b. first-born
   c. patriotic d. divided
2. congregation a. anthill b. gathering c. hearing
   d. church
3. temperance a. wrath b. modesty c. moderation
   d. alcoholic
4. nominal a. trifling b. important c. by name d. serious
5. legate a. heritage b. gift c. ambassador d. letter
6. comprehend a. misjudge b. confirm c. grasp d. gather
7. effluent a. discharge b. effort c. excess d. wealth
8. purgative a. secret agent b. bleaching agent c. road
   agent d. cleansing agent
9. semicolon a. small intestine b. punctuation mark
   c. low hill d. partial stop
10. reprehensible a. understandable b. reptilian
    c. disgraceful d. approachable
11. tempera a. anger b. character c. degree d. paint
12. millipede a. thousand-year blight b. many-legged
    arthropod c. hundred million d. obstacle
13. purgatory a. near heaven b. place of punishment
    c. evacuation d. place of earthly delights
14. semitone a. soft sound b. half note c. shade of color
    d. half step
15. aggregate a. nuisance b. assembly c. pile d. sum total

C. Fill in each blank with the correct letter:

a. mellifluous
b. expatriate
c. millefleur
d. paternalistic
e. affluence
f. purge
g. nomenclature
h. segregate
i. temper
j. misnomer
k. semiconductor
l. legacy
m. prehensile
n. millenarianism
o. delegation

1. Thousands of microscopic transistors often made of the same ____ are embedded in each chip.
2. Each generation hopes to leave the next a ____ of peace and prosperity.
3. Each time a new insect is discovered, an elaborate ____ helps determine what its name will be.
4. We sent a two-person ____ off to the restaurant to choose supper for everyone.
5. The hands of even a newborn infant are ____ and surprisingly strong.
6. We should ____ the rotten fruit from the rest to prevent the rot from spreading.
7. The ____ attitude of the corporation was at times helpful and at times just irritating.
8. The ____ tones of a Mozart flute concerto poured from the window.
9. "An artistic triumph" is a ____ for this pleasant but mediocre film.
10. Imperial Rome was a city of great ____ as well as terrible poverty.
11. He poured milk into his tea to ____ its heat and its acidity.
12. The outburst seemed to ____ the crowd of its anger.
13. Believers in ____ eagerly await the dawning of a new age in the year 2000.
14. The number of ____ Americans increases as economic involvement with other countries increases.
15. A design with a detailed ____ background is a challenge for even a needlepoint expert.

Unit 21

SUB means "under," as in *subway*, *submarine*, and *substandard*. A *subject* is a person who is under the authority of another. The word *subscribe* once meant "to write one's name underneath," and *subscription* was the act of signing at the end of a document or agreement.

---

subconscious \ˌsəb-ˈkän-chəs\ Existing in the mind just below the level of awareness.

● After dropping three dishes in a week I began to think that there might be some kind of subconscious urge to destroy behind my case of butterfingers.

We are generally not aware, or at least not fully aware, of our subconscious mental activity. But subconscious thought does affect our feelings and behavior and is often revealed in dreams, slips of the tongue, and artistic expression. The subconscious mind can be a hiding place for anxiety, a source of great creativity, and often the reason behind our own mysterious behavior, especially when subconscious motives are at work.

subjugate \ˈsəb-jə-ˌgāt\ To bring under control and rule as a subject; conquer, subdue.

● The government claimed it was just trying to protect national security, but others saw its bringing of criminal charges against reporters as an attempt to subjugate the news media.

To subjugate means literally to "bring under the yoke." In the time of ancient Rome, conquered troops were made to march under a yoke as a sign of their submission to the victor. Modern armies no longer use an actual yoke, but *subjugation* is still every bit as painful and humiliating, whether of one nation by another, one ethnic group by another, or one religious group by another. Ending the subjugation of the black majority in South Africa was for many years a goal for concerned people around the world.

subliminal \sə-'bli-mə-nəl\ Not quite strong enough to be sensed or perceived consciously.

• A few worried parents claimed that some heavy-metal songs contain subliminal messages—in the form of words recorded backwards—that urge young fans to take up devil worship.

The Latin word *limen* means "threshold," so something subliminal exists just below the threshold or border of conscious awareness. The classic example of a subliminal message is "Eat popcorn" flashed on a movie screen so quickly that the audience doesn't even notice it. The theory is that the mind perceives subliminal messages even if it doesn't know it does. Though the effectiveness of subliminal messages is still uncertain, hundreds of self-help audio tapes are produced each year, promising to deliver wonderful results by influencing you *subliminally*.

subversion \səb-'vər-zhən\ (1) An attempt to overthrow a government by working secretly from within. (2) The corrupting of someone or something by weakening morals, loyalty, or faith.

• It is often easier for a government to withstand attack from the outside than to survive subversion from within.

Subversion is literally the "turning over" of something—what was on top is turned over. During the 1950s and 1960s, many people worried about attempts at subversion of the U.S. government by communists. But it was possible to see *subversive* activities where none existed, and some innocent people suffered as a result. Similarly, some of the French have seen the appearance of words like *weekend* and *floppy disk* in their language as evidence of the subversion of French by English, though it may in fact just be part of the natural growth and development of the language.

HYPER is a Greek prefix that means "above or beyond it all." To be *hypercritical* or *hypersensitive* is to be critical or sensitive above and beyond what is normal. *Hyperinflation* is inflation that is growing at a very high rate. And *hyperextend* means to extend a joint (such as a knee or elbow) beyond its usual limits. A little-used but useful *hyper-* word is *hyperhidrosis*, meaning "excessive sweating."

---

hyperactive \‚hī-pər-'ak-tiv\ Excessively active.

● Stephen King's hyperactive imagination has produced many fantastic stories, and probably many more nightmares in his readers.

In medical or psychological terms, *hyperactive* describes a condition with unpleasant consequences. A hyperactive child usually has a very short attention span and cannot sit still, and this *hyperactivity* can lead to a learning disability or simply get the child in trouble for being disruptive. But not every high-spirited child is hyperactive. *Hyper-* means "beyond what is normal," but having a high energy level is quite normal for many children.

hyperbole \hī-'pər-bə-lē\ Extreme exaggeration.

● The food in the restaurant was quite good, but it couldn't live up to the hyperbole that had been used to describe it.

Advertisers and sports commentators make their living by their skillful use of hyperbole. Presenting each year's Superbowl as "the greatest contest in the history of sports" certainly qualifies as hyperbole, especially since the final scores are usually so lopsided. Equally *hyperbolic* are advertisers' claims that this year's new car model is "the revolutionary car you've been waiting for" when it's only slightly different from last year's—which of course was once described in the same glowing terms.

hypertension \‚hī-pər-'ten-chən\ High blood pressure.

● Pregnancy is often accompanied by mild hypertension that doesn't threaten the mother's life.

You might think that hypertension is what happens when tension builds to an excruciating level, but *hypertension* actually refers to high blood pressure, a condition in which arteries or veins become blocked or narrowed, making the heart work harder to pump blood. A *hypertensive* condition can lead to a heart attack or stroke, but there are often no warning symptoms associated with it. When detected, however, hypertension can generally be controlled with medication and changes in diet.

hyperventilate \hī-pər-'ven-tə-,lāt\ To breathe rapidly and deeply.

● They laughed so hard they began to hyperventilate and feel giddy.

Hyperventilating can be a response to fear and anxiety, among other causes. A test pilot who panics and hyperventilates faces a dangerous situation. When the level of carbon dioxide in the bloodstream goes down and the oxygen level goes up, blood vessels constrict and the body can't get enough oxygen even though it is available in the blood, and the pilot can become lightheaded and may even faint. To guard against this, pilots are taught to control their breathing. On the ground, the usual remedy for *hyperventilation* is breathing into a paper bag, which raises the level of carbon dioxide in the bloodstream and restores normal breathing. But athletes such as swimmers may intentionally hyperventilate before a race to fill their bodies with needed oxygen.

Quizzes

A. Fill in each blank with the correct letter:

a. hyperactive
b. subliminal
c. hypertension
d. subversion
e. subjugate
f. hyperventilate
g. subconscious
h. hyperbole

1. Their efforts at _____ were eventually successful in toppling the repressive military regime.
2. A tall tale uses _____, such as the giant size of Paul Bunyan, for its effect.
3. Accident-prone people may have a _____ desire to do themselves harm.
4. The yoga instructor warned the group not to _____ during their breathing exercises.
5. Napoleon hoped to _____ all of Europe and make it his empire.
6. The doctor medicated him for _____ but continued to monitor his blood pressure regularly.

7. Advertising constantly sends out _____ messages hoping to persuade people to buy the advertised products.

8. A _____ imagination can transform every little noise in a dark house into a threat.

B. Match the word on the left to the correct definition on the right:

1. hyperactive	a. breathe deeply and rapidly
2. subjugate	b. secret effort to overthrow
3. hyperventilate	c. extreme overstatement
4. subconscious	d. not strong enough to be
5. hypertension	sensed
6. subversion	e. beneath the level of
7. hyperbole	consciousness
8. subliminal	f. overly active
	g. conquer
	h. high blood pressure

PRE, one of the most common of all English *prefixes*, comes from *prae*, the Latin word meaning "before" or "in front of." A television program *precedes* another by coming on the air earlier. You make a *prediction* by saying something will happen before it occurs. A person who *presumes* to know makes an assumption before he or she has all the facts. Someone with a *prejudice* against a class of people has formed an opinion of individuals before having met them.

precept \'prē-,sept\ A command or principle that is a general rule of action or conduct.

• Our writing teacher never tires of reminding us of that fundamental precept of creative writing: Write about what you know.

Precept includes the root *capere*, the Latin verb meaning "to take." Thus, a precept is a rule or principle that one takes in before doing something. A precept is usually advice that is broadly worded and intended to serve as a guide for individual conduct. Ever since Hippocrates, physicians have tried to follow the precept laid down by the Father of Medicine himself: "First, do no harm." The precept known as the Golden Rule states "Do unto others as you would have them do unto you." The precept "If you can't say anything nice about someone, then say nothing at all" is one that almost everyone remembers—and disregards.

precocious \prē-'kō-shəs\ Showing the qualities or abilities of an adult at an unusually early age.

• Some thought the precocious child star of the new sitcom was witty and cute; others thought she was just a brat.

Growing from a child to an adult is like the slow ripening of fruit, and that is the image that gave us *precocious*. The word is based on the Latin verb *coquere*, meaning "to ripen" or "to cook," but it comes most directly from the adjective *praecox*, which means "ripening early or before its time." The Latin word was first used to describe plants and fruits, but later also to describe a child who is unusually mature at an early age. *Precocity* can occasionally be annoying; but precocious children do not come precooked, only "preripened."

predispose \prē-di-'spōz\ (1) To influence in advance in order to create a particular attitude. (2) To make one more likely to develop a particular disease or physical condition.

• Growing up in a house full of sisters had predisposed her to find her friendships with other women.

Predispose and *dispose* both mean putting someone in a frame of mind to be ready or willing to do something. Thus, good teachers know techniques that will predispose children to learn. *Predispose* differs from *dispose* by implying that the frame of mind is created some time before it becomes obvious. A belief in the essential goodness of people will predispose us to trust a stranger. Viewing television violence may predispose young people to accept real violence as normal. And in the medical sense, malnutrition over a long period can predispose a person to all kinds of infections.

prerequisite \prē-'re-kwə-zət\ Something that is required in advance to achieve a goal or to carry out a function.

• In most states, minimal insurance coverage is a prerequisite for registering an automobile.

Prerequisite comes from combining *pre-* with *requirere,* the Latin verb meaning "to need or require." A prerequisite can be anything that must be accomplished or acquired before something else can be done. Possessing a valid credit card is often a prerequisite for renting a car. A physical exam may be a prerequisite for receiving a life-insurance policy. As every college student knows, successful completion of an introductory course is often a prerequisite for enrollment in an intermediate-level course.

PARA can mean "beside": *parallel* lines run beside each other. It can mean "beyond or outside": *paranormal* activity is beyond normal experience, and *paranoid,* in which *para-* combines with the Greek word *nous,* "mind," means a little outside of one's mind. Finally, *para-* can mean "associated with, especially as an assistant": *paramedics* and *paralegals* assist doctors and lawyers, and a *paramilitary* force assists regular military forces.

---

paradigm \\'par-ə-ˌdīm\\ A very clear or typical example showing how something is to be done.

● American corporate executives have been forced to ask if Japanese-run companies present a useful paradigm of successful business management.

Paradigm has several closely related and often confusing meanings, including "typical example," "outstanding example," "typical pattern of behavior," and "theoretical framework." Still, it has its uses. Political analysts, for instance, will write that Jimmy Carter's original campaign for the presidency in 1976 serves as a paradigm of late-20th-century political strategy. When we say that modern medicine needs to find new paradigms for health-care delivery, the "excellent example" and "theoretical framework" meanings overlap. *Paradigm* can also be very close in meaning to *paragon,* discussed below.

paradox \\'par-ə-ˌdäks\\ (1) A statement that seems to go against common sense but may still be true. (2) A person or thing with qualities that seem to be opposites.

• They had to face the paradox that their family, which was the source of so much love and affection, could also be the source of great hurt and anger.

Paradox comes from a Greek word meaning "contrary to expectations"; combining the *para-* root with the Greek word for "thought," a paradox is something that takes us outside our normal thinking. No one has yet solved the paradox that an infinitely large universe and a universe that ends somewhere are equally unimaginable. Closer to home, we have the simpler paradox faced at one point or another by most people in regard to their mates: we can't live with them, and we can't live without them.

paragon \'par-ə-ˌgän\ A model of excellence or perfection.

• Mother Teresa has often been described as a paragon of saintliness and compassion.

A paragon is usually someone we hold up beside ourselves for comparison. Stories about Abraham Lincoln walking miles to school each day from his log cabin home and studying law books by the dim light from a fireplace present him as a paragon of hard work and self-reliance. Florence Nightingale is considered a paragon of bravery and determination for her efforts to care for wounded soldiers in the Crimean War. And we are all often invited to see our own mothers as paragons of virtue—at least around Mother's Day.

parameter \pə-'ram-ə-tər\ (1) A physical quality whose value determines the characteristics or behavior of a system; a characteristic element. (2) A limit or boundary.

• Weather forecasters monitor all the parameters of atmospheric behavior, including temperature, pressure, and wind direction.

Up until this century, *parameter* was used only as a technical term referring to things that could be measured and that affected the characteristics of other things. But today, in addition to being the element that determines how something behaves, a parameter can be any distinctive element. So we can say that political dissent is one of the parameters of modern life. Similarly, *parameter* has come to mean a limit or boundary to a system or concept. So all is well on the starship *Enterprise* when systems are functioning within established parameters.

Quizzes

A. Choose the closest definition:

1. prerequisite   a. pattern b. requirement c. preference
    d. direction
2. paragon   a. geometric figure b. imposing figure
    c. model of excellence d. location
3. predispose   a. recycle b. eliminate c. demonstrate
    d. influence
4. paradigm   a. example b. punishment c. tale
    d. characteristic
5. precept   a. general rule b. teacher
    c. contradiction d. model
6. paradox   a. contrary belief b. instructive example
    c. opposing truths d. painful truth
7. precocious   a. nearly cooked b. maturing early c. self-
    contradictory d. necessary
8. parameter   a. rule b. requirement c. large
    framework d. characteristic element

B. Indicate whether the following pairs have the same or different meanings:

1. paradigm / example   same ___ / different ___
2. precept / rule   same ___ / different ___
3. paragon / ideal   same ___ / different ___
4. predispose / eliminate   same ___ / different ___
5. paradox / logical proof   same ___ / different ___
6. precocious / very young   same ___ / different ___
7. prerequisite / requirement same ___ / different ___
8. parameter / edge   same ___ / different ___

META is a prefix in English with several different meanings. It can mean "after" or "behind," as it does in several terms referring to bones; for example, the *metacarpal* bones are the hand bones that come right after the *carpus*, or wrist bones. It can also mean "change," as in *metamorphosis*, a "change in shape." And it can mean "beyond": *metalanguage* is language used to talk about language, which requires going beyond normal language.

metabolism \mə-'ta-bə-,li-zəm\ The biological processes by which substances in a living thing are built up or broken down.

● Some small animals have such a high rate of metabolism that they must eat several times their own weight each day to stay alive.

Metabolism means specifically the chemical changes inside cells relating to the breaking down of food molecules to release energy and the building up of new material. More broadly, metabolism is the total process by which a particular substance, such as a food or medicine, is handled in the body. If one person's metabolism is fast, she may stay thin no matter how much she eats; if another's is slow, he puts on weight just by looking at food.

metaphorical \,me-tə-'fȯr-i-kəl\ Relating to a figure of speech in which a word or phrase meaning one kind of object or idea is used in place of another to suggest a similarity between them.

● "The eyes are the windows of the soul" and "You ain't nothin' but a hound dog" may be different kinds of poetry, but both are metaphors.

Metaphor comes from a Greek word meaning "transfer"; thus, a metaphor transfers the meaning of one word or phrase to another. Often, as in the examples above, metaphors include a form of the verb *be*, and they are often contrasted with similes, which are usually introduced by *like* or *as* ("O, my luve's like a red, red rose"). But, metaphors don't have to include the verb *be*. When we say that the teacher gave us a mountain of homework or that someone is drowning in paperwork, these too are metaphorical statements.

metaphysics \,me-tə-'fi-ziks\ The part of philosophy having to do with the ultimate causes and basic nature of things.

● Most members of the congregation preferred to hear their minister preach about virtue, and would become restless when his sermons headed in the direction of metaphysics.

Just as *physics* deals with the laws that govern the physical world (such as those of gravity or the properties of different types of particles), metaphysics describes what is beyond physics—the nature and origin of reality itself, the immortal soul, and the existence of a supreme being. Opinions about these *metaphysical* topics vary widely, since what is being discussed cannot be observed or measured or even truly known to exist. So most metaphysical questions are still as far from a final answer as they were when Plato and Aristotle were asking them.

metonymy \mə-'tä-nə-mē\ A figure of speech in which the name of one thing is used for the name of something else that is associated with it or related to it.

● When Wall Street has the jitters, the White House issues a statement, and the people wait for answers from City Hall, metonymy is having a busy day.

At first glance, *metaphor* and *metonymy* seem close in meaning, but there are differences. In a metaphor we substitute one thing with something else that is usually quite different; for example, *information superhighway* equates electronic data traveling over wires with cars and trucks on a highway. In metonymy, we replace one word or phrase (such as "stock market" or "local government officials" in the examples above) with another word or phrase associated with it. Most familiar *metonyms* are place-names, such as *Madison Avenue* for "the advertising business," or *Detroit* for "the auto industry." But using the word *bench* to refer to a judge or a court, and *crown* to refer to a king or queen, are also examples of metonymy.

PER, a Latin preposition that generally means "through," "throughout," or "thoroughly," has been a thoroughly useful root throughout its history and through all its many meanings. The "through" and "throughout" meanings are seen in *perforate*, "to bore through," *perennial*, "throughout the years," and *permanent*, "remaining throughout." And the "thoroughly" sense shows up in *persuade*, for "thoroughly advise," and *perverted*, "thoroughly turned around."

---

percolate \'pər-kə-ˌlāt\ (1) To trickle or filter through something porous. (2) To become spread through.

● Her idea was that the money she spent on luxuries would eventually percolate down to the needy.

Percolate comes from a Latin verb meaning "to put through a sieve." Something that percolates filters through something else, just as small particles pass through a sieve. Water, for instance, is drawn through soil by gravity or absorption, and this *percolation* usually cleans the water. Unfortunately, pesticides and liquid chemical wastes can also percolate through soil and contaminate groundwater. But just as water percolates through the ground, an awareness of the dangers of chemical and industrial wastes has slowly percolated through the population.

peremptory \pə-'remp-tə-rē\ (1) Putting an end to an action, debate, or delay. (2) Urgent or commanding in tone; showing an attitude of self-assurance.

• The staff was utterly intimidated by the new boss's icy stare and her peremptory tone when turning down all requests for special favors.

Peremptory comes from a Latin word meaning "to take entirely" or "destroy." Something peremptory takes away entirely a person's right to make further comments or requests. *Peremptory* suggests a dictatorial manner and a refusal to permit delays or objections of any kind, no matter how valid. A tough boss will call you to his office with a peremptory summons, tell you exactly what is expected of you, and then *peremptorily* dismiss you, perhaps with a peremptory wave of the hand. In the courtroom, a lawyer's peremptory challenge is usually a refusal to seat a juror in which the lawyer isn't required to state any reason.

permeate \'pər-mē-,āt\ (1) To spread throughout. (2) To pass through the pores or small openings of.

• The aroma of the apple pie permeated the entire house while it was baking.

A sense of dread permeates the campus at the approach of exams, with so much to learn and so little time. When the exams are over, a sense of relief permeates the student body, along with a strong desire to celebrate. A boot can be permeated by water; untreated leather is easily permeated, but certain oils make it much less *permeable*. The best boots to have are those made of *impermeable* material.

persevere \,pər-sə-'vir\ To keep at something in spite of difficulties, opposition, or discouragement.

• Despite their lack of success so far, research scientists have persevered in their search for a cure for AIDS.

The early settlers of the New World persevered in the face of overwhelming danger. The whole settlement of Roanoke Island disappeared mysteriously without a trace. The Pilgrims of Plymouth Plantation lost half their number in the first winter to disease and hunger. But their *perseverance* paid off: within five years, their community was healthy and self-sufficient.

Quizzes

A. Fill in each blank with the correct letter:

a. metaphorical	e. permeate
b. persevere	f. metonymy
c. metaphysics	g. peremptory
d. percolate	h. metabolism

1. The smaller an animal is, the higher the rate of _____ required to keep it alive.

2. Don't think of giving up; _____ in the face of these difficulties.

3. When the Gypsy Carmen sings ''Love is a wild bird,'' she is being _____.

4. As we approached the border, we were startled by a _____ order to halt from the guards.

5. ''Green Berets,'' the nickname for the U.S. Special Forces, is a good example of _____.

6. The heat from the fire gradually began to _____ the room, driving back the cold.

7. In philosophy he loved _____ most, because it dealt with the deepest mysteries.

8. The liquid began to _____ through the blend of herbs and spices, giving off a delicious scent.

B. Match the word on the left to the correct definition on the right:

1. persevere	a. seep
2. metonymy	b. equating one thing with another

3. permeate
4. metaphysics
5. peremptory
6. percolate
7. metaphorical
8. metabolism

c. spread throughout
d. keep going
e. use of an associated term
f. study of the nature of things
g. biological absorption processes
h. abrupt and final

ANT/ANTI is opposite to or opposes something else. An *antiseptic* or an *antibiotic* fights germs; an *anticlimax* is the opposite of a climax; an *antidote* is given against a poison; and an *antacid* fights acid in the stomach. Be careful not to confuse *anti-* with *ante-*, meaning "before": *antebellum* means "before a war," not "opposed to war."

---

antagonist \an-'ta-gə-nist\ A person who opposes or is unfriendly toward another; an opponent.

• Each time he gets the best of his not very wily antagonist, Wile E. Coyote, Road Runner's eloquent comment is "Meep-meep."

On stage or screen or in a story or novel, the *protagonist* is the main character and the antagonist is the opposing one. *Pro-* and *ant-* usually mark the good and bad characters, but not always; there may instead be an evil protagonist and a good antagonist. In the drama of the real world, it is especially hard to sort out which is which, so we usually speak of both parties to a conflict as antagonists. During a strike, representatives of labor and management become antagonists; they often manage to *antagonize* each other, and the *antagonism* often remains after the strike is over.

antigen \'an-ti-,jen\ A chemical substance (such as a protein) that, when introduced into the body, causes the body to form antibodies against it.

• Our bodies fight off disease and infection with white blood cells that recognize antigens on the surface of invading organisms and produce antibodies to combat them.

The *anti-* in *antigen* refers to *antibodies,* and the *-gen* means "producer." So just as an *allergen* produces an allergy and a *pathogen* produces a pathology or disease, so an antigen produces an antibody, a substance that fights off harmful outside elements. Antigens are rodlike structures that stick out from the surface of an invading organism and allow it to attach itself to cells in the invaded body. But in doing so, they signal the body that they are present and it immediately goes to work to fight off the invader.

antipathy \an-'ti-pə-thē\ A strong dislike.

• Having worked his way up from the factory floor to the executive suite, he felt an antipathy toward anyone whose advancement was based on inherited money or privilege.

Before and during the Civil War, many citizens of northern states felt a decided antipathy for slavery and those who practiced and defended it. In the southern states, many citizens felt antipathy toward busybody Northerners who would meddle in their affairs and destroy the basis of their economy and way of life. This kind of antipathy can develop into warfare. But not all feelings of antipathy are so intense.

antithesis \an-'ti-thə-səs\ (1) The contrast or opposition of ideas. (2) The exact opposite.

• Life on the small college campus, with its personal freedom and responsibility, was the antithesis of what many students had known in high school.

Writers and speechmakers use the traditional pattern known as antithesis for its resounding effect: John Kennedy's famous "ask not what your country can do for you—ask what you can do for your country" is an example. But *antithesis* normally means "opposite": war is the antithesis of peace; wealth is the antithesis of poverty; love is the antithesis of hate. Holding two *antithetical* ideas in your head at the same time—for example, that you are the sole master of your fate but also the helpless victim of your terrible upbringing—is so common as to be almost normal.

CONTRA is the Latin equivalent of *anti-* and it too means essentially "against" or "contrary to" or "in contrast to." *Contrary* itself comes directly from this prefix and means simply "opposite" or "opposed." A *contrast* "stands against" something else to which it is compared. *Contrapuntal* music sets one melody against another and produces harmony, which no one is opposed to.

---

contraband \'kän-trə-ˌband\ (1) Goods that are forbidden by law to be owned or brought into or out of a country. (2) Smuggled goods.

• He would drive up the interstate after midnight, peddling his contraband to wary gas-station attendants.

In Latin a *bannus* was an order or decree, so a *contrabannum* was something that went against a decree. The Latin word helped create the Italian word *contrabbando*, from which we get *contraband*. Contraband items are not always illegal; they may simply be things (such as cigarettes) that are taxed. So a dealer in such contraband can charge a little less and still make enormous profits. Of course, if the item is actually forbidden, like illegal drugs, then the potential profit is much greater.

contraindication \ˌkän-trə-ˌin-də-ˈkā-shən\ Something (such as a symptom or condition) that makes a particular treatment, medication, or procedure likely to be unsafe.

• A history of stomach ulcers is a contraindication to regular use of aspirin.

Doctors use the word *indication* to mean a symptom or circumstance that makes a particular medical treatment desirable. Serious anxiety, for example, is often an indication for prescribing a tranquilizer. A contraindication, then, is a symptom or condition that makes a treatment risky, such as taking certain other medications at the same time. Drugs and conditions that are *contraindicated* for a medication are often listed on its label. Patients can guard against the dangers of drug interaction by reading labels carefully and telling their doctors what else they are currently taking.

contravene \ˌkän-trə-ˈvēn\ (1) To go against or act contrary to; to violate. (2) To oppose in an argument, to contradict.

• The levels of pollutants coming from the new power plant were found to contravene both state and federal environmental standards.

Contravene is often used in legal documents and writing. A legal scholar may write, for instance, that no state law may contravene the U.S. Constitution or federal laws based on it. But nonlegal uses are also common. An experimental filmmaker may make a movie in a way that contravenes Hollywood traditions. In a small town, it's easy to get in trouble for any *contraventions* of usual patterns of behavior, such as failing to mow your lawn.

contretemps \'kän-trə-ˌtäⁿ\ An embarrassing occurrence or situation.

● He tried to make light of his angry argument with the boss by referring to it as "our recent little contretemps."

This is not a word you will hear or need to use very often, but it has its uses. Its original meaning in French was "against the time" or "out of time," thus indicating a misstep in a dance or a mistake in one's social "rhythm." It is normally used today to refer to an embarrassing argument, or to any argument or dispute. With its slightly French pronunciation and its extremely polite tone, it is a word that can lighten a moment or ease some tension. *Contretemps* has often been used to refer to displays of anger among diplomats and other government officials. For example, the President and the Speaker of the House might have to patch things up after a contretemps over the budget bill.

Quizzes

A. Complete the analogy:

1. champion : hero :: antagonist : _____
   a. comrade b. supporter c. opponent d. thug
2. harm : benefit :: contraindication : _____
   a. denial b. refusal c. injection d. indication
3. truth : fact :: antithesis : _____
   a. same b. opposite c. enemy d. friend
4. agreement : compromise :: contretemps : _____
   a. treaty b. dispute c. surrender d. meeting
5. misery : joy :: antipathy : _____
   a. disgust b. confusion c. opposition d. liking
6. accept : oppose :: contravene : _____
   a. go around b. violate c. obey d. distrust

7. cause : effect :: antigen : _____
   a. germs b. blood c. antibody d. genes
8. idol : adored :: contraband : _____
   a. useful b. illegal c. smuggled d. expensive

B. **Indicate whether the following pairs of words have the same or different meanings:**

1. antithesis / opposite   same ___ / different ___
2. contretemps / embarrassment   same ___ / different ___
3. antipathy / affection   same ___ / different ___
4. contraindication / benefit   same ___ / different ___
5. contravene / violate   same ___ / different ___
6. antigen / antibody   same ___ / different ___
7. antagonist / enemy   same ___ / different ___
8. contraband / antidote   same ___ / different ___

Greek and Latin Borrowings

in memoriam \ˌin-mə-ˈmȯr-ē-əm\ In memory of.

● The message on the pedestal begins "In memoriam" and then lists the names of those who died in World War I.

In memoriam is found on monuments and gravestones, but also in dedications of books and other creative works. Alfred Tennyson's greatest poem is his immense *In Memoriam,* mourning the death of a dear friend, which he wrote over a period of 17 years.

magnum opus \ˈmag-nəm-ˈō-pəs\ A great work, especially the greatest achievement of an artist, composer, or writer.

● We're not sure what it's meant to represent, but we're convinced that it's his magnum opus.

The greatest work of a great artist may be hard to agree on. Many would pick Rembrandt's *The Night Watch,* Mozart's *Don Giovanni,* Ovid's *Metamorphoses,* Dante's *Divine Comedy,* Wren's St. Paul's Cathedral, and Michelangelo's Sistine Chapel murals. But for Shakespeare, would it be *Hamlet* or *King Lear*? For Mahler, *The Song of the Earth* or the Ninth Symphony? For the Marx Brothers, *A Day at the Races* or *A Night at the Opera*?

memento mori \mə-'men-tō-'mȯr-ē\ A reminder of mortality especially a human skull symbolizing death.

● The first twinges of arthritis often serve as a vivid memento mori for middle-aged jocks trying to ignore their advancing years.

Memento mori literally means "Remember you must die." The early Puritan settlers were particularly aware of death and fearful of what it might mean, so they used symbols on their tombstones that served as memento mori to the living. These death's-heads or skulls may strike us as ghoulish, but they helped keep the living on the straight and narrow for fear of eternal punishment. Educated Europeans in earlier centuries would place an actual skull on their desk or elsewhere to keep the idea of death always present in their minds.

non sequitur \'nän-'se-kwə-tər\ A statement that does not follow logically from anything previously said.

● The professor's lectures were fascinating but hard to follow, as they were often a jumble of anecdotes, non sequiturs, and personal observations.

In Latin, *non sequitur* means "it does not follow," and it was borrowed into English by people who made a formal study of logic. For them it meant a conclusion that does not follow from the statements that are supposed to lead to it. But we now use *non sequitur* for any kind of statement that seems to come out of the blue. In business meetings, for instance, productive discussion can grind to a halt when the boss throws in an unexpected non sequitur and others try to respond to it.

rigor mortis \'ri-gər-'mȯr-təs\ The temporary rigidity of muscles that sets in after death.

● The coroner could tell from the degree of rigor mortis approximately when death had occurred.

Rigor mortis (which translates from Latin as "stiffness of death") sets in quickly and usually ends three or four days after death. Muscular activity before death and the external temperature both affect the course of rigor mortis, which results from a lack of certain chemicals in the muscles. Many mystery writers make use of rigor mortis as a means by which the star detective can determine when the victim died.

sine qua non \,si-ni-,kwä-'nōn\ An essential or indispensable thing.

● Good planning is the sine qua non of a successful dinner party.

Sine qua non can be translated literally as "without which, not." This may sound like gibberish, but it means something *without which* there would *not* be anything. *Sine qua non* sounds slightly literary, and it shouldn't be used just anywhere. But it does show up in such places as business magazines (a solid customer base is the sine qua non to success), show-business magazines (a good agent is a sine qua non for an actor's career), and books about publishing (careful editing is the sine qua non of staying in business when publishing reference books).

tabula rasa \'ta-byu̇-lə-'rä-sə\ (1) The mind in its blank or unmarked state before receiving any impressions from outside. (2) Something existing in its original pure state.

● As for knowing what life in the real world was like, he was practically a tabula rasa.

Tabula rasa literally means "smoothed or erased tablet." The term comes from the ancient custom of using wooden tablets covered with a layer of wax on which students would write using a sticklike implement. At the end of the day, the marks could be smoothed over, leaving a fresh, unmarked tabula rasa for the next day's lessons. *Tabula rasa* came to mean a mind ignorant of life or knowledge.

terra incognita \'ter-ə-,in-,käg-'nē-tə\ An unexplored country or field of knowledge.

● We've been to Phoenix once; otherwise Arizona is terra incognita.

Terra incognita can be translated literally as "unknown territory." When Columbus and his successors first crossed the Atlantic, they entered upon terra incognita, a new and completely unknown land. But the term is just as useful for mental exploration. The whole history of Americans before the arrival of Columbus, for example, is terra incognita for most present-day Americans. The term *terra incognita* was originally written by Roman mapmakers on those land areas that no one had yet explored.

Quiz

Fill in each blank with the correct letter:

a. rigor mortis   e. in memoriam
b. magnum opus   f. terra incognita
c. sine qua non   g. memento mori
d. non sequitur   h. tabula rasa

1. The entire field of quantum physics is _____ to me.
2. She claimed there was no such thing as the _____ of a successful novel, since great novels are so different.
3. *Bleak House* may well be Charles Dickens's _____.
4. To judge from the degree of _____, she appeared to have died during the night.
5. The monument listed the brave men and women who had died in the war, under the words "_____."
6. As for knowledge about home repair, his mind is a _____.
7. It was hard to make any sense out of his latest _____.
8. Just accept those first gray hairs as a little _____.

Review Quizzes

A. Complete the analogy:

1. brief : extended :: hyperactive : _____
   a. exaggerated   b. young   c. required   d. peaceful
2. unconscious : aware :: subliminal : _____
   a. underneath   b. noticeable   c. deep   d. regular
3. masterpiece : magnum opus :: precept : _____
   a. teacher   b. investment   c. rule   d. model
4. awareness : ignorance :: hyperbole : _____
   a. exaggeration   b. understatement   c. calm
   d. excitement
5. permit : allow :: permeate : _____
   a. ignore   b. move   c. penetrate   d. recover
6. night : dark :: sine qua non : _____
   a. indispensable   b. nonessential   c. thorough
   d. objective
7. fondness : affection :: antipathy : _____
   a. love   b. rejection   c. solution   d. distaste

8. tunnel : passageway :: paradigm : _____
   a. problem b. pattern c. form d. design
9. friendship : affection :: parameter : _____
   a. characteristic b. perimeter c. air-speed indicator
   d. comparison
10. dispute : agreement :: antithesis : _____
    a. dislike b. argument c. danger d. match

B. Fill in each blank with the correct letter:

a. peremptory	i. rigor mortis
b. memento mori	j. contraindication
c. metaphysics	k. antigen
d. antagonist	l. subconscious
e. metabolism	m. paragon
f. in memoriam	n. contretemps
g. precocious	o. subjugate
h. hyperventilate	

1. She was a _____ child who could read by the age of three.
2. As the car approached the checkpoint, the soldiers uttered a _____ command to stop.
3. The preserved body seated behind glass was like a strange _____.
4. Every child must learn to _____ his or her own desires to the desires of the group.
5. She was tired of hearing that his ex-wife was a _____ of patience.
6. The death was recent; _____ had not yet set in.
7. Late-night discussions in the dorm often turned to arguments about _____.
8. Pregnancy is a _____ to taking the measles vaccine.
9. Scientists have found the _____ associated with the tumor.
10. Researchers say that the rate of _____ decreases with age; we eat less and weigh more.
11. She asked that only "_____" and her dates appear on her tombstone.
12. The chief _____ of the Republican party is the Democratic party.

13. He felt embarrassed about the recent ___ with his girlfriend.
14. You may be dizzy because you have started to ___.
15. Was it some ___ fear that made her forget the interview?

C. Choose the closest definition:

1. metaphorical   a. symbolic b. literary c. descriptive
   d. extensive
2. subversion   a. sabotage b. undertow c. turnover
   d. overture
3. predispose   a. recycle b. subdue c. spread d. influence
4. non sequitur   a. unknown subject b. area of
   ignorance c. stray comment d. moment of weakness
5. antithesis   a. opponent b. opposite c. disadvantage
   d. argument
6. paradox   a. philosophy b. nonsense c. contradiction
   d. insight
7. tabula rasa   a. partial truth b. complete ignorance
   c. slight contamination d. pure trash
8. percolate   a. boil b. spread c. restore d. seep
9. contravene   a. go against b. retrieve c. dance d. object
10. terra incognita   a. new information b. unknown
    cause c. unexplored territory d. old suspicion
11. contraband   a. smuggled goods b. trade surplus
    c. customs d. imports
12. prerequisite   a. requirement b. reservation
    c. influence d. decision
13. metonymy   a. rate of growth b. exaggeration c. model
    of perfection d. use of a related word
14. persevere   a. carry off b. resume c. inquire d. carry on
15. hypertension   a. anxiety b. tightness c. high blood
    pressure d. duodenal ulcer

Unit 22

ACERB/ACRI comes from the Latin adjective *acer,* meaning "sharp" or "sour." Grapefruit and limes have an *acid* taste, and *acid* can also describe a person's manner or sense of humor.

acerbic \ə-'sər-bik\ Sharp or biting in temper, mood, or tone.

• His acerbic humor delighted some people and offended others.

Acerbic often describes wit. An acerbic critic may not make many friends among novelists or actors or artists, but might keep his or her readers amused and entertained. *Acerbity* is normally a bit less sharp than sarcasm; it tingles like lemon but isn't intended to hurt too much.

acrid \'a-krid\ Unpleasantly sharp and harsh; bitter.

• The acrid odor of gunpowder hung in the air long after the shots' echoes had died away.

Acrid exactly fits the smoke from a fire—a burning building or forest, for example. Dense smog may cast an acrid pall over a city, making throats burn and eyes sting. But *acrid* also describes non-physical things, such as the remarks or the writings of a bitter person.

acrimony \'a-krə-ˌmō-nē\ Harsh or bitter sharpness in words, manner, or temper.

• "If you want to leave, just leave," he said, his voice sharp with acrimony.

Acrimony is usually angry harshness that springs from resentment and bitterness. An *acrimonious* exchange is full of cutting, unpleasant remarks designed to hurt. A civil war is usually more acrimonious and bloody than a foreign war; in the same way, divorces may be more acrimonious than any other kinds of legal battles.

exacerbate \ig-'za-sər-ˌbāt\ To make worse, more violent, or more severe.

• An increase in coal-burning power plants will only exacerbate the greenhouse effect.

Because an excess of blood in the body was once thought to exacerbate fevers, it was common to remove the excess blood through draining it or applying leeches. (Since internal bleeding really *can* exacerbate wounds or hinder operations, leeches are again being used in some hospitals, long after the practice had been dismissed as worthless.) The loss of a major industry in a city exacerbates its unemployment; making an *acrimonious* remark can exacerbate a quarrel. Building a new mall may exacerbate existing traffic problems, and the wrong drug can exacerbate psychotic symptoms. To exacerbate is not to cause; it is only to make something bad even worse.

STRING/STRICT, from the Latin verb *stringo, stringere*, "to draw tight, bind, or tie," appears most simply in the English word *string*, something used to tie or bind, and in *strict*, which means tightly controlled.

---

astringent \ə-'strin-jənt\ (1) Able to draw together or pucker the soft tissues. (2) Rigidly severe; harsh, bitter.

• The herbal tea was refreshing but so astringent that it could only be drunk in small sips.

Dry wines are often described as astringent; raw cranberries and lemons are much more so. Cosmetic companies sell a variety of *astringents*, which may get rid of oil and tighten the skin to give it a smoother appearance. An astringent aftershave lotion will stop the bleeding from small shaving nicks. The tingle of such astringents can be rather pleasant; but an astringent comment may be unpleasantly biting.

constrict \kən-'strikt\ (1) To draw together or make narrow. (2) To limit or inhibit.

● She felt constricted by small-town life, where everyone seemed to know every move you made.

Arteries constricted by cholesterol and other deposits slow the flow of blood. Traffic arteries or highways constricted by accidents slow the flow of traffic. A constricted life is one that is narrow and limited; such *constriction* may be caused by poverty or lack of opportunity. Economic growth may be constricted by trade barriers. And an actress may feel constricted by the roles she played as a child.

prestigious \pre-'sti-jəs\ Having high status or eminence.

● He told anyone who would listen how his brilliant daughter had been accepted by the most prestigious universities in the country.

The words *prestige* and *prestigious* have had confusing histories, and they originally referred to stage magic and deception. But their meanings have since turned around deceptively, and now they are used to describe the best colleges and universities, the most powerful law firms, the most important awards—as well as the most expensive dress shops. These words turn up constantly in novels about the rich and glamorous; prestige today is something that can often be bought with money.

stringent \'strin-jənt\ Tight or constricted; severely or strictly regulated.

● The rules for the laboratory tests were so stringent that most of the results had to be thrown out.

Stringent often means simply "strict." But whereas *strict* often emphasizes the sternness with which something is enforced, *stringent* tends to emphasize the narrowness of what is permitted. Stringent requirements are extremely limited and specific; stringent customs laws greatly limit what comes into a country; and stringent standards of proof in court may be so narrow that they are very hard to meet. The stringent regulations that St. Benedict formulated for the Christian monasteries in the 6th century demanded absolute obedience, prayers throughout the day and night, and a life devoted to work and study.

Quizzes

A. Indicate whether the following pairs of words have the same or different meanings:

1. exacerbate / worsen   same __ / different __
2. acrid / dry   same __ / different __
3. acrimony / alimony   same __ / different __
4. acerbic / harsh   same __ / different __
5. stringent / puckering   same __ / different __
6. constrict / limit   same __ / different __
7. prestigious / respected   same __ / different __
8. astringent / tight   same __ / different __

B. Fill in each blank with the correct letter:

a. astringent   e. acerbic
b. prestigious   f. acrimony
c. constrict   g. acrid
d. stringent   h. exacerbate

1. The list of new demands only served to ___ the crisis.
2. The wine was too ___ and tasted a bit like vinegar.
3. The ___ fumes in the plant irritated his eyes and nose for several days.
4. With four or five ___ comments she managed to annoy or insult almost everyone in the room.
5. Soon after the banking scandal hit the newspapers, a new set of ___ regulations was announced.
6. It's not certain that he would give up the presidency of the university even for such a ___ position.
7. These deposits are beginning to ___ the coronary arteries to a dangerous degree.
8. Even for a child-custody case, the ___ between the parties was unusual.

STRU/STRUCT comes from the Latin verb *struere,* meaning "to put together," "to put in order," and "to build or devise." A *structure* is something *constructed,* "built" or "put together"; *instructions* tell how the pieces should be arranged. Something that *obstructs* is "built up in the way." And something *destructive* "unbuilds."

---

deconstruction \,dē-kən-'strək-shən\ Analysis of texts, works of art, and cultural patterns that is intended to expose the assumptions on which they are based.

• True deconstruction is a highly intellectual realm, but the word is being used more and more freely by nonintellectuals.

Deconstruction doesn't actually mean "demolition"; instead it means "breaking down" or analyzing something into its separate parts (especially its words) to discover its true significance, which is almost never what the author probably intended. A feminist may *deconstruct* an old novel to show in what ways even an innocent-seeming story somehow depends on the oppression of women. A new western may deconstruct the myths of the old West and show lawmen as vicious and criminals as flawed but decent. Today almost anything can be deconstructed; table manners, the Virgin Mary, and Tchaikovsky's symphonies have all been the subjects of *deconstructionist* books.

infrastructure \'in-frə-,strək-chər\ (1) The underlying foundation or basic framework. (2) A system of public works.

• The public loved her speeches about crime but dozed off when she brought up highway repair and infrastructure deterioration.

Infra- means "below"; so the infrastructure is the "underlying structure" of a country and its economy, the fixed installations that it needs in order to function. These include roads, bridges, dams, the water and sewer systems, railways and subways, airports, and harbors. These are generally government-built and publicly owned. Some people speak about such things as the infrastructure of science research or the intellectual infrastructure, but the meaning of such terms can be extremely vague.

construe \kən-'strü\ (1) To explain the arrangement and meaning of words in a sentence. (2) To understand or explain; interpret.

• "So how did you construe that last remark he made?" she asked.

Construe can usually be translated as "interpret." It is often used in law; thus, an Attorney General might construe the term "serious injury" in a child-abuse law to include bruises, or a judge might construe language about gifts to "heirs" to include spouses. The IRS's *construal* of some of your activities might be quite different from your own—and much more expensive at tax time. Construing is close to translating; when the British say "public school" it should be construed or translated as "prep school" in American terms.

instrumental \ˌin-strù-'men-təl\ (1) Acting as a means, agent, or tool. (2) Relating to an instrument, especially a musical instrument.

• His mother was instrumental in starting the new arts program at the school.

An *instrument* is a tool, something used to *construct*. It is often a tool for making music. (A musical saw happens to be a carpenter's tool that can be bowed with a violin bow.) The musical meaning of *instrumental*—usually, "performed on instruments"—is very common. But the word can also mean "helpful," "useful," "essential," or "indispensable," especially when speaking of achieving a specific goal.

PROP/PROPRI comes from the Latin word *proprius,* meaning "own." A *proprietor* is an owner. *Property* is what he or she owns.

appropriate \ə-'prō-prē-ˌāt\ (1) To take exclusive possession of, often without right. (2) To set apart for a particular purpose or use.

• Since there was no one else around, we quickly appropriated the tennis court for our own use.

Each year the President and Congress create a budget and appropriate—or "make their own"—funds for each item in it, funds which mostly come in the form of taxes from the public. But formal and legal *appropriation* isn't the only kind. "*Misappropriation* of funds" is a nice way of saying theft or embezzlement. If someone appropriated pieces of your novel, you might take him or her to court. And if you appropriated trade secrets from your former employers, you might be the one sued.

expropriate \ek-'sprō-prē-ˌāt\ (1) To take away the right of possession or ownership. (2) To transfer to oneself.

• It was only when the new government threatened to expropriate the U.S. oil refineries that Congress became alarmed.

In ancient Rome an emperor could condemn a wealthy senator, have him killed, and expropriate his property. In 1536 Henry VIII expropriated the lands and wealth of the monasteries after declaring himself head of the new Church of England. And nearly all of North America was expropriated from the Native Americans. Today, whenever a highway or other public project is to be built, the government may carry out legal *expropriations* in which the owners are *properly* paid for their land.

proprietary \prə-'prī-ə-,ter-ē\ (1) Relating to an owner or proprietor; made or sold by one who has the sole right to do so. (2) Privately owned and run as a profit-making organization.

• The local hospital was a not-for-profit institution, whereas the nearby nursing homes were proprietary.

Baseball fans tend to take a proprietary attitude toward their favorite team, although the only right they have in it is to call it their own; only for the team's owners is baseball a proprietary proposition from which they intend to make a profit. A proprietary process is a manufacturing process that others are forbidden to use, and a proprietary trademark can't be *appropriated* by a "copycat" company. These legal rights are ensured by such things as copyrights and patents. However, after a certain period of time, inventions and processes lose their legal protection and cease to be proprietary.

propriety \prə-'prī-ə-tē\ (1) The state of being proper; appropriateness. (2) Acting according to what is socially acceptable, especially in conduct between the sexes.

• Propriety used to forbid unmarried men and women to go almost anywhere unaccompanied.

In an earlier era when social manners were far more elaborate than they are today, *propriety* and *impropriety* were words in constant use. But today we use them in more limited ways. We may talk about the propriety of government officials' dealings with private citizens, the propriety of the relationship between a lawyer and a judge, or the propriety of a particular procedure in a formal meeting that follows standard rules of order. Relations between men and women in the workplace is increasingly an area in which we speak of propriety and impropriety. In other words, propriety can become an issue wherever rules, standard procedures, and ethical principles have been clearly stated.

Quizzes

A. Complete the analogy:

1. grant : award :: expropriate : _____
   a. find b. want c. move d. claim
2. architecture : design :: infrastructure : _____
   a. foundation b. surface c. exterior d. amphitheater
3. finance : fund :: appropriate : _____
   a. send b. lose c. assign d. offer
4. explain : confuse :: construe : _____
   a. build b. misspell c. destroy d. misunderstand
5. habit : practice :: propriety : _____
   a. appropriateness b. property c. behavior
   d. proportion
6. description : portrayal :: deconstruction : _____
   a. demolition b. interpretation c. transference
   d. translation
7. monetary : money :: proprietary : _____
   a. prosperity b. property c. profit
   d. protection
8. emotional : feeling :: instrumental : _____
   a. means b. construction c. music d. toolkit

B. Indicate whether the following pairs of terms have the same or different meanings:

1. proprietary / public   same __ / different __
2. construe / explain   same __ / different __
3. appropriate / offer   same __ / different __
4. infrastructure / foundation   same __ / different __
5. propriety / ownership   same __ / different __
6. instrumental / musical   same __ / different __
7. expropriate / take down   same __ / different __
8. deconstruction / demolition   same __ / different __

TORS/TORT comes from two forms of the Latin verb *torquere*, meaning "to twist" or "to wind" or "to wrench." A sideshow *contortionist* twists his or her body into bizarre shapes. This may appear to be a form of *torture*, which itself often involves a merciless wrenching and twisting of the body.

tort \'tȯrt\ A wrongful act that does not involve breach of contract and for which the injured party can receive damages in a civil action.

• The insulation manufacturer was almost bankrupted by the massive tort actions brought by employees harmed by asbestos.

Tort came into English straight from French many centuries ago, and it still looks a little odd. Its root meaning of "twisted" (as opposed to "straight") obviously came to mean "wrong" (as opposed to "right"). Every first-year law student must take a course in the important subject of torts. Torts include all the so-called "product-liability" cases against manufacturers of cars, household products, children's toys, and so on. They also cover dog bites, slander and libel, and a huge variety of other very personal cases of injury, both mental and physical—the Torts class is never dull. Individuals are generally compensated through "damages," or money awards.

extort \ik-'stȯrt\ To obtain from a person by force, threats, or illegal power.

• Having found out the whole story, he could now extort the information from her in exchange for his silence.

To extort is literally to wrench something out of someone. *Extortion* is a mainstay of organized crime. Thugs extort "protection" money from business owners with threats of violence, in much the way the school bully extorts lunch money from smaller kids in exchange for not beating them up. And mobsters might extort favors from politicians with threats of revealing some dark secret, just as you might extort a favor from a brother or sister by promising not to tell on them.

torsion \'tȯr-shən\ The twisting or wrenching of a body when one end or part is turned while the other is held fast or turned in the opposite direction.

• The release of the torsion of the rubber band attached to the propeller can send a toy airplane a considerable distance.

Automobile torsion bar suspension uses twisted steel bars to absorb and reduce the effects of bumps. Torsion springs are used in common things such as clothespins and window shades. Torsion testing determines the strength of certain materials when they are twisted. The twisting motion itself is called *torque* (which can also refer to a simple turning motion, such as a car engine delivers to a driveshaft). *Torsion* is also a medical and veterinary term that means the twisting of an internal organ such as the stomach.

tortuous \'tȯr-chù-wəs\ (1) Having many twists, bends, or turns; winding. (2) Crooked or tricky; involved, complex.

• The road over the mountains was long and dangerously tortuous.

A labyrinth is a tortuous maze. The first was built as a prison for the monstrous Minotaur, half bull and half man; only by holding one end of a thread was the heroic Theseus able to enter and slay the Minotaur and then exit. A tortuous problem, a tortuous history, and the tortuous path of a bill through Congress all have many unexpected twists and turns; a tortuous explanation or argument may be too crooked for its own good. (Don't confuse *tortuous* with *torturous*, which means "tortured" or "painfully unpleasant"; *tortuous* has nothing to do with torture.)

VIV comes from *vivere*, the Latin verb meaning "to live or be alive." A *survivor* has lived through something terrible. A *revival* brings something back to life, whether an old film, interest in a long-dead novelist, or the religious faith of a group.

---

convivial \kən-'vi-vē-əl\ Fond of feasting, drinking, and good company.

• It was a relaxed and convivial gathering, and the wine flowed freely.

Convivial, beginning with the prefix *con-,* "with," has come to describe a particularly hearty and enthusiastic manner of enjoying oneself with others. When he wasn't feeling suspicious and paranoid, Henry VIII of England was noted for his *conviviality*, which led to his becoming hugely fat. But *convivial* doesn't mean "drunken" or "rowdy" and needn't involve overeating; what it really means is "merry."

revivify \rē-'vi-və-,fī\ To give new life to; bring back to life.

• All their efforts to revivify the boys' club seemed to be getting them nowhere.

Under President Charles de Gaulle after World War II, the economy and cultural life of France were revivified, enabling it to play a large role in the postwar world. A new recruit can revivify a discouraged football team, and a new director can bring about the *revivification* of a school or museum. Worn-out soil may be revivified by careful organic tending. Notice that *revivify* looks like some other words with very similar meanings, such as *revive, revitalize,* and *reinvigorate.*

vivacious \vī-'vā-shəs\ Lively or sprightly.

• For the cheerleading squad they insisted on only the most outgoing, energetic, and vivacious of the students.

Vivacious today generally describes people, and particularly women. The main female characters in Shakespeare's plays—Beatrice in *Much Ado About Nothing,* Portia in *The Merchant of Venice,* Mistress Quickly in *Henry IV,* and many others—are often full of humor, spirit, and *vivacity.* But *vivacious* can also at times be used to describe a piece of music or writing, or a bright and alert mind.

vivisection \'vi-və-,sek-shən\ Operation on living animals, often for experimental purposes; animal experimentation.

• They agreed to avoid research that involved vivisection and concentrate instead on alternative methods.

Vivisection includes the Latin root *sect,* meaning "cut." The Greek physician Galen, who lived during the 2nd century A.D., practiced vivisection on live monkeys and dogs to learn such things as the role of the spinal cord in muscle activity and whether veins and arteries carry air or blood; his findings formed the basis of medical practice for more than a thousand years. Vivisection continues to be used in drug and medical research today, though often in secret, since some groups are violently opposed to it and want to ban it altogether.

Quizzes

A. Fill in each blank with the correct letter:

a.	revivify	e.	extort
b.	tort	f.	vivisection
c.	vivacious	g.	torsion
d.	tortuous	h.	convivial

1. He was horrified by _____, and even protested the dissecting of frogs in biology class.
2. If the tubes pass the _____ test, we can begin assembly immediately.
3. The party began slowly, but after an hour everyone was in a _____ mood.
4. Two years of steady work had managed to _____ the organization.
5. A toxic _____ is an injury inflicted by a hazardous substance.
6. We carefully made our way down the steep and _____ trail.
7. Marie is the _____ one and Jan is the serious one.
8. He tried to _____ a B from his math teacher, saying that if he couldn't play because of bad grades, they would lose and everyone would blame her.

B. Choose the closest definition:

1. vivacious   a. sweet-tempered b. loud c. lively   d. gluttonous
2. extort   a. obtain by force b. pay up c. engage in crime d. exterminate
3. vivisection   a. living area b. animal experimentation   c. experimental treatment d. removal of organs
4. torsion   a. elasticity b. twisting c. body trunk d. axis
5. convivial   a. life-giving b. drunk c. contrary   d. sociable

6. tortuous a. painful b. winding c. harmful
   d. monstrous
7. revivify a. revive b. reclaim c. retain d. restrain
8. tort a. deformity b. law c. product d. injury

SERV means "to be subject to." A *servant* is the person who *serves* you with meals and provides other necessary *services*. A tennis or volleyball *serve* puts the ball in play much as a servant puts food on the table.

serviceable \'sər-və-sə-bəl\ (1) Helpful or useful. (2) Usable.

• In the attic they found some chairs and a table, which, with a new coat of paint, became quite serviceable for informal get-togethers.

Someone who speaks serviceable Spanish isn't fluent in it but gets by pretty well. A serviceable jacket is practical and maybe even rugged. But *serviceable* sometimes damns with faint praise. A serviceable performance is adequate but not inspired. Serviceable curtains are not the ideal color or pattern, though they *serve* their purpose. A serviceable pair of shoes is sturdy but won't win you any fashion points.

servile \'sər-ˌvīl\ (1) Suitable to a servant. (2) Humbly submissive.

• The dog's manner was servile, and it lacked a healthy independence.

During the Middle Ages, most of the farming was done by a servile class known as *serfs* who enjoyed hardly any personal freedom. This began to change in the 14th century; but the Russian serfs weren't freed until the 1860s, when the servile class in the United States was also freed. *Servile* today often refers to a personal manner; a person who shows *servility* is too eager to please and seems to lack self-respect.

servitude \'sər-və-ˌtüd\ A state or condition of subjection to another; slavery, bondage.

• She spent an entire summer working at the resort under conditions that felt like complete servitude.

Servitude is slavery or anything resembling it. The entire black population of colonial America lived in permanent servitude. And millions of the whites who populated this country arrived in "indentured servitude," obliged to pay off the cost of their journey with several years of labor. Servitude comes in many forms, of course: in the bad old days of the British navy, it was said that the difference between going to sea and going to jail was that you were less likely to drown in jail.

subservient \səb-'sər-vē-ənt\ (1) Serving or useful in an inferior situation or capacity. (2) Slavishly obedient; servile.

• The butler was always careful to make himself subservient to his master's wishes.

Since *sub-* means "below," it emphasizes the lower position of the subservient one. Soldiers of a given rank are always subservient to those of a higher rank, and this *subservience* is constantly symbolized by the requirement that they salute their superior at every opportunity and address him or her in highly respectful terms. Women have often been forced into subservient relationships with men. A small nation may feel subservient to its more powerful neighbor, obliged to obey even when it doesn't want to. So subservience usually brings with it a good dose of resentment.

CLUD/CLUS, from the Latin *claudere*, "to close," appears in *include*, which originally meant "to shut up or enclose" and now means "to contain." *Exclude*, its opposite, means "to expel or keep out"—that is, to close the door to something.

occlusion \ə-'klü-zhən\ An obstruction or blockage; the act of obstructing or closing off.

• The surgeon worried that a loosened piece of plaque from the artery wall would lead to an occlusion of a brain artery resulting in a stroke.

Occlusion, formed with the prefix *ob-*, here meaning "in the way," occurs when something has been closed up or blocked off. Almost all heart attacks are the result of the occlusion of one of the coronary (heart) arteries by a blood clot. When a person's upper and lower teeth form a *malocclusion*, they close incorrectly or badly. An occlusion, or *occluded* front, happens when a fast-moving cold front overtakes a slow-moving warm front and slides underneath it, lifting the warm air and blocking its movement.

preclude \prē-'klüd\ To make impossible or rule out in advance; prevent.

● Phyllis hoped that her decisive action would preclude any possibility that blame would fall on her.

In the 13th century, Genghis Khan and his conquering Mongol hordes would burn the bridges they had just crossed to preclude any possibility of their own retreat. So today, "burning your bridges" usually means leaving a person or job in anger, which precludes you from ever going back. Prejudice may still preclude many Americans from winning public office. And the size of large ships may preclude them from using shallow harbors.

recluse \'re-ˌklüs\ A person who lives withdrawn from society.

● He had long been known in the town as a recluse, so the police were surprised when he called for help.

Greta Garbo and Howard Hughes were probably the most famously *reclusive* celebrities of modern times. She had been a great international star, called the most beautiful woman in the world; he had been an aircraft manufacturer and film producer, with one of the greatest fortunes in the world. It seems that her *reclusiveness* resulted from her desire to leave her public with only the youthful image of her face, and that he desperately wanted to avoid catching germs.

seclusion \si-'klü-zhən\ A screening or hiding from view; a place that is isolated or hidden.

● The police immediately placed him in seclusion in a hospital room, with armed guards at the door.

The addition of the prefix *se-*, "apart," gives the meaning of a place or condition that is "closed away." Presidents and their staffs may go into seclusion before making critical decisions. A lone island may be *secluded*. Monastery life is purposely secluded. The deadly brown *recluse* spider prefers seclusion but is sometimes disturbed by very unlucky people.

Quizzes

A. Complete the analogy:

1. freedom : liberty :: servitude : _____
   a. determination b. arrangement c. bondage d. work
2. permit : allow :: preclude : _____
   a. oppose b. conclude c. avoid d. delay
3. considerate : thoughtless :: subservient : _____
   a. boastful b. commanding c. decisive d. unique
4. monk : pray :: recluse : _____
   a. deny b. receive c. reclaim d. hide
5. fashionable : stylish :: serviceable : _____
   a. useless b. devoted c. fundamental d. adequate
6. progress : advance :: occlusion : _____
   a. dismissal b. obstruction c. prevention d. denial
7. dominant : aggressive :: servile : _____
   a. saving b. sensitive c. submissive d. forgetful
8. conclusion : termination :: seclusion : _____
   a. refusal b. servility c. isolation d. denial

B. Indicate whether the following pairs of words have the same or different meanings:

1. occlusion / stroke   same ___ / different ___
2. subservient / military   same ___ / different ___
3. recluse / hermit   same ___ / different ___
4. serviceable / usable   same ___ / different ___
5. preclude / prevent   same ___ / different ___
6. servitude / slave   same ___ / different ___
7. seclusion / submission   same ___ / different ___
8. servile / humble   same ___ / different ___

Greek and Latin Borrowings

acme \\'ak-mē\\ Highest point; summit, peak.

● Last Saturday's upset victory over Michigan may prove to have been the acme of the entire season.

In Greek, *acme* meant a mountain peak, but in English we hardly ever use it in the physical sense. Instead we speak of someone's new job as the acme of her career, or of a certain leap as the acme of classical dance technique. In old cartoons, the Acme Company seemed to be the provider of every known service and device. It is possible that something called the Acme Bar & Grill may not be the ideal example of a bar and grill, however. (Don't confuse *acme* with *acne*, the skin disorder, even though both actually come from the same word.)

catharsis \kə-'thär-səs\ A cleansing or purification of the body, the emotions, or the spirit.

• He broke down sobbing at the funeral; afterwards, feeling much calmer, he felt that it had been a catharsis.

One of the earliest uses of *catharsis* is in Aristotle's *Poetics,* where the philosopher claims that watching a tragedy provides the spectators with a desirable catharsis because of the buildup and release of the emotions of pity and fear. Freud borrowed the term as a name for the process of bringing a set of repressed desires and ideas back into one's consciousness in order to eliminate their bad effects. Today some people speak of merely expressing anger, grief, or other strong emotions, in order to "get them out of your system," as being *cathartic*. Laxatives are also called cathartic, since they provide a physical catharsis that some people believe to be healthful. But there is no general agreement about any of this, and the notion of catharsis remains a very personal one.

colossus \kə-'lä-səs\ (1) A gigantic statue. (2) A person or thing that resembles such a statue in size or activity or influence.

• Even if *Citizen Kane* had been his only movie, Orson Welles would be regarded as a colossus in the history of film.

The original colossi were the larger-than-life statues made by the Greeks and Romans. The most famous of these was the Colossus of Rhodes, a statue of the sun god Helios that was over 100 feet tall and took more than 12 years to build. The Statue of Liberty is a modern colossus, enormous and stately, at the entrance to New York Harbor. And someone who has played a *colossal* role in history, such as Winston Churchill, may be called a colossus as well.

detritus \di-'trī-təs\ Loose material that results from disintegration; debris.

• The base of the cliff was littered with the detritus of centuries of erosion.

After the first hard freeze of fall, the garden is sadly littered with the detritus of the summer's plants and produce: stalks, leaves, vines, rotted vegetables, and maybe even a hand trowel left behind. As the flooding Mississippi River recedes within its banks, it leaves detritus behind in its wake, debris gathered from everywhere by the raging waters. The detritus of civilization may include junkyards and abandoned buildings; one's mental detritus includes all kinds of useless trivia.

icon \'ī-ˌkän\ (1) An image, symbol, or emblem. (2) A religious image usually painted on a small wooden panel.

• By his death he had become a national icon, symbolizing everything the country stood for in its proud citizens' eyes.

The icons of the Eastern Orthodox church are usually portraits of saints, apostles, or the holy family done in a simple and distinctive style. Worshipers use these images as a focus for their prayers. Nonreligious icons generally represent things or concepts just as simply. A company icon is its symbol, which is generally designed to make it immediately recognizable, especially for advertising purposes. *Icon* today also can often be used in place of *idol*. Pop superstars are frequently called idols or icons, since they are objects of adoration. And we also use the word constantly for the little symbols on a computer screen that lead you to a new function or program. Something *iconic* is usually iconlike or symbolic.

kudos \'kü-ˌdōz\ (1) Fame and renown that result from an achievement; prestige. (2) Praise.

• Anne Tyler earns well-deserved kudos for every new book she writes.

Kudos is an odd word in English. In Greek, *kudos* means a single bit of praise or prestige. But the word looks like an English plural and is therefore often treated as one. So people now sometimes use the form *kudo*, with *kudos* as its plural.

onus \'ō-nəs\ (1) A burden; a disagreeable necessity or obligation. (2) Blame.

• Now that the Congress has passed the bill, the onus is on the President to live up to his promise and sign it into law.

An onus in Latin is literally a "burden," like a particularly heavy backpack. But in English an onus is more frequently a burden of responsibility or blame. In legal language, the *onus probandi* is the "burden of proof" which normally falls on the prosecutor and the plaintiff. It is up to them to prove guilt, since the accused is innocent until proved guilty.

regimen \'re-jə-mən\ A systematic plan of action or treatment, especially one designed to improve and maintain health; a regular course of physical training.

• Her daily regimen included at least an hour of vigorous physical exercise, preferably outdoors.

In Latin *regimen* simply means "rule." But it comes into English meaning a system of rules or guidelines, possibly for living a healthy life or taking a regular dose of exercise. A practical physical regimen includes vigorous exercise for at least 20 minutes several times a week; but dancers, boxers, and other serious athletes may require a regimen as merciless as the *regime* of the cruelest tyrant. A writer or scholar may have just as demanding a regimen, and one that is just as carefully planned and timed.

Quiz

Fill in each blank with the correct letter:

a. kudos	e. icon
b. colossus	f. detritus
c. acme	g. regimen
d. catharsis	h. onus

1. Now that they have apologized, the _____ is on you to do the same.
2. After the storm, _____ washed up by the waves lay all along the beaches.
3. Toni Morrison has become a _____ among modern American novelists.
4. By following a strict _____ of nutrition and exercise, they kept up their strength despite a grueling competition schedule.

5. The billboards on the highway displayed many a familiar _____ of corporate identity.
6. At the _____ of his racing career, Bold Ruler won the Kentucky Derby.
7. During the death scene the theater was filled with sobs, as if the film were providing a _____ for the viewers.
8. The winner of each year's pennant race wins _____ from the commentators.

Review Quizzes

A. Complete the analogy:

1. sharp : blunt :: astringent : _____
   a. biting b. mild c. puckering d. harsh
2. demanding : effortless :: tortuous : _____
   a. twisting b. winding c. straight d. descending
3. include : omit :: preclude : _____
   a. occur b. permit c. prevent d. decide
4. criticism : error :: kudos : _____
   a. praise b. prestige c. blame d. achievement
5. experiment : subject :: vivisection : _____
   a. botany b. biology c. bacteria d. animals
6. rise : descend :: construe : _____
   a. condemn b. continue c. contend d. confuse
7. appropriate : take :: expropriate : _____
   a. proclaim b. seize c. expel d. complete
8. warm : passionate :: acerbic : _____
   a. distrustful b. sarcastic c. witty d. cheerful
9. praise : compliment :: onus : _____
   a. load b. habit c. obligation d. reputation
10. capable : helpless :: serviceable : _____
    a. useless b. useful c. practical d. formal

B. Fill in each blank with the correct letter:

a. extort   c. appropriate
b. exacerbate   d. constrict

e. detritus	k. vivacious
f. convivial	l. colossus
g. servitude	m. stringent
h. infrastructure	n. propriety
i. icon	o. occlusion
j. seclusion	

1. The collapsing bridge was only the latest evidence of the city's deteriorating _____.

2. The company's _____, a winged horse, stood for the speed of gasoline-powered travel.

3. The _____ of the mountain hut was just what she needed to begin serious work on her book.

4. On the remote farm the foster children lived in a condition of genuine _____, often working from dawn to dusk.

5. They often joined their neighbors for a _____ evening of Scrabble or charades.

6. The steep bank had become a dumping ground, and _____ of all kinds lay at the bottom.

7. His diet had been terrible for years, so he wasn't surprised when the doctor reported a near _____ of one coronary artery.

8. The company's new standards of _____ prohibited taking any large gifts from salespeople.

9. All the machine parts had to meet _____ government requirements for strength and durability.

10. The statue for the plaza would be a 30-foot-high _____ representing Atlas holding the globe.

11. She had been a _____ teenager but became rather quiet and serious in her thirties.

12. She was forced to practically _____ the money from her husband with threats.

13. Dr. Moss warned him that any drinking would only _____ his condition.

14. The legislature had decided to _____ funds for new harbor facilities.

15. She feared that marriage and a family would _____ her life unbearably.

C. Choose the closest definition:

1. prestigious   a. massive b. solemn c. ancient d. honored
2. deconstruction   a. analysis b. destruction
      c. breaking d. theory
3. acme   a. monument b. peak c. honor d. award
4. subservient   a. arrogant b. submissive c. demanding
      d. underneath
5. torsion   a. wrenching b. tension c. suspension
      d. portion
6. instrumental   a. instructive b. intelligent
      c. important d. fortunate
7. catharsis   a. explosion b. cleansing c. pollution
      d. cough
8. acrid   a. pleasant b. crazed c. irritating d. soothing
9. regimen   a. law code b. training plan c. rule of
      thumb d. government
10. recluse   a. spider b. hermit c. request d. hiding place
11. acrimony   a. breakup b. dispute c. bitterness
      d. custody
12. propriety   a. misbehavior b. suitability
      c. harassment d. drama
13. servile   a. efficient b. pleasant c. submissive
      d. unnerving
14. tort   a. cake b. twist c. wrong d. law
15. revivify   a. retreat b. rewrite c. reappear d. restore

Unit 23

TEXT comes from a Latin verb that means "to weave." Individual words are "woven" into sentences and paragraphs to form a *text*. A *textile* is a woven or knitted cloth. The material the cloth is made from determines its *texture*, the smoothness or roughness of its surface.

context \\'kän-ˌtekst\\ (1) The surrounding spoken or written material in which a word or remark occurs. (2) The conditions or circumstances in which an event occurs; environment or setting.

• The politician claimed his remarks were taken out of context, and that if we would look at the whole speech we would get a more favorable impression.

Context reveals meaning. The context of an unfamiliar word can give us *contextual* clues to help us determine what the word means. Taking a remark out of context can change its meaning entirely. Likewise, people's actions sometimes have to be understood as having occurred in a particular context. The behavior of historical figures should be seen in the context of their time and culture, in which ethical standards may have differed greatly from our own.

pretext \\'prē-tekst\\ A purpose, motive, or appearance put forward to conceal the real intention or condition.

• She managed to go along on the expedition under the pretext of providing help with recording information.

A pretext provides an excuse—a false reason for doing something when it's necessary or desirable to keep the real reason hidden. Often the real reason just doesn't seem good enough. Someone bored with a chore might use a minor or imaginary illness as a pretext for quitting. Hostile nations sometimes use minor incidents as a pretext for going to war.

subtext \'səb-ˌtekst\ The underlying meaning of a spoken or written passage.

• The tough and cynical tone of the story is contradicted by its romantic subtext.

A literary text often has more than one meaning: the literal meaning of the words on the page, and the hidden meaning of the work as a whole—the subtext. The subtext of a play is found in what exists "between the lines." Arthur Miller's play *The Crucible*, for example, is literally about the Salem witchcraft trials of the 17th century. The subtext of the play, however, is the comparison of those trials with the "witch hunts" of the 1950s, when many people were unfairly accused of being communists.

textual \'teks-chù-wəl\ Having to do with or based on a text.

• The class spent several hours doing a detailed textual analysis of the poem.

Before the invention of the printing press, books were produced by hand. When the *text* of a book is copied this way, textual errors can creep in, and a text that has been copied again and again can contain many such errors. By comparing different copies of a work, textual critics try to figure out where the copyists went wrong and restore the text to its original form so that modern readers can again enjoy the correct versions of ancient texts.

PLAC/PLAIS comes from the Latin *placere*, "to please or be agreeable to," or *placare*, "to soothe or calm." *Pleasant, pleasurable,* and *pleasing* all derive from this root.

---

complaisant \kəm-'plā-zənt\ (1) Seeking to please or oblige. (2) Consenting to the wishes of others.

• The legislature was criticized at first for being too complaisant, agreeing to everything the White House wanted.

Complaisant comes from Latin by way of French. It is easily confused with *complacent*, a related adjective that comes directly from Latin and has the meaning "self-satisfied" or "unconcerned." Someone who readily goes along with what you want to do is complaisant. Someone who doesn't care about what you want to do may be complacent.

placebo \plə-'sē-bō\ A harmless substance given to a patient in place of genuine medication, either for experimental purposes or to soothe the patient.

• The placebo worked miraculously: his skin rash cleared up, his sleep improved, and he even ceased to hear voices.

Doctors doing research on new treatments for disease often give one group a placebo while a second group takes the new medication. Since those in the placebo group usually believe they are getting real medication, their own hopeful attitude may bring about improvement in their physical condition. The real medication must thus produce even better results than the placebo in order for the drug to be considered effective. Placebos have another use as well. If a doctor suspects that a patient's symptoms are psychologically produced, he or she may prescribe a placebo in the hope that mentally produced symptoms can also be mentally cured.

placidity \pla-'si-də-tē\ Serene freedom from interruption or disturbance; calmness.

• Her placidity seemed eerie in view of the destruction she had recently witnessed and the huge loss she had suffered.

Someone with a *placid* disposition has an inner peacefulness that is not easily disturbed. The placidity of such a person is not always admired. The ability to bear bad news *placidly* can suggest a strong character, but it can also suggest a dull mind. Few creatures are more placid, after all, than a contented cow.

implacable \im-'pla-kə-bəl\ Not capable of being pleased, satisfied, or changed.

• Attempts to negotiate a peace settlement between such implacable enemies seem doomed to failure.

Implacable adds the negative prefix *im-* to the root to describe something that cannot be calmed or soothed or altered. A person who carries a grudge feels an implacable resentment—a resentment that can't be soothed. The surest way to achieve a goal is to set your mind to it with implacable determination.

Quizzes

A. Fill in each blank with the correct letter:

a. placebo
b. textual
c. complaisant
d. context

e. subtext
f. implacable
g. pretext
h. placidity

1. His calm response taken out of _____ made him sound rash and unreasonable.
2. No one thought she could do it, but they didn't count on her _____ determination.
3. She came over to talk to us about her own predicament on the _____ of giving us advice about our problems.
4. He wanted to be helpful without seeming to be too _____.
5. The deeper meaning of a literary work lies in its _____.
6. The group of patients given a _____ did as well as those who were given the drug.
7. Careful _____ analysis is important in the study of poetry.
8. The _____ of the quiet countryside was soothing after a week in the city.

B. Match the word on the left to the correct definition on the right:

1. complaisant
2. context
3. placebo
4. textual
5. placidity
6. subtext
7. implacable
8. pretext

a. relating to written matter
b. unchangeable
c. underlying meaning
d. eager to please
e. setting of spoken or written words
f. harmless substance
g. excuse hiding a real motive
h. peacefulness

AUT/AUTO comes from the Greek word for "same" or "self." Something *automatic* operates by itself, and an *automobile* is a vehicle that moves by itself, without a horse or locomotive. An *autograph* is written by the person him- or herself, and an *autopsy* is an inspection of a corpse by an examiner's own eyes.

automaton \ȯ-'tä-mə-tən\ (1) An automatic machine, especially a robot. (2) An individual who acts mechanically.

• John's position as a welder in the assembly plant had been taken over by a sophisticated automaton designed overseas.

Early automatons included such machines as clocks and mechanical dolls. Today the robots in industrial plants often mimic human workers. The plural of *automaton* may be written *automata,* just as in Latin.

autodidact \ˌȯ-tō-'dī-ˌdakt\ A self-taught person.

• While his friends shied away from schoolwork, Kingsley consumed text after text at home with the intensity of a born autodidact.

The word *didactic,* taken from the Greek, refers to teaching. Autodidacts, or self-teachers, have frequently been the most serious students. Since college and even high school were available to few Americans before this century, some of our most brilliant figures have been autodidacts—among many others, Benjamin Franklin, Walt Whitman, and Thomas Edison.

autonomy \ȯ-'tä-nə-mē\ (1) The power or right of self-government. (2) Self-directing freedom and especially moral independence.

• Normally respectful of their son's autonomy, the Slocums drew the line at his request to take a cross-country motorcycle trip.

Since *nomos* is Greek for "law," an *autonomous* person or unit makes its own laws. The amount of autonomy enjoyed by French-speaking Quebec, or of Palestinians in certain towns in Israel, or of independent-minded regions of Russia, have become major issues. The autonomy of individual states in the United States has posed serious constitutional questions for two centuries.

autism \'ȯ-ˌti-zəm\ Absorption in self-centered mental activity such as fantasies, delusions, and hallucinations, often accompanied by withdrawal from reality.

• He had been watching Sophie drift into a kind of autism that November—sitting all day in her apartment with the shades drawn, refusing to answer the phone.

Autism, in its strict sense, becomes evident before the age of 3 and afflicts about 1 in 3,000 children, mostly boys. The *autistic* child generally refuses to talk, becomes obsessive about toys, resists any change vehemently, and sometimes flies into unexplained rages. Autism is believed to be biological in origin. The word is now used more loosely by writers to describe psychological withdrawal of a much more common sort in adults.

GRAT comes from *gratus,* the Latin word meaning "pleasing, welcome, or agreeable," or from *gratia,* meaning "grace, agreeableness, or pleasantness." A meal that is served *graciously* will be received with *gratitude* by *grateful* diners, unless they want to risk being called *ingrates.*

---

gratify \'gra-tə-ˌfī\ (1) To be a source of pleasure or satisfaction; give pleasure or satisfaction to. (2) To give in to; indulge or satisfy.

• It gratified him to see that his daughter had worked so hard and become an important member of the team.

A *gratifying* experience is quietly pleasing or satisfying. Gratifying an impulse involves giving in to it, which is not always such a good idea. Some people, though, seem to want instant *gratification* of every impulse and desire they feel, failing to recognize that the truly gratifying accomplishments in life take time.

gratuity \grə-'tü-ə-tē\ Something, especially a tip, given freely.

• They left a generous gratuity for the waiter as thanks for his excellent service.

Gratuity is a fancier and more formal word than *tip*. It occurs most often in written notices along the lines of "Gratuities Accepted."

Its formality makes it best suited for describing tips of the dignified, expensive variety. For the taxi driver who takes you to the famous French restaurant, it's a tip. For the restaurant's maitre d', it's a gratuity.

gratuitous \grə-'tü-ə-təs\ (1) Done or provided freely. (2) Not called for by the circumstances.

• The members of the committee were objecting to what they considered gratuitous violence on television.

In its original sense, *gratuitous* can refer to anything given freely, but the word now almost always applies to something that is seen as unnecessary and unwelcome. Sex and violence on television are called gratuitous by people who feel that they serve no purpose other than to improve ratings. To insult or criticize someone *gratuitously* is to make a hurtful remark that is uncalled for and undeserved.

ingratiate \in-'grā-shē-ˌāt\ To gain favor or acceptance by making a deliberate effort.

• Her attempts to ingratiate herself with the teacher did nothing to improve her grade.

To ingratiate yourself is to put yourself in someone's good graces, which means to gain someone's approval or favor. People often try to ingratiate themselves by engaging in an activity known by such unflattering names as *bootlicking, apple-polishing,* and *brownnosing,* to name only a few. But some people are able to win favor just by relying on their *ingratiating* smiles.

Quizzes

A. Complete the analogy:

1. ratify : approve :: gratify : _____
   a. use b. please c. thank d. repay
2. victory : surrender :: autonomy : _____
   a. restraint b. freedom c. law d. self-repair
3. entertain : amuse :: ingratiate : _____
   a. seek gratitude b. seek fame c. seek favor d. seek thanks

4. automation : manual labor :: automaton : _____
   a. robot b. computer c. gadget d. human being
5. necessary : unwelcome :: gratuitous : _____
   a. thankless b. unthinking c. welcome d. uncalled for
6. autograph : self-written :: autodidact : _____
   a. oneself b. self-taught c. self-reliant d. learned
7. bonus : salary :: gratuity : _____
   a. obligation b. thankfulness c. refusal d. bill
8. paranoia : suspicion :: autism : _____
   a. sleep b. withdrawal c. anger d. fear of cars

**B. Indicate whether the following pairs of words have
the same or different meanings:**

1. august / grand   same ___ / different ___
2. gratuity / tip   same ___ / different ___
3. auxiliary / essential   same ___ / different ___
4. gratuitous / deserved   same ___ / different ___
5. augment / dignify   same ___ / different ___
6. gratify / please   same ___ / different ___
7. authorize / bar   same ___ / different ___
8. ingratiate / contribute   same ___ / different ___

CLAM/CLAIM comes from the Latin verb *clamare,* meaning "to shout or cry out." An *exclamation* is a cry of shock, joy, or surprise. A *proclamation* is read loudly enough so that all can hear its important message.

acclamation \,a-klə-'mā-shən\ (1) A loud, eager indication of approval, praise, or agreement. (2) An overwhelming yes vote by cheers, shouts, or applause.

• The students agreed by long and loud acclamation to the principal's suggestion that Friday be made a holiday honoring the victors in the math olympics.

Approval can come from a single person, but acclamation requires a larger audience. An *acclaimed* movie is widely praised, winning the kind of critical *acclaim* that usually leads to box-office success.

If a proposal at a political meeting is greeted by thunderous cheers and shouts of approval, it may be said to have passed by acclamation, with no counting of votes being necessary.

clamor \\'kla-mər\\ (1) Noisy shouting or loud, continuous noise. (2) Strong and active protest or demand.

• The clamor of the construction being done next door made it hard for her to concentrate on reading.

City traffic makes a clamor, as does a group of schoolchildren at recess. The clamorous noise of a typewriter is heard less and less in this age of computers. Another kind of clamor is quieter but can be just as hard to ignore. A political scandal might lead to a public clamor for the resignation of an elected official, and a newspaper's editorials might *clamor* for the passage of a new law.

declaim \\di-'klām\\ To speak in the formal manner of someone delivering a speech.

• Almost any opinion can sound convincing if declaimed loudly and with conviction.

Declaim suggests an unnatural kind of speech best suited to a stage or podium. Listening to an actor declaim a literary passage can be enjoyable. Listening to Aunt Gertrude at Sunday dinner declaiming on the virtues of roughage, however, is not so enjoyable. Most people don't appreciate being treated as an audience, and good advice is usually more welcome when it's not given in a *declamatory* style.

reclamation \\ˌre-klə-'mā-shən\\ The act or process of restoring to use through reformation or rehabilitation or recovery.

• The reclamation of that land, once the site of a huge landfill, took several years and a lot of work.

Making wild or overgrown land suitable for farming or other human uses is one kind of reclamation. Allowing cultivated or otherwise altered land to be *reclaimed* by nature, returning it to its wild state, is another kind. Both kinds of land reclamation are widely practiced, but the second kind is becoming more and more popular as people throughout the world gain a greater appreciation for the importance of wild things.

CRAC/CRAT comes from the Greek word meaning "power." Attached to another root, it indicates which group holds the power. With *demos,* the Greek word for "people," it forms *democracy,* a form of government in which the people rule. In a *meritocracy,* people earn power by their own merit. A *theocracy,* from the Greek *theos,* "god," is government based on divine guidance.

aristocrat \ə-'ris-tə-ˌkrat\ (1) A member of the hereditary nobility or of a government by a small privileged class. (2) One thought to be superior of its kind.

• Although raised as a wealthy aristocrat, she took up the cause of the poor and homeless.

Aristos means "best" in Greek. Aristocrats hold power or position because they are thought somehow to be the "best people,"usually because of their birth. The French Revolution was aimed at taking power from the *aristocracy* whose lives of privilege contrasted so greatly with the lives of ordinary citizens. In the course of the Revolution, many French aristocrats were sent to the guillotine, including King Louis XVI and his wife, Marie Antoinette. In the United States there is no formal aristocracy—no noble titles or hereditary right to rule—but certain people and families have achieved an almost *aristocratic* status because of their wealth or political influence.

autocratic \ˌȯ-tə-'kra-tik\ (1) Having to do with a form of government in which one person rules. (2) Resembling the ruler of such a government.

• She was a good teacher, but her autocratic manner made her hard to like.

Autos in Greek means "same" or "self." In an autocratic government—an *autocracy*—one person holds all the power. A dictatorship is an autocratic form of government. True *autocrats* are relatively rare, but teachers, parents, and football coaches can all be autocratic in their own way.

bureaucrat \'byu̇r-ə-ˌkrat\ (1) An appointed government official. (2) An official of a government or system that is marked by fixed and complex rules that often result in long delays.

● To settle his insurance claim he had to make his way through a dozen bureaucrats, every one of them with new forms to fill out.

Despite the bad-mouthing they often get, bureaucrats do almost all of the day-to-day work that keeps a government running. The idea of a *bureaucracy* is to split up the complicated task of governing a large country into smaller jobs that can be handled by specialists. *Bureaucratic* division of government is nothing new. The Roman Empire had an enormous and complex bureaucracy, with the bureaucrats at lower levels reporting to bureaucrats who were their superiors, and so on up to the Emperor himself.

plutocracy \plü-'tä-krə-sē\ (1) Government by the wealthy. (2) A controlling class of wealthy people.

● American social reformers in the early 20th century sought to limit the power held by the plutocracy of wealthy industrialists.

Pluto was the Roman god of the underworld, and thus keeper of all the mineral wealth of the earth. So a plutocracy governs or wields power through its money. The economic growth in the United States in the late 19th century produced a group of enormously wealthy *plutocrats*. The new wealth and the economic importance of huge companies like John D. Rockefeller's Standard Oil conferred very real political power on those companies' owners. Not only was Rockefeller able to get special treatment from other businesses, but he was also able to influence legislation in states where his businesses operated. For this reason, it was said in 1905 that Ohio and New Jersey were plutocracies, not democracies.

Quizzes

A. Fill in each blank with the correct letter:

a.	plutocracy	e. reclamation
b.	declaim	f. bureaucrat
c.	aristocrat	g. acclamation
d.	clamor	h. autocratic

1. It took forever for the application to make its way from one _____ to another.
2. The assembly approved the proposal by enthusiastic _____.

3. Their _____ grandfather ran the family as if it were a dictatorship.

4. I got tired of hearing him _____ about how much better things were when he was young.

5. She had the expensive education and fine manners of a true _____.

6. The town has voted funds for the _____ of that tract of contaminated land out by the airport.

7. His enormous wealth made him a member of a small _____ of powerful industrialists.

8. The proposed new tax was met with a _____ of protest.

B. Match the word on the left to the correct definition on the right:

1. autocratic   a. recovery
2. declaim   b. noble
3. plutocracy   c. noisy din
4. acclamation   d. government official
5. reclamation   e. speak formally
6. bureaucrat   f. ruled by one person
7. clamor   g. rule by the rich
8. aristocrat   h. acceptance with cheers

PUNG/PUNC comes from the Latin verb *pungere*, meaning "to prick or stab," and the noun *punctum*, meaning "point." A period is a form of *punctuation* that is literally a point. A *punctured* tire, pricked by a sharp point, can make it hard to be *punctual*—that is, to arrive "on the dot" or at a precise point in time.

compunction \kəm-'pəŋk-shən\ (1) Anxiety caused by guilt. (2) A slight misgiving or scruple.

● Speeding is something many people seem to do without compunction.

To feel compunction is to feel the sharp sting or prick of conscience. The word *compunction* is most often used in describing people who don't feel it. Hardened criminals have no compunctions about committing their crimes. Ruthless businessmen steal clients and contracts from other ruthless businessmen without compunction.

expunge \ik-'spənj\ To remove, erase, or destroy.

• After years of good behavior, all mention of his juvenile criminal career was expunged from his record.

Expunge comes directly from the Latin *expungere,* which means ''to mark for deletion with dots.'' In English, the material expunged is no longer marked with dots but is erased or removed completely. It is easier to expunge something written down than it is to expunge a memory.

punctilious \ˌpəŋk-'ti-lē-əs\ Marked by exact agreement or conformity to the details of codes or conventions.

• A good proofreader has to be punctilious about matters of spelling and punctuation.

A *punctilio* is a small point—a minor detail of conduct in a ceremony or in the observance of a code. A person who pays close attention to such minor details is punctilious. *Punctiliousness* can be valuable in the right circumstances, but you don't want to become so concerned about small points that you fail to pay attention to the large ones.

pungent \'pən-jənt\ (1) Having a sharp, cutting quality. (2) Sharp or harsh to the sense of taste or smell.

• We could smell the pungent aroma of the spicy Indian food before we even entered the restaurant.

Someone with a pungent wit has a sharp sense of humor. Many people enjoy the aroma and flavor of pungent food, even if it does make their eyes water. The *pungency* of a cheap cigar can have the same effect, but it's more likely to clear a room than to draw a crowd.

PLIC comes from the Latin verb *plicare,* ''to fold.'' A *complicated* subject has many folds or wrinkles. A person who is *implicated* in a crime is ''wrapped up'' in it somehow. The person's involvement may become *explicit*—"unwrapped" or revealed—when the details of the crime unfold.

implicit \im-'pli-sət\ (1) Understood though not put clearly into words. (2) Being without doubt; absolute.

• Even though no one said so, the implicit assumption was that they'd all meet for lunch as usual.

Implicit has the root meaning of "wrapped up in" or "contained in." It is one of the adjective forms of *imply,* so it often means "implied" or "understood." Truly close friends have an implicit understanding. They know without saying it that they can call on each other for help. Friends like that trust each other *implicitly,* having a kind of faith that is so complete and absolute that it "goes without saying."

explicate \'ek-splə-ˌkāt\ (1) To explain in detail. (2) To analyze logically and clearly.

• The entire class was spent in explicating a difficult passage in the novel.

When students are asked to explicate a poem in an English class, they are expected to "unfold" it and explain its meaning. An *explication* includes not just a summary of a literary work, but also a detailed discussion and analysis of its themes and images. A long poem like T.S. Eliot's *The Waste Land* might require separate explications for each section before the whole poem is understood.

replicate \'re-plə-ˌkāt\ To copy or reproduce.

• The results of the experiment proved to be impossible to replicate.

Exact *replication* of a scientific experiment shows that the results of the experiment are valid and can be trusted. A genetic experiment might involve the process by which DNA replicates, producing an exact copy or *replica* of itself every time a cell divides. Scientists are finding ways to replicate this natural process in the laboratory.

supplication \ˌsə-plə-'kā-shən\ A humble and earnest request or prayer.

• The convicted criminal fell to his knees in supplication, begging the judge for mercy.

In the biblical story, Daniel continues his daily supplications to his God even though such prayers have been outlawed by the Babylonian king Darius. The king's princes and ministers are jealous of Daniel and insist that he be thrown into the lion's den as the law requires. But the God of the Hebrews protects his loyal *supplicant*: Daniel escapes unharmed, the princes who condemned him are themselves thrown to the lions, and no amount of *supplicating* can save them.

Quizzes

A. Choose the closest definition:

1. explicate a. explain b. bend c. fold d. mutilate
2. expunge a. mop up b. partially restore c. remove completely d. hesitate slightly
3. supplication a. substitution b. plea c. use d. subdivision
4. pungent a. sharp b. rotten c. round d. funny
5. punctilious a. pointed b. careful c. prompt d. unusual
6. replicate a. reflect b. breed c. copy d. measure
7. compunction a. desire b. bravery c. scruple d. conviction
8. implicit a. difficult b. unspoken c. written d. faithful

B. Indicate whether the following pairs of words have the same or different meanings:

1. pungent / smoky   same ___ / different ___
2. replicate / divide   same ___ / different ___
3. expunge / erase   same ___ / different ___
4. supplication / prayer   same ___ / different ___
5. compunction / threat   same ___ / different ___
6. explicate / analyze   same ___ / different ___
7. punctilious / absurd   same ___ / different ___
8. implicit / unclear   same ___ / different ___

Greek and Latin Borrowings

ambrosia \am-'brō-zhə\ (1) The food of the Greek and Roman gods. (2) Something extremely pleasant to taste or smell.

• To the hungry hikers, the simple stew tasted like ambrosia.

Ambrosia literally means ''immortality'' in Greek, and only immortals—gods and goddesses—could eat ambrosia in Greek and Roman mythology. Their drink was *nectar* (though sometimes the two are reversed). Both may have been divine forms of honey. Both were also used like oils for ceremonial anointing by the gods, and a mixture of water, oil, and fruits called ambrosia came to be used in human ceremonies as well. Since we cannot know what the mythical ambrosia tasted or smelled like, we mere mortals are free to give the name to our favorite *ambrosial* dessert.

dogma \'dȯg-mə\ (1) Something treated as established and accepted opinion. (2) A principle or teaching, or a body of principles or teachings, set forth by a church.

• New findings about the ways in which animals communicate challenge the current dogma in the field.

Religious dogma and scientific dogma are sometimes at odds, as they are in arguments between those who believe in the biblical story of creation and those who believe in evolution. Arguments of any kind are harder to resolve when both sides are *dogmatic* in their beliefs, since it's the nature of any dogma to resist change.

gratis \'gra-təs\ Without charge; free.

• Refreshments were supplied gratis for everyone attending the convention.

Gratis is used both as an adjective—''The drinks were gratis''— and as an adverb—''The drinks were furnished gratis.'' However it's used, it means ''free.'' *Gratis* comes from the Latin word for ''favor.'' In English, a party favor is a small item given gratis to everyone attending a party.

eureka \yu̇-'rē-kə\ An exclamation used to express triumph and delight on a discovery.

• The town of Eureka in the California mountains is named for the cries of delight by prospectors when they discovered gold in them there hills.

Eureka, or *heurēka,* means "I have found" in Greek. The story goes that the Greek inventor Archimedes, given the task of determining the purity of gold in a crown, shouted "Eureka!" one day after he stepped into a bath, making water slop over the side, and realized that the amount of water displaced indicated the bulk of his body, but that a larger body made of lighter matter might weigh the same but would displace more water. Thus, a crown in which lighter metal had secretly been mixed with the gold would reveal itself in the same way. The story may not be true, but we still shout "Eureka!" when we make a sudden, welcome discovery.

factotum \fak-'tō-təm\ (1) A person with many different jobs or responsibilities. (2) A general servant responsible for a variety of housework.

• His job title was "Executive Assistant," but basically he was a factotum who did all the jobs nobody else had time for.

In Latin *factotum* means literally "do everything," and that's just what a modern-day factotum does. Every organization seems to have a factotum responsible for all the daily details that fall outside everyone else's job description. This person often goes unnoticed until he or she is absent or gone—when suddenly no one makes the coffee, or picks up the mail, or takes messages, or just generally makes it easier for work to get done.

opus \'ō-pəs\ A creative work, especially a musical composition or set of compositions numbered in order of publication.

• Beethoven's Ninth Symphony is also known as Opus (Op.) 125.

A literary opus is often a single novel, though the word may sometimes refer to all of a writer's works. But *opus* normally is used for musical works. Mendelssohn's Opus 90 is his *Italian Symphony,* for example, and Brahms's Op. 77 is his Violin Concerto. Since many composers' works were never given opus numbers in an orderly way, they now often have catalog numbers assigned by later scholars. Haydn's Symphony No. 104 is Hob. 104 (Hob. is short for Anthony van Hoboken, the cataloger), and Mozart's *Marriage of Figaro* is K.492 (K. stands for Ludwig Köchel).

impetus \'im-pə-təs\ (1) A driving force or impulse; something that makes a person try or work hard; incentive. (2) Momentum.

● The promise of a bonus gave everyone an added impetus for finishing the project on time.

An impetus can be something positive and pleasant, or it can be something negative and unpleasant, but in either case it stimulates action. The need to earn a living provides many people with an impetus to drag themselves out of bed five mornings a week. On the other two days, the impetus might be the smell of bacon cooking or the anticipation of an early-morning round of golf.

thesis \'thē-səs\ (1) An opinion or proposition that a person presents and tries to prove by argument. (2) An extended paper that contains the results of original research, especially one written by a candidate for an academic degree.

● She's done all the classwork needed for her Master's degree, but she hasn't yet completed her thesis.

In college and graduate school, students often have to write a thesis on a topic in their major field of study. A student studying history might write a thesis on the economic causes of the War of 1812, based on original research. In an extended essay of this type, the student may put forth several theses (note the plural form) and prove or disprove each in turn, depending on how they support or contradict the main thesis or argument of the paper.

Quiz

Fill in each blank with the correct letter:

a.	gratis	e.	thesis
b.	ambrosia	f.	opus
c.	factotum	g.	eureka
d.	impetus	h.	dogma

1. With composers like Handel or Schubert, each _____ seems greater than the one before.
2. This sauce could be _____, it tastes so delicious.
3. Medical _____ used to call for treating epilepsy and depression by stimulating the muscles with electrical current.

4. He's the office _____, and we really couldn't function without him.
5. She wrote her _____ on the portrayal of women in the works of Nathaniel Hawthorne.
6. _____! I found my mittens!
7. The souvenirs were distributed _____ to anyone who stopped to see the display.
8. The looming deadline provided everyone with an _____ for working late.

Review Quizzes

A. Complete the analogy:

1. shout : whisper :: clamor : _____
   a. noise b. din c. quiet d. confusion
2. barrier : stop :: impetus : _____
   a. force b. go c. trip d. work
3. explanation : reason :: pretext : _____
   a. intention b. article c. excuse d. disguise
4. helpful : servant :: autocratic : _____
   a. friend b. enemy c. teacher d. tyrant
5. turmoil : war :: placidity : _____
   a. peace b. dullness c. trouble d. smoothness
6. alas : disappointment :: eureka : _____
   a. distress b. woe c. distance d. discovery
7. professor : students :: autodidact : _____
   a. self b. government c. mechanism d. instruction
8. praise : applaud :: replicate : _____
   a. reduce b. pursue c. copy d. unfold

B. Fill in each blank with the correct letter:

a. acclamation
b. ingratiate
c. supplication
d. context
e. declaim
f. ambrosia
g. automaton
h. dogma
i. plutocracy
j. thesis
k. autonomy
l. complaisant

m. punctilious   o. expunge

n. subtext

1. To her fellow workers she resembled an _____ as she sped around the office with never a sideways glance.

2. He had such a _____ attitude that he was willing to agree to almost anything.

3. By taking his remarks out of _____, the papers made him look like a crook.

4. The government was controlled by a _____ of wealthy businessmen.

5. Her attempts to _____ herself with the new management were resented by the other workers.

6. She was always so _____ about being on time that everyone worried when she was late.

7. He had to revise his _____ twice before he was able to receive his degree.

8. He was ready to refuse the request, but her earnest and desperate _____ for help changed his mind.

9. Shouts and cheers of _____ greeted the winning candidate.

10. The dinner was nothing special, but the dessert was pure _____.

11. He finally had to sue to get the Army to _____ the information from his file.

12. She stood before the crowd and began to _____ in the tones of a practiced politician.

13. The remote tribe was granted limited _____, including self-policing rights and freedom from taxation.

14. Her theory was controversial because it disagreed with the established _____.

15. The deeper meaning of a literary work is found in its _____.

C. Choose the closest definition:

1. aristocrat   a. noble   b. power   c. ruler   d. office worker

2. pungent   a. sweet   b. sharp   c. blunt   d. explosive

3. gratuity   a. fee   b. service   c. obligation   d. tip

4. opus   a. achievement   b. composition   c. burden   d. talent

5. reclamation   a. return b. retreat c. restoration
      d. resumption
6. explicate   a. detain briefly b. maintain indefinitely
      c. explain clearly d. regain eventually
7. autism   a. self-absorption b. self-governance
      c. authenticity d. authority
8. gratis   a. irritating b. grateful c. inexpensive d. free
9. gratify   a. unify b. donate c. satisfy d. modify
10. factotum   a. computer printout b. carved pole
      c. plumber d. servant
11. implacable   a. impossible to place b. impossible to
      change c. impossible to say d. impossible to like
12. textual   a. of an idea b. of a manuscript c. on an
      assumption d. on a hunch
13. placebo   a. one-celled animal b. medical instrument
      c. harmless substance d. peaceful mood
14. implicit   a. unforeseen b. unsaid c. unintended
      d. unexpected
15. bureaucrat   a. furniture maker b. politician
      c. official d. servant

Unit 24

MAND/MEND comes from *mandare*, Latin for "entrust" or "order." A *command* and a *commandment* are both orders. A *commando* unit carries out orders for special military actions. A *recommendation* may entrust, praise, or advise.

commendation \,kä-men-'dā-shən\ (1) The awarding of praise, often with a formal citation or a recommendation. (2) A formal citation of merit or thanks.

● The city awarded him a commendation for exceptional bravery in rescuing two children from the fire.

One is generally *commended* for a particular act or quality. We may commend a child for her hard work or commend a dog for his patience. A commendation likewise recognizes something specific—a high grade on an exam, an extraordinary athletic performance, or 25 years of working at the same company.

mandate \'man-,dāt\ (1) A formal command; permission to act, given by the people to their representatives. (2) To order or direct; require.

● The new President claimed that his landslide victory was a mandate from the people to enact his programs.

Mandate is both a noun and a verb. The Clean Air Act mandated new restrictions on pollution from industries; that is, the Act was a mandate from Congress to clean up pollutants. Elections are often interpreted as mandates from the public for certain kinds of action. But since a politician is always an individual as well as the symbol of certain beliefs or policies, it can often be risky to interpret election as mandating anything at all.

mandatory \'man-də-ˌtȯr-ē\ Required, compulsory.

● Unfortunately, attendance at the meeting was mandatory; otherwise she would have just gone home.

Something mandatory is the result of a *mandate* or order. Today there seem to be a lot of mandates: mandatory seat belts, mandatory inspections for cars and industries, mandatory prison sentences for violent crimes, mandatory retirement at certain ages, and so on, are regularly in the news. What is mandatory is the result of laws, rules, and regulations; and schools, companies, and religions, as well as governments and parents, may all lay down their own requirements.

remand \ri-'mand\ (1) To order a case sent back to another court or agency for further action. (2) To send a prisoner back into custody to await further trial or sentencing.

● The state supreme court remanded the case to a lower court, instructing it to consider the new evidence.

Remand means "order back" or "send back." After losing a case in a lower court, lawyers will frequently appeal it to a higher court. If the higher court looks at the case and sees certain kinds of errors made by the lower court, it will simply send the case back, telling the lower court what it failed to do the first time: the judge's instructions to the jury may have been incorrect, for example, or a recent related court decision may not have been considered.

UND comes into English from the Latin words *unda*, "wave," and *undare*, "to rise in waves," "to surge or flood." *Undulations* are waves or wavelike things or motions. To *undulate* is to rise and fall in a wavelike way.

---

inundate \'i-nən-ˌdāt\ (1) To cover with a flood or overflow. (2) To overwhelm.

● The radio station was inundated with requests for the new song.

In the summer of 1993, record rains in the Midwest caused the Mississippi River to overflow its banks, break through levees, and inundate the entire countryside. Such an *inundation* had not been seen for at least a hundred years. The area was soon inundated with phone calls from friends checking to see if everyone was safe, which were followed by inundations of food, blankets, clothing, and medicines.

redound \ri-'daůnd\ (1) To have an effect for good or bad. (2) To rebound or reflect.

• Such generous actions redound to the credit of the entire community.

Redound has had a confusing history. The modern meaning "result" may have arisen because flowing back is a result of the original flowing—on a beach, for example. *Redound* has long been confused with other words such as *resound* and *rebound,* and today "rebound" is another of its standard meanings. So we can say that the prohibition of alcohol in 1919 redounded unintentionally to the benefit of gangsters such as Al Capone, and that the jailing of Capone on tax evasion charges redounded to the credit of the famous "Untouchables."

redundancy \ri-'dən-dən-sē\ (1) The state of being superfluous, extra, or unnecessary. (2) Needless repetition.

• A certain amount of redundancy can help make a speaker's points clear, but too much can be annoying.

Redundancy, closely related to *redound,* has stayed close to the original meaning of "overflow" or "more than necessary." Avoiding redundancy is one of the prime rules of good writing. "In the modern world of today" contains a redundancy; so does "he died of fatal wounds" and "for the mutual benefit of both parties." But redundancy occurs in more than just language. "Data redundancy" means the keeping of the same computer data in more than one place, and a backup system in an airplane may provide redundancy for the sake of safety.

undulant \'ən-jů-lənt\ (1) Rising and falling in waves. (2) Wavy in form, outline, or surface.

• The dancer's movements became sinuous, undulant—almost snakelike.

The surface of a freshly plowed field is undulant, and so is the edge of a scallop shell. A field of wheat or hay will *undulate* or sway in the wind, like the waves of the sea. In fact, any wavy surface can be described as undulant, from the shifting sands of the Sahara Desert to the mattress of a waterbed.

Quizzes

A. Fill in each blank with the correct letter:

a. redound	e. remand
b. commendation	f. inundate
c. undulant	g. mandate
d. mandatory	h. redundancy

1. Because an ''adage'' is an ''old saying,'' to say ''old adage'' is a _____.
2. This _____ for valor above and beyond the call of duty comes with our deepest thanks.
3. The _____ water of the pool beckoned them into its cool depths.
4. This court decision was interpreted as a _____ to continue to work toward absolute equality in the workplace.
5. Such generosity in victory will _____ to the credit of the whole team.
6. The judge will probably _____ this case to the lower court for further study.
7. Requests for private interviews _____ the office these days.
8. The session on business ethics is _____ for all employees.

B. Match the definition on the left to the correct word on the right:

1. needless repetition	a. mandate
2. required	b. undulant
3. flood	c. commendation
4. formal citation	d. redundancy
5. reflect	e. inundate
6. direct	f. remand
7. wavy	g. mandatory
8. send back	h. redound

SACR/SANCT, meaning "holy," comes from the Latin words *sacer* and *sanctus*. A *sacrament* such as the bread and wine of Christian communion is a way of receiving holy grace. The person who receives it is *sanctified* or "made holy" by it; this holiness or *sanctity* is believed to result from God's grace.

sanction \'saŋk-shən\ (1) To give approval to. (2) Official approval; a measure intended to enforce a law or standard.

• The bill's opponents claimed that legalization of drugs would officially sanction drug use.

Sanction originally meant "make holy"—that is, "give official church approval to." Now it often has nothing to do with a church but generally involves an institution of some kind. A government may sanction, or "give its blessing to," a private transaction, or a college may sanction the use of office space by a gay organization. With its noun form, *sanction* can be slightly confusing, since it often means an enforcement measure and thus is rather negative. Government sanctions against a country (usually sanctions forbidding trade) are extremely unfriendly, and criminal sanctions against selling marijuana can be harsh. But a company sanction for leaving work early on a snowy day is simply approval.

sacrilege \'sa-krə-lij\ Gross disrespect toward a revered person, place, or thing; blasphemy.

• The barbarians who sacked the Roman temples committed gross sacrilege.

Sacrilege contains the root *leg-*, meaning "to steal," and describes the acts of vandalism and theft of *sacred* objects of the kind that marked almost every conquest in the ancient world. *Sacrilegious* acts continue to this day in areas of religious conflict, such as India, with its long history of strife between Muslim and Hindu believers, and the Middle East. But the word is more widely used in its broader meaning. A booklover may regard the harming of books as almost sacrilegious, and environmentalists see the plundering of old forests and the destruction of wetlands as a *desecration* and a sacrilege.

sacrosanct \'sa-krō-ˌsaŋkt\ (1) Most sacred or holy. (2) Treated as if holy and therefore immune from criticism or disturbance of any kind.

• The governor's education program is sacrosanct to members of her own party.

Sacrosanct means literally "made holy by a sacred rite," and in its original use *sacrosanct* was reserved for things of the utmost holiness. But generally *sacrosanct* now tends to imply a supposed but not genuine sacredness that nevertheless makes something immune from attack or violation. That is, the speaker usually doesn't regard the thing in question as at all sacred. Thus, to call a government program sacrosanct is to imply that others regard it as untouchable. And a piece of writing is more likely to be regarded as sacrosanct by its author than by the editor who has to fix it up.

sanctuary \'saŋk-chů-ˌwer-ē\ (1) A holy place, such as a church or temple, or the most holy part of one. (2) A place of safety, refuge, and protection.

• The midtown park is a tranquil sanctuary amidst the city's heat, noise, and bustle.

Historically, churches have been places where fugitives could seek at least temporary refuge from the law. In Anglo-Saxon England, churches and churchyards generally provided 40 days of immunity. But gradually the right of sanctuary was eroded. In 1486 sanctuary for the crime of treason was disallowed; sanctuary for most other crimes was severely restricted by Henry VIII and later abolished. In the 1980s U.S. churches often provided sanctuary to political refugees from El Salvador and the U.S. government mostly chose not to interfere. Today, *sanctuary* is used for other places providing safety and protection. A wildlife sanctuary provides protection for the species within its boundaries. A monastery can be a sanctuary from the turmoil of the modern world.

LOC/LOQU comes from the Latin verb *loqui,* "to talk." An *eloquent* preacher speaks fluently, forcefully, and expressively. A dummy's words come out of a *ventriloquist's* mouth (or perhaps out of his belly, or *venter*).

---

circumlocution \ˌsər-kəm-lō-ˈkyü-shən\ (1) The use of an unnecessarily large number of words to express an idea or to avoid stating a position or opinion directly. (2) Evasion in speech.

• When faced with a hard question, the senator would resort to pleasant-sounding circumlocution.

Circumlocution is "talking around" a subject, usually to avoid making a direct statement, and can include all kinds of long-winded language. Many businesspeople specialize in circumlocutions. The elaborate courtesy of phrases like "I wonder if it might be at all possible that . . ." is a harmless variety of circumlocution. The Defense Department has long been fond of euphemism and circumlocution: in Operation Desert Storm for example, the "collateral damage" caused by U.S. bombs actually referred to the killing of thousands of unarmed Iraqi citizens. "Metabolically challenged" may be a nice new way of saying "dead," but there are several nice old ways as well.

elocution \ˌe-lə-ˈkyü-shən\ The art of effective public speaking.

• Elocution is no longer taught in school, and our appreciation for eloquence has suffered as a result.

The Greek orator Demosthenes was one of the greatest public speakers of the ancient world, but his *eloquence* did not come easily. Legend has it that he originally had a speech defect, but he taught himself proper elocution by reciting poetry while running or out of breath, practicing in front of a mirror, and speaking with his mouth full of pebbles. To keep himself working at it, he shaved half his head so he would be embarrassed to go out in public. His hard work paid off: he became an important leader in Athens, and his speeches are still studied today. But great speeches are rare in the United States today; only three or four speakers are widely admired for their elocution.

colloquial \kə-ˈlō-kwē-əl\ Conversational or informal in style.

• The author, though obviously a professional writer, had chosen to use a colloquial style for her new book.

Colloquial language is the language almost all of us speak. It uses contractions ("can't," "aren't," "wouldn't"), possibly some slang, lots of short words and not many long ones. But when we write, our language usually changes, becoming more formal and sometimes even "literary." Many people will never write a contraction or use the word "I" except in notes and letters, and avoid informal words completely. But colloquial language isn't necessarily bad in writing and sometimes is the most appropriate style to use.

loquacious \lō-'kwā-shəs\ Apt to talk too much; talkative.

• She just wanted to read quietly on the plane, but the loquacious salesman in the next seat made it nearly impossible.

A loquacious writer might write a 1,200-page novel; luckily, book-binding technology often won't allow them to go on any longer. Loquacious letters used to go on for pages, though they seem to be a thing of the past. But *loquacity* in speech has gone on and on for centuries and will always be with us.

Quizzes

A. Choose the closest definition:

1. sanction   a. criminalize b. punish c. trade d. approve
2. elocution   a. public opinion b. public speaking
    c. public platform d. public transportation
3. sacrilege   a. religion b. blasphemy c. priest
    d. conviction
4. sacrosanct   a. sacred b. churchlike c. Christian
    d. priestly
5. loquacious   a. abundant b. silent c. talkative
    d. informative
6. sanctuary   a. belief b. holiness c. cemetery d. refuge
7. colloquial   a. slangy b. disrespectful
    c. conversational d. uneducated
8. circumlocution   a. exaggeration b. excess of words
    c. falsehood d. confusion

B. Indicate whether the following pairs of words have the same or different meanings:

1. elocution / memorization   same ___ / different ___
2. sanction / permit   same ___ / different ___
3. loquacious / long-winded   same ___ / different ___

4.	sacrosanct / converted	same ___ / different ___
5.	circumlocution / correction	same ___ / different ___
6.	sanctuary / morgue	same ___ / different ___
7.	colloquial / informal	same ___ / different ___
8.	sacrilege / outrage	same ___ / different ___

VIR is Latin for "man." A *virtue* is a good quality—originally, the kind of quality an ideal man possessed. And *virtuous* behavior is morally excellent. All in all, the Romans seemed to believe that being a man was a good thing.

---

triumvirate \trī-'əm-və-rət\ (1) A commission or government of three. (2) A group or association of three.

• Slowly a triumvirate emerged as the inner circle of the White House, and the Vice President was not among them.

The first triumvirate of the Roman Republic, which consisted of Julius Caesar, Pompey, and Crassus, was not a formal institution of the government but simply an alliance or partnership. The alliance did not last long, however, and Caesar emerged finally with total power. After his assassination, a second triumvirate took over, with Octavian, Mark Antony, and Lepidus dividing the Roman world between themselves. But these *triumvirs* also soon turned on one another, and Octavian alone held power as the Emperor Augustus. From these historical alliances the word has come into English, and now we can talk about a triumvirate of city council members—or even perhaps a triumvirate of sanitation workers.

virago \və-'rä-gō\ (1) A loud, bad-tempered, overbearing woman. (2) A woman of great stature, strength, and courage.

• The staff called her a virago and other things behind her back, but everyone was awed by her abilities.

The most famous virago in English literature is the ferocious Kate in Shakespeare's *The Taming of the Shrew*. Some historical viragoes have also become famous. Agrippina poisoned her husband, the Emperor Claudius, so that her son Nero could take his place, but was eventually killed by Nero himself. And Queen Eleanor of Aquitaine, a powerful and respected virago of the 12th century, was imprisoned by her husband, King Henry II of England, after she encouraged their sons to rebel against their father. Today *virago* is often used admiringly, which was not always the case.

virility \və-'ri-lə-tē\ Energetic, vigorous manhood; masculinity.

• He was convinced that anyone who had been a Marine had established his virility beyond any doubt.

Luckily, there is no doubt about what virility is, since it is depicted on the covers of dozens of new romance novels every month. A masterful and dominating manner, a splendid bared chest, a full head of lustrous hair, and an array of stunning costumes seem to be what is required. And such *virile* men can probably be expected to be perfect in almost every other way as well.

virtuosity \,vər-chù-'wä-sə-tē\ Great technical skill, especially in the practice of a fine art.

• The guitarist's virtuosity doesn't show through in the band; you have to hear him solo to appreciate him.

Virtuosity is used particularly to describe musicians but also often for writers, actors, dancers, and athletes. A *virtuoso* is a highly skilled performer, especially a musician, and a *virtuoso* performance is one that astonishes the audience by its feats. In ancient Greece the cities would hold male competitions in acrobatics, conjuring, public reciting, blowing the trumpet, and acting out scenes from Homer's epics, the winners of which would have been praised as *virtuous,* or "full of manly virtues."

VAL has as its basic meaning "strength," from the Latin verb *valere,* meaning "to be worthy, strong, or healthy" and "to have power or influence." A *valid* proof is one that provides strong evidence and can be used to *validate* or *invalidate* a claim. Of course, the evidence must be *evaluated* to confirm its *validity.*

---

equivalent \i-'kwi-və-lənt\ (1) Equal in force, amount, value, area, or volume. (2) Similar or virtually identical in effect or function.

• A square can be equivalent to a triangle in area, but not in shape.

Modern democracies have institutions and offices that are roughly equivalent to those found in others: the President of the United States has his British equivalent in the Prime Minister, and the U.S. Congress finds its equivalent in the British Parliament. The heavily armored knight on his great armored horse has been called the Middle Ages' equivalent of the army tank. Obviously, none of these examples are identical to each other; they are simply very similar in their effect or purpose or nature, which is what *equivalence* usually implies.

prevalent \\'pre-və-lənt\\ Widely accepted, favored, or practiced; widespread.

• On some campuses Frisbees seem to be more prevalent than schoolbooks, especially in the spring.

Many diseases that were prevalent a century ago have been controlled by advances in medicine. The most dramatic example may be smallpox. Throughout history, smallpox epidemics were prevalent all over the world; Europeans brought it with them to the Americas, where it killed more Native Americans than the armed settlers did. As late as 1967, over two million deaths were caused by smallpox. But medical science *prevailed* over the disease: after years of an aggressive vaccination program, scientists announced that the disease had been wiped out.

valorous \\'va-lə-rəs\\ Courageous, brave, heroic.

• The gun duels of the Old West were the invention of a novelist, who modeled them on the tournaments of valorous knights of the Middle Ages.

Valor, or "bravery," in uniform is still rewarded by medals, but *valorous* is a word that tends to describe warriors of the past, as does *valiant,* which means the same thing. The knights of the Middle Ages often engaged in activities we wouldn't consider particularly valorous, however. In the 10th century the Catholic Church had to declare a policy designed to prevent the "valorous" knights from attacking unarmed peasants, pilgrims, merchants, and clergymen, and to prevent them from burning crops and villages. And during the Crusades, the Christian knights couldn't be kept from looting and destroying Constantinople, the capital city of the Christian Byzantine Empire that they were supposed to be saving.

validate \'va-lə-ˌdāt\ (1) To make legally valid; give official approval to. (2) To support or confirm the validity of.

● Only experiments of this kind will be able to validate Tompkins's theory.

Validating a pass might require getting an official stamp on it. Validating experimental data might require checking it against data from further experiments. An A on a test might validate a student's abilities. A President might try to validate a foreign dictator who is serving our national interest. And a trusted friend can validate your decision to buy a pet iguana or to sell everything and move to Las Vegas.

Quizzes

A. Fill in each blank with the correct letter:

a. virago	e. valorous
b. virtuosity	f. validate
c. triumvirate	g. prevalent
d. virility	h. equivalent

1. Some people think a man's _____ fades with age.
2. He's desperate for someone to _____ his artwork, but none of his friends really like it.
3. The orchestra has a new soloist whose _____ has already made her a star.
4. Colds and flu threaten to be unusually _____ this winter.
5. Like the _____ she is, she strode forcefully out and ordered the hunters off her land.
6. We may not be able to find an identical chair, but surely we'll be able to find an _____ one.
7. The company is really run by a _____; that is, Bailey, Sanchez, and Dr. Ross.
8. Each winter some unwise skater falls through thin ice and needs to be rescued by a _____ passerby.

B. **Match the word on the left to the correct definition on the right:**

1. prevalent   a. brave
2. virago   b. masculinity
3. virtuosity   c. confirm
4. virility   d. strong woman
5. valorous   e. skill
6. triumvirate   f. widespread
7. equivalent   g. three-person board
8. validate   h. similar in value

CRE/CRET comes from the Latin verb *crescere,* which means both "to come into being" and "to grow." A *crescendo* in music occurs when the music is growing louder, a *decrescendo* when it is growing softer.

accretion \ə-'krē-shən\ (1) Growth or enlargement by gradual buildup. (2) A product of such buildup.

• The house and barn were linked by an accretion of outbuildings, each joined to the one next to it.

The land area of the Mississippi Delta increases every year from the accretion of soil washed down the Mississippi River, but the accretions usually happen so slowly that it is difficult to detect any increase at all. The slow accretion of scientific knowledge over many centuries has turned into an avalanche in our time.

crescent \'kre-sənt\ (1) The moon between new moon and first quarter and between last quarter and the next new moon. (2) Anything shaped like the crescent moon, with a convex and a concave edge.

• The symbol of Islam is a crescent moon with a star between the points, an astronomical impossibility.

The roughly crescent-shaped area stretching from the Persian Gulf up the Tigris and Euphrates Rivers across to Lebanon and Israel and into Egypt down the Nile River, all known as the Fertile Crescent, was the birthplace of civilization. It was here that weaving, pottery, irrigation farming, and writing all first appeared, as well as numerous other aspects of culture. The civilization that developed in the Fertile Crescent formed the basis of Greek and Roman civilization. Other crescents aren't nearly so exotic: a *crescent wrench* can be found in almost any household, and a *croissant*, or crescent pastry, is a breakfast staple. *Crescent* simply means "growing," since a crescent moon is in the process of growing to a full moon.

excrescence \ek-'skre-səns\ (1) A projection of growth, especially when abnormal. (2) A disfiguring, unnecessary, or unwanted mark or part.

• The new building squatted like some hideous excrescence on the landscape.

Warts and pimples are common excrescences that can usually be wiped out with medication; other excrescences such as cysts and tumors need to be removed surgically. Mushrooms are excrescences from underground fungus networks. Some people consider slang words vulgar excrescences on the language, while others consider slang the most colorful words of all.

increment \'iŋ-krə-mənt\ (1) Something gained or added, especially as one of a series of regular additions or as a tiny increase in amount. (2) The amount or extent of change, especially the positive or negative change in value of one or more variables.

• Her bank account had grown weekly by increments of $30 for the past two years.

Increment is used in many technical fields, but also nontechnically. *Incremental* increases in drug dosages are used for experimental purposes. Incremental tax increases are easier to swallow than sudden large increases. Rome wasn't built in a day, as the saying goes; instead it was built up by increments from a couple of villages in the 10th century B.C. to the capital of the Mediterranean world in the 1st century A.D.

FUND/FUS, from the Latin verb *fundere*, "to pour out" or "to melt," pours forth English words. A *fuse* depends on melting metal to break an overloaded circuit. A *refund* pours money back into your pocket. *Confusion* results when so many things are poured together that they can't be sorted out.

diffuse \di-'fyüz\ To pour out and cause to spread freely; to extend or scatter.

• Around 1000 B.C. the use of iron was diffused along ancient trade routes, along with knowledge of how to work with it.

Lamplight can be diffused and softened by pointing the lamp at a light-colored ceiling. Diffusing your creative energies (by trying to do several things at once, for instance) is the opposite of focusing them, just as diffused light is the opposite of focused light. The adjective *diffuse* (meaning "unfocused" or "unorganized and long-winded") is spelled the same but pronounced differently. Don't mix up *diffuse* and *defuse,* which means "to make less harmful."

effusive \i-'fyü-siv\ (1) Given to excessive display of feeling. (2) Freely expressed.

• She repaid all her supporters with effusive thanks that lasted nearly a half hour.

Since to *effuse* is to "pour out," an effusive person makes a habit of pouring out emotions. Greeting someone *effusively* may include giving great hugs and wet kisses. Academy Award winners tend to become embarrassingly effusive once they've grabbed the microphone. But at least *effusiveness* is generally an expression of positive rather than negative emotions.

profusion \prə-'fyü-zhən\ Great abundance.

• In May the trees and flowers bloom with almost delirious profusion.

A profusion is literally a "pouring forth," so a profusion of gifts is a wealth or abundance of gifts. *Profuse* apologies are abundant, as are profuse thanks and profuse relief. A *profusely* illustrated book is lavishly filled with pictures, and a profusely planted garden is overflowing with different plants. And this paragraph has now supplied a profusion of examples.

suffuse \sə-'fyüz\ To spread over or through as fluid or light spreads; to flush or fill.

• As the soft light of dawn suffused the landscape, they could hear the loons crying over the lake.

The odors of baking may suffuse a room, and so may the light of a sunset. Emotions may spread as well. A face may be suffused (that is, filled, but also probably flushed) with joy, or hope, or love. A group may be suffused with a glow of pleasure. And a novel may be suffused with anger.

Quizzes

A. Choose the closest definition:

1. excrescence   a. disgust b. outgrowth c. extremity
        d. unusual formation
2. suffuse   a. overwhelm b. flow c. spread through
        d. inject
3. accretion   a. layer b. eruption c. decision d. buildup
4. effusive   a. emotional b. gradual c. continual
        d. general
5. increment   a. entrance b. slight increase
        c. construction d. income
6. diffuse   a. consider b. make harmless c. spread
        widely d. pour in
7. crescent   a. pie-shaped b. half-full c. sickle-shaped
        d. increasing
8. profusion   a. distinction b. abundance c. addition
        d. completion

B. Indicate whether the following pairs of words have the same or different meanings:

1. effusive / gushy   same __ / different __
2. crescent / graceful   same __ / different __
3. diffuse / scatter   same __ / different __
4. excrescence / grotesqueness same __ / different __
5. suffuse / fill   same __ / different __
6. increment / excess   same __ / different __
7. profusion / amount   same __ / different __
8. accretion / destruction   same __ / different __

Greek and Latin Borrowings

apologia \ˌa-pə-'lō-jē-ə\ A defense, especially of one's own ideas. opinions, or actions.

● His resignation speech was an eloquent apologia for his highly controversial actions as chairman.

An apologia and an *apology* are not always the same thing. An apology is generally an admission of wrong and an excuse, but an apologia rarely *apologizes* in this sense. In 1992 some of the books published for the 500th anniversary of Columbus's voyage were apologias explaining why European powers such as Spain acted as they did in the New World: because, for example, the Aztecs were a cruel and barbaric people, practicing human sacrifice in grotesque ways (victims were skinned, and their skins were worn by the high priests), and Christianity would do them good. The Christian Spanish Inquisition, however, was also committing atrocities at the same time—but that is the subject of other apologias. These apologias. instead of apologizing for the acts, attempt to explain and justify them.

atrium \'ā-trē-əm\ An open rectangular patio around which a house is built; a court with a skylight in a many-storied building.

● Best of all, their new home had a large atrium, where they could have a summer breakfast in the fresh air.

The enclosed atriums of several buildings in New York City have full-size trees growing in them and are lined with balconies from which hang ivies and other vines. This is a far cry from the atrium open to the sky that stood at the center of an ordinary Roman villa. This open courtyard allowed air to circulate and light to enter; and its plantings added to the comfort and coolness of the house.

oligarchy \'ä-lə-ˌgär-kē\ A government in which power is in the hands of a small group.

● The nation's people were shackled by an iron-willed oligarchy that dictated every aspect of their lives and ruthlessly crushed any hint of rebellion.

In ancient Greece, an aristocracy was government by the "best" (in Greek, *aristos*) citizens. An oligarchy was a corrupted aristocracy, one in which a few evil men unjustly seized power and used it to further their own ends. *Oligarchy* combines the Greek words *oligos,* meaning "few," and *archos,* meaning "leader or ruler." It has been used in English to describe and condemn oppressive governments since at least 1542.

encomium \en-'kō-mē-əm\ Glowing, enthusiastic praise, or an expression of such praise.

• She was overwhelmed by the encomiums heaped on her after winning the Most Valuable Player award.

Encomium comes from the Greek and literally means "in celebration." The British Poet Laureate is expected to compose poetic encomiums to mark special events or to praise a person honored by the state. Any awards banquet is thick with encomiums, with each speaker effusively praising the person being honored.

neurosis \nù-'rō-səs\ A mental and emotional disorder that is less severe than a psychosis and may involve various pains, anxieties, or phobias.

• He had a neurosis about dirt, and was constantly washing his hands because of it.

A neurosis is a form of mental disorder: unexplained attacks of anxiety, unreasonable fears such as a fear of cats (called ailurophobia), and mentally-caused illnesses are all examples of *neurotic* conditions. A superstitious person might be suffering from a harmless neurosis, compulsively knocking on wood or avoiding anything with the number 13. But a severe neurosis such as agoraphobia (the fear of crowds or open spaces) can be very harmful, making a person a prisoner of his or her home. *Neurosis* is based on the Greek word for "nerve," since until quite recently neurotic behavior was often blamed on the nerves.

opprobrium \ə-'prō-brē-əm\ (1) Something that brings disgrace. (2) A public disgrace that results from conduct considered wrong or bad.

• The writers of the New Testament hold the Pharisees up to opprobrium for their hollow spirituality.

Witches have long been the objects of opprobrium, especially in the 16th and 17th centuries when they were burned by the thousands. The *opprobrious* crime of treason could result in the most hideous torture and execution. The sin of adultery in Puritan times brought opprobrium on Hester Prynne in *The Scarlet Letter*. But today mere smokers, or even overweight people, may feel themselves to be the objects of mild opprobrium.

referendum \ˌre-fə-'ren-dəm\ (1) The referring of legislative measures to the voters for approval or rejection. (2) A vote on such a measure.

• The referendum on the new tax needed for construction of the new hospital passed by seven votes.

A referendum is a measure that is *referred* to the people. Such referenda tend to be local and state issues, and a few questions usually appear on the ballot at election time. A pressing issue might result in a special referendum. Typical referenda items involve new zoning ordinances, new taxes for schools, and limits on spending.

ultimatum \ˌəl-tə-'mā-təm\ A final proposal, condition, or demand, especially one whose rejection will result in forceful action.

• Saddam Hussein ignored the ultimatum to withdraw from Kuwait, which resulted in U.S. and U.N. intervention.

An ultimatum is usually issued by a stronger power to a weaker one, since it wouldn't carry much weight if the one giving the ultimatum couldn't back up its threat. Near the end of World War II, the Allied powers issued an ultimatum to Japan: surrender unconditionally or face the consequences. Japan rejected the ultimatum, and eight days later the United States dropped an atomic bomb on Hiroshima, leveling the city and killing almost 200,000 people.

Quiz

Fill in each blank with the correct letter:

a. encomium   c. neurosis
b. ultimatum   d. atrium

e. apologia   g. referendum
f. oligarchy   h. opprobrium

1. His particular _____ was a fear of heights.
2. After twenty years, the shadowy ruling _____ was facing growing accusations of corruption and brutality.
3. The committee voted to submit the new zoning plan to the voters in a special _____.
4. The new office building was designed around a wide, sunlit _____ with a fountain and small trees.
5. He offered an _____ for the tough measures but refused to change his mind about enforcing them.
6. _____ was heaped on the school board from angry parents on both sides of the issue.
7. When peace negotiations fell apart, an angry _____ was issued by the government.
8. In her speech, the new company president gave a glowing _____ to her staff members.

Review Quizzes

A. Complete the analogy:

1. church : temple :: sanctuary : _____
   a. destination b. parish c. destiny d. refuge
2. relaxed : stiff :: colloquial : _____
   a. conversational b. talkative c. casual d. formal
3. portion : segment :: increment : _____
   a. inroad b. inflation c. increase d. instinct
4. reprimand : scolding :: encomium : _____
   a. warm drink b. warm thanks c. warm toast d. warm praise
5. truce : treaty :: ultimatum : _____
   a. decision b. negotiation c. threat d. attack
6. sentence : convict :: remand : _____
   a. case b. jury c. court d. judge
7. monarchy : king :: oligarchy : _____
   a. dictator b. ruling group c. emperor
   d. totalitarian

8. cavity : hole :: excrescence : ____
    a. growth b. deposit c. residue d. toad
9. rare : scarce :: prevalent : ____
    a. unique b. commonplace c. thick d. preferred
10. evaporate : dry up :: inundate : ____
    a. flood b. drain c. wash d. irrigate
11. reprimand : dishonor :: commendation : ____
    a. invention b. bravery c. valor d. honor
12. seductress : kitten :: virago : ____
    a. cub b. cow c. tigress d. hen
13. generous : stingy :: effusive : ____
    a. emotional b. thoughtful c. restrained d. passionate
14. release : restrain :: sanction : ____
    a. disapprove b. bless c. train d. welcome
15. femininity : man :: virility : ____
    a. female b. girl c. woman d. lady

B. Fill in each blank with the correct letter:

a. referendum   i. apologia
b. profusion   j. opprobrium
c. crescent   k. diffuse
d. validate   l. equivalent
e. virtuosity   m. loquacious
f. circumlocution n. sacrosanct
g. redundancy   o. redound
h. mandate

1. Although he was shy at first, he became downright ____ once he felt at home.
2. The crystal globes would ____ the light and cast a series of soft rainbows.
3. This award will ____ to your honor for years to come.
4. The Russian flag's hammer and sickle resemble the Islamic star and ____.
5. The planning board submitted their proposal to the voters as a nonbinding ____.
6. He resorted to ____ rather than own up to his part in the disaster.
7. Every politician claims he or she has a ____ from the voters, no matter how small their margin of victory was.

8. Under the new boss, no one here is ____ and anyone could be fired tomorrow.

9. She was renowned for her ____ in the kitchen, whipping up delicious meals from any ingredients that came to hand.

10. The bower was hung with roses blooming in great ____.

11. His public ____ for his conduct toward his staff members helped clear up some of the misunderstandings.

12. He hoped the new sales figures would ____ his belief that he was the company's best salesman.

13. The neo-Nazi group marching down Pennsylvania Avenue was greeted with ____ from passersby.

14. The computer files contain a great deal of data ____ which should be removed.

15. Driving 60 miles per hour is ____ to driving about 100 kilometers per hour.

C. Match the definition on the left to the correct word on the right:

1. open courtyard   a. elocution
2. emotional disorder   b. undulant
3. spread over   c. valorous
4. accumulation   d. triumvirate
5. courageous   e. suffuse
6. public speaking   f. accretion
7. blasphemy   g. atrium
8. wavelike   h. neurosis
9. required   i. sacrilege
10. three-person group   j. mandatory

Unit 25

VERB comes from the Latin *verbum*, meaning "word." A *verb*— or action word—appears in some form in every complete sentence. To express something *verbally*—or to *verbalize* something—is to say it or write it.

verbose \vər-'bōs\ Using more words than are needed; wordy.

• The writing style in government publications has often been both dry and verbose—a deadly combination.

Americans brought up on fast-paced television have lost any patience they once had for *verbosity*. So most American writing is brisk, and American speakers usually don't waste many words. But many of us love our own voices and opinions and don't know we're being verbose until our listeners start stifling their yawns. And students still try to get ahead by stuffing their term papers with unneeded verbosity.

proverb \'prä-,vərb\ A brief, often-repeated statement that expresses a general truth or common observation.

• A favorite proverb in many households is "Waste not, want not."

Proverbs probably appeared with the dawn of language. Sayings such as "A stitch in time saves nine," or "Pride goeth before a fall," or "Least said, soonest mended," or "To everything there is a season" *verbalize* nuggets of homespun wisdom. The convenient thing about proverbs is that there is often one for every point of view. For every "Look before you leap" there is a "He who hesitates is lost." "A fool and his money are soon parted" can be countered with "To make money you have to spend money." A cynic once observed, "Proverbs are invaluable treasures to dunces with good memories."

verbatim \vər-'bā-təm\ In the exact words; word for word.

• The desperate writer lifted verbatim long passages from an earlier, forgotten biography of the statesman.

Verbatim comes directly from Latin into English with the same spelling and meaning. Memorizing famous speeches, poems, or literary passages is a good way to both train the memory and absorb the classic texts of our literature and culture. At one time the ability to recite verbatim the Gettysburg Address, the beginning of the Declaration of Independence, and classic speeches from Shakespeare was the mark of the well-educated person.

verbiage \'vər-bē-ij\ An excess of words, often with little content; wordiness.

• The agency's report was full of the verbiage for which bureaucrats are justly famous.

Verbiage generally tries to disguise a lack of real substance or clarity of thought. Doctoral dissertations, government reports, and political speeches are only a few of the literary forms that have shown an unfortunate tendency toward empty verbiage.

SIMIL/SIMUL look very *similar* to each other and, not surprisingly, come from a similar source. *Simil* comes from the Latin adjective *similis,* meaning "like," "resembling," or "similar." *Simul* comes from the Latin verb *simulare,* "to make like." Between them, these two roots are responsible for a host of English words, such as *simultaneous,* "at the same time," and *facsimile,* "an exact copy."

---

assimilate \ə-'si-mə-ˌlāt\ (1) To take in and thoroughly understand. (2) To take into the culture or customs of a population or group.

• One of the traditional strengths of American society has been its ability to assimilate one group of immigrants after another.

Assimilate comes from the Latin verb *assimulare,* "to make similar." *Assimilate* originally applied to the process by which food is taken into the body and absorbed into the system. In a similar way, a fact can be taken into the mind, thoroughly digested, and absorbed into one's store of knowledge. A newcomer to a job or a subject must assimilate an often confusing mass of information; only after it has been thoroughly absorbed can the person make intelligent use of it. A general population assimilates a group of outsiders by gradually removing their language and other foreign characteristics and having them adopt those of the larger group.

simile \'si-mə-lē\ A figure of speech, introduced by *as* or *like,* that makes a point of comparison between two things distinctly different in all other respects.

• When composing his love poems, Evan strives to create similes that go beyond the tried-and-true "your lips are like cherries."

Fiction, poetry, and philosophy have been full of similes for centuries; in fact, the oldest literature known to us uses similes, along with their close relatives known as metaphors. This suggests that they are an essential part of imaginative writing, probably in all times and all cultures. "And like a thunderbolt he falls" is a simile, since it makes a specific comparison. "The road was a ribbon of moonlight" can be called a metaphor, though "The road was like a ribbon of moonlight" would be a simile.

simulacrum \ˌsim-yu̇-'la-krəm\ (1) An image or representation of something. (2) A superficial likeness or imitation.

• The jeweled eagle statuette was a reasonable simulacrum of the original, she thought, and probably good enough to fool the buyer.

In the original sense of the word, a simulacrum is simply a representation of something, such as an oil painting, a marble statue, a wax figure, or a plastic figurine. Because a simulacrum, no matter how skillfully done, is not the real thing, the usual sense of the word today emphasizes the notion of superficiality or insubstantiality. A simulacrum is usually a pale or even very inadequate imitation of the original. A faded, once-grand hotel may be a pitiful simulacrum of its former self. A gossipy biography will often turn out to present an unconvincing simulacrum of a complex person's life.

simulate \'sim-yə-ˌlāt\ (1) To take on the appearance or effect of something, often in order to deceive. (2) To make a realistic imitation of something, such as a physical environment.

● The Air Force uses sophisticated machines to simulate actual flying conditions in its training program.

The zircon, that favorite of home shopping channels, simulates a diamond—more or less. A skilled furrier can dye lower-grade furs to simulate real mink. A skilled actor can simulate a range of emotions, from absolute joy to crushing grief. A complex apparatus can simulate an environment by reproducing under test conditions what is likely to occur in the real world; one that simulates the hazards of driving while intoxicated is likely to provide some very real benefits.

Quizzes

A. Fill in each blank with the correct letter:

a.	simulacrum	e.	proverb
b.	verbiage	f.	simile
c.	simulate	g.	verbose
d.	verbatim	h.	assimilate

1. Please quote me _____ or don't "quote" me at all, was what she told the reporter.
2. Most students can't _____ so much information all at once, so they approach it gradually.
3. He turned out to be a _____ old windbag, and I slept through the whole lecture.
4. I can't offer you real maple syrup; just an inferior _____.
5. She tried to _____ pleasure at the news, but she could barely manage a smile.
6. Our grandmother recites one _____ after another, hoping to instruct us in the truths of life.
7. The use of unnecessary _____ often makes it harder to make sense of what is being said.
8. An occasional _____ can make any explanation clearer.

B. Complete the analogy:

1. garbage : food :: verbiage : _____
    a. boxes b. verbs c. words d. trash

2. create : invent :: assimilate : _____
   a. wring b. absorb c. camouflage d. drench
3. frequently : often :: verbatim : _____
   a. later b. closely c. differently d. exactly
4. painting : portrays :: simulacrum : _____
   a. imitates b. shows c. demonstrates d. calculates
5. cartoon : reality :: proverb : _____
   a. instinct b. experience c. authority d. fantasy
6. inflate : expand :: simulate : _____
   a. reveal b. entrap c. devote d. imitate
7. dense : sparse :: verbose : _____
   a. poetic b. concise c. fictional d. musical
8. contrast : different :: simile : _____
   a. near b. equal c. like d. clear

SCAND/SCEND comes from the Latin verb *scandere,* ''to climb.'' *Ascend,* ''go up,'' and *descend,* ''go down,'' are the most familiar of the English words it has produced.

---

transcend \tran-'send\ To rise above the limits of; overcome, surpass.

• Charlotte made every attempt to transcend her in-laws' small-minded bickering and gossip.

A great leader can occasionally transcend the limitations of politics, especially during wartime and national crises. A great writer may transcend geographical boundaries to become internationally respected. Certain laws of human nature may seem to transcend historical periods and hold true for all times and all places. A *transcendent* experience seems to surpass everything familiar and somehow go beyond normal human experience.

condescend \ˌkän-di-'send\ (1) To stoop to a level of lesser importance or dignity. (2) To behave as if superior.

• Every once in a while their big brother condescended to take them to a children's movie.

When society was more rigidly structured, *condescend* did not always have negative overtones. People of higher rank, power, or social position had to overlook certain established formalities if they wished to have social dealings with those regarded as their inferiors, but condescending normally involved graciousness and courtesy. Today's more classless society takes a dimmer view of *condescension*. Nowadays the term implies a patronizing manner that the other person will find offensive. Employees at an office party may not be thrilled when the boss's wife condescends to mingle with them. A poor relation is unlikely to be grateful to a condescending relative intent on palming off useless junk. Often the word is used ironically, as in "After they had finished their chitchat, the sales clerks condescended to wait on me."

descendant \di-'sen-dənt\ (1) One that has come down from another or from a common stock. (2) One deriving directly from a forerunner or original.

• Their grandfather liked nothing better than to be surrounded by his descendants on the big holidays.

Descendant includes the prefix *de-*, "down from." We have all "stepped down" from someone else. If one anthropological theory is correct, we are all the descendants of a single woman who lived in Africa millions of years ago. Not all descendants are human, however; publishing, for instance, also has its family trees. The Merriam-Webster dictionaries of today are the direct descendants of those published by Noah Webster in the early 19th century, and any modern thesaurus is the spiritual descendant of the one devised by Peter Mark Roget in 1852.

ascendancy \ə-'sen-dən-sē\ Governing or controlling interest; domination.

• China's growing ascendancy over Tibet was capped by the invasion of 1950.

In the course of a year, the sun appears to pass through the twelve constellations of the zodiac in sequence, and all the planets but Pluto also lie close to the solar path. The constellation and planet that are just rising, or *ascendant,* above the eastern horizon in the sun's path at the moment of a child's birth are said by astrologers to exercise lifelong dominating or controlling influence over the child. This idea lies at the heart of *ascendancy,* even though the word today no longer even hints at supernatural powers.

TEN/TENU comes from the Latin adjective *tenuis,* meaning "thin." The Latin words for "thin," "stretch," and "hold" are similar and related; the physical connection is obvious in the image of someone holding *tenaciously* to something and stretching it till it *extends* and becomes *thin.*

---

attenuate \ə-'ten-yə-ˌwāt\ (1) To make thin or slender. (2) To reduce in amount, force, size, or value; weaken.

• Now that we have been out of touch for so many years, our friendship is so attenuated that I couldn't ask him for a favor.

Attenuate can apply to actual thinning by means of some mechanical process; that is, one can attenuate wire by drawing it through successively smaller holes, or attenuate gold by hammering it into thin sheets. But *attenuate* also is used to refer to the loss (or thinning out) of whatever gives a thing its strength, vitality, or effectiveness. An overly intellectualized theatrical performance can attenuate the emotional effectiveness of a character. And too long an absence can attenuate the love two people feel for each other.

extenuating \ik-'sten-yù-ˌwā-tiŋ\ Reducing or trying to reduce the seriousness of something by making partial excuses.

• To lessen the sentence, she pleaded extenuating circumstances—her desperate poverty and her child's illness.

Extenuate comes from the Latin verb *extenuare,* meaning "to make thin or small." Originally *extenuate* meant "to treat as of small importance, make light of," so to extenuate one's faults meant to try to put them in the best possible light. Today the word no longer implies dishonesty, and it is generally used in the term "extenuating circumstances." Extenuating circumstances are those that partly excuse the person of wrongdoing. The classic defense of soldiers accused of war crimes is to cite their military obligation to follow orders as an extenuating circumstance.

tenure \'ten-yər\ The act, right, manner, or period of holding something, such as property, a position, or an office.

• During his tenure in office, Franklin D. Roosevelt helped engineer the nation's recovery from the Great Depression.

Tenure always emphasizes the notion of holding on to something. It usually means the status granted to some teachers, and especially some college professors, that enables them to hold on to their teaching positions for as long as they want them—which normally extends to pension-collecting retirement age. Generally, *tenured* faculty members can be dismissed only under extraordinary circumstances.

tenuous \'ten-yù-wəs\ Having little substance or strength; flimsy, weak.

• He based his argument on tenuous grounds that did not stand up to close examination.

Tenuous always refers to thinness. It can describe a wire, for example, or the atmosphere of a planet. But generally it is not used for physical things. We may say, for instance, that Don Quixote has only a tenuous grasp on reality; that some of the Kennedy assassination conspiracy theories established only tenuous connections between the alleged conspirators; that a lawyer has made only a tenuous argument for her client's innocence; or that a churchgoer has only a tenuous faith in God.

Quizzes

A. Choose the closest definition:

1. ascendancy   a. growth   b. climb   c. control
       d. rank
2. extenuating   a. partly balding   b. partly excusing
       c. partly specific   d. partly mending
3. descendant   a. offspring   b. ancestor   c. cousin
       d. forerunner
4. tenure   a. teaching   b. term of office   c. election
       d. grasp
5. transcend   a. exceed   b. astound   c. fulfill   d. transform
6. attenuate   a. make free   b. make late   c. make friends
       d. make thin

7. condescend   a. stoop b. remove c. agree d. reject
8. tenuous   a. stretching b. tender c. insubstantial
       d. arranged

**B. Indicate whether the following words have the same
or different meanings:**

1. condescend / inherit   same __ / different __
2. attenuate / weaken   same __ / different __
3. ascendancy / altitude   same __ / different __
4. tenure / resemblance   same __ / different __
5. transcend / surpass   same __ / different __
6. extenuating / justifying   same __ / different __
7. descendant / elder   same __ / different __
8. tenuous / atmospheric   same __ / different __

SCRIB/SCRIP comes from the Latin verb *scribere,* "to write."
Scribble is an old word meaning to write or draw carelessly. A
written work that hasn't been published is a *manuscript.* To
describe is to picture something in words.

conscription \kən-'skrip-shən\ Enforced enlistment of persons,
especially for military service; draft.

• The first comprehensive system for nationwide conscription was
instituted by France for the Napoleonic wars that followed the
French Revolution.

Conscription has existed at least since ancient Egypt's Old Kingdom (27th century B.C.). Universal conscription has been rare
throughout history, but modified forms were used by Prussia, Swit-
zerland, Russia, and other European powers during the 17th and
18th centuries. In the United States, conscription was first applied
during the Civil War, by both the North and the South. In the North
there were pockets of resistance, and the draft provoked riots in
several cities. The United States abandoned conscription at the end
of the war and did not revive it again until World War I.

circumscribe \'sər-kəm-ˌskrīb\ (1) To clearly limit the range or
activity of something. (2) To draw a line around or to surround
with a boundary.

• Some children thrive when their freedom is clearly circumscribed and their activities supervised.

The area in which a boxing match takes place is clearly circumscribed by a barrier of ropes. Whether the boxers are contenders for the heavyweight championship or raw amateurs at the local gym, the way in which they are allowed to fight is also carefully circumscribed by rules—no hitting below the belt, no rabbit punches, no long clinches. The prefix *circum-*, "around," is the key to the word's basic meaning.

inscription \in-'skrip-shən\ (1) Something permanently written, engraved, or printed, particularly on a building, coin, medal, or piece of currency. (2) The dedication of a book or work of art.

• All U.S. coins bear the inscription "E pluribus unum," meaning "From many, one."

The principal monument of the Vietnam memorial in Washington, D.C., is a black wall on which are inscribed the names of all who died during the war—each name in full, row upon seemingly endless row. This monument stands as a sorrowful testimonial to the cost of that war. The prefix *in-*, meaning "in" or "on," reinforces the notion that an inscription is either written on or engraved into a surface.

proscribe \prō-'scrīb\ To forbid as harmful or unlawful; prohibit.

• Despite thousands of laws proscribing littering, the streets and public spaces of American cities continue to be regarded as common dumping grounds.

With its prefix *pro-*, meaning "before," *proscribe* refers basically to a "writing before"—that is, a written law to prevent something from happening. (It is often the opposite of *prescribe*, which means "to order or direct," including ordering someone to take a medication.)

MENS comes from the Latin noun *mensura*, "measure," and the verb *metiri*, "to measure."

---

commensurate \kə-'men-sür-ət\ Similar in size, extent, amount, or degree; proportionate, corresponding.

● His skill was commensurate with the varsity's level of play.

The prefix *com-*, "with," accounts for the sense of "equal measure" in *commensurate*. The crudeness of a makeshift shelter is usually commensurate with the haste in which it was constructed. The salary for a job should be commensurate with the required skills and experience.

dimension \di-'men-chən\ (1) Measurement in one direction or all directions; size. (2) The range or scope of something.

● What are the dimensions of the doorway through which all this furniture must pass?

Dimension is used so often to refer to literal measurement that the plural *dimensions* is used to refer to the overall scope of things that can't actually be precisely measured. It can take weeks or even months before the dimensions of a natural disaster are known. The dimensions of the legends attached to celebrities who die young—Marilyn, Elvis, James Dean—grow relentlessly with each passing year.

immensity \i-'men-sə-tē\ Greatness, especially of size or degree, that may exceed ordinary means of measurement.

● The immensity of the distances involved makes travel to other galaxies impossible with today's technology

The negative prefix *im-*, "not," gives *immensity* its basic meaning: the impossibility of measurement. To the pioneers of the American West, the immensity of the wilderness must have seemed adequate to protect it from ever becoming spoiled or overdeveloped. The immensity of today's social problems—drugs, crime, homelessness—tends to overwhelm and discourage even the most concerned citizens.

mensurable \'men-sùr-ə-bəl\ Capable of being measured; measurable.

● To speak of the declining "quality of life" in American cities is meaningless unless it can be defined in mensurable terms such as crime rates.

Mensurable is usually used in connection with information that can be measured and evaluated precisely. Since "progress" is itself a vague term, it may become meaningful only if it is converted into such mensurable terms as literacy rates and per-capita incomes. Hard-nosed scientists generally view studies in ESP and similar subjects with skepticism, because the information reported is rarely mensurable.

Quizzes

A. Fill in each blank with the correct letter:

a. proscribe	e. mensurable
b. dimension	f. circumscribe
c. inscription	g. commensurate
d. immensity	h. conscription

1. They plan to ＿＿＿ their yard with rows of annuals and perennials.
2. The punishment, life in prison, didn't seem ＿＿＿ with the crime of armed robbery.
3. The ＿＿＿ on her gravestone read, "She done the best she could."
4. The ＿＿＿ of Einstein's contribution to physics has hardly ever been equaled.
5. Officials saw fit to ＿＿＿ beer drinking during the games to help prevent fistfights and accidents.
6. With luck, both ＿＿＿ and warfare will become outmoded concepts in our lifetime.
7. Her hot temper is a ＿＿＿ of her personality we don't see very often.
8. These aspects of the problems aren't yet accurately ＿＿＿.

B. Match each word on the left with its correct definition on the right:

1. commensurate		a. prohibit
2. proscribe		b. aspect
3. immensity		c. engraving
4. conscription		d. equivalent
5. dimension		e. measurable
6. circumscribe		f. limit
7. mensurable		g. hugeness
8. inscription		h. draft

SOLV/SOLU comes from the Latin verb *solvere,* "to loosen, free, release." The number of English words that have been spawned by this root is seemingly without end. For example, to *solve* a problem—that is, to find its *solution*—is to free up a situation, and a *solvent dissolves* and releases oil or paint.

absolve \ab-'zälv\ To set free from an obligation or from guilt for a sin or mistake.

• The committee absolved two senators of responsibility for the wrongdoing but charged two others.

In Wagner's opera *The Flying Dutchman,* the ship's captain can only absolve himself of a curse by finding true love; until he finds *absolution,* he is doomed to sail the seas forever. *Absolution* is a formal term, not much used today. But *absolve* can be used both formally (that is, like *acquit*) and informally (more like *excuse*). And you may say either "absolved of" or "absolved from."

dissolution \di-sə-'lü-shən\ The act or process of breaking down or apart into basic components, as through disruption or decay.

• The dissolution of the U.S.S.R. has been the most momentous event of the last quarter of the 20th century.

The prefix *dis-,* "apart," produces the sense of something "exploding." With the independence of India in 1948, the dissolution of the once-global British Empire was all but complete, and a chapter in world history was closed. The dissolution of marriages has become far more common in the last 30 years. The unholy trinity of crime, drugs, and homelessness has contributed greatly to the dissolution of contemporary society's moral fabric.

resolve \ri-'zȯlv\ (1) To deal with successfully; clear up. (2) To reach a decision about; determine, decide.

• At the start of every new year, we resolve to become better than we were the year before.

Resolve comes directly from the Latin verb *resolvere,* "to unloose" or "to dissolve." But the word often suggests careful separation or analysis. One resolves a problem or situation by sorting out its various aspects or phases. The process of resolving brings order out of chaos and clarity out of confusion, and in the course of resolving an issue, dispute, or mystery, one finds a satisfactory *solution*. In its second sense, an organization may formally resolve—by passing a resolution—to support a cause or honor a member. And an alcoholic may resolve never to lift another glass.

soluble \\'säl-yù-bəl\\ (1) Able to be dissolved in a liquid, especially water. (2) Able to be solved or explained.

• To the optimistic young principal, the school's problems looked challenging but soluble.

Soluble looks like a word that should be confined to chemistry labs. Certainly, it is used by chemists and nonchemists alike to refer to substances that can be dissolved in liquids. On the other hand, the sense of *soluble* meaning "solvable" is also quite common. In this sense, *soluble* (like its opposite, *insoluble*) is usually paired with *problem*. If only all of life's problems were soluble by stirring them in a container filled with water.

HYDR flows from the Greek word for "water." In the Northwest, rushing rivers provide an abundance of *hydrodynamic* power to convert to electricity. "Water" can also be found in the lovely flower called *hydrangea*: its seed capsules resemble ancient Greek water vessels.

---

dehydrate \\dē-'hī-ˌdrāt\\ (1) To remove water from. (2) To deprive of energy and zest.

• The boy appeared at dusk staggering out of the desert, dangerously sunburned and dehydrated.

Dehydrating food is a good way to preserve it; raisins, which are dehydrated grapes, are a good example. *Dehydration* through industrial processes makes it possible to keep food even longer and store it in a much smaller space as well. Freeze-drying produces food that only needs *rehydration* by the addition of water to restore its original consistency. Since water is a life-sustaining element, the word *dehydrate* has developed a related sense that is used whenever something inorganic is regarded as "dry" or "lifeless." Thus, a dull teacher can dehydrate American history—a subject that should be fascinating—and an unimaginative staging can dehydrate even the greatest of Shakespeare's plays.

hydraulic \hī-'drȯ-lik\ (1) Relating to water; operated, moved, or brought about by means of water. (2) Operated by the resistance or pressure of liquid forced through a small opening or tube.

• Without any hydraulic engineers, the country is unlikely to build many dams or reservoirs on its own.

By means of a hydraulic lift, the driver can lift the bed of a dump truck with the touch of a button. He can proceed to repair the hydraulic steering, the hydraulic brake, and the hydraulic clutch, all of which, like the lift that holds everything up, take advantage of the way liquids act under pressure. Somewhat like a pulley or a lever, a hydraulic system magnifies the effect of moderate pressure exerted over a longer distance into powerful energy for a shorter distance.

hydroelectric \ˌhī-drō-i-'lek-trik\ Having to do with the production of electricity by waterpower.

• The massive hydroelectric project seemed to hold the key to the future for the small African country.

The prime component of most hydroelectric systems is a dam. A high dam funnels water downward at high pressure to spin turbines, which in turn drive generators to produce high-voltage electricity. Mountainous countries with rushing rivers can produce the most *hydroelectricity,* which is the cleanest and most renewable of our three major energy sources today (the others being nuclear power and fossil fuels).

hydroponics \ˌhī-drō-'pä-niks\ The growing of plants in nutrient solutions, with or without supporting substances such as sand or gravel.

• Hydroponics has been used extensively in the floral industry.

Hydroponics comes from combining *hydro* with *ponos,* "labor." (It is patterned after such words as *geoponics,* "earth labor," which means simply agriculture.) Hydroponics is also known as "aquaculture" or "tank farming." The practice began as a way of studying scientifically the mechanisms of plant nutrition. The principal advantage to hydroponics is the savings that result from reduced labor costs, since it is generally carried on in enclosed areas and the irrigation and fertilizing are done mechanically. Tomatoes, cucumbers, and various other vegetables are produced *hydroponically* in huge quantities.

Quizzes

A. Complete the analogy:

1. freezing : melting :: dissolution : _____
   a. unification b. separation c. death d. defiance
2. romantic : love :: hydraulic : _____
   a. solid b. gas c. liquid d. evaporation
3. acquit : incriminate :: absolve : _____
   a. accuse b. forgive c. require d. lose
4. sterile : bacteria :: hydroponic : _____
   a. water b. soil c. air d. fire
5. determined : hesitant :: soluble : _____
   a. moist b. dry c. unexplainable d. possible
6. nuclear : uranium :: hydroelectric : _____
   a. coal b. petroleum c. dynamics d. water
7. involve : include :: resolve : _____
   a. determine b. delay c. detect d. demand
8. drain : replenish :: dehydrate : _____
   a. find b. dry out c. rehydrate d. add

B. Indicate whether the following pairs of words have the same or different meanings:

1. hydraulic / electric   same ___ / different ___
2. soluble / believable   same ___ / different ___
3. dehydrate / dry   same ___ / different ___
4. dissolution / disintegration same ___ / different ___
5. hydroelectric / solar-powered same ___ / different ___
6. resolve / decide   same ___ / different ___
7. hydroponics / waterworks   same ___ / different ___
8. absolve / recreate   same ___ / different ___

Greek and Latin Borrowings

aegis \'ē-jəs\ (1) Something that protects or defends; shield. (2) Sponsorship or guidance by an individual or organization.

• The conference was held under the aegis of the World Affairs Council.

The original aegis was a goatskin shield or breastplate, symbolizing majesty, that was worn by Zeus and his daughter Athena in Greek mythology. *Aegis* came to be used for any kind of seemingly invulnerable shield. But today we almost always use *aegis* in the phrase "under the aegis of . . . ," which means "under the authority, sponsorship, or control of."

charisma \kə-'riz-mə\ (1) An extraordinary gift for leadership that attracts popular support and enthusiasm. (2) A special ability to attract or charm; magnetism.

• Few figures in world history have possessed as much charisma as Napoleon Bonaparte, whom many of his followers genuinely believed to be immortal.

Charisma comes from Christian belief, where it originally referred to an extraordinary power—the power of healing, the gift of tongues, or the gift of prophecy—bestowed upon a Christian individual for the good of all the church. Charisma is believed to be a gift of the Holy Spirit; in fact, *charisma* is Greek for "gift." The first nonreligious use of *charisma* didn't appear until this century, when it was applied to that mysterious personal magnetism that a lucky few seem to possess, and especially to the magnetism that enables a political leader to arouse great popular enthusiasm. This sense really came into vogue when John F. Kennedy was elected President in 1960; its frequent use by journalists popularized the term in the mass media. Since then, the word has generally been used to mean "appeal" or "magnetism." Evangelists, movie actors, rock stars, athletes, military commanders, and business entrepreneurs are some of the celebrities who are now constantly said to possess charisma.

ego \'ē-gō\ (1) An exaggerated sense of self-importance; conceit. (2) A sense of confidence and satisfaction in oneself; self-esteem.

● His raging ego was what his fellow lawyers remembered about him—his tantrums, his vanity, his snobbery, and all the rest of it.

If a person with an overbearing ego seems to begin every sentence with "I," the habit is only natural: "ego" is Latin for "I." In the field of philosophy, *ego* has often been used to mean the innermost self, and it has a special meaning in Freudian psychology as well. But usually *ego* simply refers to one's sense of self-worth, whether exaggerated or healthy. When used in the "exaggerated" sense, *ego* is almost the same thing as *conceit* and *narcissism*. Meeting a superstar athlete without a trace of this kind of ego would be a most refreshing experience. But having a reasonable sense of one's worth or position is no sin, and life's little everyday victories, are good—in fact, necessary—for the ego.

ethos \'ē-ˌthäs\ The features, attitudes, moral code, or basic beliefs that define a person, a group, or an institution.

● Some social critics have observed that since the end of the Second World War, the United States has become increasingly immersed in an ethos of materialism.

Ethos literally means "custom" or "character" in Greek. As originally used by Aristotle, it referred to the man's character or personality, especially with respect to the balance between passion and caution. Today it is used to refer to the traits, practices, beliefs, or values that distinguish a person, organization, subculture, or society from others. One may speak of the ethos of rugged individualism and personal self-sufficiency on the American frontier in the 19th century. Sociologists study the ethos of permissiveness in the suburbs and the ethos of violence in the inner cities. Observers of pop culture note, with a mixture of puzzlement and scorn, that an ethos of vanity and self-indulgence has become well-established in Tinseltown.

hubris \'hyü-brəs\ Unreasonable or unjustified pride or self-confidence.

● Their boastful pregame hubris bumped into the embarrassing reality of defeat.

To the Greeks, *hubris* referred to extreme arrogance, especially when directed toward the gods. Hubris was the flaw most frequently attributed to the heroes of classical Greek tragedy; it was the pride, usually brought about by overwhelming success, that went before the fall. Typically, this overconfidence led to a violation of moral law or the natural order and an attempt to exceed the boundaries of fate and mortality and to assume godlike status. Inevitably, the tragic hero was brought low by the gods themselves.

id \\'id\\ In psychoanalytic theory, the division of the psyche that is unconscious and gets its energy from instinctual needs and drives.

• Exploration of the id has revealed that even the most normal-appearing individual can feel irrational and antisocial impulses.

In Freudian theory, the id, ego, and superego make up the human personality. The id (which means simply "it" in Latin) is the first to develop. It is the home of the body's basic instincts particularly those involving sex and aggression. Since it lacks logic, reason, or even organization, it can contain conflicting impulses. Primitive in nature, the id tends to seek immediate gratification. Although the working processes of the id are completely unconscious, its contents can be revealed in works of art, in slips of the tongue, and through other nonrational modes of expression, and can also be discovered by free association and the analysis of dreams.

libido \\lə-'bē-dō\\ (1) In psychoanalytic theory, energy that is derived from primitive biological urges and is usually goal-oriented. (2) Sexual drive.

• She would sit at home trying not to think about where his unmanageable libido had led him this time.

Once again, it was Sigmund Freud who conceived and named the libido. At first Freud defined *libido* to mean the psychic or instinctual energy associated with the sex drive. Later he used the word for the psychic energy behind purposeful human activity of any kind. The libido, or *eros,* came to be regarded as the life instinct and the opposite of *thanatos,* the death instinct and the source of destructive urges. But outside of psychoanalytic circles, *libido* is popularly used simply as a synonym for the sex drive.

trauma \\'trȯ-mə\\ (1) An injury to living tissue caused by an external agent. (2) Psychic or behavioral disorder caused by mental or emotional stress or physical injury.

• Fifteen years later, their adopted Cambodian daughter was still having nightmares in which she relived the trauma of those terrible years.

Trauma is the Greek word for "wound." Although the Greeks used the term only for physical injuries, nowadays *trauma* is just as likely to refer to psychic or emotional wounds. We now know that emotional trauma often remains long after any physical injuries that may have caused it have healed. The psychological reaction to emotional trauma now has an established name: *post-traumatic stress disorder*. The reaction usually occurs after an extremely stressful event, such as wartime combat, a natural disaster, or sexual or physical abuse. Typical symptoms include depression, anxiety, flashbacks, and recurring nightmares.

Quiz

Fill in each blank with the correct letter:

a.	charisma	e.	ethos
b.	libido	f.	trauma
c.	aegis	g.	ego
d.	id	h.	hubris

1. It seems like _____ to brag about a victory before it has been won.
2. She recovered from the physical _____ in a few weeks, but not from the emotional one.
3. He has such a massive _____ that no praise seems to satisfy him.
4. Those who enter the monastery do not lose their _____, just their option to satisfy it.
5. They traveled to Egypt under the _____ of the State Department.
6. She has a lot of personal _____, and this helps her run an effective team.
7. In and out of jail for assault and drug use, Crawford seemed to be driven by a powerful and uncontrollable _____.
8. The novelist Sinclair Lewis made fun of the _____ of conformity that he saw as the basis of small-town American life.

Review Quizzes

A. Complete the analogy:

1. solid : firm :: tenuous : _____
   a. thick b. fast c. flimsy d. large
2. drama : play :: trauma : _____
   a. wound b. harm c. mind d. emotion
3. flee : seek :: proscribe : _____
   a. hesitate b. stick c. permit d. lead
4. tune : melody :: proverb : _____
   a. poem b. song c. story d. saying
5. extent : length :: simile : _____
   a. shape b. contrast c. kind d. comparison
6. mob : crowd :: ego : _____
   a. self b. other c. friend d. same
7. provoke : argument :: simulate : _____
   a. trial b. disease c. environment d. pain
8. disease : cure :: dissolution : _____
   a. disintegration b. unification c. departure d. solidity
9. acorn : oak tree :: descendant : _____
   a. brother b. offspring c. child d. ancestor
10. investigate : check :: dehydrate : _____
    a. liquidate b. dry c. dissolve d. adjust

B. Fill in each blank with the correct letter:

a. transcend
b. libido
c. verbose
d. tenure
e. circumscribe
f. absolve
g. simile
h. verbatim
i. id
j. condescend
k. hydroponics
l. ethos
m. proscribe
n. resolve
o. conscription

1. The doctor warned her that her _____ would be reduced while she was on the medication.
2. The use of _____ and greenhouses enables the florist industry to operate year-round.
3. Nothing can _____ society of its obligation to provide educational opportunities for all.

4. During Lincoln's _____ as President, the nation tore itself apart in a civil war.
5. These rules will clearly _____ the boundaries of permissible behavior.
6. Whatever possessed that snooty couple to _____ to invite us to their cocktail party?
7. Since the tape recorder wasn't turned on, we don't have a _____ record of the meeting.
8. His poetic _____ compared his beloved to a rose.
9. The outbreak of war made _____ unavoidable.
10. Within months General Ramirez had begun to _____ antigovernment opinion in the newspapers.
11. Let us _____ the Orotech matter once and for all.
12. Only rarely did the talk show manage to _____ the level of trivia and gossip.
13. A "question" from the most _____ student in the class could go on for five minutes.
14. The _____ reacts unthinkingly according to the pleasure-pain principle.
15. The company's _____ didn't correspond to my own beliefs, so I left.

C. Match each word on the left to its correct definition on the right:

1. inscription   a. domination
2. verbiage   b. personal magnetism
3. immensity   c. to stretch thin
4. simulacrum   d. absorb
5. soluble   e. protection
6. hubris   f. proportional
7. commensurate   g. dissolvable
8. dissolution   h. breakup
9. aegis   i. excessive pride
10. hydraulic   j. involving liquid
11. ascendancy   k. image
12. attenuate   l. wordiness
13. assimilate   m. excusing
14. charisma   n. hugeness
15. extenuating   o. dedication

Answers

UNIT 1

p.4 A 1.d 2.g 3.f 4.c 5.h 6.e 7.b 8.a
      B 1.e 2.a 3.f 4.d 5.c 6.h 7.b 8.g

p.7 A 1.c 2.b 3.b 4.a 5.a 6.d 7.b 8.d
      B 1.b 2.d 3.a 4.b 5.d 6.d 7.b 8.a

p.11 A 1.S 2.D 3.D 4.D 5.D 6.D 7.S 8.D
      B 1.e 2.a 3.b 4.f 5.d 6.h 7.g 8.c

p.14 A 1.d 2.f 3.c 4.h 5.b 6.a 7.e 8.g
      B 1.f 2.a 3.g 4.b 5.c 6.h 7.d 8.e

p.17   1.d 2.b 3.a 4.c 5.b 6.d 7.a 8.c

p.18 A 1.e 2.d 3.k 4.b 5.h 6.l 7.f 8.j 9.g 10.c 11.n 12.a 13.m
         14.i
      B 1.d 2.a 3.d 4.c 5.b 6.b 7.d 8.a 9.c 10.c 11.c 12.a
      C 1.f 2.c 3.e 4.d 5.h 6.g 7.j 8.a 9.b 10.i

UNIT 2

p.23 A 1.c 2.b 3.d 4.a 5.d 6.b 7.c 8.b
      B 1.a 2.b 3.c 4.d 5.b 6.b 7.b 8.a

p.27 A 1.h 2.g 3.d 4.a 5.b 6.f 7.e 8.c
      B 1.f 2.d 3.b 4.g 5.h 6.c 7.e 8.a

p.30 A 1.d 2.c 3.a 4.b 5.d 6.c 7.b 8.a
      B 1.d 2.e 3.h 4.f 5.g 6.a 7.c 8.b

p.34   A   1.b 2.c 3.e 4.a 5.g 6.h 7.d 8.f
          B   1.h 2.d 3.a 4.f 5.e 6.b 7.g 8.c

p.37   1.a,c 2.d,b 3.b,a 4.c,b 5.c,a 6.a,b 7.c,a 8.d,a

p.38   A   1.c 2.b 3.b 4.d 5.b 6.c 7.d 8.a 9.c 10.b
          B   1.c 2.f 3.e 4.a 5.i 6.d 7.b 8.g 9.j 10.h
          C   1.f 2.h 3.c 4.i 5.d 6.e 7.j 8.b 9.g 10.a

UNIT 3

p.43   A   1.b 2.c 3.f 4.d 5.e 6.a 7.g 8.h
          B   1.c 2.f 3.e 4.h 5.a 6.d 7.b 8.g

p.47   A   1.b 2.c 3.c 4.b 5.d 6.c 7.a 8.a
          B   1.D 2.D 3.S 4.D 5.D 6.S 7.D 8.D

p.51   A   1.a 2.g 3.f 4.d 5.c 6.b 7.h 8.e
          B   1.D 2.D 3.S 4.D 5.S 6.S 7.D 8.D

p.55   A   1.b 2.b 3.a 4.d 5.b 6.d 7.b 8.a
          B   1.d 2.g 3.h 4.a 5.f 6.e 7.b 8.c

p.59   1.c 2.b 3.a 4.c 5.a 6.a 7.b 8.c

p.59   A   1.d 2.b 3.a 4.d 5.c 6.a 7.b 8.a
          B   1.m 2.j 3.c 4.l 5.f 6.i 7.e 8.g 9.d 10.k 11.b 12.n 13.h
              14.a 15.o
          C   1.S 2.D 3.S 4.D 5.D 6.S 7.S 8.D 9.D 10.S 11.D 12.D
              13.S 14.S 15.S

UNIT 4

p.65   A   1.S 2.D 3.D 4.S 5.D 6.S 7.D 8.S
          B   1.f 2.g 3.e 4.h 5.b 6.c 7.d 8.a

p.69   A   1.h 2.b 3.a 4.c 5.g 6.e 7.f 8.d
          B   1.a 2.c 3.h 4.g 5.f 6.b 7.e 8.d

p.73   A   1.c 2.b 3.e 4.f 5.g 6.h 7.a 8.d
          B   1.h 2.a 3.g 4.b 5.c 6.f 7.d 8.e

p.77   A 1.c 2.b 3.b 4.c 5.d 6.b 7.a 8.a
             B 1.b 2.c 3.c 4.d 5.b 6.a 7.a 8.d

p.81   1.b 2.c 3.f 4.a 5.d 6.e 7.h 8.g

p.81   A 1.a 2.b 3.d 4.d 5.b 6.c 7.a 8.b 9.b 10.c
             B 1.D 2.D 3.S 4.D 5.S 6.D 7.S 8.D 9.S 10.S
             C 1.b 2.d 3.d 4.a 5.a 6.c 7.c 8.b

UNIT 5

p.86   A 1.c 2.c 3.c 4.b 5.d 6.c 7.b 8.d
             B 1.D 2.D 3.S 4.S 5.S 6.D 7.S 8.D

p.89   A 1.d 2.g 3.c 4.b 5.a 6.e 7.h 8.f
             B 1.f 2.e 3.d 4.a 5.h 6.g 7.b 8.c

p.93   A 1.c 2.b 3.d 4.b 5.d 6.b 7.c 8.a
             B 1.D 2.S 3.D 4.D 5.D 6.S 7.S 8.D

p.97   A 1.a 2.g 3.c 4.e 5.f 6.d 7.h 8.b
             B 1.c 2.e 3.f 4.g 5.a 6.h 7.b 8.d

p.101   1.h 2.f 3.d 4.e 5.b 6.g 7.a 8.c

p.102   A 1.d 2.b 3.c 4.b 5.c 6.d 7.b 8.a 9.a 10.d
            B 1.g 2.i 3.a 4.o 5.b 6.n 7.m 8.k 9.c 10.e 11.f 12.d 13.h
                 14.j 15.l
            C 1.S 2.D 3.S 4.S 5.D 6.D 7.D 8.S 9.D 10.D 11.S 12.D
                 13.S 14.D 15.D

UNIT 6

p.107   A 1.c 2.c 3.c 4.c 5.b 6.a 7.b 8.d
             B 1.g 2.b 3.c 4.d 5.e 6.f 7.a 8.h

p.111   A 1.d 2.f 3.h 4.g 5.e 6.a 7.b 8.c
             B 1.b 2.c 3.d 4.a 5.b 6.a 7.c 8.d

p.115   A 1.S 2.D 3.S 4.S 5.D 6.D 7.D 8.S
             B 1.b 2.e 3.c 4.h 5.g 6.a 7.f 8.d

p.118 A 1.c 2.a 3.d 4.c 5.d 6.a 7.c 8.b
       B 1.f 2.c 3.e 4.b 5.d 6.a 7.h 8.g

p.122   1.c 2.c 3.b 4.a 5.a 6.b 7.c 8.a

p.122 A 1.g 2.a 3.j 4.c 5.i 6.b 7.d 8.e 9.h 10.f
       B 1.c 2.a 3.a 4.a 5.b 6.c 7.b 8.b 9.b 10.a
       C 1.e 2.j 3.a 4.i 5.f 6.h 7.c 8.b 9.d 10.g

UNIT 7

p.128 A 1.b 2.d 3.g 4.f 5.a 6.h 7.a 8.e
       B 1.c 2.e 3.f 4.h 5.a 6.g 7.d 8.b

p.132 A 1.c 2.d 3.c 4.b 5.b 6.a 7.d 8.b
       B 1.S 2.D 3.D 4.S 5.S 6.S 7.D 8.D

p.135 A 1.a 2.e 3.b 4.f 5.c 6.g 7.d 8.h
       B 1.d 2.c 3.c 4.a 5.b 6.b 7.d 8.a

p.139 A 1.S 2.D 3.D 4.S 5.D 6.D 7.D 8.D
       B 1.c 2.f 3.d 4.a 5.e 6.g 7.h 8.b

p.143   1.a 2.d 3.c 4.h 5.f 6.g 7.b 8.e

p.144 A 1.c,a 2.b,c 3.b,a 4.d,b 5.a,b 6.b,c 7.c,a 8.a,b 9.d,c
          10.c,a 11.c,b 12.d,a 13.a,c 14.c,b 15.c,d
       B 1.c 2.a 3.b 4.c 5.d 6.a 7.b 8.a 9.d 10.a 11.b 12.c 13.c
          14.a 15.c
       C 1.i 2.f 3.c 4.h 5.e 6.j 7.g 8.a 9.b 10.d

UNIT 8

p.150 A 1.c 2.a 3.b 4.a 5.c 6.d 7.b 8.c
       B 1.f 2.b 3.e 4.a 5.g 6.c 7.h 8.d

p.155 A 1.a 2.g 3.b 4.h 5.e 6.c 7.d 8.f
       B 1.D 2.S 3.D 4.S 5.S 6.D 7.D 8.D

p.158 A 1.D 2.D 3.S 4.D 5.D 6.D 7.D 8.S
       B 1.b 2.f 3.d 4.c 5.g 6.h 7.a 8.e

p.162 A 1.c 2.c 3.d 4.a 5.b 6.c 7.d 8.c
        B 1.e 2.d 3.g 4.h 5.c 6.f 7.a 8.b

p.166   1.g 2.f 3.e 4.d 5.a 6.h 7.b 8.c

p.167 A 1.a,c 2.d,b 3.a,d 4.b,a 5.c,a 6.d,b 7.d,a 8.a,b 9.d,c
           10.d,a
        B 1.D 2.D 3.S 4.D 5.S 6.S 7.S 8.D 9.D 10.D 11.D 12.D
           13.S 14.S 15.S 16.D 17.D 18.S 19.S 20.D
        C 1.h 2.g 3.i 4.b 5.a 6.f 7.d 8.j 9.c 10.e

UNIT 9

p.172 A 1.a 2.g 3.f 4.b 5.c 6.e 7.h 8.d
        B 1.a 2.b 3.c 4.d 5.a 6.b 7.d 8.c

p.176 A 1.b 2.a 3.b 4.a 5.b 6.b 7.d 8.d
        B 1.d 2.c 3.e 4.f 5.g 6.h 7.a 8.b

p.180 A 1.a 2.a 3.a 4.a 5.c 6.d 7.b 8.c
        B 1.S 2.D 3.S 4.D 5.S 6.S 7.D 8.D

p.183 A 1.h 2.c 3.g 4.d 5.e 6.b 7.f 8.a
        B 1.g 2.f 3.b 4.c 5.h 6.a 7.e 8.d

p.187   1.c 2.b 3.b 4.b 5.c 6.d 7.b 8.c

p.187 A 1.b 2.c 3.a 4.d 5.b 6.c 7.a 8.d 9.d 10.b
        B 1.d 2.g 3.a 4.b 5.j 6.e 7.c 8.i 9.h 10.f
        C 1.a 2.h 3.i 4.b 5.e 6.d 7.g 8.c 9.j 10.f

UNIT 10

p.192 A 1.S 2.D 3.D 4.D 5.D 6.D 7.D 8.S
        B 1.a 2.c 3.d 4.b 5.a 6.c 7.d 8.a

p.195 A 1.c 2.c 3.d 4.c 5.b 6.a 7.b 8.d
        B 1.f 2.h 3.g 4.e 5.d 6.a 7.c 8.b

p.199 A 1.a 2.g 3.c 4.f 5.b 6.h 7.e 8.d
        B 1.c 2.a 3.d 4.c 5.b 6.c 7.a 8.b

p.202   A 1.b 2.d 3.a 4.c 5.a 6.d 7.a 8.d
             B 1.e 2.h 3.f 4.a 5.g 6.b 7.c 8.d

p.206   1.e 2.b 3.d 4.c 5.g 6.f 7.a 8.h

p.206   A 1.D 2.S 3.D 4.D 5.D 6.S 7.S 8.D 9.D 10.S 11.S 12.D
               13.D 14.S 15.D 16.D 17.S 18.D 19.D 20.D
             B 1.d 2.a 3.d 4.b 5.a 6.c 7.b 8.a 9.d 10.a
             C 1.f 2.e 3.a 4.d 5.c 6.b 7.h 8.g

UNIT 11

p.212   A 1.b 2.d 3.a 4.c 5.c 6.b 7.a 8.b
             B 1.D 2.D 3.S 4.D 5.D 6.D 7.D 8.D

p.215   A 1.a 2.g 3.b 4.h 5.e 6.c 7.d 8.f
             B 1.c 2.c 3.b 4.a 5.d 6.c 7.b 8.b

p.219   A 1.d 2.b 3.a 4.d 5.c 6.a 7.c 8.a
             B 1.b 2.e 3.h 4.a 5.f 6.g 7.d 8.c

p.222   A 1.a 2.d 3.e 4.b 5.h 6.c 7.f 8.g
             B 1.S 2.D 3.S 4.D 5.D 6.D 7.D 8.S

p.226   1.a 2.g 3.f 4.d 5.c 6.e 7.b 8.h

p.227   A 1.c,d 2.c,b 3.a,b 4.a,d 5.c,d 6.c,b 7.a,c 8.a,d 9.d,a
               10.c,b 11.b,c 12.d,a 13.b,c 14.b,a 15.d,c 16.c,a
             B 1.D 2.D 3.D 4.S 5.S 6.D 7.D 8.S 9.S 10.S
             C 1.f 2.b 3.e 4.g 5.i 6.j 7.l 8.h 9.a 10.d 11.k 12.c

UNIT 12

p.232   A 1.f 2.c 3.g 4.d 5.e 6.a 7.b 8.h
             B 1.f 2.h 3.g 4.c 5.b 6.e 7.a 8.d

p.236   A 1.a 2.g 3.c 4.b 5.f 6.e 7.d 8.h
             B 1.c 2.f 3.h 4.e 5.d 6.g 7.a 8.b

p.239   A 1.b 2.c 3.a 4.b 5.c 6.b 7.d 8.c
             B 1.S 2.D 3.S 4.D 5.D 6.S 7.D 8.D

p.243   A   1.g 2.b 3.a 4.f 5.c 6.h 7.e 8.d
            B   1.b 2.d 3.g 4.c 5.f 6.a 7.e 8.h

p.246   1.a 2.f 3.b 4.g 5.e 6.h 7.d 8.c

p.247   A   1.b 2.d 3.c 4.a 5.c 6.a 7.c 8.a 9.d 10.d 11.a 12.c 13.b
                 14.d 15.c 16.b
            B   1.f 2.b 3.g 4.j 5.d 6.e 7.i 8.a 9.h 10.c
            C   1.h 2.j 3.g 4.a 5.i 6.c 7.d 8.f 9.e 10.b

UNIT 13

p.253   A   1.b 2.d 3.c 4.b 5.c 6.a 7.b 8.a
            B   1.g 2.h 3.b 4.f 5.a 6.e 7.d 8.c

p.256   A   1.c 2.b 3.f 4.g 5.a 6.h 7.e 8.d
            B   1.S 2.D 3.S 4.S 5.D 6.S 7.S 8.S

p.260   A   1.c 2.a 3.c 4.d 5.d 6.a 7.b 8.c
            B   1.e 2.f 3.a 4.g 5.b 6.c 7.h 8.d

p.264   A   1.e 2.b 3.c 4.g 5.a 6.h 7.f 8.d
            B   1.a 2.c 3.d 4.a 5.b 6.d 7.a 8.c

p.267   1.D 2.S 3.D 4.D 5.S 6.S 7.D 8.D

p.267   A   1.h 2.i 3.o 4.r 5.c 6.s 7.f 8.n 9.e 10.p 11.m 12.a 13.b
                 14.t 15.g 16.d 17.j 18.l 19.q 20.k
            B   1.b,d 2.d,b 3.b,d 4.a,d 5.d,b 6.b,c 7.b,d 8.d,a 9.c,d
                 10.b,c
            C   1.c 2.b 3.d 4.b 5.a 6.c 7.a 8.d 9.a 10.d

UNIT 14

p.273   A   1.d 2.g 3.a 4.e 5.f 6.b 7.h 8.c
            B   1.g 2.a 3.d 4.c 5.h 6.f 7.e 8.b

p.277   A   1.D 2.D 3.S 4.S 5.D 6.S 7.S 8.S
            B   1.d 2.e 3.f 4.c 5.g 6.h 7.a 8.b

p.280   A   1.b 2.f 3.e 4.c 5.a 6.d 7.h 8.g
            B   1.d 2.a 3.f 4.c 5.e 6.g 7.b 8.h

p.284 A 1.b 2.a 3.c 4.d 5.b 6.c 7.a 8.d
       B 1.S 2.S 3.D 4.D 5.D 6.D 7.S 8.D

p.288   1.b 2.h 3.g 4.c 5.e 6.a 7.f 8.d

p.288 A 1.b 2.a 3.b 4.a 5.b 6.c 7.b 8.a 9.b 10.d 11.a 12.a 13.b
          14.b 15.d 16.d 17.c 18.c 19.b 20.a
       B 1.a 2.b 3.h 4.i 5.d 6.e 7.f 8.c 9.g 10.j
       C 1.S 2.D 3.D 4.D 5.S 6.S 7.D 8.S 9.S 10.S

UNIT 15

p.293 A 1.a 2.d 3.c 4.c 5.d 6.a 7.b 8.c
       B 1.h 2.c 3.f 4.b 5.e 6.a 7.d 8.g

p.297 A 1.c 2.c 3.a 4.b 5.a 6.d 7.a 8.d
       B 1.d 2.g 3.f 4.e 5.a 6.h 7.b 8.c

p.301 A 1.S 2.D 3.S 4.S 5.S 6.S 7.S 8.D
       B 1.d 2.f 3.e 4.h 5.c 6.g 7.a 8.b

p.305 A 1.a 2.b 3.c 4.c 5.b 6.a 7.c 8.b
       B 1.c 2.e 3.f 4.g 5.h 6.d 7.b 8.a

p.309   1.h 2.e 3.a 4.d 5.f 6.g 7.b 8.c

p.310 A 1.q 2.f 3.h 4.o 5.m 6.k 7.d 8.n 9.r 10.l 11.p 12.c 13.e
          14.s 15.b 16.a 17.i 18.t 19.g 20.j
       B 1.d,a 2.b,c 3.b,d 4.b,a 5.b,c 6.a,d 7.b,a 8.c,d 9.c,a
          10.d,b
       C 1.a 2.b 3.a 4.b 5.c 6.a 7.c 8.c 9.d 10.c

UNIT 16

p.316 A 1.c 2.e 3.h 4.b 5.g 6.f 7.d 8.a
       B 1.e 2.d 3.f 4.b 5.h 6.g 7.c 8.a

p.319 A 1.b 2.c 3.c 4.c 5.b 6.a 7.c 8.a
       B 1.c 2.d 3.c 4.d 5.c 6.c 7.c 8.a

p.323 A 1.a 2.e 3.c 4.b 5.f 6.g 7.h 8.d
       B 1.f 2.c 3.e 4.h 5.d 6.g 7.b 8.a

p.327 A 1.b 2.a 3.c 4.a 5.b 6.c 7.d 8.a
B 1.c 2.g 3.h 4.f 5.d 6.e 7.b 8.a

p.331   1.b 2.c 3.b 4.c 5.b 6.c 7.d 8.b

p.331 A 1.m 2.k 3.i 4.e 5.s 6.l 7.f 8.t 9.b 10.a 11.j 12.p 13.q
14.g 15.d 16.o 17.n 18.r 19.c 20.h
B 1.c 2.a 3.a 4.c 5.b 6.a 7.c 8.b 9.d 10.a
C 1.i 2.d 3.f 4.j 5.g 6.b 7.h 8.a 9.e 10.c

UNIT 17

p.337 A 1.a 2.g 3.f 4.e 5.b 6.c 7.h 8.d
B 1.D 2.S 3.S 4.D 5.D 6.S 7.D 8.S

p.340 A 1.c 2.b 3.c 4.b 5.d 6.b 7.a 8.c
B 1.c 2.d 3.f 4.e 5.g 6.h 7.b 8.a

p.344 A 1.f 2.c 3.b 4.h 5.d 6.a 7.e 8.g
B 1.D 2.S 3.D 4.D 5.S 6.D 7.D 8.S

p.348 A 1.b 2.a 3.c 4.d 5.a 6.b 7.d 8.a
B 1.c 2.e 3.f 4.a 5.d 6.g 7.h 8.b

p.352   1.f 2.g 3.e 4.b 5.a 6.c 7.h 8.d

p.352 A 1.a,c 2.d,b 3.b,d 4.d,a 5.c,a 6.d,b 7.b,c 8.b,c 9.d,b
10.c,a
B 1.c 2.i 3.k 4.o 5.a 6.t 7.s 8.l 9.n 10.j 11.f 12.g 13.b
14.e 15.h 16.d 17.m 18.r 19.p 20.q
C 1.g 2.i 3.d 4.a 5.c 6.f 7.b 8.h 9.j 10.e

UNIT 18

p.358 A 1.d 2.f 3.b 4.h 5.g 6.a 7.e 8.c
B 1.d 2.e 3.a 4.g 5.h 6.f 7.c 8.b

p.361 A 1.a 2.c 3.b 4.d 5.a 6.a 7.b 8.b
B 1.D 2.S 3.S 4.D 5.D 6.S 7.D 8.D

p.365 A 1.b 2.c 3.a 4.d 5.a 6.b 7.c 8.a
B 1.h 2.b 3.f 4.g 5.a 6.e 7.c 8.d

p.368   A 1.D 2.D 3.S 4.D 5.D 6.S 7.S 8.S
         B 1.f 2.e 3.h 4.b 5.c 6.d 7.a 8.g

p.372   1.f 2.g 3.d 4.e 5.a 6.h 7.c 8.b

p.372   A 1.d,a 2.b,c 3.d,b 4.a,d 5.d,b 6.c,a 7.b,d 8.c,a 9.c,b
            10.d,a
         B 1.k 2.d 3.i 4.f 5.l 6.e 7.o 8.b 9.m 10.a 11.h 12.c 13.j
            14.g 15.n
         C 1.c 2.a 3.d 4.c 5.c 6.a 7.c 8.d 9.c 10.a 11.d 12.a 13.c
            14.d 15.b

UNIT 19

p.378   A 1.f 2.g 3.c 4.d 5.e 6.b 7.h 8.a
         B 1.S 2.D 3.D 4.S 5.S 6.S 7.S 8.D

p.382   A 1.c 2.b 3.a 4.d 5.b 6.a 7.b 8.c
         B 1.a 2.c 3.c 4.b 5.c 6.d 7.b 8.b

p.386   A 1.d 2.f 3.b 4.a 5.g 6.h 7.e 8.c
         B 1.c 2.d 3.g 4.a 5.f 6.b 7.h 8.e

p.390   A 1.c 2.a 3.d 4.b 5.a 6.c 7.d 8.b
         B 1.D 2.D 3.D 4.D 5.S 6.D 7.D 8.S

p.394   1.d 2.e 3.h 4.g 5.c 6.b 7.a 8.f

p.394   A 1.a,b 2.b,d 3.d,a 4.c,a 5.d,b 6.a,d 7.d,a 8.c,d 9.a,c
            10.b,a 11.c,b 12.d,b 13.c,b 14.a,c 15.d,b
         B 1.f 2.k 3.d 4.l 5.g 6.n 7.i 8.m 9.b 10.j 11.h 12.c 13.o
            14.e 15.a
         C 1.D 2.S 3.D 4.D 5.D 6.D 7.S 8.S 9.D 10.S

UNIT 20

p.401   A 1.d 2.f 3.b 4.h 5.e 6.c 7.g 8.a
         B 1.c 2.e 3.d 4.a 5.h 6.g 7.f 8.b

p.405   A 1.b 2.c 3.c 4.a 5.d 6.a 7.b 8.c
         B 1.h 2.g 3.c 4.e 5.f 6.d 7.a 8.b

p.409 A 1.d 2.a 3.b 4.b 5.c 6.a 7.d 8.c
B 1.D 2.S 3.D 4.S 5.S 6.D 7.D 8.S

p.413 A 1.e 2.f 3.g 4.a 5.b 6.c 7.d 8.h
B 1.h 2.g 3.f 4.e 5.d 6.c 7.b 8.a

p.417 1.f 2.b 3.h 4.d 5.a 6.g 7.c 8.e

p.417 A 1.b 2.d 3.c 4.d 5.a 6.c 7.c 8.b 9.c 10.b
B 1.a 2.b 3.c 4.a 5.c 6.c 7.a 8.d 9.a 10.c 11.d 12.b 13.b
14.c 15.d
C 1.k 2.l 3.g 4.o 5.m 6.h 7.d 8.a 9.j 10.e 11.i 12.f 13.n
14.b 15.c

UNIT 21

p.423 A 1.d 2.h 3.g 4.f 5.e 6.c 7.b 8.a
B 1.f 2.g 3.a 4.e 5.h 6.b 7.c 8.d

p.428 A 1.b 2.c 3.d 4.a 5.a 6.c 7.b 8.d
B 1.S 2.S 3.S 4.D 5.D 6.D 7.S 8.S

p.432 A 1.h 2.b 3.a 4.g 5.f 6.e 7.c 8.d
B 1.d 2.e 3.c 4.f 5.h 6.a 7.b 8.g

p.436 A 1.c 2.d 3.b 4.b 5.d 6.c 7.c 8.c
B 1.S 2.S 3.D 4.D 5.S 6.D 7.S 8.D

p.440 1.f 2.c 3.b 4.a 5.e 6.h 7.d 8.g

p.440 A 1.d 2.b 3.c 4.b 5.c 6.a 7.d 8.b 9.a 10.d
B 1.g 2.a 3.b 4.o 5.m 6.i 7.c 8.j 9.k 10.e 11.f 12.d 13.n
14.h 15.l
C 1.a 2.a 3.d 4.c 5.b 6.c 7.b 8.d 9.a 10.c 11.a 12.a 13.d
14.d 15.c

UNIT 22

p.446 A 1.S 2.D 3.D 4.S 5.D 6.S 7.S 8.D
B 1.h 2.a 3.g 4.e 5.d 6.b 7.c 8.f

p.450 A 1.d 2.a 3.c 4.d 5.a 6.b 7.b 8.a
         B 1.D 2.S 3.D 4.S 5.D 6.D 7.D 8.D

p.454 A 1.f 2.g 3.h 4.a 5.b 6.d 7.c 8.e
         B 1.c 2.a 3.b 4.b 5.d 6.b 7.a 8.d

p.458 A 1.c 2.c 3.b 4.d 5.d 6.b 7.c 8.c
         B 1.D 2.D 3.S 4.S 5.S 6.D 7.D 8.S

p.461   1.h 2.f 3.b 4.g 5.e 6.c 7.d 8.a

p.461 A 1.b 2.c 3.b 4.d 5.d 6.d 7.b 8.b 9.c 10.a
         B 1.h 2.i 3.j 4.g 5.f 6.e 7.o 8.n 9.m 10.l 11.k 12.a 13.b
            14.c 15.d
         C 1.d 2.a 3.b 4.b 5.a 6.c 7.b 8.c 9.b 10.b 11.c 12.b 13.c
            14.c 15.d

UNIT 23

p.468 A 1.d 2.f 3.g 4.c 5.e 6.a 7.b 8.h
         B 1.d 2.e 3.f 4.a 5.h 6.c 7.b 8.g

p.471 A 1.b 2.a 3.c 4.d 5.c 6.b 7.d 8.b
         B 1.S 2.S 3.D 4.D 5.D 6.S 7.D 8.D

p.475 A 1.f 2.g 3.h 4.b 5.c 6.e 7.a 8.d
         B 1.f 2.e 3.g 4.h 5.a 6.d 7.c 8.b

p.479 A 1.a 2.c 3.b 4.a 5.b 6.c 7.c 8.b
         B 1.D 2.D 3.S 4.S 5.D 6.S 7.D 8.D

p.482   1.f 2.b 3.h 4.c 5.e 6.g 7.a 8.d

p.483 A 1.c 2.b 3.c 4.d 5.a 6.d 7.a 8.c
         B 1.g 2.l 3.d 4.i 5.b 6.m 7.j 8.c 9.a 10.f 11.o 12.e 13.k
            14.h 15.n
         C 1.a 2.b 3.d 4.b 5.c 6.c 7.a 8.d 9.c 10.d 11.b 12.b 13.c
            14.b 15.c

UNIT 24

p.489 A 1.h 2.b 3.c 4.g 5.a 6.e 7.f 8.d
         B 1.d 2.g 3.e 4.c 5.h 6.a 7.b 8.f

p.493   A   1.d 2.b 3.b 4.a 5.c 6.d 7.c 8.b
          B   1.D 2.S 3.S 4.D 5.D 6.D 7.S 8.D

p.497   A   1.d 2.f 3.b 4.g 5.a 6.h 7.c 8.e
          B   1.f 2.d 3.e 4.b 5.a 6.g 7.h 8.c

p.501   A   1.b 2.c 3.d 4.a 5.b 6.c 7.c 8.b
          B   1.S 2.D 3.S 4.D 5.S 6.D 7.D 8.D

p.504   1.c 2.f 3.g 4.d 5.e 6.h 7.b 8.a

p.505   A   1.d 2.d 3.c 4.d 5.c 6.a 7.b 8.a 9.b 10.a 11.d 12.c 13.c
              14.a 15.c
          B   1.m 2.k 3.o 4.c 5.a 6.f 7.h 8.n 9.e 10.b 11.i 12.d 13.j
              14.g 15.l
          C   1.g 2.h 3.e 4.f 5.c 6.a 7.i 8.b 9.j 10.d

UNIT 25

p.511   A   1.d 2.h 3.g 4.a 5.c 6.e 7.b 8.f
          B   1.c 2.b 3.d 4.a 5.b 6.d 7.b 8.c

p.515   A   1.c 2.b 3.a 4.b 5.c 6.d 7.a 8.c
          B   1.D 2.S 3.D 4.D 5.S 6.D 7.D 8.D

p.519   A   1.f 2.g 3.c 4.d 5.a 6.h 7.b 8.e
          B   1.d 2.a 3.g 4.h 5.b 6.f 7.e 8.c

p.523   A   1.a 2.c 3.a 4.b 5.c 6.d 7.a 8.c
          B   1.D 2.D 3.S 4.S 5.D 6.S 7.D 8.D

p.527   1.h 2.f 3.g 4.b 5.c 6.a 7.d 8.e

p.528   A   1.c 2.a 3.c 4.d 5.d 6.a 7.c 8.b 9.b 10.b
          B   1.b 2.k 3.f 4.d 5.e 6.j 7.h 8.g 9.o 10.m 11.n 12.a 13.c
              14.i 15.l
          C   1.o 2.l 3.n 4.k 5.g 6.i 7.f 8.ḥ 9.e 10.j 11.a 12.c 13.d
              14.b 15.m

Index

AB/ABS, 271
aberrant, 115
abjure, 367
abnegation, 389
abrogate, 104
abscond, 272
absolve, 520
abstemious, 272
abstinence, 283
abstraction, 272
abstruse, 273
accede, 117
acclamation, 472
accord, 250
accretion, 498
ACERB/ACRI, 443
acerbic, 443
Achilles' heel, 140
acme, 458
acquisitive, 107
acrid, 443
acrimony, 443
acropolis, 240
ad hoc, 56
ad hominem, 57
adaptation, 257
adept, 258
adherent, 169
adjacent, 28
adjunct, 177
admonish, 201
adumbrate, 229
advent, 21

aegis, 524
aeolian harp, 163
affidavit, 67
affinity, 25
affluence, 406
a fortiori, 98
AG, 20
aggregate, 403
agitate, 20
alleviate, 13
allude, 210
alter ego, 57
AM/IM, 6
AMBI/AMPHI, 40
ambient, 40
ambiguous, 40
ambivalent, 41
ambrosia, 480
amicable, 6
amorphous, 298
amphitheater, 41
anachronism, 326
ANIM, 334
animated, 334
animosity, 334
ANN/ENN, 337
annuity, 338
ANT/ANTI, 433
antagonist, 433
ANTE, 88
antebellum, 1
antecedent, 117
antechamber, 88

antedate, 88
ante meridiem, 89
anterior, 89
ANTHROP, 356
anthropoid, 356
anthropology, 357
anthropomorphic, 298
antigen, 433
antipathy, 434
antithesis, 434
apathetic, 196
apiary, 265
apocryphal, 270
apollonian, 35
apologia, 502
a posteriori, 99
apotheosis, 233
appease, 3
appendage, 148
apprehensive, 407
approbation, 9
appropriate, 448
a priori, 99
APT/EPT, 257
aptitude, 258
aquamarine, 194
aquiline, 244
arachnid, 184
arcadia, 140
aristocrat, 474
arrogate, 104
ART, 259
artful, 259
artifact, 259
artifice, 259
artisan, 260
ascendancy, 513
asinine, 244
assignation, 346
assimilate, 509
astringent, 444
atheistic, 233
atrium, 502
attenuate, 514
AUD, 112

audition, 113
auditor, 112
auditory, 112
Augean stable, 119
auspicious, 126
AUT/AUTO, 469
autism, 470
autocratic, 474
autodidact, 469
automaton, 469
autonomy, 469
aver, 214
avert, 297
bacchanalian, 35
BELL, 1
bellicose, 1
belligerence, 1
BI/BIN, 308
biennial, 308
binary, 308
BIO, 375
biodegradable, 375
bionic, 375
biopsy, 376
biosphere, 295
bipartisan, 308
bipolar, 309
bona fide, 99
bovine, 245
bureaucrat, 474
cacophony, 130
CAD/CID/CAS, 261
cadaver, 261
calliope, 184
calypso, 78
canine, 245
CANT, 209
cantata, 209
cantor, 210
CAP/CEP/CIP, 24
caper, 265
CAPIT, 355
capitalism, 355
capitulate, 355
carcinogenic, 376

CARN, 63
carnage, 63
carnal, 64
carnival, 64
carnivorous, 62
carpe diem, 99
Cassandra, 141
casualty, 261
CATA, 84
cataclysm, 84
catacomb, 85
catalyst, 85
catatonic, 85
catharsis, 459
caveat emptor, 100
CED/CESS, 117
CENT, 392
centenary, 392
centigrade, 393
centimeter, 393
CENTR/CENTER, 314
centrifugal, 170
centurion, 393
cereal, 203
charisma, 524
CHRON, 326
chronic, 326
chronology, 327
cicerone, 15
CIRCU/CIRCUM, 242
circuitous, 242
circumference, 242
circumlocution, 492
circumscribe, 516
circumspect, 242
circumvent, 243
CIS, 262
CLAM/CLAIM, 472
clamor, 473
CLUD/CLUS, 456
codex, 345
CODI/CODE, 345
codicil, 345
codify, 346
coeval, 339

cognate, 275
cognitive, 255
cohesion, 169
collate, 364
colloquial, 492
collusion, 211
colossus, 459
commendation, 486
commensurate, 517
commutation, 380
compel, 182
complaisant, 466
complement, 108
component, 281
comprehend, 408
compunction, 476
concession, 117
concise, 262
concordance, 250
concurrent, 70
condescend, 512
conducive, 31
confection, 220
configuration, 335
conform, 300
congenial, 377
congregation, 404
conjecture, 28
conscientious, 174
conscription, 516
consequential, 33
conspicuous, 127
constrict, 445
construe, 447
contemporary, 324
contentious, 147
context, 465
CONTRA, 434
contraband, 435
contraindication, 435
contravene, 435
contretemps, 436
convivial, 452
convoluted, 218
CORD, 250

cordial, 251
CORP, 341
corporal, 342
corporeal, 341
corpulent, 342
corpus delicti, 100
correlate, 364
COSM, 173
cosmetic, 173
cosmology, 173
cosmopolitan, 174
cosmos, 174
CRAC/CRAT, 474
CRE/CRET, 498
CRED, 66
credence, 66
creditable, 66
credulity, 67
creed, 67
crescent, 498
CRIM, 8
criminology, 8
CRIT, 366
criterion, 366
critique, 366
Croesus, 120
CRYPT/CRYPH, 270
crypt, 271
cryptic, 270
cryptography, 271
CULP, 251
culpable, 251
CUMB/CUB, 358
CUR, 132
curative, 132
curator, 133
CURR/CURS, 70
curriculum vitae, 101
cursory, 70
cyclopean, 141
cynosure, 164
DE/DIV, 234
DEC, 391
decadent, 262
decalogue, 391

decapitate, 356
decathlon, 391
decibel, 391
decimate, 392
declaim, 473
decode, 346
deconstruction, 447
decriminalize, 8
deduction, 31
de facto, 57
deferential, 277
definitive, 26
deflect, 74
degrade, 362
dehydrate, 521
deity, 234
dejected, 28
de jure, 58
delegation, 402
delphic, 35
DEMI/HEMI/SEMI, 415
DEMO, 236
demographic, 237
demotic, 238
deplete, 109
derogatory, 105
descant, 210
descendant, 513
detract, 29
detritus, 460
deus ex machina, 235
devolution, 218
DI/DUO, 306
diagnosis, 255
diaphanous, 213
DIC, 253
dichotomy, 306
diffident, 68
diffraction, 54
diffuse, 500
dimension, 518
Dionysian, 36
diplomatic, 307
DIS, 54
discordant, 251

discursive, 70
disjunction, 177
disposition, 282
disprove, 10
disputatious, 189
disseminate, 54
dissension, 54
dissipate, 55
dissolution, 520
dissonant, 113
distend, 147
divert, 296
divest, 230
divinatory, 235
divinity, 235
DOC/DOCT, 302
docile, 303
doctrinaire, 303
doctrine, 302
dogma, 480
DOM, 316
domicile, 317
domination, 317
dominion, 318
draconian, 141
dragon's teeth, 120
dryad, 185
DUC, 31
duplex, 307
duplicity, 307
DYNAM, 360
dynamic, 360
dynamo, 360
dynasty, 361
DYS, 96
dysfunctional, 96
dyslexia, 96
dyspeptic, 97
dystrophy, 97
eccentric, 314
ectopic, 313
edict, 253
effigy, 336
effluent, 406
effusive, 500

ego, 524
egocentric, 315
egregious, 404
elevate, 13
elocution, 492
elucidate, 157
emissary, 181
empathy, 196
enamored, 6
encomium, 503
encyclopedic, 274
endemic, 237
EP/EPI, 41
ephemeral, 42
epicenter, 315
epiphyte, 42
epitaph, 42
epithet, 43
equestrian, 265
equivalent, 495
equivocate, 129
ERR, 115
errant, 116
erratic, 116
erroneous, 116
ethnocentric, 315
ethos, 525
EU, 94
eugenic, 94
eulogy, 190
euphemism, 95
euphoria, 95
eureka, 480
EV, 339
evangelism, 95
evince, 292
evolution, 218
ex post facto, 58
exacerbate, 444
excise, 263
excrescence, 499
exculpate, 252
execute, 33
exhibitionist, 318
expatriate, 399

expedient, 71
expedite, 72
expel, 182
expend, 149
explicate, 478
expropriate, 448
expunge, 477
expurgate, 411
extemporaneous, 325
extenuating, 514
extort, 451
EXTRA, 153
extramundane, 153
extraneous, 154
extrapolate, 153
extrovert, 154
FAC/FEC/FIC, 220
facile, 220
factotum, 481
fauna, 185
feline, 245
FER, 277
fertile, 278
FID, 67
fiduciary, 68
FIG, 335
figment, 336
figurative, 336
FIN, 25
finite, 26
FLECT/FLEX, 74
flexor, 74
flora, 185
FLU/FLUCT, 406
fluctuation, 406
FORM, 300
formality, 300
format, 301
formative, 301
fractious, 383
FRAG/FRACT, 383
fragmentary, 383
FUG, 170
fugitive, 171
fugue, 171

functionary, 379
FUND/FUS, 499
FUNG/FUNCT, 379
fungible, 380
GEN, 376
genealogy, 191
generic, 377
genuflect, 74
GNI/GNO, 255
GRAD, 362
gradation, 363
graduate, 363
GRAT, 470
gratify, 470
gratis, 480
gratuitous, 471
gratuity, 470
GRAV, 11
gravid, 11
gravitas, 12
gravitate, 12
gravity, 12
GREG, 403
HABIT/HIBIT, 318
habitation, 318
habitual, 319
Hades, 120
hector, 15
hedonism, 15
hematocrit, 367
hemiplegia, 416
hemisphere, 295
HER/HES, 169
herbivorous, 62
herculean, 186
HOM/HOMO, 52
homogeneous, 52
homologous, 53
homonym, 52
homophone, 53
HOSP/HOST, 5
hospice, 5
hostage, 5
hostel, 5
hubris, 525

HYDR, 521
hydraulic, 522
hydrodynamic, 361
hydroelectric, 522
hydroponics, 522
HYPER, 421
hyperactive, 422
hyperbole, 422
hypercritical, 366
hypertension, 422
hyperventilate, 423
HYPO/HYP, 44
hypochondriac, 44
hypocrisy, 44
hypothermia, 45
hypothetical, 45
icon, 460
id, 526
ignominious, 397
immensity, 518
immortality, 159
immutable, 381
impart, 178
impartial, 179
impediment, 72
impel, 183
impetus, 482
implacable, 467
implement, 109
implicit, 478
impunity, 197
impute, 189
inanimate, 335
inaudible, 113
incantation, 209
incarnation, 65
incipient, 24
incisive, 263
incognito, 256
incoherent, 169
incorporate, 342
increment, 499
incriminate, 9
incubate, 359
inculpate, 252

incumbent, 359
indeterminate, 291
indigenous, 377
indoctrinate, 303
induce, 32
inept, 258
inference, 278
infinitesimal, 26
inflection, 75
infraction, 384
infrastructure, 447
ingratiate, 471
inherent, 170
inhibit, 319
inhospitable, 6
inimical, 6
injunction, 177
in memoriam, 437
innate, 276
inquisition, 106
inscription, 517
instrumental, 448
intact, 343
intemperate, 409
interdiction, 254
interminable, 291
internecine, 161
intractable, 30
introspection, 127
intuition, 304
inundate, 487
investiture, 231
invincible, 293
iridescent, 224
irrevocable, 129
JAC/JEC, 28
jovial, 36
JUNCT, 177
Junoesque, 203
junta, 178
JUR, 367
jurisdiction, 254
jurisprudence, 368
kudos, 460
laconic, 164

LAT, 364
leavening, 13
LEGA, 402
legacy, 402
legate, 402
leonine, 246
lethargic, 121
LEV, 13
levity, 13
libido, 526
litigate, 20
LOC/LOQU, 491
LOG, 190
longevity, 339
loquacious, 493
LUC, 157
lucent, 157
lucubration, 158
LUD/LUS, 210
ludicrous, 211
lupine, 266
lycanthropy, 266
magnanimous, 334
magnum opus, 437
MAL/MALE, 83
malediction, 255
malevolent, 83
malfunction, 379
malicious, 83
malign, 83
malnourished, 84
MAND/MEND, 486
mandate, 486
mandatory, 487
manumission, 181
MAR, 194
marina, 194
mariner, 194
maritime, 195
martial, 204
maternity, 200
MATR/METR, 200
matriculate, 200
matrilineal, 200
mausoleum, 224

mea culpa, 252
medieval, 340
megalopolis, 241
mellifluous, 407
memento mori, 438
MENS, 517
mensurable, 518
mentor, 224
mercurial, 36
META, 428
metabolism, 429
metamorphosis, 299
metaphorical, 429
metaphysics, 429
metonymy, 430
METR, 110
metric, 110
metropolitan, 201
Midas touch, 121
MILL, 414
millefleur, 414
millenarianism, 414
millennium, 338
millipede, 415
millisecond, 415
misanthropic, 357
misnomer, 397
missive, 181
MIT/MIS, 180
mnemonic, 164
modus operandi, 58
modus vivendi, 58
MONI, 201
monitor, 202
monitory, 201
MONO, 285
monogamous, 285
monograph, 285
monolithic, 285
monologue, 191
monotheism, 286
MOR/MORT, 159
moribund, 159
MORPH, 298
morphology, 299

mortician, 160
mortify, 160
muse, 223
MUT, 380
myrmidon, 142
narcissism, 225
NASC/NAT/NAI, 275
nascent, 276
NEC/NIC/NOX, 161
necrosis, 161
NEG, 388
negligible, 389
nemesis, 142
neologism, 191
nestor, 16
neurosis, 503
NOM, 397
nomenclature, 398
nominal, 398
non sequitur, 438
noxious, 161
objurgate, 368
obsequious, 33
occlusion, 456
odometer, 110
odyssey, 78
oenophile, 387
olfactory, 220
oligarchy, 502
olympian, 37
omniscience, 175
omnivorous, 63
onus, 460
opprobrium, 503
opus, 481
ornithologist, 266
ORTH/ORTHO, 90
orthodontics, 91
orthodox, 91
orthography, 92
orthopedics, 91
PAC/PEAS, 2
pacifist, 3
pacify, 2
pact, 3

palladium, 78
PAN, 151
panacea, 151
pandemic, 237
pandemonium, 152
Pandora's box, 186
panegyric, 152
panoply, 152
pantheistic, 233
PARA, 426
paradigm, 426
paradox, 426
paragon, 427
parameter, 427
paramour, 7
PART, 178
parterre, 192
participle, 179
partisan, 179
PATER/PATR, 399
paternalistic, 399
PATH, 196
pathology, 197
patrician, 400
patrimony, 400
PED, 274
PED, 71
pedagogy, 274
pedant, 275
pedestrian, 72
pediatrician, 275
PEL/PULS, 182
PEN/PUN, 197
penal, 198
penance, 198
PEND/PENS, 148
Penelope, 79
PENT, 369
pentagram, 370
pentameter, 370
Pentateuch, 370
pentathlon, 369
penumbra, 229
PER, 430
perceptible, 25

percolate, 430
peremptory, 431
perennial, 339
perfidy, 68
perfunctory, 380
PERI, 134
perimeter, 134
periodontal, 134
peripatetic, 135
peripheral, 135
perjury, 367
permeate, 431
permutation, 381
pernicious, 162
perquisite, 106
persevere, 431
perspicacious, 127
perturb, 216
perverse, 296
PHAN/PHEN, 212
phantasm, 212
phantasmagoria, 213
phenomenon, 213
PHIL, 387
philanthropy, 357
philatelist, 387
philology, 388
philter, 388
PHON, 130
phonetic, 130
PHOS/PHOT, 155
phosphorescent, 156
photogenic, 156
photon, 156
photosynthesis, 157
PLAC/PLAIS, 466
placebo, 467
placidity, 467
platonic, 164
PLE, 108
PLIC, 477
plutocracy, 475
POLIS/POLIT, 240
politic, 241
politicize, 241

POLY, 48
polychromatic, 48
polyglot, 49
polymer, 49
polyphonic, 131
polyphony, 49
PON/POS, 281
POPUL, 238
populace, 238
populist, 238
populous, 239
porcine, 246
portend, 148
POST, 75
posterior, 75
posthumous, 76
postmodern, 76
postmortem, 76
PRE, 424
precedent, 118
precept, 424
precision, 263
preclude, 457
precocious, 425
precursor, 71
predispose, 425
predominant, 317
PREHEND/PREHENS, 407
prehensile, 408
prelate, 364
prelude, 211
premonition, 202
prerequisite, 425
prerogative, 105
prescient, 175
prestigious, 445
pretext, 465
prevalent, 496
PRIM, 50
primal, 50
primeval, 340
primiparous, 50
primogeniture, 50
primordial, 51
PRO, 320

PROB/PROV, 9
probity, 10
procrastinate, 320
procrustean, 79
procure, 133
prodigal, 21
prodigious, 321
proficient, 220
profusion, 500
prognosis, 256
proliferate, 278
Promethean, 204
PROP/PROPRI, 448
propensity, 149
prophylaxis, 321
propitious, 321
proprietary, 449
propriety, 449
proscribe, 517
PROT/PROTO, 86
protagonist, 87
protean, 80
protocol, 87
protoplasm, 87
prototype, 88
protracted, 29
provenance, 22
proverb, 508
provincial, 293
provoke, 129
punctilious, 477
PUNG/PUNC, 476
pungent, 477
punitive, 198
PURG, 411
purgative, 411
purgatory, 412
purge, 412
PUT, 189
putative, 190
pyrrhic victory, 121
QUADR/QUART, 349
quadrennial, 349
quadrille, 349
quadriplegic, 349

quartile, 350
quincentennial, 371
QUINT, 370
quintessential, 371
quintet, 371
quintile, 372
QUIS, 106
rebellion, 2
recapitulate, 356
reception, 24
recidivism, 262
reclamation, 473
recluse, 457
recrimination, 9
RECT, 92
rectify, 92
rectilinear, 93
rectitude, 92
rector, 93
recumbent, 359
redound, 488
redundancy, 488
referendum, 504
refraction, 384
regimen, 461
relativity, 364
relegate, 403
remand, 487
remittance, 181
renaissance, 276
renegade, 389
renege, 389
replete, 109
replicate, 478
repository, 282
reprehensible, 408
reprobate, 10
repulsion, 183
reputed, 190
requisition, 107
resign, 347
resolve, 520
resonance, 114
retraction, 30
RETRO, 322

retroactive, 322
retrofit, 322
retrograde, 363
retrogress, 323
retrospective, 323
revivify, 453
rigor mortis, 438
ROG, 104
SACR/SANCT, 490
sacrilege, 490
sacrosanct, 491
sanction, 490
sanctuary, 491
sapphic, 165
SCAND/SCEND, 512
SCI, 174
SCRIB/SCRIP, 516
Scylla and Charybdis, 186
SEC/SEQU, 33
seclusion, 457
seduction, 32
segregate, 404
semiconductor, 416
semicolon, 416
semitone, 415
sensational, 136
sensuous, 138
SENT/SENS, 136
sentient, 137
sentiment, 137
sequential, 34
serpentine, 266
SERV, 455
serviceable, 455
servile, 455
servitude, 455
sibyl, 80
SIGN, 346
signatory, 347
signet, 347
simian, 267
SIMIL/SIMUL, 509
simile, 510
simulacrum, 510
simulate, 511

sinecure, 133
sine qua non, 439
siren, 80
Sisyphean, 204
sociopath, 197
Socratic, 165
solecism, 166
soluble, 521
SOLV/SOLU, 520
SON, 113
sonic, 114
SOPH, 138
sophisticated, 138
sophistry, 138
sophomoric, 139
spartan, 16
SPHER, 294
spherical, 296
SPIC/SPEC, 126
stentorian, 16
stipend, 149
stoic, 17
stratosphere, 294
STRING/STRICT, 444
stringent, 445
STRU/STRUCT, 446
stygian, 121
SUB, 420
subconscious, 420
subjugate, 420
subliminal, 421
subservient, 456
subterfuge, 171
subterranean, 193
subtext, 466
subversion, 421
succumb, 360
suffuse, 500
superannuated, 338
superimpose, 282
supplication, 478
susceptible, 25
sustenance, 283
sybaritic, 17
symbiosis, 376

symmetrical, 110
symphony, 131
synagogue, 21
synchronous, 327
tabula rasa, 439
tachometer, 111
tactile, 343
TANG/TACT, 343
tangential, 343
tangible, 343
tantalize, 225
TELE, 384
telegenic, 384
telemetry, 385
teleological, 385
telepathic, 386
TEMPER, 409
temper, 410
tempera, 410
temperance, 410
TEMPOR, 324
temporal, 325
temporize, 326
TEN/TENU, 514
TEN/TIN/TAIN, 282
tenable, 283
tenacious, 283
TEND/TENT, 147
tendentious, 148
tenuous, 515
tenure, 514
TERM/TERMIN, 291
terminal, 292
terminology, 292
TERR, 192
terra incognita, 439
terrarium, 193
terrestrial, 193
TESSAR/TETR, 350
tetracycline, 350
tetrahedron, 351
tetralogy, 351
tetrapod, 351
TEXT, 465
textual, 466

THE/THEO, 233
theocracy, 234
theosophy, 139
THERM/THERMO, 45
thermal, 46
thermocline, 46
thermocouple, 46
thermonuclear, 47
thesis, 482
thespian, 225
titanic, 205
TOP, 313
topiary, 313
topical, 313
topography, 314
TORS/TORT, 451
torsion, 451
tort, 451
tortuous, 452
TRACT, 29
trajectory, 28
TRANS, 279
transcend, 512
transcendent, 280
transfiguration, 279
transfuse, 279
transient, 280
translucent, 158
transmute, 381
transvestite, 231
trauma, 526
travesty, 231
TRI, 328
triceratops, 328
tricolor, 329
trident, 329
trilogy, 329
trimester, 330
trinity, 330
triptych, 330
Triton, 205
triumvirate, 494
trivial, 330
Trojan horse, 142
tuition, 304

TURB, 216
turbid, 217
turbine, 216
turbulent, 217
TUT/TUI, 304
tutelage, 304
tutorial, 305
ultimatum, 504
ultrasound, 114
umber, 230
UMBR, 229
umbrage, 230
unconscionable, 175
UND, 487
undulant, 488
UNI, 286
unicameral, 286
unilateral, 286
unison, 287
unitarian, 287
usufruct, 221
usury, 221
UT/US, 221
utilitarian, 222
utility, 222
VAL, 495
validate, 497
valorous, 496
VEN/VENT, 21
venereal, 37
venturesome, 22
venue, 22
VER, 214
VERB, 508

verbatim, 509
verbiage, 509
verbose, 508
verify, 214
verisimilitude, 214
verity, 215
versatile, 297
VERT/VERS, 296
VEST, 230
victimize, 293
VID/VIS, 125
VINC/VICT, 292
VIR, 494
virago, 494
virility, 495
virtuosity, 495
visage, 125
vis-a-vis, 125
visionary, 126
visitation, 126
VIV, 452
vivacious, 453
vivisection, 453
VOC/VOK, 129
vociferous, 130
VOLU/VOLV, 217
voluble, 218
VOR, 62
voracious, 63
vox populi, 239
vulcanize, 205
vulpine, 246
zephyr, 226